History Alive!

The Ancient World

Student Edition

TCi

Teachers' Curriculum Institute

Managing Editor: Laura Alavosus
Developmental Editor: John Bergez
Production Editor: Mali Apple
Editorial Assistant: Anna Embree
Art Director: Tim Stephenson
Production Manager: Lynn Sanchez
Senior Graphic Designer: Christy Uyeno
Graphic Designers: Katy Haun, Paul Rebello, Don Taka
Photo Editor: Lindsay Kefauver
Audio Director: Katy Haun
Operations Manager: Ellen Mapstone

 Teachers' Curriculum Institute
P.O. Box 50996
Palo Alto, CA 94303

ISBN 13: 978-1-58371-351-8   ISBN 10: 1-58371-351-4
15 16 17 18 19 20 -WC- 15 14 13 12 11

Manufactured by Webcrafters, Inc., Madison, WI
United States of America, May 2011, Job# 90731

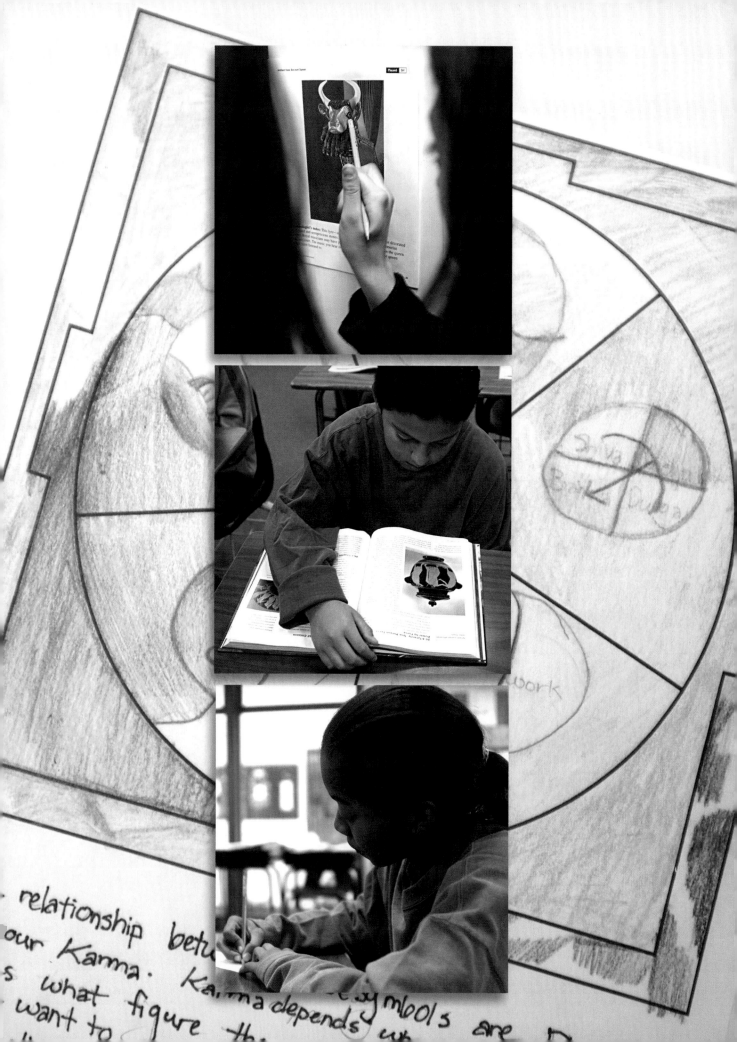

Welcome to *History Alive!*
The Ancient World

History Alive! The Ancient World was developed by middle school teachers at Teachers' Curriculum Institute (TCI). We, Bert Bower and Jim Lobdell, are two former high school teachers who started TCI. Our goal is to help students like you succeed in learning about history in a way that is fun and exciting. With the help of teachers from around the nation, we've created the TCI Approach to learning. This chapter explains how the TCI Approach will make ancient world history come alive for you.

The TCI Approach has three main parts. First, during class you'll be involved in a lot of exciting activities. For example, you'll learn about early humans by crawling into a "cave" to bring out ancient artifacts. You'll travel the famous Silk Road to learn about ancient China's silk trade. You'll explore Greek civilization by taking a walking tour of ancient Athens. Every lesson is built around an activity like these.

Second, during and after these activities, you get to read this book. You'll discover that your reading connects closely to the activities that you experience. We've worked hard to make the book interesting and easy to follow.

Third, during each lesson you'll write about your learning in an Interactive Student Notebook. You'll end up with your very own personal account of ancient world history.

With the TCI Approach, you'll not only learn more about history than ever before, but you'll have fun doing it. Let's take a closer look at how this approach will help you learn ancient world history.

Two teachers, Bert Bower (above) and Jim Lobdell (below) started TCI. They work with teachers and students like you to develop new ways to learn history.

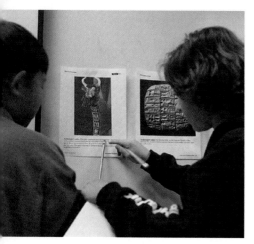

Researchers have found that students learn best when they are given the opportunity to use their multiple intelligences, work cooperatively with their peers, and build on what they already know.

Theory-Based, Active Instruction

History Alive! The Ancient World is probably unlike any other history program you have ever encountered. Perhaps you have been in history classes where you listen to the teacher and then read a textbook and answer chapter questions. Does this approach make you excited about learning history? Most students would say no, and educational researchers would tend to agree. Researchers have discovered new ways of reaching all students in the diverse classroom. This program relies on three of their theories.

Students learn best through multiple intelligences. Howard Gardner, an educational researcher, discovered that people use their brains in very different ways to learn the same fact or concept. From this discovery, he created a theory called multiple intelligences. There are at least seven intelligences. You can think of them as different ways of being smart—with words, with pictures, with numbers, with people, with your body, with music and rhythms, and with who you are. Everyone has multiple intelligences. Using one or more of these ways of being smart can make learning easier.

Cooperative interaction increases learning gains. Through research, Elizabeth Cohen discovered that students learn more when they interact by working in groups with others. Interactive learning includes working with your classmates in many kinds of activities. You'll work in groups, do role plays, and create simulations. This kind of learning requires you and your classmates to share your ideas and work together well.

All students can learn via the spiral curriculum. Researcher Jerome Bruner believed that learning isn't just up to students. Teachers need to make learning happen for all students. Bruner believed, as the TCI Approach does, that all students can learn through a process of step-by-step discovery. This process is known as a spiral curriculum.

These three theories are the foundation of the TCI Approach. Putting them into practice in *History Alive! The Ancient World* gives you what you need to succeed.

Standards-Based Content

A lot of people care about what you are learning in history. These people include your parents, your school administrators, your teachers, and even your state and national elected officials. In fact, if you're like students in most states, you take tests at the end of the year to measure your progress.

Most end-of-year tests are based on standards. Standards are the key pieces of information about history that elected officials think are important for you to remember. When you read most standards, you might scratch your head and think, "These seem really hard to understand, and they're probably even harder to learn and remember." There's no need to worry about that with *History Alive! The Ancient World*. Every lesson is based on standards. So every day, while you're having fun learning ancient history, you are also learning key standards.

You'll be recording everything you learn in your Interactive Student Notebook. When it's time to prepare for tests, your notebook will make it easy to review all the standards you've learned.

In fact, students across the nation using the TCI Approach are getting better scores than ever on standardized tests. A big reason for this success is that the TCI Approach is based on interactive learning. That means you won't just read about history. You'll be actively involved in experiencing it and recording what you learn. Let's take a look at what you'll do during each part of a lesson with the TCI Approach.

History Alive! The Ancient World has been carefully developed to provide the information and learning you need to succeed on state tests.

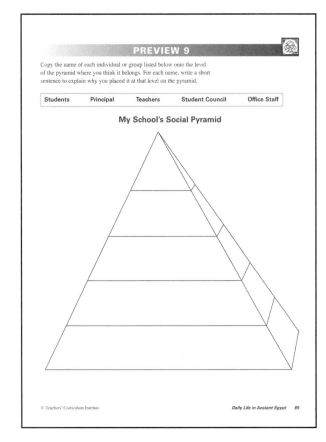

Preview assignments like the one shown here help introduce you to new topics

Preview Assignments

With the TCI Approach, learning starts even before you begin studying. Most of the lessons in *History Alive! The Ancient World* begin with a Preview assignment. Previews are short assignments that you complete in your Interactive Student Notebook. They allow you to make a personal connection to what you will study.

After you complete a Preview assignment, your teacher will hold a brief class discussion. Several students will share their answers. Your teacher will then reveal how the assignment "previews" what is to come in the lesson.

Here are some examples of the kinds of Preview assignments you will complete:

- Before studying the early civilization of Sumer in Chapter 5, you will complete a spoke diagram. You'll use the diagram to show what you think are the characteristics of a civilization.

- Before studying ancient Egypt's social pyramid in Chapter 9, you'll draw a social pyramid for your school. You will arrange individuals and groups on your pyramid, including students, the principal, teachers, and the student council.

- Before learning about the golden age of India's Gupta Empire in Chapter 18, you will write a paragraph about a "golden age" (a time of special accomplishment) in your own life.

- Before learning about Alexander the Great in Chapter 30, you will draw a figure to represent a good leader. You'll use the figure to show five qualities that you believe make a good leader.

Preview assignments like these will spark your interest and get you ready to tackle new concepts. Next come the exciting activities that make up the heart of each lesson. As you're about to see, these activities draw on many ways of being smart—our multiple intelligences.

Multiple-Intelligence Teaching Strategies

The teaching strategies in the TCI Approach are based on hands-on learning. Every lesson in *History Alive! The Ancient World* is built around a fun and exciting activity. We mentioned some examples earlier. Here are some other things you and your classmates will do to experience ancient history:

- For Chapter 7, you'll use your bodies to model the physical geography of ancient Egypt, Kush, and Canaan.
- For Chapter 14, you'll pretend to be archeologists digging up the ancient Indian city of Mohenjodaro.
- For Chapter 35, you'll take a journey back in time to experience life as a teenager during the Roman Empire.

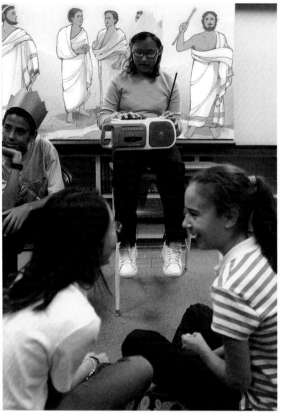

Activities like these will challenge you to use your multiple intelligences. Think about times when learning new things has been easier for you. Were you looking at pictures about the new ideas? Were you writing about them? Does acting out an event help you to better understand what happened? Studying history is a lot easier and more fun when you learn new ideas in ways that best suit your learning styles. Here's a list of seven different intelligences:

Using your multiple intelligences helps you learn and remember what you study.

- Linguistic (word smart)
- Logical-mathematical (number/reasoning smart)
- Spatial (picture smart)
- Body-kinesthetic (body smart)
- Musical (music smart)
- Interpersonal (people smart)
- Intrapersonal (self smart)

While you're engaged in fun and exciting activities, you'll also be reading this book to learn more about ancient history. The next page explains why this book is so easy to read.

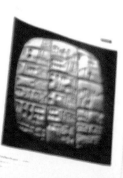

You'll use *History Alive! The Ancient World* during classroom activities. You'll be turning to it over and over again to find the information you need to know.

Considerate Text

The TCI Approach is all about being successful and having fun while you learn. You're about to discover that reading *History Alive! The Ancient World* is interesting to read and easy to understand. That's because this book is "reader friendly," which is another of saying that it makes readers want to read it. Some people call this *considerate text*. The writers of this book considered your needs as a reader and made sure you would have fun reading.

Here are some of the ways this book is considerate of all levels of readers:

- Each chapter is organized around key concepts. Introduction and summary sections point out the big ideas in the chapter.
- Each chapter begins with a graphic organizer—a picture that represents the main ideas of the chapter. The graphic organizer also appears in the Reading Notes in your Interactive Student Notebook. It will help you remember key ideas long after you've read the chapter.
- Short chapters make it easier for you to understand and remember what each one is about.
- Each section has a clear focus and a subtitle that provides an outline for your reading. Research shows that presenting new information in easy-to-manage chunks makes it easier to understand.
- Important new words are in bold type. These words are defined in the margins and in the Glossary at the back of the book.
- Photos and illustrations provide additional information about the topic on the page. A great way to check your understanding is to ask yourself, "How does this picture show what I just read?"

Most importantly, *History Alive! The Ancient World* is as exciting to read as a good story. The next section explains a special way of taking notes that will help you remember what you read.

Graphically Organized Reading Notes

Note taking is very important in the TCI Approach. As you read this book, you'll complete Reading Notes in your Interactive Student Notebook. You'll answer important questions, find main ideas, and connect new ideas to what you already know.

Your Reading Notes will leave you with a picture in your mind of each chapter's key ideas. The graphic organizers at the start of each chapter will help be a visual reminder of what you read. In your Reading Notes, you'll use those same graphic organizers to record key ideas. For example, in Chapter 1, you'll be taking notes on an illustration of a cave wall. Your notes will show archeologists' hypotheses (guesses) about some ancient paintings you discover in a cave. For Chapter 16, you will take notes on an illustrated path. The path represents the experiences of Prince Siddhartha, the founder of Buddhism. For Chapter 33, you will take notes on and around a drawing of a pan balance. You'll use the balance to show how political power in the Roman Republic was divided between two key groups, patricians and plebeians.

Completing your Reading Notes will help you study in two ways. First, it will encourage you to think carefully about what you read. Second, recording key ideas will help you remember them for a long time.

There's one more part of the TCI Approach that will help you remember the important ideas you are learning. Read the next page to find out out.

You'll record key ideas on the Reading Notes pages in your Interactive Student Notebook. This will help you remember what you learned long after the lesson is over.

Hindu Beliefs Mandala

In the top symbol it shows how the one all-powerful god, Brahman, is everything and everyone. This relates to the second figure after that because it shows all four other powerful gods and how they are all part of Brahman. The third symbol shows Dharma. The second symbol goes with this because when people were trying to live a good Dharma they had to worship Brahman. The fourth symbol is Karma. In Karma good and bad actions affect your life. This goes with the third symbol because the gods and

In Processing assignments, you'll show that you understand the new ideas of the lesson.

Processing Assignments

At the end of each lesson, you'll complete a Processing assignment in your Interactive Student Notebook. Here you'll show that you understand the key concepts of the lesson.

These pages encourage you to relate ideas to one another. You'll make connections between the past and present. You'll show your understanding of concepts by creating illustrations, diagrams, flowcharts, poetry, and cartoons. As one student told us, "It's really cool to have a place in our notebooks where we can record our own ideas. It makes learning history a lot more fun."

Here are some examples of the kinds of Processing assignments you'll complete:

• In Chapter 13, you will learn how the physical geography of India affected where people chose to settle. In the Processing assignment, you'll create a real estate ad to convince people to settle in a desirable region.

• For Chapter 20, you will dig up an ancient tomb to learn about China's Shang dynasty. In the Processing assignment, you'll decorate a bronze vessel by drawing two artifacts you found. Then you'll write a paragraph explaining what each artifact shows about the Shang dynasty.

• In Chapter 34, you will study the growth of the Roman Empire. In the Processing assignment, you'll write a poem using key terms to praise the growth of the empire.

Students across the country report that their Processing assignments have helped them understand and remember what they have learned. As a result, they are earning higher test scores.

Multiple-Intelligence Assessments

Do you dread taking chapter and unit tests? If so, maybe you feel that most tests don't let you show what you've learned. The tests for *History Alive! The Ancient World* are different. They let you show how well you understand each lesson's key ideas.

These tests also allow you to use your multiple intelligences. Each test has some of the usual multiple-choice questions. These will help prepare you for taking more formal tests. But other parts of the assessments will challenge you to use more than just your "word smart" intelligence. They'll give you a chance to shine if you are good in other areas, such as reading maps, using charts and graphs, drawing, understanding music, or analyzing historical paintings. You may also be asked to show how well you read. You'll be invited to express your ideas and your understanding of historical events in writing, too.

The secret to doing well on tests is preparation. You have the perfect tool for this purpose: your Interactive Student Notebook. Right there on those pages are your notes about all the key ideas in each chapter. Students who study their Reading Notes and Processing assignments before a test usually earn good test scores.

Success on tests is important, but the most important thing of all is learning. We've designed our tests not just to assess your understanding but to help you remember key ideas. That's because the lessons you learn from ancient history can help you make sense of your world and guide your future decisions. We hope that what you learn in *History Alive! The Ancient World* will remain with you for years to come.

Your teacher may give you test pages to complete at the end of a lesson. These tests include questions with multiple-choice answers as well as questions that let you draw or write your answers.

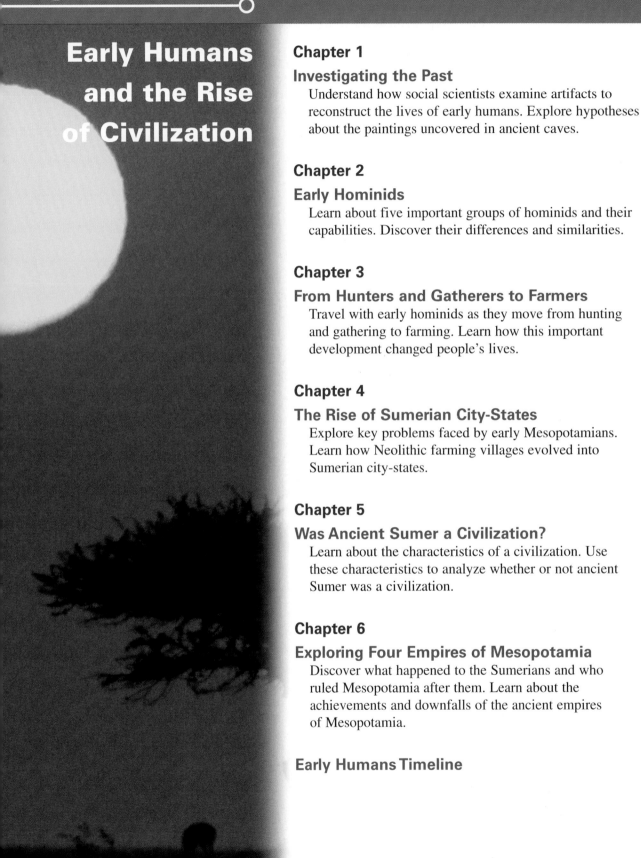

UNIT 1

Early Humans and the Rise of Civilization

UNIT 2

Ancient Egypt and the Near East

UNIT 3

Ancient India

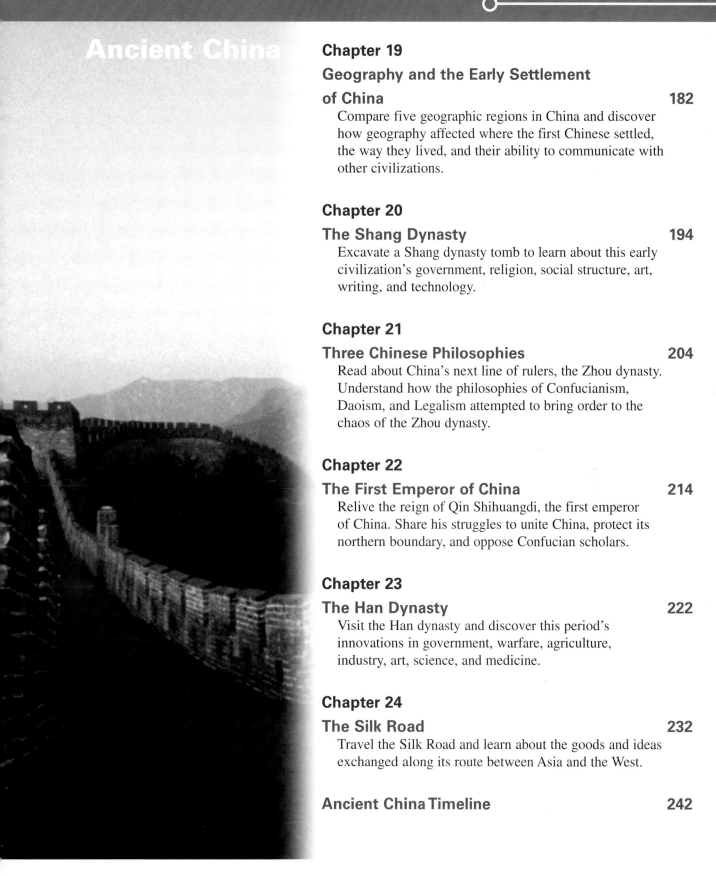

UNIT 4

Ancient China

UNIT 5

Ancient Greece

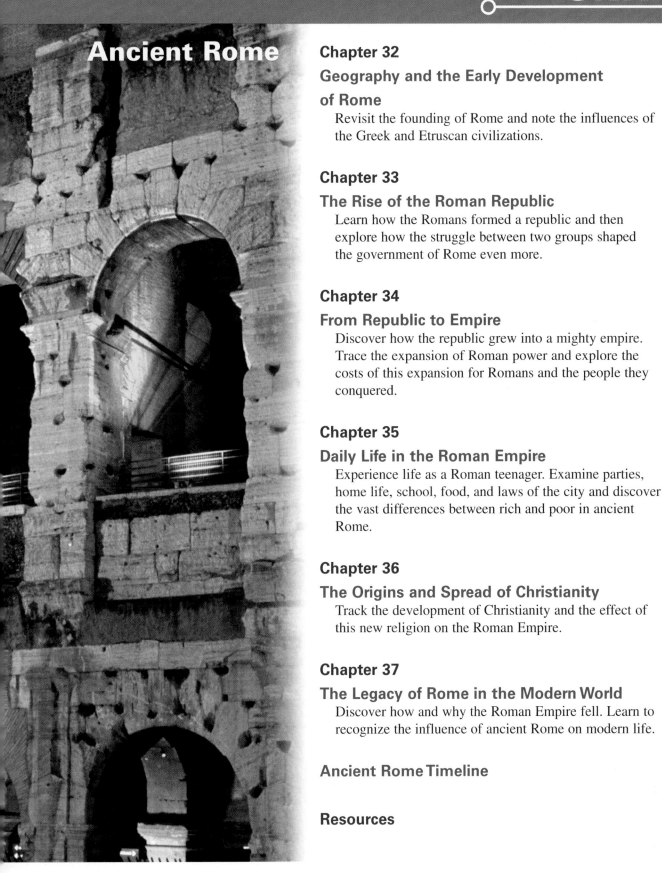

UNIT 6

Ancient Rome

UNIT 1

Early Humans and the Rise of Civilization

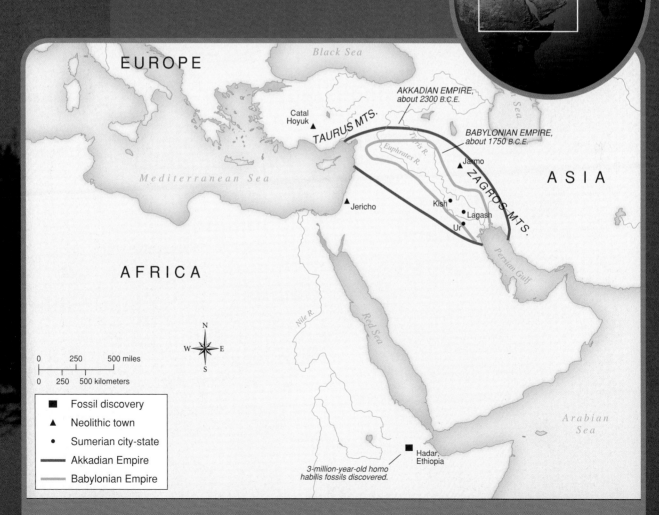

Early Humans and Civilizations, 3 Million to 1750 B.C.E.

CHAPTER 1

◀ ◀ ◀ Prehistoric paintings of bulls were found in a cave in Lascaux, France.

Investigating the Past

1.1 Introduction

Welcome to the world of ancient history! Studying history involves investigating what happened in the past and why. **Ancient history** concerns the distant past, from the earliest humans through the first great civilizations.

How can we learn about events that happened so long ago? People who study history are a lot like detectives conducting an investigation. They ask questions, study the evidence for clues, and form hypotheses (educated guesses).

Our investigation of the ancient past starts near the very beginning of human history. What was life like long, long ago?

One of the most amazing clues about what life was like long ago was discovered by four teenagers at Lascaux, France. On September 12, 1940, the four boys found a cave. All over the walls and ceiling of the cave were paintings of animals. The paintings seemed to be very old. Who had created them? What did they mean?

How would you solve a mystery like this one? The clues are centuries old, and the witnesses are gone. An expert detective might help, but whom should you ask?

In this chapter, you'll meet three kinds of experts who study the past: **archeologists, historians,** and **geographers**. Then you'll look at some fascinating examples of cave art to see what this evidence can teach us about life long ago.

Use this graphic organizer to help you learn more about how scientists investigate the past.

1.2 Detectives Who Study the Past

Scholars who study human society are called *social scientists*. Many social scientists can help us study the past. Among these "history detectives" are archeologists, historians, and geographers.

Archeologists: Digging Up the Past Archeologists study the past by examining objects that people have left behind. These **artifacts** are anything made or used by people, such as clothing, tools, weapons, and coins. When archeologists discover a place that has artifacts, they ask, Who lived in this place? When did they live? What were they like? Then they study the artifacts for clues.

Historians: Recording the Past Historians are the recorders of the past. Human beings have been around a very long time. Historians are most interested in the last few thousand years, when people began leaving written records. The first question historians ask is, What happened in the past? To find out, they study all kinds of artifacts and documents. They read diaries and letters. Besides asking what happened, they try to understand why events happened the way they did.

Geographers: Mapping the Past Geographers study natural features of the Earth, such as water, landforms, plants, and animals. They also look at humanmade features, such as towns, roads, bridges, and dams. They can help us answer questions like these: Where did people live? How did they use their environment to survive? Geographers often create maps to show what they have learned.

Social scientists who study prehistoric history face a unique challenge because there is very little evidence from prehistoric times. There are huge gaps of time for which there is no evidence at all. This means that scientists can look at the same evidence and come up with different answers, or theories, about how humans came to be.

artifact an object made or used by people in the past

Archeologists carefully study artifacts for clues about the past.

1.3 Cave Art: Treasures of the Past

Cave paintings like those at Lascaux, France, provide clues about what life was like in **prehistoric** times, before writing was invented. Caves with paintings thousands of years old have been found all over the world. The paintings show what animals roamed the Earth. They show how people hunted. Often they offer hints about what people believed.

Many of the rooms that are decorated with paintings are deep inside the caves. Scientists guess that cave artists used torches as they worked in these dark places. Some of the paintings are very large and taller than a person. Some were done on high ceilings. Scientists guess that prehistoric artists built scaffolding, or planks raised above the floor, to reach the highest places.

Caves have also provided clues in the form of artifacts. Scientists have found lamps for burning animal fat, bits of rope, and tools for painting and engraving. Cave paintings and artifacts are amazing treasures, because they can help answer many questions about how ancient humans lived. But, as you will see, they also raise new questions for scientists to puzzle over.

prehistoric before written history

Cave painters developed different methods for applying paint to the walls of a cave. This museum exhibit shows one such technique.

1.4 Cave Painting of a Human

This painting was found inside the cave at Lascaux in France. It was painted between 11,000 and 18,000 years ago.

The painting shows a scene from a hunt. The man is about to be gored (pierced by the horn of an animal). The animal, which is a wooly mammoth or a bison (a kind of buffalo), is wounded. It has a spear in its side, and its insides are spilling onto the ground. The man is lying in front of it. He is wearing a mask that looks like a bird. Next to him is a long stick with a bird on top. The stick is probably a spear thrower, a kind of handle used to hurl a spear.

Paintings of humans are rare in cave art. Notice that the man is drawn simply, like a stick figure. The animal is much more realistic.

Most social scientists think this painting was created as part of a hunting **ritual**. The artist may have been asking for a successful hunt. Or the painting might be a record of an actual event or simply a decoration.

This hunting scene may show items used in special ceremonies. Notice the man's bird mask and the bird on top of the stick.

1.5 Cave Painting of Animals

This painting is a copy of one found at Lascaux. The part of the cave where the painting was found was closed to protect the art.

The painting was created about 17,000 years ago. It shows many prehistoric animals, such as bulls, bison, and horses.

The painters used the cave's uneven walls as part of their composition. At the lower left, a ledge juts out from the wall. The artists painted horses to look as if they are running along it.

Look at the bull in the center of this painting. Do you see how its neck is stretched out, as if the bull is running away?

Scientists have many ideas about why animal paintings were created. Some believe that the artists tried to capture the "magical powers" of certain animals. Some think the painters believed in spirits and created the art to honor or influence them. Some speculate that the cave was a place of worship and that paintings were used in rituals or ceremonies.

1.6 Cave Painting of Shapes and Handprints

This painting was found in a cave in Argentina, South America. It shows a circular shape, a sticklike animal, and several handprints.

The handprints in this cave painting are very small. Prehistoric people were probably much smaller than people are today.

Paintings of shapes and handprints are fairly common in cave art. Their meaning, though, is a bit of a mystery. Many scientists believe that the handprints were the way an artist signed a painting. Some think geometric shapes had special meanings in rituals.

Researchers tried singing inside one painted cave in France. They discovered that the sound was loudest in the areas that were painted. They guess those areas were used for special gatherings.

The horse carved on this spear thrower looks full of energy.

These clay sculptures may offer clues about the people who made them and why they made them.

1.7 Spear Thrower

This prehistoric spear thrower was found in France. Made from a reindeer antler bone, it is 10 inches long. It was probably made about 18,000 years ago.

The spear thrower has a leaping horse carved into the top. The artist engraved, or carved, hundreds of tiny dashes to show details in the horse's head. The artist must have cared a great deal about decorating this important hunting tool.

Some scientists believe that the artist carved the horse for decoration. It could have been a good-luck charm to protect the hunter or make him or her more successful. It might have been related to the hunter's name. Or it could have been a way of identifying the clan that the hunter belonged to.

1.8 Clay Sculptures

These clay sculptures of two bison were found in a low room, deep inside a cave in France. They were made about 10,000 to 14,000 years ago. They are 23 inches long. The artist sculpted them from gold-colored clay. Carved lines show details such as the animals' faces, coat markings, and the fringe of fur below their powerful necks.

Scientists have two main ideas about why these sculptures were created. One is that the sculptures showed that the cave belonged to a certain clan. The other idea is that they were used in an important ceremony that was held deep inside the cave. It might have been a coming-of-age ceremony to show that a child had become an adult. One clue that supports this idea is that footprints of young people have been found near the sculptures.

1.9 Cave Art Tools

The prehistoric tools and materials you see here include two piles of colored, rock-hard minerals and a grindstone for grinding the minerals. There are also a sculptor's pick and an engraving tool.

Scientists study tools like these and try to guess how they were used. For example, scientists believe that cave artists made paints by grinding colored minerals into powder. They probably mixed the powder with animal fat or vegetable oil to create various colors.

You've already seen how prehistoric artists engraved some of their art. For painting, they might have used brushes made of moss, fur, or human hair. They may also have blown paint through hollow bird bones to create softer textures, such as shaggy winter coats on horses.

Cave artists used tools made of sharpened stones to sculpt and engrave objects and cave walls.

1.10 Chapter Summary

In this chapter, you've learned how archeologists, historians, and geographers are like detectives who solve the mysteries of the past: they ask questions, study the evidence for clues, and form hypotheses. You've also studied examples of prehistoric cave art to find clues about how people lived long ago.

No one knows for sure why these colorful images and sculptures were created. Some might simply have been decorations. Others might be records of important events. Or they may have been used in rituals or to influence or honor the spirit world.

Scientists are always learning more about the distant past. Are you ready to join them by studying clues and weighing the evidence? In the next chapter, you'll explore the first hominids and how they lived.

CHAPTER 2

◀ ◀ Humans living 2 million years ago shaped
stone and animal bones into simple tools.

Early Hominids

2.1 Introduction

In Chapter 1, you explored cave paintings made by prehistoric humans. Scientists call these prehistoric humans **hominids**. In this chapter, you will learn about five important groups of hominids.

You've already met three kinds of "history detectives"—archeologists, historians, and geographers. The study of hominids involves a fourth type, paleoanthropologists. Anthropologists study human development and culture. Paleoanthropologists specialize in studying the earliest hominids. (*Paleo* means "ancient.")

In 1974, an American paleoanthropologist, Donald Johanson, made an exciting discovery. He was searching for artifacts under a hot African sun when he found a partial skeleton. The bones included a piece of skull, a jawbone, a rib, and leg bones.

After careful study, Johanson decided the bones came from a female hominid who lived more than 3 million years ago. He nicknamed her "Lucy" while he was listening to the song "Lucy in the Sky with Diamonds," by the Beatles. She is one of the earliest hominids ever discovered.

What have scientists found out about Lucy and other hominids? How were these hominids like us? How were they different? What **capabilities,** or skills, did each group have? Let's find out.

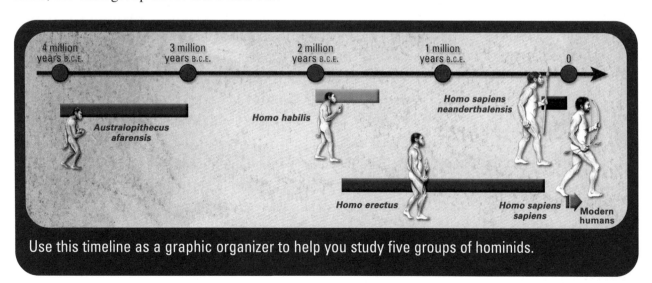

Use this timeline as a graphic organizer to help you study five groups of hominids.

2.2 *Australopithecus Afarensis:* Lucy and Her Relatives

Traditionally, scientists have given Latin names to groups of living things. (Latin was the language of the ancient Romans. You will learn about the Romans in a later unit.) An **anthropologist** in Africa called the earliest known group of hominids *Australopithecus,* or "southern ape." Donald Johanson decided to call the group Lucy belonged to *Australopithecus afarensis.* The second part of this name refers to the Afar Triangle, the part of Africa where Lucy was found.

Scientists have learned a lot about early hominids by studying Lucy. By assembling her bones, they know something about what she looked like. Lucy was short compared to humans today, about 3 feet tall. She had a mix of ape and human features. Her arms were long, but her hands and feet were similar to a modern human's. She had a large head, and her forehead and jaw stuck out from her face.

2.3 Lucy and Her Relatives: Walking on Two Feet

The **remains** of other hominids like Lucy have been found in the same area. Scientists guess that Lucy's relatives lived in Africa, about 3 to 4 million years ago.

Exactly how are hominids like Lucy related to later hominids and to us? Anthropologists often disagree about questions like this. One reason is that they have so few clues to work with. Bones as old as Lucy's are very hard to find. Still, most anthropologists agree that Lucy and her relatives were very early forms of humans.

One discovery about Lucy was especially exciting. By studying her skeleton, scientists found out that she was a **biped**. That means she walked on two feet. This gave Lucy and her relatives many advantages compared to such animals as gorillas and chimpanzees. With their hands free, they could gather and carry food more easily. They could also use their hands to defend themselves and their children.

Being a biped is one important way that Lucy resembled us. In other ways, hominids like Lucy were quite different from modern humans. Lucy's brain was only about one third the size of ours. Scientists have found no tools from Lucy's time. They also don't think these early hominids were able to talk.

Australopithecus afarensis

Because *Australopithecus afarensis* walked on two feet, adults were able to carry their young children in their arms.

2.4 *Homo Habilis:* Handy Man

A second group of hominids was discovered by the husband-and-wife team of Louis and Mary Leakey. The Leakeys were searching for evidence of early hominids in Africa when they discovered some hominid bones. The bones were scattered among artifacts that looked like tools. The Leakeys named their discovery *Homo habilis,* or "Handy Man," in honor of its ability to make tools.

Handy Man lived a little closer to our time than Lucy, about 1.5 to 2 million years ago. Like Lucy, the hominids in this group had a combination of ape and human features. They also walked on two feet. But they were taller than Lucy. Their features were slightly more humanlike, and their brains were twice the size of hers.

Scientists have found Handy Man remains only in Africa. They have also discovered the bones of more than one Handy Man together. This means these hominids probably lived in groups. Living with others would have helped them survive. They could work together to protect themselves against animal attacks. They could also collect food over larger areas of land.

Homo habilis

2.5 Handy Man: The Toolmaker

The tools found by the Leakeys were a very important clue. Along with a larger brain, the ability to use tools was a key difference between Handy Man and hominids like Lucy. It shows that Handy Man was more advanced and more like modern humans than Lucy was.

Handy Man's tools were very simple. These hominids used rocks as chopping tools. They made sharp pieces of stone for cutting. They used animal bones as digging sticks.

Making a tool, even a simple one, takes some thought. First, the hominids had to imagine what kind of tool to make. Then they had to plan how to make it. Finally, they had to craft what they wanted. They may also have passed on what they learned to others.

The ability to make tools helped Handy Man live better and longer than Lucy and hominids like her. Using cutting tools allowed these hominids to take meat from dead animals. They may have used crushing tools to crack animal bones and then eaten the marrow inside. They may even have dug or made traps for small animals.

Homo habilis may have used stone tools to skin animals.

2.6 *Homo Erectus:* Upright Man

A third type of hominid was discovered in 1891 by a Dutchman named Eugene Dubois. He and his team were searching for artifacts on the island of Java, off the southern coast of Asia, when they found a new type of hominid skull.

Eventually, Dubois' team discovered the bones of many more hominids. When they assembled the bones, they could see that these hominids stood up straight. Dubois named this hominid group *Homo erectus,* or "Upright Man." (Lucy and Handy Man had not yet been discovered.)

Upright Man was around longer than any other hominid group, from 1.8 million to 200,000 B.C.E. Scientists believe they were the first hominids to **migrate** out of Africa. Their remains have been found in Asia and Europe.

It's no wonder that scientists have found Upright Man bones in many places. This group of hominids was made for traveling. They were taller and thinner than earlier hominids—some even reaching the height of modern humans. Their bones were very strong. And they were good walkers and runners.

The face of Upright Man looked more like a modern human than those of earlier hominids did. Their foreheads were round and smooth. But they still had a large ridge above the eyes, a thicker skull, and a jaw that stuck out.

2.7 Upright Man: Traveling with Fire

Like Handy Man, hominids in the Upright Man group were toolmakers. But with their larger brains, they were able to invent more complex tools, including strong hand-axes made of stone.

Upright Man's greatest advantage was the ability to use fire. Anthropologists have found burned animal bones in the same places as Upright

Homo erectus

Man remains. This clue means that Upright Man probably used fire to cook animal meat.

Scientists aren't sure whether these hominids were hunters or whether they found dead animals to eat. But studies of their tools and teeth show that they ate more meat than earlier hominids did. They feasted on red deer, elephant, rhinoceros, goat, boar, and oysters.

The remains of an ancient campsite in France have provided additional clues about how Upright Man lived. Scientists guess that they built oval huts by covering posts with tree branches. In the center of the hut, they kept a fire burning. They sat and slept on animal skins. They may have decorated their bodies with yellow-colored mud called *ocher*.

Scientists believe that Upright Man groups moved from place to place, creating shelters with tools and using fire to keep warm. These abilities helped them travel farther and survive longer than earlier hominids. Building shelters allowed them to live in colder climates and in places where there were no caves to provide natural shelter. Being able to control fire helped them survive the cold and protect themselves against animals.

Homo erectus was the first hominid to use fire for warmth and cooking. These hominids probably carried a glowing ember when they moved from place to place.

2.8 *Homo Sapiens Neanderthalensis:* Neanderthals

In 1856, some mine workers in Germany's Neander Valley found a skeleton. It had thick bones and a ridge above the eyes, but it was also very humanlike. Today most scientists consider this group of hominids to be a distinct type of *Homo sapiens* ("Wise Man"), the large-brained group that modern humans belong to. Scientists call this group *Homo sapiens neanderthalensis,* or Neanderthal Man.

Neanderthals lived after Upright Man, from 230,000 to 30,000 years ago. They lived in Africa, the Near East, Europe, and parts of Asia.

The appearance of the skeleton found in Germany led people to imagine that Neanderthals walked hunched over, with their hands dragging on the ground. As it turned out, the skeleton was of an older man who had a bone disease. In reality, Neanderthals walked upright. They were shorter and stockier than modern humans, but they were also much stronger.

Most important, Neanderthals had large brains. They used their intelligence to become skilled toolmakers. More than 60 types of Neanderthal tools have been found. These tools required much more planning, skill, and knowledge than those of earlier hominids. Neanderthals created knives, scrapers, and spear points. They learned how to make sharp, thin blades by slicing off the top of a rock and then creating two or three sharp flakes from the original piece.

The ability to make better tools certainly helped Neanderthals survive. But they were helped even more by their ability to work together. They lived and traveled in groups. And they were the first early hominids to hunt in an organized group.

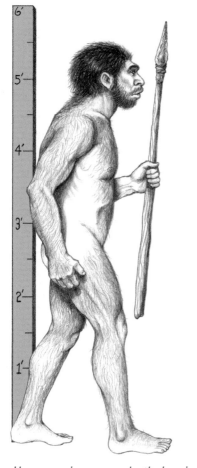

Homo sapiens neanderthalensis

2.9 Neanderthals: A Sense of Community

Scientists believe that Neanderthals had a sense of community. When members of a group died, they were laid in burial mounds along with hunting tools and flowers. This shows that Neanderthals cared about one another and had a sense of ritual.

When they hunted, Neanderthals worked together to surround and trap an animal. They then moved in close to kill it with spears. Sometimes they would be injured. But if they got hurt, it seems that other members of the group would take care of them. Scientists have found Neanderthal bones that were broken and then healed. These clues lead them to think that Neanderthals cared for their injured and sick.

This evidence of caring for each other is another sign of a sense of community. And if Neanderthals lived as a community, they were also able to learn from the experience and wisdom of older members of the group.

Exactly how are Neanderthals related to early modern humans? Scientists aren't sure. Judging from the remains that have been found of both groups, Neanderthals existed side by side with early modern humans for about 10,000 years. No one knows exactly why they disappeared. All we know for sure is that only one type of *Homo sapiens* survived to become early modern humans.

Evidence suggests that *Homo sapiens neanderthalensis* lived in communities and cared for each other.

land bridge a piece of land connecting two continents

2.10 *Homo Sapiens Sapiens:* Early Modern Humans

In 1879, an eight-year-old Spanish girl named Maria was exploring a cave with her father when she made an amazing discovery. She found a cave room filled with ancient paintings of deer, bison, wild horses, and boars. They were the first prehistoric cave paintings ever discovered.

The people who created these paintings were the earliest members of our own group, *Homo sapiens sapiens,* or "Doubly Wise Man." These early modern (or prehistoric) humans lived from 35,000 to 12,000 B.C.E. Most scientists believe they originated in Africa. From there they spread to Europe, Asia, and Australia. Eventually they migrated to North and South America, probably traveling across **land bridges,** which were later covered by water.

The first modern humans looked more like us than Neanderthals did. They had high, rounded skulls, large brains, small teeth, and slender bones. But their bodies were not as well adapted to the cold as those of Neanderthals. They survived because of their ability to create better tools, shelter, and clothing.

As toolmakers, early modern humans were even more skilled than Neanderthals. They attached thin blades to bone, antler, and stone to create a wide variety of tools. They made tools for engraving and sculpting. They fashioned needles for sewing animal skins together. They also built shelters of earth and stone.

These prehistoric humans were also better hunters than earlier hominids. They made hooks and spears to catch fish. Most important, they invented the spear thrower and the bow and arrow. With these weapons, they could hunt from a distance, which meant hunting was much safer.

2.11 Early Modern Humans: The First Artists

Early modern humans left behind a fascinating record of their lives through their artwork. They painted on the walls of their caves. They carved and shaped images out of clay, bone, flint (a hard mineral), and ivory. They even created musical instruments.

Prehistoric artists created a variety of images. Some images came from the world around them, like the animals they hunted. Some came from their imaginations, such as mythical creatures. As you learned in Chapter 1, these early artists also made patterns using shapes, and they may have signed their work with handprints.

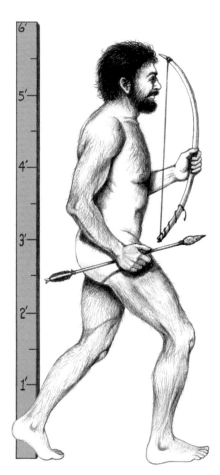

Homo sapiens sapiens

Why did early modern humans create art? Many scientists believe they painted to express themselves. Some think they used pictures to teach their children. Others think they created images for religious purposes.

One thing is certain. These early humans didn't just exist in their world. They had feelings about it and created images to express those feelings. They had the ability to imagine, dream, and communicate thoughts to others through pictures and symbols. Some scientists believe these abilities contributed to the development of complex language, one of the capabilities that make us fully human.

Once *Homo sapiens sapiens* had food and shelter, these prehistoric humans had time to create art that expressed their feelings about the world.

2.12 Chapter Summary

In this chapter, you learned about five hominid groups and their different capabilities. Each change along the way—from walking upright to creating better tools—was a key step in the development of early modern humans.

The next chapter looks at another dramatic change. Early hominids gathered or hunted their food. Next you'll discover how life changed when people learned to grow their own food.

CHAPTER 3

By learning to plant and harvest crops, hunter-gatherers became farmers.

From Hunters and Gatherers to Farmers

3.1 Introduction

In the last chapter, you learned about five important groups of hominids. Like the hominids before them, early modern humans hunted and gathered their food. In this chapter, you'll read about how people learned, over thousands of years, to farm their own food.

Humans discovered farming toward the end of the Stone Age. The **Stone Age** gets its name from the tools people made of stone. It began with the first toolmaking hominids about 2 million years ago. It lasted until around 3000 B.C.E., when people learned to make tools and weapons out of metal.

Historians divide the Stone Age into periods. The first is the **Paleolithic Age,** or Old Stone Age. During this time, people got their food by hunting wild animals and gathering nuts, berries, and other plants. They lived much of their lives out in the open and rarely stayed in one place for long.

By about 8000 B.C.E., some groups of people had learned how to raise animals and crops for food. With this discovery, the **Neolithic Age,** or New Stone Age, began. For the first time, people settled down to live in one place.

The shift from being hunter-gatherers to being farmers is one of the most important advances people have ever made. In this chapter, you'll explore the many ways it changed human life.

The cartoon characters in this graphic organizer will help you understand what life was like during Neolithic times.

3.2 From Old Stone Age to New Stone Age

The Old Stone (Paleolithic) Age began about 2 million years ago and lasted until about 8000 B.C.E. It was during this time that early modern humans developed. Like the hominids who came before them, early humans were hunter-gatherers. They wandered from place to place, looking for animals to hunt and plants to gather for food. Often they took shelter in caves, like the cave painters you read about in Chapter 1.

The New Stone (Neolithic) Age began when people learned to farm and produce their own food. The discovery of farming did not happen all at once. Over thousands of years, people gradually learned to raise animals and plant crops. Eventually they began to rely on farms for their food. Now they could settle down in one place instead of roaming in search of things to eat.

The Neolithic Age began around 8000 B.C.E. and lasted until about 3000 B.C.E., when people learned to make tools out of metal instead of stone. Farming developed in many parts of the world during this time, including parts of Europe, Africa, Asia, and the Americas.

Many Neolithic settlements were located east of the Mediterranean Sea, where the land was fertile (good for growing crops). Here, people built towns and villages such as Jericho, Catal Hoyuk, and Jarmo (see map).

People in settlements like these lived very different lives from earlier hunter-gatherers. With farms to provide their food, they could build permanent shelters and form larger communities. They could make better tools and clothing. And they could trade with people in other places for resources they wanted. As you will see, these changes made life safer, more comfortable, and more interesting.

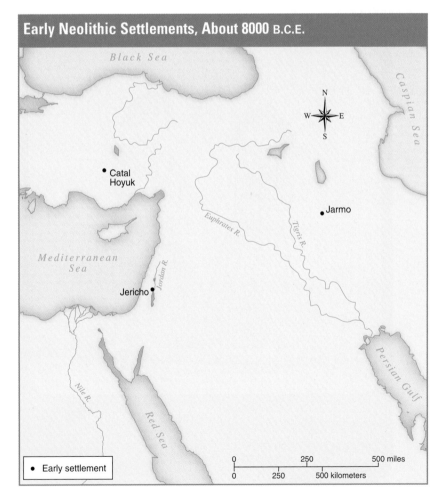

Early Neolithic Settlements, About 8000 B.C.E.

Black Sea

Caspian Sea

Catal Hoyuk

Jarmo

Euphrates R.

Tigris R.

Mediterranean Sea

Jordan R.

Jericho

Nile R.

Red Sea

Persian Gulf

- Early settlement

0   250   500 miles
0   250   500 kilometers

3.3 Creating a Stable Food Supply

During the Paleolithic Age, people obtained food by hunting animals and gathering plants. But hunting and gathering did not provide a very stable, or dependable, food supply. Wild plants and animals grew scarce when people stayed in one area for too long. And hunting was dangerous. Hunters were often injured or killed.

Gradually, people discovered they didn't have to depend on hunting and gathering. Instead of gathering wild plants, they could plant seeds and harvest crops. Over time, they learned which seeds produced the most crops in the areas where they lived.

Early farmers also learned how to **domesticate** animals, raising and using them for their own purposes. They raised sheep, goats, and cattle for their meat. They got milk from both goats and cattle. They used mules to carry heavy loads and pull plows.

Together, the growing of crops and the domestication of animals are called **agriculture**. The Neolithic Age began with the invention of agriculture. For the first time, people had a stable food supply. Let's explore why this change was one of the most important advances in all of history.

domesticate to train a wild animal to be useful to humans
agriculture the business of farming

In this Neolithic painting, herdsmen are shown with cattle.

3.4 Making Permanent Shelters

The first great change brought about by agriculture was the development of permanent shelters. During the Paleolithic Age, people had lived in caves or rough, tentlike structures. These shelters were temporary because hunter-gatherers often moved to follow wild animals or find new plants to eat. As people settled down to farm during the Neolithic Age, they built more permanent shelters.

In many areas, people packed mud bricks together to build round or rectangular houses. Sometimes they added stones and tree branches to strengthen the walls and roof. The houses had openings high in the walls. People probably climbed a ladder to reach the openings and enter the house.

Inside were several rooms. Places to store food were built into the floor. Pits for cooking were dug into the floor and lined with clay. People may have filled the pits with water and dropped in hot stones to make the water boil for cooking.

The development of permanent shelters was important in several ways. Houses gave people protection from harsh weather and wild animals. They made life more comfortable. They allowed new ways of cooking food. And living in permanent shelters allowed people to form larger communities.

Neolithic houses were made of packed mud, which helped keep people warm in winter and cool in summer.

3.5 Establishing Communities

Along with permanent shelters, farming allowed people to form larger communities. In Paleolithic times, small bands of 20 to 60 people wandered from place to place in search of food. Once people began farming, they could settle down near their farms. As a result, towns and villages grew up, like those at Jericho (in present-day Israel) and Catal Hoyuk (Turkey).

Living in communities allowed people to organize themselves more efficiently. They could divide up the work of producing food and other things they needed. While some workers grew crops, others built new houses and made tools.

Village dwellers also learned to work together to do a task faster. For example, toolmakers could share the work of making stone axes and knife blades. By working together, they could make more tools in the same amount of time.

With their basic needs met, people had more time and energy for other activities. They could invent new ways of making their lives safer and more comfortable. Larger communities could also defend themselves more easily against enemies. The Neolithic town of Jericho, for example, was protected by strong stone walls. All these changes helped populations to grow where farming villages developed.

Neolithic villages were the first real communities.

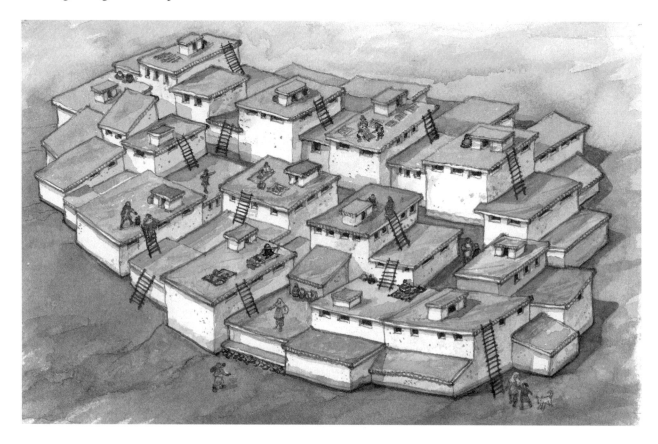

People in Neolithic communities had time and tools to create works of art.

3.6 Developing New Jobs

Having a stable food supply allowed people to develop new kinds of jobs. In Paleolithic times, people's main job was finding enough food to survive. With farms to provide their food, Neolithic people could develop more specialized skills.

A good example is the town of Catal Hoyuk, which dates back to about 6000 B.C.E. Historians believe that the town's people worked in a number of different jobs. Besides farmers, there were weavers, basket makers, toolmakers, and traders.

Focusing on one job allowed people to get better at their work. In Catal Hoyuk, farmers learned how to grow more than 14 kinds of food plants. Clothing makers developed a way to spin and weave. They wove natural fibers such as wool and linen into comfortable cloth. In some regions, people mined flint so that stoneworkers could create sharper tools.

Neolithic people didn't just want to survive. They wanted to make themselves, and their surroundings, more beautiful. They decorated their pottery and baskets with geometric shapes. Stoneworkers learned to polish stones to make shiny jewelry and mirrors. House builders added special rooms to honor the gods and goddesses they believed in.

The development of different jobs encouraged people to become highly skilled at their crafts. This led to new and better ways of doing things. And different jobs created much more variety in community life.

3.7 Beginning to Trade

Another major change in Neolithic times was the growth of **trade**. Paleolithic hunter-gatherers rarely traded with other groups. They usually used only the plants, animals, and other resources they found nearby. Once people settled in towns and villages, trade became much more common.

People trade to get resources they don't have in their own area. As Neolithic people became more skilled in their crafts, they wanted materials to improve the strength and beauty of the things they made. Getting those resources became the job of traders.

Traders often traveled hundreds of miles to find what they wanted. They crossed mountains on foot, rode donkeys across deserts, and sailed the Mediterranean Sea on ships.

What were the traders looking for? Popular items included flint and obsidian. Obsidian is a black glass from volcanic mountains. Craftspeople used it to make knife blades, arrowheads, and mirrors. People also traded for "beauty products" like shell ornaments and a red **ore** called *hematite*. Women rubbed hematite on their lips and cheeks to make them redder.

The growth of trade allowed people to make use of more resources. It also brought them into contact with people from distant places. These contacts helped spread ideas and knowledge around the ancient world.

trade the business of buying and selling or exchanging items

ore a mineral mined for its valuable uses

This arrowhead is made from obsidian. Neolithic traders all around the Mediterranean region prized this resource. It was found mostly in the area that is now Turkey.

3.8 Chapter Summary

In this chapter, you learned how the development of farming changed people's lives. For the first time, people had a stable supply of food. As a result, they could build permanent shelters and communities. They created new jobs and traded for the resources they needed. In the next chapter, you'll explore another dramatic change: the building of large cities.

CHAPTER 4

◄ ◄ ◄ These ruins in the Syrian desert reveal
an ancient Sumerian walled city.

The Rise of Sumerian City-States

4.1 Introduction

In Chapter 3, you learned how people began farming and living in small villages during Neolithic times. In this chapter, you'll discover how some small villages grew into large, complex cities.

These villages were located in a land of rolling hills and low plains called **Mesopotamia** (modern-day Iraq). *Mesopotamia* is a Greek word that means "the land between the rivers." The two rivers are the Tigris River and the Euphrates River. Cities first appeared in the southern part of this land, an area called **Sumer**.

The earliest cities in Sumer date back to about 3500 B.C.E. These first cities were like small, independent countries. They each had their own ruler and their own farmland to provide food. For this reason, they are called **city-states**.

Imagine that you are visiting one of these early cities. You see a walled settlement surrounded by farmland that supplies food for the city. The strong city walls are built of sunbaked bricks. Moats, or ditches filled with water, surround the walls. The moats help to keep out enemies. During an attack, people living outside the city walls fled inside for protection.

As you gaze on the city, you may wonder how it came to be built. Why didn't people in Mesopotamia go on living in small villages, as their ancestors had done for thousands of years? Why did large city-states grow up here, in the "Land Between the Rivers"? In this chapter, you'll find out.

Use this graphic organizer to help remember the changes that occurred in Mesopotamia.

4.2 Mesopotamia: A Difficult Environment

Mesopotamia was not an easy place to live. The northern part was hilly and received rain. The southern part was low plains, or flat land. The sun beat down fiercely on the plains between the Tigris River and the Euphrates River. There was little rain. The Mesopotamians were farmers, and farms need water. The rivers brought water to the plains when they flooded, but for most of the year the soil was hard and dry.

On the plains, building materials were difficult to find. There were plenty of reeds (weeds that grow near rivers). But there were few trees to provide wood. Even stones were scarce. And there were few natural barriers to keep out enemies.

Mesopotamians faced four key problems as they tried to survive in this environment:

- food shortages in the hills
- an uncontrolled water supply on the plains
- difficulties in building and maintaining **irrigation systems** to serve the needs of several villages at once
- attacks by neighboring communities

Over time, Mesopotamians found solutions to these problems. Let's explore how their solutions led to the building of some of the first cities in the world.

irrigation system
a means of supplying land with water

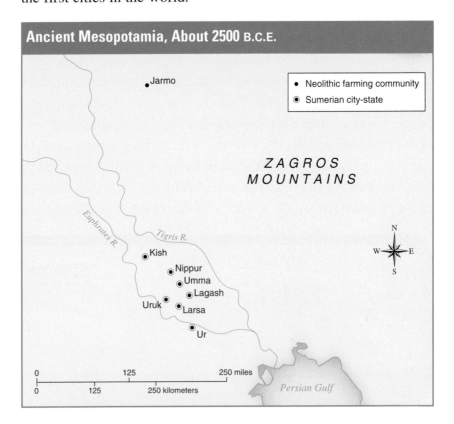

Ancient Mesopotamia, About 2500 B.C.E.

- Neolithic farming community
- Sumerian city-state

Jarmo

ZAGROS MOUNTAINS

Euphrates R.

Tigris R.

Kish
Nippur
Umma
Lagash
Uruk
Larsa
Ur

Persian Gulf

0   125   250 miles
0   125   250 kilometers

4.3 Food Shortages in the Hills

As you learned in the last chapter, in Neolithic times people in some areas of the world began farming. One of these areas was the rolling foothills of the Zagros Mountains in northern Mesopotamia.

Mild weather and plentiful rains made the foothills a good place to farm. The wooded hills provided timber for building shelters. There were plenty of stones in the hills for toolmaking. Over several thousand years, these conditions allowed the population in Mesopotamia to grow dramatically.

Then problems arose. By 5000 B.C.E., some historians believe, farmers in the Zagros foothills did not have enough land to grow food for the increasing number of people. As a result, villages began to suffer from food shortages.

Below the foothills and to the south, the Euphrates and Tigris Rivers ran through flat plains. The plains covered a large area of land, and no one lived there. During most of the year, the land was very hard and dry. And the plains lacked trees and stones for making shelters and tools.

Yet the plains held promise, too. In the spring the rivers flooded, bringing precious water. Perhaps farms could be built there.

Driven by the need for food, people moved out of the foothills and onto the plains. This region became known as Sumer, and its people would be called the **Sumerians**.

Sumerians ancient people who lived in the geographic region of Sumer

The Zagros foothills were an ideal place to farm.

4.4 Uncontrolled Water Supply in the River Valley

The farmers who moved to Sumer faced many challenges. One of the biggest problems was the uncontrolled water supply.

During the spring, rain and melted snow from the mountains flowed into the Tigris and Euphrates Rivers, causing them to flood across the plains. But no one could be sure exactly when the floods would come. If it happened after farmers planted their crops, their young plants would be washed away. For much of the rest of the year, the sunbaked soil was dry and hard as stone. Hot, strong winds blew thick layers of dust across the ground.

Faced with such dramatic seasonal changes, farmers had to constantly struggle to raise crops. Either they had too little water, or they had too much. To succeed in growing food, they needed a way to control the water so they would have a reliable water supply all year round.

So, Sumerian farmers began to create irrigation systems to provide water for their fields. They built earth walls, called **levees,** along the sides of the river to prevent flooding. When the land was dry, they poked holes in the levees. The water flowed through the holes and into the thirsty fields.

Over time, the Sumerians learned other ways to control the supply of water. They dug canals to shape the paths the water took. They also constructed dams along the river to block the water and force it to collect in pools they had built. The water was stored in these reservoirs for later use.

levee a wall of earth built to prevent a river from flooding its banks

The Euphrates is the longest river in southwestern Asia.

4.5 Difficulties in Building and Maintaining a Complex Irrigation System

Irrigation systems provided enough water for Sumerian farmers to grow plenty of food. But now a new problem arose: how to maintain the irrigation system across village boundaries.

The irrigation system passed through many villages as it carried water from the river to the fields. The system had to be maintained constantly. The canals had to be cleaned regularly as they became clogged with silt (very fine mud). One clogged canal could spoil the entire system.

Farmers could no longer live apart, or in small groups. They were connected for miles around by the canals. They had to work together for the common good.

Gradually, villages came to depend on each other to build and maintain their complex irrigation system. Workers from different villages probably worked together. They cleared the silt from the canals to keep them from clogging. They scooped water from one reservoir into another to make sure the water levels were balanced.

As the Sumerians worked together, they began to create larger communities. Between 3500 and 3000 B.C.E., villages grew into towns. Some towns in Sumer became cities with populations as great as several thousand people.

The Euphrates River still irrigates fields in Iraq today.

4.6 Attacks by Neighboring Communities

As Sumerian cities grew, they fought over the right to use more water. Sometimes cities located upriver (closer to where the river begins) built new canals or blocked other cities' canals. In this way, they kept water from reaching the cities that were downriver (farther from where the river begins). Fights over water became so intense that they led to bloodshed and killing.

Sumerians began to look for ways to protect their cities from their neighbors. The plains provided no natural barriers for protection. There were no mountain ranges or rushing rivers to keep out enemies. So, Sumerians began to build strong walls around their cities. The walls were made of mud bricks that were baked in the sun until they were hard. The Sumerians also dug moats outside the city walls to prevent enemies from entering the city. Most people lived in houses behind the walls, while the farms lay outside. In case of attack, farmers fled the fields and took safety inside the city walls.

The walled cities of Sumer were like independent countries. Historians call them city-states. By 3000 B.C.E., most Sumerians lived in city-states.

A stele is an upright slab of stone inscribed with letters and pictures in memory of important events. This part of the Stele of the Vultures, which was found in Iraq, pictures an attacking army.

4.7 From Small Farming Villages to Large City-States

As you've seen, beginning around 3500 B.C.E., the Sumerians went from living in small farming villages to building large, walled cities. How and why did this happen? The answer lies in the problems the Sumerians faced and how they solved them.

A basic challenge for any group is how to provide food for itself. Food shortages had forced settlers in Mesopotamia to move from the foothills down to the river valley. There, farmers faced the problem of having either too much water or too little.

To control the water supply, Sumerians built a complex irrigation system. The system crossed village boundaries, so the Sumerians had to cooperate with one another. This led them to live in larger communities—the first cities.

Each of these cities was like an independent country. Often these city-states fought with one another. To defend themselves, Sumerians built walls and dug moats around their cities. By 3000 B.C.E., most Sumerians lived in walled city-states.

A Sumerian city-state was like a tiny country. The city walls helped protect the city against enemies.

4.8 Chapter Summary

In this chapter, you've learned how villages in Mesopotamia grew into large cities. The people of Mesopotamia had to solve a series of problems in order to live successfully in their challenging environment. Their solutions to these problems gradually led them to build the large communities we call *city-states*.

Living in cities led to a new way of life. In the next chapter, you'll take a closer look at the culture that developed in the Sumerian city-states.

◀ ◀ ◀ Panels from the Standard of Ur depict scenes of war and peace in ancient Sumer.

Was Ancient Sumer a Civilization?

5.1 Introduction

In the last chapter, you read about the rise of Sumerian city-states. In this chapter, you'll take a closer look at Sumerian **culture**. Like an archeologist, you'll consider evidence to try to answer a question about the distant past. The question is this: Was Sumer a **civilization**?

Until about 150 years ago, archeologists had no idea that the Sumerian people had lived at all. Then, in the mid 1800s, archeologists began finding artifacts in the area we call Mesopotamia. They dug up tablets, pottery, and the ruins of cities. They were surprised to find writing in a language they had never seen before.

By studying artifacts, archeologists have learned a lot about Sumer. One artifact is called the Standard of Ur. It was found where the ancient city of Ur once stood. You can see the standard on the opposite page. It is made of wood and decorated with pieces of shell and lapis lazuli, a semi-precious blue stone. It shows Sumerians in times of peace and war. Artifacts like this one can tell us a great deal about daily life in ancient Sumer.

We now know that the Sumerians had a complex society. Some of the things they invented, like the plow and writing, are still in use today. But can we call Sumer a civilization? Let's consider the evidence.

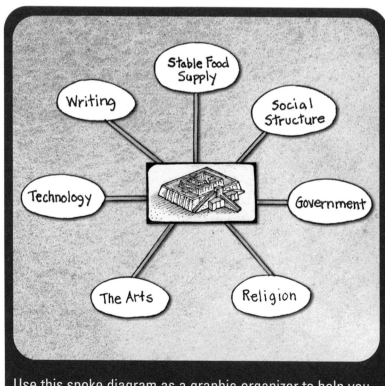

Use this spoke diagram as a graphic organizer to help you think about the characteristics of civilization.

5.2 Characteristics of Civilization

As you learned in the last chapter, Sumer was a challenging place to live. It had hot summers, little rain, and rivers that flooded the plains. Yet the Sumerians overcame these challenges. They built complex irrigation systems and large cities. By 3000 B.C.E., most Sumerians lived in powerful city-states like Ur, Lagash, and Uruk. But can we say that the Sumerians had created a civilization?

To answer this question, we need to think about what *civilization* means. What characteristics make a culture a civilization? Historians name several such characteristics, including these:

- a *stable food supply,* so that the people of a society have the food they need to survive
- a **social structure** with different social levels and jobs
- a *system of government,* so that life in the society is orderly
- a *religious system,* which involves a set of beliefs and forms of worship
- a *highly developed culture* that includes arts such as painting, architecture, music, and literature
- *advances in* **technology**
- a highly developed written *language*

Did Sumer have these characteristics? Let's find out what the evidence can tell us.

social structure the way a civilization is organized
technology the use of tools and other inventions for practical purposes

These two artifacts—one modern and one ancient Sumerian—are both examples of one characteristic of a civilization. Can you name the characteristic?

5.3 Stable Food Supply

Civilizations need a stable food supply. A complex society can thrive only if its members have the food they need to survive.

Sumerians invented two things to help them create a stable food supply. You already know about one of these inventions—their complex irrigation systems. The Sumerians built networks of canals, dams, and reservoirs to provide their crops with a regular supply of water.

Their second invention was the plow. A plow is a tool for tilling (turning) the soil to prepare it for planting. Before the plow was invented, farmers used animal horns or pointed sticks to poke holes in the earth. Then they would plant seeds in the holes. This was a very slow way to farm. Farmers needed a faster way to prepare the land for planting.

The Sumerians made the first plow out of wood. One end was bent for cutting into the ground to turn the soil. Farmers pushed and pulled the plow along the ground themselves, or they used animals such as oxen to pull it.

Sumerians invented the plow. Today, families in Iraq (ancient Sumer) still farm the land using ox-drawn plows.

This man and child are standing in the ruins of the ancient city of Uruk.

status importance

5.4 Social Structure

Civilizations have a complex organization, or social structure. A social structure includes different jobs and social levels. People at higher levels have greater **status** than others.

Archeologists have found evidence that several classes of people lived in Sumer. At the top was an upper class, which included priests, land owners, and government officials. These people had the largest and most luxurious homes, near the center of the city. Their houses were two stories high. Evidence suggests they had whitewashed mud walls.

In the middle was the common class. This included merchants and craftspeople. The craftspeople included highly skilled metal-workers. They worked with such metals as gold, silver, tin, lead, copper, and bronze. With these materials, they made swords and arrowheads for the army. They made tools like plows and hoes for farmers. They also made luxury items, such as mirrors and jewelry, for the upper class.

The common class also included farmers and fishermen. They lived in small, mud-brick houses at the edge of the city. Farmers often worked to build or repair the irrigation systems. In times of war, they were forced to serve in the army.

At the very bottom of the social structure were slaves. They lived in their owners' homes and had no property of their own.

5.5 Government

All civilizations have a system of government to direct people's behavior and make life orderly. Sumerian city-states were ruled by kings. The Sumerians believed that their kings were chosen by the gods to rule in their place. This belief made their kings very powerful. It also helped strengthen the social order, since Sumerians believed they must obey the will of the gods.

Sumerian kings enforced the laws and collected taxes. They built temples and made sure irrigation systems were maintained.

A king also led his city-state's army. All the city-states needed armies because they were constantly fighting over land boundaries and the use of water. Leading the army was one of the king's most important jobs.

A Sumerian army included both professional soldiers and temporary citizen-soldiers. Some were foot soldiers. Others drove **chariots,** wheeled vehicles pulled by horses.

Kings had officials under them to help them with their duties. Governors ruled over outlying towns. **Scribes** helped record laws. The Sumerians were the first people to develop a system of written laws.

One special group of officials patrolled the canals. They looked for damage and made sure farmers didn't take water illegally.

A king looks out from his palace walls over the city-state he rules.

5.6 Religion

All civilizations have a religious system. A religious system includes a set of beliefs, usually in a god or gods, together with forms of worship.

In Sumer, religious beliefs influenced every part of daily life. Sumerians tried to please the gods in all things, from growing crops to settling disputes. Religion bound them together in a common way of life.

Sumerians expressed their religious beliefs by building temples and religious towers called **ziggurats**. It was the king's duty to build and maintain the ziggurats. The towers were made of mud bricks and located near temples. They were so large that they could be seen from 20 miles away. Some were as high as eight stories and as wide as 200 feet.

The Sumerians believed that the gods lived in the ziggurats, and they built special temples at the top for them. Outside the ziggurat, they attached a long staircase so the gods could climb down to Earth. Kings and priests stood inside the towers to ask for the gods' blessings.

Sumerian statues also expressed their religious beliefs. Many of these statues were detailed and lifelike. They showed people worshipping the gods, often with their eyes gazing upward. The Sumerians believed that the gods were pleased when people showed them devotion, or love and obedience.

Sumerians had many kinds of religious ceremonies. Often musicians played at these ceremonies. Some ceremonies may have involved human sacrifice, the ritual killing of a person as an offering to the gods.

ziggurat an ancient Mesopotamian temple tower

This is a reconstruction of the ziggurat that once rose over the ancient city of Ur.

5.7 The Arts

All civilizations have a highly developed culture, including the arts. Arts include creative forms of expression such as painting, architecture, and music.

There were many kinds of artists and craftspeople in Sumer. Sumerian metalworkers made practical objects, like weapons and cups. They also made decorative items, such as mirrors and jewelry. Sumerian architects designed temples and ziggurats.

Music was another important art in Sumer. The Sumerians believed that music brought joy to the gods and people alike. Musicians played instruments and sang during temple ceremonies. They wrote love songs and entertained guests at feasts.

Musicians played many instruments, including drums and pipes. One favorite was a small harp called a *lyre*. Lyres were wooden instruments made of a sound box and strings. A wooden bar held the strings in place at the top. Lyre makers often decorated their instruments with precious stones and carvings made of horn. These decorations show how much the Sumerians valued music.

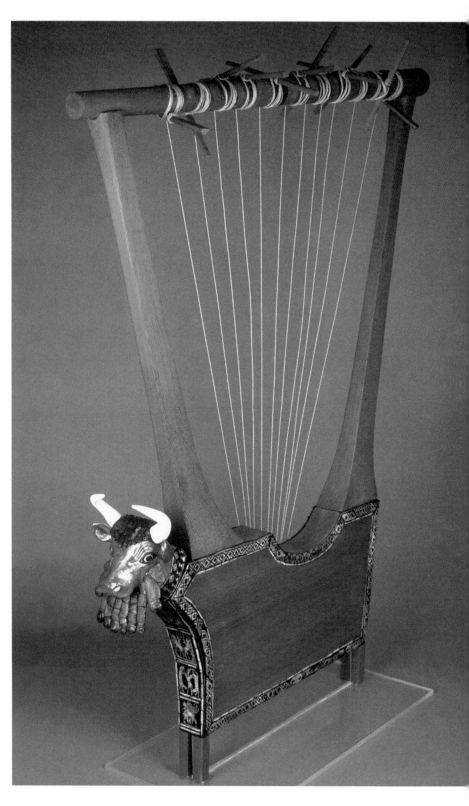

This fancy lyre has the head of a bull decorating its sound box. A musician would strum the strings to play musical notes.

5.8 Technology

All civilizations create new forms of technology, or practical tools and inventions. The Sumerians made several technological advances.

The Sumerians' most important invention was the wheel. The earliest examples of the wheel date back to 3500 B.C.E. Sumerian potters, or pottery makers, used wheels as a surface for shaping clay into pots. Potters' wheels spun, flat side up, on an axle. Sumerians discovered that a wheel that was flipped onto its edge could be rolled forward. They used this discovery to create wheeled carts for farmers and chariots for the army. They built the wheels by clamping pieces of wood together.

This model shows a wheeled chariot used in the Sumerian army. Chariots were pulled by a horse while a soldier stood behind the shield.

arch an upside-down U- or V-shaped structure that supports weight above it, as in a doorway

It would be hard to imagine a more powerful invention than the wheel. Before the wheel, people had to drag their goods on flat-bottomed carts called *sledges*. The sledges often got stuck in mud, and they couldn't support heavy loads. Wheeled carts made it much easier to move goods over long distances. Oxen could pull three times more weight on wheeled carts than they could on sledges.

Another technological advance was the **arch**. Sumerian arches were inverted (upside down) U- or V-shaped structures built above doorways. To build arches, the Sumerians stacked bricks made of clay and straw so that they rose in steps from the walls until they met in the center.

Arches added strength and beauty to Sumerian buildings. They became a common feature of temple entrances and upper-class homes. Some historians say the arch is the Sumerians' greatest architectural achievement.

5.9 Writing

A final characteristic of civilizations is a highly developed written language. The Sumerians created a written language called **cuneiform**. This name comes from the Latin word for "wedge." The Sumerians used a wedge-shaped stylus (a sharp, pointed tool) to etch their writing in clay tablets.

Sumerians developed cuneiform around 2400 B.C.E. The earliest examples of cuneiform show that it was used to record information about the goods Sumerians exchanged with one another. At first, they may have used as many as 2,000 symbols to stand for ideas and sounds. Over time, they were able to reduce this number to about 700.

Cuneiform was based on an earlier, simpler form of writing that used pictographs. **Pictographs** are symbols that stand for real objects, such as a snake or water. Scribes drew the symbols with a sharpened reed on wet clay. When the clay dried, the marks became a permanent record.

This relief sculpture shows scribes using a clay tablet and stylus.

5.10 Chapter Summary

Was Sumerian culture a civilization? It had all the characteristics you read about at the start of this chapter. The people of Sumer created a stable food supply. Their society had a complex social structure. They had a system of government, headed by kings. They had a religious system with priests, temples, and ziggurats. They had highly developed arts, technologies, and written language. For these reasons, historians call Sumer one of the world's first civilizations.

Sumerian civilization lasted about 1,500 years, from 3500 to 2000 B.C.E. What happened to the Sumerians? What new cultures developed in Mesopotamia? In the next chapter, you'll find out.

An Assyrian carving from the king's palace depicts soldiers marching off to battle.

CHAPTER 6

Exploring Four Empires of Mesopotamia

6.1 Introduction

In Chapter 5, you read about the ancient civilization of Sumer. In this chapter, you will discover what happened to the Sumerians and who ruled Mesopotamia after them.

As you have learned, the city-states of Sumer were like independent countries. They often fought over land and water rights. They never united into one group. Their lack of unity left them open to attacks by stronger groups.

About 2300 B.C.E., a group called the Akkadians conquered Sumer. They made the Sumerian city-states a part of an empire. An **empire** is a large territory where several groups of people are ruled by a single powerful leader or government. Empire builders like the Akkadians first conquer other lands. Then they use their power to keep these lands under their control.

In this chapter, you will learn about four empires that rose up in Mesopotamia between 2300 and 539 B.C.E. They were the **Akkadian Empire,** the **Babylonian Empire,** the **Assyrian Empire,** and the **Neo-Babylonian Empire**.

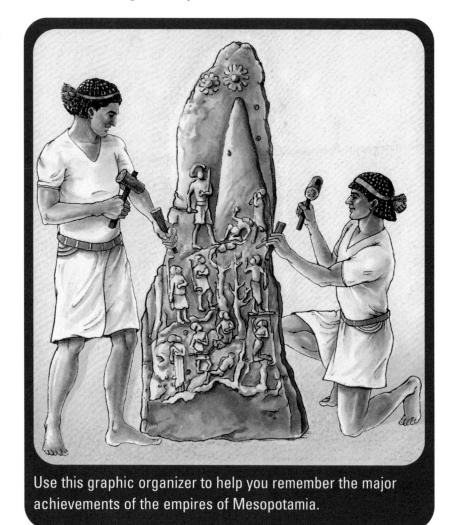

Use this graphic organizer to help you remember the major achievements of the empires of Mesopotamia.

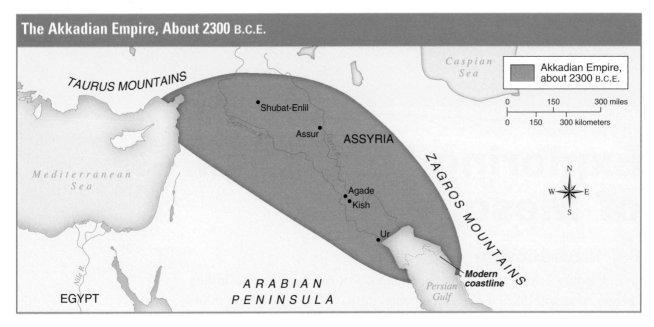

6.2 The Akkadian Empire

For 1,500 years, Sumer was a land of independent city-states. Then, around 2300 B.C.E., the Akkadians conquered the land. The Akkadians came from northern Mesopotamia. They were led by a great king named Sargon. Sargon became the first ruler of the Akkadian Empire.

Sargon was both a strong king and a skilled general. He created his empire through powerful military strategies. First he assembled a large army. He taught his soldiers to fight in tight formations. Soldiers carrying shields stood at the front of the formation. Behind them stood soldiers carrying spears. The spear carriers extended their weapons between the shields.

Sargon used his military skills to win territory for his empire. After defeating the king of the city-state of Uruk, Sargon controlled all of Mesopotamia, including Sumer.

To keep control of his empire, Sargon used smart political strategies. He destroyed the walls of cities to make it harder for people to rebel. He also made sure the governors of city-states were loyal to him. If they were not, he replaced them with his own men. And he became the first king to demand that his sons rule after his death.

Sargon died in very old age. His name soon passed into legend. He and the Akkadians had created the world's first empire. This was their greatest achievement.

This metal sculpture is of the head of Sargon. Based on what you see, how would you describe this famous king?

6.3 Life Under Akkadian Rule

Sargon ruled his empire for 56 years. During that time, he made the city of Agade in northern Mesopotamia the empire's **capital**. He built up the city with **tributes,** or money and goods, collected from the people he conquered. Agade became a cultural center with many beautiful temples and palaces. It was one of the richest and most powerful cities in the world.

The Akkadians ruled Sumer, but the Sumerians' culture lived on. The Akkadians used Sumerian irrigation techniques to farm. To record information, they used the Sumerians' system of cuneiform writing. They even worshiped the same gods and goddesses, although they called them by different names. Religion remained central to the social order, and kings continued to rule in the name of the gods.

The Akkadians had cultural achievements of their own. Their language gradually replaced the Sumerian language. In art, they became especially well known for their beautiful three-dimensional sculptures. Craftspeople carved relief sculptures on stones. These carved stones are called *steles*. One famous example is called the Victory Stele. It was created to celebrate a military victory by Sargon's grandson, King Naram-Sin. The stele shows Naram-Sin leading his victorious army up the slopes of a mountain. Some of his enemies are crushed underfoot. Others die, flee, or beg for mercy.

Sargon had hoped that his empire would last for a thousand years. But later kings found it difficult to rule such a large territory. The empire became weaker and weaker. After about 200 years, the Akkadian Empire fell to new invaders from the north.

On the Victory Stele, King Naram-Sin is pictured as taller than the other men. He wears a horned crown to make him look like a god.

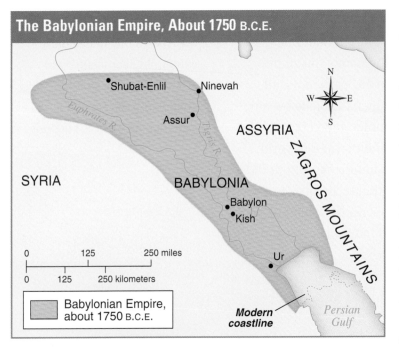

Shubat-Enlil
Ninevah
Euphrates R.
Assur
ASSYRIA
N
W E
S
SYRIA
BABYLONIA
ZAGROS MOUNTAINS
Babylon
Kish

0   125   250 miles
0   125   250 kilometers

Ur

Babylonian Empire, about 1750 B.C.E.

Modern coastline

Persian Gulf

6.4 Hammurabi and the Babylonian Empire

For a time after the fall of the Akkadians, Sumer was once again a collection of city-states. The next ruler to unite all of Mesopotamia was a king named Hammurabi.

Hammurabi was the king of Babylon, a small city-state in central Mesopotamia. After conquering the rest of Mesopotamia, he made Babylon the capital of his empire. The region under his rule became known as Babylonia.

Hammurabi is best known for his code of laws, which he wrote from 1792 to 1750 B.C.E. Hammurabi used the code of laws to unify his empire and to preserve order. He based the laws not just on his own authority, but on the word of the gods. He claimed that the gods had told him to create laws that applied to everyone in the empire. Because they were based on the gods' will, the laws could never be changed. The code of laws was written on a stele and placed in a temple for everyone to see.

Hammurabi's code was very detailed. It covered many situations, such as trade, payment for work, marriage, and divorce. The code spelled out punishments for stealing, causing injury, and other crimes. For example, a builder who sold a poorly built house that collapsed and killed its owner could be put to death. If the owner's son rather than the owner was killed in the collapse, the builder's son could be put to death.

Laws like this one seem harsh to us now. Yet Hammurabi's code was an important achievement. Although it did not treat all people equally in terms of laws and punishments, it was the first code of laws to apply to everyone.

Hammurabi's code was carved on a stele so that all people would know their rights and responsibilities.

6.5 Life in the Babylonian Empire

Babylonia thrived under Hammurabi. He worked to unite the people of his empire. He made the Babylonian god, Marduk, supreme over other gods. He built roads and created a postal service.

Agriculture and trade flourished. Hammurabi carefully kept irrigation systems working properly, so the land remained fertile and provided plenty of food. The city of Babylon was on the banks of the Euphrates River, and it became an important center of trade. Babylonians traded with people all along the Persian Gulf. They traded grain and woven cloth for wood, gold, silver, precious gems, and livestock (animals).

This woman is weaving cloth on a simple loom. One end of the loom is tied around a tree or post, and the other end is tied around her back.

Trade helped the empire's economy. Many kinds of crafts-people used materials brought from distant lands. The arts also flourished. Writers wrote historical poems that survive to this day.

Most important, Babylonian society was unusually fair for its time. The laws treated different classes differently, but even slaves had some rights. Slaves could work elsewhere and keep their wages. They could own property. If they saved enough money, they could even buy their freedom.

Women also had more rights than they did in most ancient societies. Even though their fathers chose their husbands, women could own property. They could also keep money of their own.

Hammurabi was proud of his achievements. He once wrote:

I rooted out the enemy above and below.
I made an end of war.
I promoted the welfare of the land....
I have governed the people in peace.
I have sheltered them in my strength.

This carving shows an army breaking through the walls of a city with a battering ram.

siege a military blockade and attack on a city to force it to surrender

6.6 The Assyrian Empire

The line of kings begun by Hammurabi did not rule Babylonia for long. Over the next several hundred years, a number of groups ruled parts of Babylonia. The next great empire in Mesopotamia was created by a warlike people called the Assyrians.

Assyria lay to the north of Babylon. The Assyrians had lived in Mesopotamia for a long time. They had even briefly had their own empire before being conquered by Hammurabi. They rose to power again toward 900 B.C.E., when a series of rulers began training them for war. With their trained army, the Assyrians began to expand their territory.

The Assyrians were feared for their military might and their cruelty. Their greatest achievements were their new weapons and war strategies. They perfected the use of horses and iron weapons in battle. They also became extremely good at siege warfare. In a **siege,** an army camps outside a city and attacks it over and over again until the city falls. The Assyrians developed new ways of attacking cities. They were the first to use battering rams. These were long poles on wheels that were used for punching holes in walls. The Assyrians also built moveable towers that could be rolled up to a city's walls. Soldiers used the towers to climb over the walls.

The Assyrians were often ruthless. They made entire populations leave conquered areas.

The Assyrians spread tales of their cruelty far and wide. Creating fear among their enemies was part of their military strategy. One such tale was that after cutting off the heads of enemy leaders, they forced defeated soldiers to march barefoot wearing their leaders' heads around their necks.

The Assyrian Empire, About 650 B.C.E.

ASIA MINOR

TAURUS MOUNTAINS

Caspian Sea

Ninevah

Assur   ASSYRIA

Euphrates R.

Tigris R.

ZAGROS MOUNTAINS

PHOENICIA

SYRIA

Jerusalem

Mediterranean Sea

Babylon

BABYLONIA

Modern coastline

Persian Gulf

EGYPT

ARABIAN PENINSULA

Nile R.

Red Sea

0   150   300 miles

0   150   300 kilometers

N W E S

Assyrian Empire, about 650 B.C.E.

6.7 Life Under the Assyrians

The Assyrian Empire was ruled by powerful kings. Religion, however, remained very important in the social and political order. Even kings were obliged to obey the gods.

The Assyrians believed that kings were special beings. So it's not surprising that they built beautiful palaces for them. The great palace in the capital city of Nineveh had many, many rooms. Some palaces were built on tall mounds so they were higher than all the surrounding buildings. Huge sculptures of winged and human-headed bulls or lions stood at the entrances.

While the kings ruled, ordinary people farmed the land. Like other groups in Mesopotamia, the Assyrians dug canals to irrigate their land and keep it fertile. They also built some of the earliest **aqueducts**. A system of canals and aqueducts brought drinking water to Nineveh from 30 miles away.

Assyrian craftspeople were known for their two-dimensional sculptures called **bas-reliefs**. Many of their most famous bas-reliefs were on palace walls. They were amazingly realistic. Often they showed the king hunting, fighting in battle, or enjoying family life. The Assyrians also used ivory to decorate thrones, beds, chairs, and doors.

The Assyrian Empire lasted about 300 years. At its height, it stretched from Egypt to the Persian Gulf. In the end, this vast territory proved too big to control. The army was stretched thin, and the Assyrians could not fight off neighbors who rose up against them. In 612 B.C.E., Nineveh was plundered by a combined army of Babylonians, Scythians, and a group called the Medes. The Assyrians' power was broken forever.

aqueduct a pipe or channel that brings water from distant places

bas-relief a sculpture in which the image projects out from a flat surface

This winged bull with five legs stood guard before a palace of an Assyrian king.

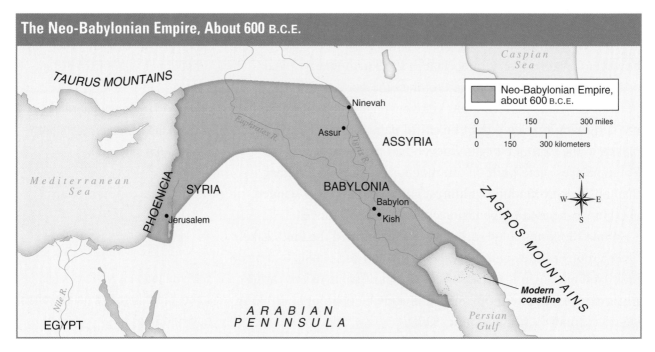

6.8 The Neo-Babylonian Empire

After the fall of Nineveh, the Babylonians regained control over Mesopotamia. They established a new empire, the Neo-Babylonian Empire. (*Neo* means "new.")

The new empire's most famous king was Nebuchadrezzar II. A ruthless military leader, he reigned from 605 to 562 B.C.E.

Nebuchadrezzar expanded his empire whenever he could. He drove the Egyptians out of Syria. He also conquered part of Canaan (present-day Israel), the home of the Hebrews. When the Hebrews rebelled, he took most of them captive and carried them off into Babylonia. Many of them never returned to their homeland.

As a military leader, Nebuchadrezzar knew it was important to keep his capital city, Babylon, safe. He built an inner wall and an outer wall around the city. The walls were so thick that two chariots could pass each other on top of them. Towers were placed on the walls for archers to stand on. Finally, a moat was dug around the outer wall and filled with water. During peacetime, people used bridges to cross the moat and enter the city. In times of war, the bridges were taken down.

The Ishtar Gate was one of the gates into Babylon. Each gate was dedicated to a Babylonian god or goddess. Ishtar was the goddess of war and love.

6.9 Life in the Neo-Babylonian Empire

Nebuchadrezzar worked hard to give Babylon the splendor it had enjoyed under Hammurabi. From 605 to 562 B.C.E., he rebuilt the city's ziggurat. This huge structure was several stories high. The Babylonians called it the "House of the Platform Between Heaven and Earth."

Nebuchadrezzar decorated his palace with fabulous gardens. They became famous as the Hanging Gardens of Babylon. The gardens were planted on rooftops and tall terraces so that lush greenery hung down over the walls. A watering system kept the gardens fresh and green. They were one of the great wonders of the ancient world.

The Babylonians were also skilled in mathematics and **astronomy**. They created the first sundial, a device for telling time using the sun. They made discoveries that led us to the 60-minute hour and the 7-day week.

The Neo-Babylonian Empire lasted only 75 years. In 539 B.C.E., a new conqueror swept into Babylon from the east. His name was Cyrus, and he was the leader of the Persian Empire.

The Persians came from the land we now call Iran. For about 200 years, they ruled the most powerful empire in the world. Later you will learn how the Persians themselves were conquered by a man named Alexander the Great.

The Hanging Gardens of Babylon were one of the wonders of the ancient world. The sight of so many trees and bushes rising above the desert landscape was stunning.

astronomy the study of stars and planets

6.10 Chapter Summary

In this chapter, you read about four empires that once ruled Mesopotamia. Each of these empires had its own achievements. And each had its own problems that eventually led to its fall.

Outside Mesopotamia, other cultures developed during this time. In the next unit, you'll explore the cultures of the ancient Egyptians, the people of Kush, and the Hebrews.

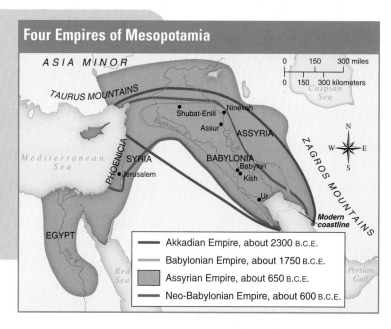

Four Empires of Mesopotamia

ASIA MINOR
TAURUS MOUNTAINS
Shubat-Enlil • Nineveh
Assur • ASSYRIA
Mediterranean Sea
PHOENICIA SYRIA BABYLONIA
Jerusalem Babylon • Kish
Ur
ZAGROS MOUNTAINS
Modern coastline
EGYPT
Red Sea
Persian Gulf
Caspian Sea

0 150 300 miles
0 150 300 kilometers

— Akkadian Empire, about 2300 B.C.E.
— Babylonian Empire, about 1750 B.C.E.
— Assyrian Empire, about 650 B.C.E.
— Neo-Babylonian Empire, about 600 B.C.E.

Early Humans Timeline

1.8 million – 200,000 B.C.E.
Homo erectus learns to make fire.

2 million B.C.E.		1.5 million B.C.E.		1 million B.C.E.

6500 – 5700 B.C.E.
People in the Neolithic town of Catal Hoyuk have different jobs, such as farmer, basket weaver, and toolmaker.

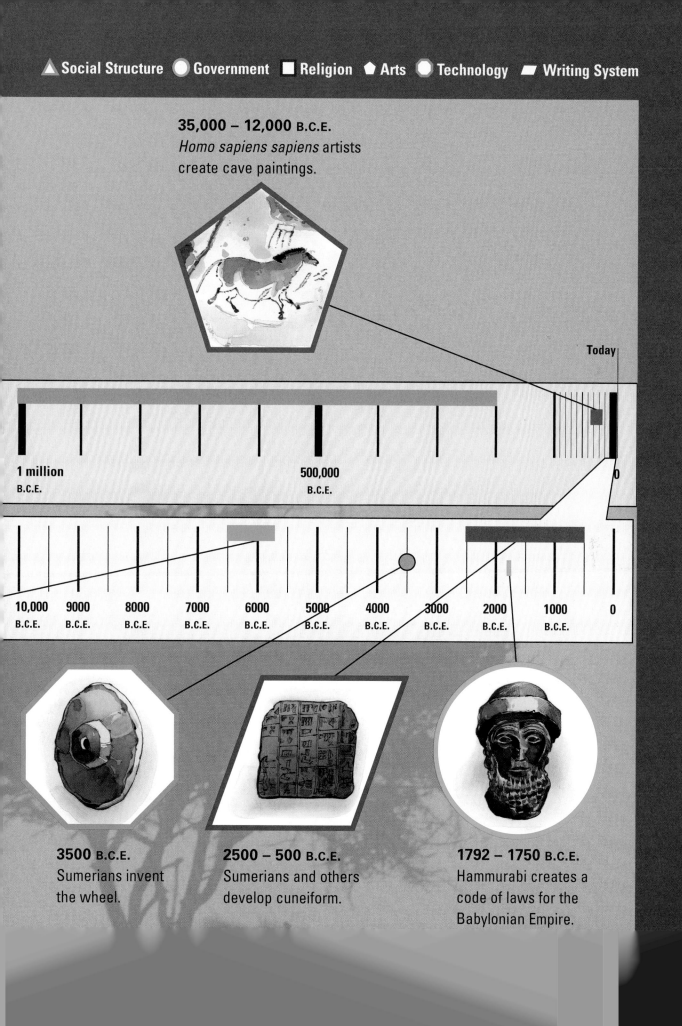

▲ Social Structure ● Government ■ Religion ◆ Arts ● Technology ▬ Writing System

35,000 – 12,000 B.C.E.
Homo sapiens sapiens artists create cave paintings.

Today

1 million B.C.E.

500,000 B.C.E.

0

10,000 B.C.E. **9000** B.C.E. **8000** B.C.E. **7000** B.C.E. **6000** B.C.E. **5000** B.C.E. **4000** B.C.E. **3000** B.C.E. **2000** B.C.E. **1000** B.C.E. **0**

3500 B.C.E.
Sumerians invent the wheel.

2500 – 500 B.C.E.
Sumerians and others develop cuneiform.

1792 – 1750 B.C.E.
Hammurabi creates a code of laws for the Babylonian Empire.

UNIT 2

Ancient Egypt and the Near East

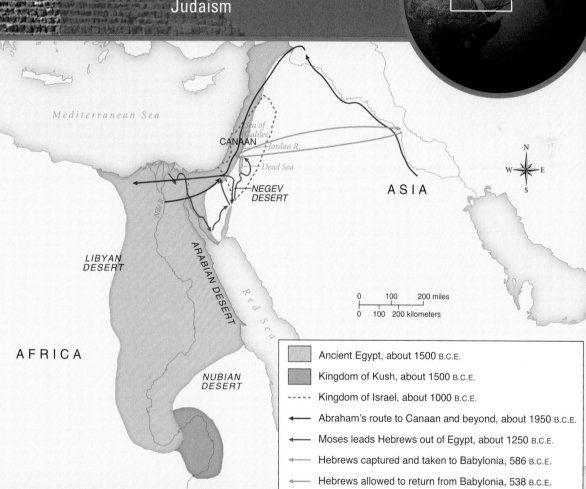

	Ancient Egypt, about 1500 B.C.E.
	Kingdom of Kush, about 1500 B.C.E.
----	Kingdom of Israel, about 1000 B.C.E.
←	Abraham's route to Canaan and beyond, about 1950 B.C.E.
←	Moses leads Hebrews out of Egypt, about 1250 B.C.E.
←	Hebrews captured and taken to Babylonia, 586 B.C.E.
←	Hebrews allowed to return from Babylonia, 538 B.C.E.

Routes of the Ancient Hebrews, About 1950–538 B.C.E.

CHAPTER 7

◀ ◀ ◀ The Nile River provided fresh water and fertile land for those living along its banks.

Geography and the Early Settlement of Egypt, Kush, and Canaan

7.1 Introduction

In Unit 1, you learned about early hominids and the empires of Mesopotamia. In this unit, you will explore three civilizations that arose in Africa and southwestern Asia. They were the **Egyptian, Kush,** and **Hebrew civilizations**.

The Egyptians settled along the Nile River, in the northeast corner of Africa. Their civilization lasted from around 3100 B.C.E. to 350 C.E.

The Kushites settled to the south of Egypt, along the southern part of the Nile. Their civilization began around 2000 B.C.E. and lasted until 350 C.E.

The Hebrews settled northeast of Egypt, in Canaan, in about 1800 B.C.E. Over time, they developed a unique civilization that thrived until their capital city was destroyed in 70 C.E.

Why did these people settle where they did? Their choices were greatly affected by **environmental factors**. Three important environmental factors were water, topography (the shape of the land), and vegetation (plant life). These factors depended upon physical features that were part of each area's **geography**. Physical features include such things as rivers, mountains, valleys, deserts, climate, and the fertility of the soil.

In this chapter, you will learn why water, topography, and vegetation were so important to early human settlement. Then you'll explore the geography of ancient Egypt, Kush, and Canaan. You'll find out how environmental factors in these places affected where people chose to live.

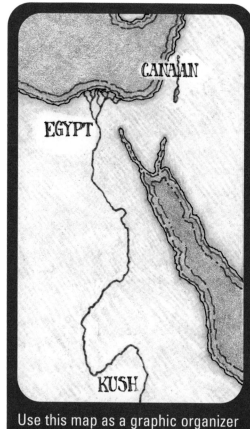

Use this map as a graphic organizer to learn more about the geography and settlement of ancient Egypt, Kush, and Canaan.

7.2 Environmental Factors and Early Human Settlement

Environmental factors influenced where people chose to settle in ancient times. Three important environmental factors were water, **topography,** and **vegetation**.

topography the surface features of a place or region, such as mountains or deserts
vegetation the plants of a place or region

Water

The most important environmental factor in early human settlement was water. Physical features like rivers, lakes, and inland seas are good sources of fresh water.

Water is important for many reasons. People need fresh drinking water to live. They also bathe and wash things in fresh water. Bathing and washing help to prevent disease.

Water is also a source of food. People catch the fish that live in rivers, lakes, and seas. They hunt water birds and other animals that gather near water. In addition, farmers need water to grow their crops. For this reason, farmers often settled near rivers. The river's natural flooding could help to irrigate their farms. Farmers could also dig canals or trenches to direct the river's water to their crops. As you've learned, farmers in Mesopotamia dug canals for this purpose.

Water can also be used for transportation. Cities and towns often used rivers as "highways." People traveled in boats to visit relatives and trade goods. Towns near the sea could trade goods with countries far away.

Topography

A second environmental factor was topography. Topography refers to the shape of the land. It includes features like mountains, hills, plains, and deserts.

The topography of an area was important for early human settlement. Farmers usually settled in flat, open areas such as plains and valleys. Large, flat spaces gave them room to grow crops. Also, the rich soil in coastal plains and river valleys was excellent for growing crops.

Mountains and deserts were less friendly to human settlement. Steep mountains were hard to cross. Their jagged peaks and rocky land made farming difficult. Deserts were hot and dry. They contained very little water for farming. The intense heat and lack of water made travel difficult. People who settled in mountains and deserts faced many challenges.

Vegetation

A third environmental factor was vegetation, or plant life. There are many kinds of vegetation, such as trees, bushes, flowers, grass, and reeds. The crops people grow are also a type of vegetation.

Many physical features affect vegetation. Mild weather, regular rain, and fresh water are good for plant life. The areas around rivers and lakes are usually green and lush. Mountains are often covered with thick groves of trees. Deserts, being dry and hot, have very little vegetation.

The vegetation in an area influenced early human settlement in several ways. Most important, plants were a source of food. People ate both wild plants and crops they had planted. But vegetation had other uses as well. People learned to make many useful products out of plants, including medicine, baskets, rope, tools, and even paper. Trees provided shade from the hot sun. And plants and flowers helped to make a place beautiful.

Water, topography, and vegetation were important wherever people settled in the ancient world. Let's look now at how these environmental factors influenced the early settlements of Egypt, Kush, and Canaan.

Can you identify three environmental factors in this photograph? Why might they be important to the people living in this place?

Africa's Nile River is the longest river in the world. It is more than 4,100 miles long and flows from south to north, draining into the Mediterranean Sea.

delta an area of sediment deposited at the mouth of a river

Key Physical Features of Ancient Egypt and Kush

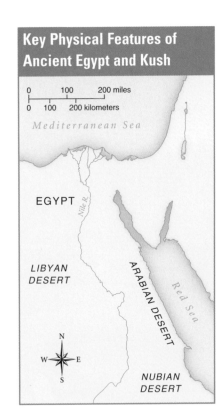

7.3 Environmental Factors and the Early Settlement of Egypt and Kush

The Egyptians and Kushites both settled near the Nile River. The Egyptians lived along the northern part of the river. The Kushites lived to the south.

Why did settlements in these areas cluster around the Nile? Let's look at the physical features of Egypt and Kush and then see how environmental factors favored settlement near the Nile.

Physical Features of Egypt and Kush

The most important physical feature in ancient Egypt and Kush was the Nile River. Flowing north from deep in Africa, the Nile created a long, fertile valley that ended in a marshy **delta** by the Mediterranean Sea.

The Nile River valley was surrounded by the Libyan Desert, the Arabian Desert, and the Nubian Desert. These sandy deserts were extremely hot and dry. Most people avoided them, yet the deserts did play one important role in the settlement of Egypt and Kush. They formed a natural barrier that helped protect people living in the Nile River valley. The deserts did not support large settlements, and few invaders wanted to cross them.

On the north, Egypt was bordered by the Mediterranean Sea. Settlers could not drink its sparkling salt water, but the sea was rich in fish and other kinds of life. It was also a waterway that linked ancient Egypt to other civilizations.

To the east of Egypt and Kush was a long, thin channel of very salty water called the Red Sea. The climate in this area was hot and dry. Much of the land near the Red Sea was desert.

Environmental Factors and Human Settlement in Egypt and Kush

Environmental factors in ancient Egypt and Kush greatly favored settlement near the Nile River. Most important, the Nile was a source of fresh water in an area that was mostly desert.

The lack of water in the deserts made them useless for farming. But in the Nile River valley, the river provided natural irrigation and **fertilization**. Every summer, the river overflowed its banks. The floodwaters soaked the dry ground. After several weeks, the waters went down. A thin ribbon of silt (rich soil) was left behind. This soil was perfect for farming.

Where there is fresh water, there are usually fish to catch and animals to hunt. The abundant wildlife in the Nile region included fish, ducks, geese, hippos, crocodiles, giraffes, and ostriches.

The topography of the river valley also encouraged human settlement. In the south, parts of the Nile ran through narrow valleys and hills. But there were also wide areas of flat land around deep bends in the river. These flat areas were good for farming. In the north, wide plains were watered by the Nile's annual flooding.

Vegetation was rare in the dry deserts, but it was plentiful in the Nile River valley. Useful plants included reeds and a tough water plant called **papyrus**. People wove reeds into baskets and roofs for their huts. They used papyrus to make rope and paper. And the rich farmland made it easy to grow crops like wheat and barley.

fertilization the process of adding fertilizer, or plant food, to soil

papyrus a tough water plant used to make paper and rope in ancient times

Deserts are natural barriers against invaders. Would you want to walk for days across this hot, dry desert to fight those who live on the other side?

While parts of the Jordan River valley were lush, the area was not as fertile as the Nile River valley.

7.4 Environmental Factors and the Early Settlement of Canaan

Canaan, where the ancient Hebrews settled, was a diverse land. Canaan's physical features and environmental factors made settlement easier in some areas than in others.

Physical Features of Canaan

Canaan's physical features included plains and valleys, hills and mountains, deserts, and bodies of water.

In the west, coastal plains bordered the Mediterranean Sea. To the north, the Lebanon Mountains rose steeply from the coast. The southern part of this range gave way to the lower hills of Galilee.

The Jordan River flowed down from a mountain range through the middle of Canaan, heading south through the Sea of Galilee to the Dead Sea. The land around the narrow river valley included hills, grassy slopes, and mountains. To the east was the hot, dry Syrian Desert. In southwestern Canaan was the Negev Desert. Rain soaked this area during the winter months, giving the Negev more water than most deserts.

Environmental Factors and Human Settlement in Canaan

In Canaan, just as in Egypt and Kush, water was a key environmental factor. The wet, fertile plains near the Mediterranean Sea were farmed in very ancient times. The Mediterranean also allowed traders from many lands to visit Canaan.

Other bodies of water played a role in the settlement of Canaan. The Sea of Galilee was actually a freshwater lake. It had plentiful fish, and fertile land was nearby. Another large lake, the Dead Sea, was so salty that nothing grew in it, not even plants. The area near the Dead Sea was hot, dry, and not very good for farming.

The most important source of fresh water was the Jordan River. People hunted, fished, and farmed along its banks. But unlike the Nile, the Jordan did not flood regularly, so its valley was not as fertile as the Nile's.

Key Physical Features of Ancient Canaan

```
0      25        50 miles
0    25     50 kilometers

                              N
                          W  ✦  E
                              S

              LEBANON☐
              MOUNTAINS

Mediterranean Sea

              Sea of Galilee

       Jordan R.

                      SYRIAN☐
                      DESERT

              Dead Sea

    NEGEV☐
    DESERT
```

Canaan's varied topography greatly influenced patterns of settlement. Farmers found it easiest to live in the coastal plains and near the Jordan River. But in many areas, the hilly land and dry soil made growing crops difficult. As a result, many people, including the ancient Hebrews, became herders rather than farmers. Herders tended flocks of sheep, goats, cattle, donkeys, and camels. Unlike farmers, herders were **nomads,** wandering from place to place in search of good land for their animals to graze.

The mountains and deserts were the hardest areas to settle. Mountainous land was difficult to farm, and the deserts were too dry for farming. Still, some people did settle in these areas. Nomads sometimes herded cattle and camels in the Negev and Syrian Deserts.

In general, Canaan's hot, dry climate discouraged abundant plant life. Vegetation was most plentiful near the Jordan River. Some places had light forests. Others had only short, scrubby plants. Grasslands were common, though, and herders made good use of them to feed their animals.

The Negev is not as dry as most deserts. After the winter rains, colorful flowers bloom there every spring.

nomad a person who moves from place to place with no permanent home

7.5 Chapter Summary

In this chapter, you learned about three environmental factors that influenced the settlement of ancient Egypt, Kush, and Canaan. In Egypt and Kush, most people farmed in the fertile Nile River valley. In Canaan, many people, including the ancient Hebrews, were nomads. They followed their herds in search of good grazing land. In the next chapter, you will learn more about ancient Egypt and meet some of its rulers.

CHAPTER 8

◀ Twin statues of the pharaoh Ramses II
guard an ancient Egyptian temple.

The Ancient Egyptian Pharaohs

8.1 Introduction

In the last chapter, you learned how early Egyptians settled in the Nile River valley. In this chapter, you will visit ancient Egypt and meet four of its leaders, called **pharaohs**.

In 1922, archeologists discovered the tomb of a pharaoh known as King Tutankhaten, or King Tut. Inside a small burial chamber, they found three coffins nested inside each other. The smallest coffin was made of solid gold. It held the king's mummy. (A mummy is a body that has been preserved after death to keep it from decaying.) On the mummy's head was a magnificent golden mask. Jewelry and good luck charms lay on the mummy and in the wrappings that protected it. Other rooms of the tomb were filled with statues, weapons, furniture, and even a chariot.

The treasures in King Tut's tomb provided an amazing glimpse into ancient Egypt. Other pharaohs also left behind fabulous riches and artwork. Many of them built great monuments to celebrate their accomplishments. Like King Tut's tomb, these artifacts have much to teach us about this ancient civilization.

In this chapter, you will learn about three important periods in ancient Egyptian history. They are called the **Old Kingdom,** the **Middle Kingdom,** and the **New Kingdom**. Then you will meet four of the pharaohs who ruled during these periods. You will learn about their achievements and explore some of the monuments they left behind.

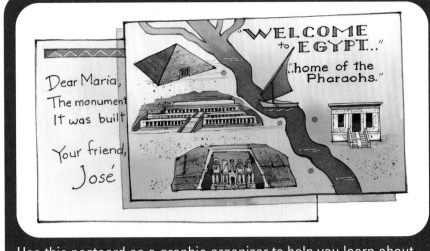

Use this postcard as a graphic organizer to help you learn about ancient Egyptian pharaohs and their achievements.

8.2 Ancient Egypt and Its Rulers

Ancient Egypt enjoyed three long periods of stability and unity under the rule of pharaohs. Historians call these periods the Old Kingdom, the Middle Kingdom, and the New Kingdom.

The Old Kingdom lasted from about 2700 to 2200 B.C.E. During this time, early pharaohs set up a strong central government. They also built great **pyramids** as tombs for themselves. Some historians call this time the Age of Pyramids.

The Middle Kingdom (about 2000 to 1800 B.C.E.) is sometimes called the Period of Reunification because it followed years of chaos and disunity. During this era Egyptians made many great achievements in literature, art, and architecture.

The New Kingdom (about 1600 to 1100 B.C.E.) is often called Egypt's Golden Age. During this time of peace and stability, Egypt's power reached its height. Pharaohs increased trade and built gigantic monuments.

As in Mesopotamia, religion played a central role in Egypt's social and political order. The pharaohs were believed to be gods. They owned all the land and were responsible for the people's well-being. They were kings, generals, and religious leaders, all at once.

After they died, the pharaohs were thought to enter an afterlife that would never end. Their great tombs were built to last forever.

The pharaohs built other monuments to glorify their power and success. The map shows the locations of some of the greatest monuments. Let's find out more about these structures and the pharaohs who built them.

pyramid a huge, triangular-shaped monument of ancient Egypt built around a tomb

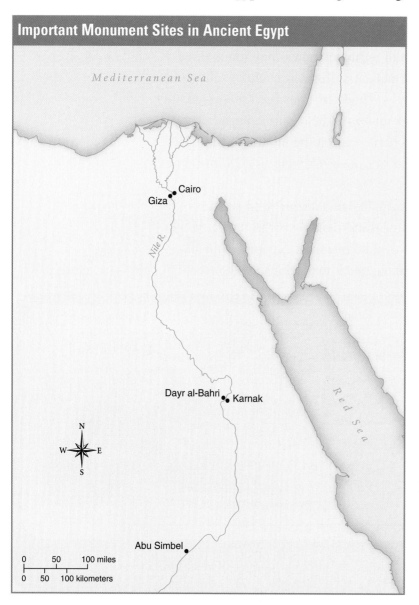

Important Monument Sites in Ancient Egypt

Mediterranean Sea

Cairo
Giza

Nile R.

Dayr al-Bahri • Karnak

Red Sea

N
W   E
S

Abu Simbel

0   50   100 miles

0   50   100 kilometers

Khufu began construction on the Great Pyramid as soon as he became pharaoh.

8.3 Pharaoh Khufu: The Pyramid Builder

The pharaoh Khufu ruled from about 2551 to 2528 B.C.E., during the Old Kingdom period. Today he is best known as the builder of a famous pyramid.

Not much is known about what Khufu was like. Some stories describe him as a cruel, harsh ruler. Others say he was powerful but kind.

We do know that Khufu helped establish the pharaoh as a central authority. For example, he kept strict control over Egypt's food supply. This involved overseeing the harvest and storing extra grain. He controlled a large network of government officials who carried out his laws. Khufu emphasized his supreme power by declaring himself a god.

Khufu and other Old Kingdom pharaohs had magnificent pyramids built as tombs for themselves and their families. Khufu himself was responsible for the building of the Great Pyramid at Giza. It is one of the wonders of the ancient world.

The Great Pyramid sat at the center of a huge complex of temples, statues, monuments, and smaller tombs. It was made of more than 2 million stone blocks that fit together perfectly. Inside, tunnels led to several burial chambers. The king's chamber had six roofs to hold up the weight of the stones above it.

Building the Great Pyramid was an amazing feat. No one knows exactly how the Egyptians did it. The pyramid took more than 20 years to complete. Khufu maintained full control of the building project. He organized and fed thousands of workers. The completed pyramid was a stunning monument to Egyptian engineering.

This three-inch-high ivory statue is a portrait of Khufu.

8.4 Pharaoh Senusret I: Patron of the Arts

The pharaoh Senusret I ruled from about 1971 to 1926 B.C.E., during the Middle Kingdom. He was a strong leader who ruled a stable, unified Egypt. Art, literature, and architecture flourished during his reign.

Craftspeople thrived under Senusret's rule. The pharaoh controlled mines loaded with gold, copper, and gems such as purple amethyst. Craftspeople fashioned these materials into beautiful pieces of jewelry. Bracelets and necklaces were often highly detailed. They were then decorated with stones like turquoise.

Some of the greatest works in Egyptian literature were written during Senusret's reign. "The Story of Sinuhe" tells of a young official named Sinuhe who overhears a plot to kill the pharaoh. Fearing for his own life, Sinuhe flees Egypt. He thrives in his new land, but he grows very homesick. When a new pharaoh calls him home, Sinuhe returns joyfully.

Senusret's greatest accomplishments were in religious architecture. He built and improved many temples, shrines, and religious monuments.

Perhaps Senusret's finest architectural achievement was the White Chapel. (A chapel is a small temple.) It was made of alabaster, a hard white stone. Some historians think the chapel was originally covered in a thin layer of gold.

Beautiful artwork decorated the chapel's pillars. Carved scenes showed the pharaoh with various gods. Birds, animals, and Egyptian symbols were also depicted.

Senusret wanted his memory to live on through his monuments. But almost none of his buildings survived the passage of time. A later pharaoh took the White Chapel apart and used the pieces in a monument of his own. Archeologists later discovered the pieces and reconstructed the White Chapel.

This statue of Senusret shows him clutching an ankh in each hand. The ankh was the Egyptian symbol of immortality, or eternal life.

8.5 Pharaoh Hatshepsut: Promoter of Egyptian Trade

The pharaoh Hatshepsut ruled from about 1473 to 1458 B.C.E. Hatshepsut was Egypt's first female pharaoh. Under her rule, Egyptian art and architecture flourished. She was also known for encouraging trade.

One of Hatshepsut's greatest accomplishments was simply gaining power. Never before had Egypt been ruled by a woman. At first she shared power with her male relatives. However, she soon took over as sole ruler.

Hatshepsut strengthened her position in several ways. She filled her government with loyal advisors. She demanded the same respect as a male ruler. Sometimes she wore men's clothing. She even wore the fake beard that was worn by male pharaohs. Artists were often instructed to portray her as a man. She also spread stories that her father was a god.

As pharaoh, Hatshepsut promoted trade with other countries. Her biggest trade expedition was to the African kingdom of Punt, at the southern end of the Red Sea. Five ships sailed to Punt bearing gifts and trade goods. In all, over 200 men made the voyage.

Hatshepsut left behind a stunning monument to her reign, a great temple at Dayr al-Bahri. The main part of the temple was built into a cliff above the Nile River. At the entrance were two tall, thin monuments called *obelisks*. The entrance was also graced by 200 sphinx statues. The sphinx is a mythical creature with the body of a lion and the head of a man.

Scenes from Hatshepsut's reign decorated the temple walls. Detailed carvings portrayed the great voyage to Punt. The carvings showed the wondrous things that the pharaoh's traders had brought back to Egypt.

Hatshepsut actively encouraged trade. During her reign, trade helped spread Egyptian influence along the Nile and in nearby lands in the Middle East (western Asia).

8.6 Pharaoh Ramses II: Military Leader and Master Builder

The pharaoh Ramses II ruled from about 1290 to 1224 B.C.E., during the New Kingdom. Called Ramses the Great, he is one of the most famous pharaohs. He reigned for more than 60 years, longer than almost any other pharaoh. He is best known for his military leadership and for building numerous monuments.

Ramses did everything in a big way. He had over 100 wives and more than 100 children. He wasn't shy about glorifying himself, either. He had hundreds of statues of himself erected all around Egypt. Some of them were over 60 feet high.

Ramses was a fearless soldier from a young age. He fought alongside his father in various battles. He was made a captain in the Egyptian army at the age of 10.

Ramses tried to defend an Egyptian empire that extended north into Canaan. His most famous military campaigns were against the Hittite Empire in Anatolia (now the country of Turkey). The Hittites constantly threatened Egypt's northern borders. In his most famous battle, Ramses reached a standoff with the Hittites even though he was badly outnumbered.

Ramses was also a peacemaker. He and the Hittites signed the world's first peace treaty. This peace lasted until the Hittite Empire collapsed around 1190 B.C.E.

One of Ramses' most impressive projects was the temple complex at Abu Simbel. The main temple was carved into the side of a cliff on a bank of the Nile River. A smaller temple honored his favorite wife, Nefertari.

This painting shows Ramses II attacking a Hittite fort.

Four giant seated statues of Ramses framed the entrance to the main temple. The figures were sculpted right out of the rock face of the cliff. They are among the finest examples of Egyptian art.

The inside of the temple was also remarkable. Visitors passed through three large rooms, called *halls,* to reach the temple's main room. The room's altar contained statues of Ramses and three Egyptian gods. The temple was built so that twice a year the sun lined up with the entrance. Beams of sunlight would shine down the halls and light up the statues.

Ramses built more temples and monuments than any other pharaoh in history. When he died, he was buried in a tomb that he had had constructed for himself. His is one of the best-preserved mummies ever found.

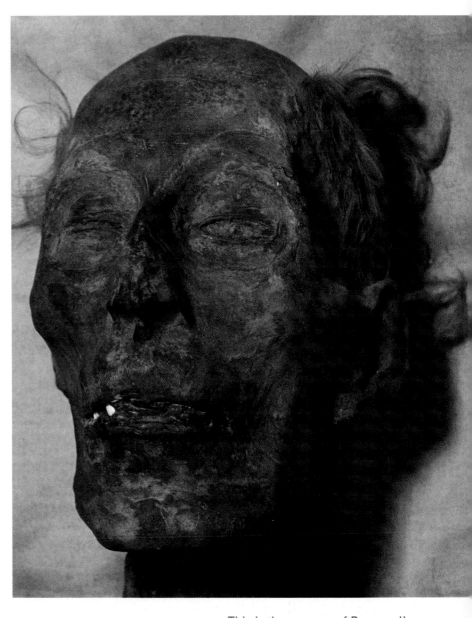

This is the mummy of Ramses II. Egyptians believed that preserving the bodies of the dead was necessary for the afterlife.

8.7 Chapter Summary

In this chapter, you learned about three long periods of stability in ancient Egypt: the Old Kingdom, the Middle Kingdom, and the New Kingdom. You explored the accomplishments of four pharaohs who ruled during these times. Khufu built the Great Pyramid. Senusret encouraged Egyptian art and literature. Hatshepsut, Egypt's first female pharaoh, promoted Egyptian trade. And Ramses the Great was a superior military leader and builder of monuments.

Pharaohs were at the top of Egyptian society. In the next chapter, you'll learn about the rest of Egypt's people and what daily life was like in the New Kingdom.

CHAPTER 9

◄ ◄ ◄ Grand festivals brought together ancient Egyptians of every social class.

Daily Life in Ancient Egypt

9.1 Introduction

In Chapter 8, you learned about four Egyptian pharaohs. In this chapter, you will meet other members of Egyptian society. You'll learn what life was like for Egyptians during the New Kingdom (about 1600 to 1100 B.C.E.).

Each year, when the Nile River flooded its banks, all of Egypt celebrated the Opet Festival. Work in the fields stopped while the people joined in a festival honoring the pharaoh and his patron, the god Amon-Re.

Almost everyone in Egyptian society took part in the festival. Priests decorated a statue of the god with jewelry. They put the statue in a shrine and placed the shrine on a ceremonial boat called a *barque*. The beautifully decorated boat was made by artisans, or craftspeople. High government officials competed for the honor of carrying the barque on poles through town. Peasant farmers lined the streets to watch the procession. Scribes made a written record of the celebration.

The Opet Festival brought all these groups together. But in everyday life, they belonged to very different **social classes**. These classes made up a **social pyramid,** with the pharaoh at the top and peasants at the bottom. In between were government officials, priests, scribes, and artisans. The daily life of each class was quite different.

In this chapter, you will learn more about Egypt's social pyramid. Then you'll explore the work and daily life of the various classes in Egyptian society.

Use this illustration as a graphic organizer to help you learn more about the Egyptian social pyramid.

artisan a craftsperson
peasant a person who
does farmwork for wealthy
landowners

9.2 Ancient Egypt's Social Pyramid

Egyptian society was structured like a pyramid. At the very top of this social pyramid was the pharaoh, Egypt's supreme ruler. Egyptian religion strengthened the pharaoh's authority. Pharaohs were looked upon as gods, and their word was law.

Below the pharaoh were several layers of social classes. The classes near the top of the pyramid had the fewest people and enjoyed the highest status. The classes nearer the bottom had more people and lower status.

Egypt's Social Classes

Government officials and priests belonged to the top two classes in the social pyramid under the pharaoh. They were the most powerful groups in Egypt.

Government officials carried out the orders of the pharaoh. Most of them came from noble families. They were powerful and wealthy, and they enjoyed a high quality of life.

Priests were also a powerful group, because religion touched every part of people's daily lives. The priests were in charge of the temples and religious rituals. They also oversaw the important ceremonies surrounding death and burial.

Next on the social pyramid were scribes. The scribes held a respected position in society. They recorded information for government and religious leaders. It took many years of schooling to become a scribe.

Artisans occupied the next layer of the social pyramid. This group included craftspeople like carpenters, metal-workers, painters, sculptors, and stone carvers. Artisans were highly skilled, but they had little social status.

At the bottom of the social pyramid were the peasants. They were the largest social class. Peasants worked the land, providing Egypt with a steady food supply. When they weren't farming, they worked on the pharaoh's massive building projects.

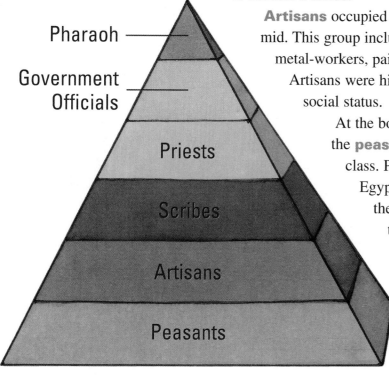

Pharaoh

Government Officials

Priests

Scribes

Artisans

Peasants

Ancient Egyptian society was organized like a pyramid. The groups near the top had the most power and status.

Egyptian women enjoyed more freedom and rights than most women in the ancient world. A few women even became pharaohs.

Life in Egypt's Social Classes

Egypt's social pyramid was fairly rigid. People usually belonged to the same social class as their parents. Most people had little chance to move to a higher class. People in different classes had some things in common, but in other ways their lives were quite different.

Egyptians in all social classes cherished family life. Most Egyptians married within their social group. Children were highly valued.

Men and women had different roles within the family. Men were the heads of their households. They worked to support the family. Fathers often trained their sons from an early age to take on their line of work. Women typically managed the home and raised the children. Noblewomen had servants or slaves to help them. Lower-class women had to do the work themselves.

Men were in charge of Egyptian society, but women enjoyed more freedom and rights than most women in the ancient world. They could own land and run businesses. They could ask for divorces and represent themselves in legal matters. Some women in the middle and upper classes worked as doctors, government officials, or priestesses. Both women and men enjoyed a better quality of life the higher they were on the social pyramid.

The Egyptians believed that their class system created a stable, well-ordered society. Each group had its own role to play. Let's take a look at the duties and daily lives of the various social classes during the time of the New Kingdom.

9.3 Government Officials

Government officials belonged to the highest class on Egypt's social pyramid, after the pharaoh. Their job was to assist the pharaoh in his or her role as supreme ruler of Egypt.

Government officials usually came from the pharaoh's family or other upper-class families. Most of them inherited their positions from family members. However, trusted servants from the royal court sometimes rose to power.

Important Government Officials

Three important officials were the vizier, the chief treasurer, and the general of the armies. Each had his own duties.

The **vizier** had more power than anyone except the pharaoh. The vizier advised the pharaoh and carried out his commands. He appointed and supervised most of the other government officials.

The vizier also served as a kind of chief judge. Judges often brought him their toughest cases. A vizier was expected to be fair and not show special favor to either side in a dispute. One vizier had this advice for those who would follow him: "Regard one you know like one you don't know, one near you like one far from you." In works of art, viziers often were shown wearing white, the color of neutrality.

The chief treasurer looked after the government's wealth. His main duty was to collect taxes. Egypt's economy was based on goods rather than money. People paid their taxes in grain, cows, cloth, silver, and even beer.

After the pharaoh, the general of the armies was the top military commander in Egypt. He advised the pharaoh in matters of war and national security, such as how to protect Egypt's borders from invaders. He also helped the pharaoh make **alliances** with other kingdoms.

This is a statue of Imhotep, an early and powerful vizier in ancient Egypt. Imhotep was famous for his role in designing and building great monuments.

Lives of Luxury

High government officials led lives of luxury. Most were nobles who had great wealth, fine homes, and plenty of time to socialize.

The lavish banquets enjoyed by these wealthy Egyptians illustrate their luxurious lifestyle. A good host made every effort to provide the best food. Cooks roasted ducks, geese, pigeons, quail, antelope, wild sheep, and goats. Dishes were piled high with figs, dates, grapes, and coconuts. Bread, cakes, honey, and plenty of beer and wine completed the meal.

Guests at banquets dressed in fine linen clothing. Both men and women wore perfume. The women often wore ropes of beads. They painted their nails, lined their eyes with makeup, and wore lipstick.

At the start of a banquet, the guests usually offered the host long blessings. They wished the host many riches, great happiness, a long life, and good health. The host often simply responded with "Welcome, welcome," or "Bread and beer," as a way of saying, "Come and eat!"

The feast began with men and women sitting on opposite sides of the room. Important guests were given chairs with high backs. Everyone else sat on stools or cushions. Servants, who were nearly all women, waited on the guests. There were no forks or spoons, so people ate with their fingers.

While the guests ate, musicians, dancers, and acrobats provided entertainment. Most of the musicians were women. They played flutes, harps, rattles, and lutes (a guitarlike instrument). Guests often clapped along with the music.

This painting shows women at a banquet.

9.4 Priests

Like government officials, priests were powerful and highly respected in Egyptian society. A large network of priests served under the pharaoh, who was considered the highest-ranked priest of all.

The Duties of Priests

Priests had different jobs. The High Priest advised the pharaoh and oversaw all religious ceremonies. Temple priests were in charge of the many temples scattered throughout Egypt. Other priests handled more common concerns and requests. They gave advice and performed healings.

Women were allowed to be priestesses in Egypt. They were generally considered to be equal to male priests. Their main duty was to oversee temples that were devoted to music and dancing.

Temple priests played an

Priests shaved their heads as an act of cleanliness and to show their religious purity.

especially important role in Egyptian religion. Every temple was home to an Egyptian god or gods. A temple priest's main job was to take care of the god.

A temple's god was thought to live in a statue. The statue was housed in a holy room called a *sanctuary*. Only a priest who had purified (cleansed) himself could enter the sanctuary. There were many things a priest had to do in order to be purified. He had to avoid certain foods, such as fish, that were associated with the lower classes. He had to cleanse his body by bathing three or four times a day in holy pools. He also had to shave off his body hair. And he had to wear clothes made of linen cloth, because animal products like leather and wool were considered unclean. Once he was purified, the priest could perform his sacred duties.

The Priests' Role in Burial Practices

Priests had a special role to play in burial practices. Egyptians believed in a life after death. They thought the spirits of the dead needed their bodies in the afterlife. For this reason, they preserved bodies from decay through **embalming**. Priests oversaw this sacred work.

The embalming process had many steps. First, the embalmers removed the body's organs, such as the brain, lungs, and liver. They used hooks to pull the brain out through the nostrils. Only the heart was left in the body. Egyptians believed that the gods used the heart to judge a dead person's soul.

The organs were packed in jars to preserve them. The organs and body were dried out with a special salt called *natron*.

After about 70 days, the embalmers washed and oiled the body. Then they wrapped it in hundreds of yards of linen. They decorated the wrapped body, or mummy, with jewelry and protective charms. Often they placed a mask over the head. Finally, they spread a black, gooey gum over the body and wrapped it a final time.

The mummy was then ready for burial. The mummy was placed in a wooden box which was then put inside a large stone coffin, called a **sarcophagus**. Because the ancient Egyptians believed that the afterlife was much like life in this world, the box or coffin was buried along with other items. These included food and drink, furniture, statues, gold, jewelry, clothes, games, and mirrors.

Not all Egyptians could afford such complicated burials. But even poor Egyptians wrapped their dead in cloth and buried them with jars of beer, loaves of bread, and other items they thought would be needed in the afterlife.

The process of embalming a body produced a mummy, such as those shown here.

embalm to treat a dead body with preservatives to prevent it from decaying

sarcophagus a large stone coffin

9.5 Scribes

Scribes were one level below priests in the social pyramid. Scribes were Egypt's official writers and record keepers. They were highly respected and well paid. Most scribes worked for the government. Others worked for priests or nobles.

Only men were allowed to be scribes. They came from all classes of society. Becoming a scribe was one of the few ways that men could rise above their parents' social class.

This engraving shows students in a scribe school working at their writing.

Scribe Schools

Boys who wanted to become scribes had to attend scribe school. The schools were run by priests. Most students came from artisan or merchant families. A very few came from the peasant class.

Schooling started around the age of five. Students typically spent 12 years or more learning **hieroglyphs,** the symbols used in the Egyptian system of writing. The system was very complicated. Most students first mastered a simpler form of writing and then worked their way up to hieroglyphs.

Students had to memorize over 700 hieroglyphs. They spent as many as four years copying the signs over and over. They practiced their writing on pieces of wood, flakes of stone, and even broken bits of pottery. When they were good enough, they were allowed to write on papyrus, a type of paper made from the papyrus plant.

Students in scribe schools did not have an easy life. Classes sometimes lasted from dawn until sunset. Teachers were strict and often treated their students harshly. They frequently yelled at students for being lazy or not paying attention. Beatings were common. One stern schoolmaster wrote, "A youngster's ear is on his back; he only listens to the man who beats him."

The Work of the Scribes

Ancient Egyptians made all kinds of records, so scribes held a wide variety of jobs. They kept records of the grain and food supply. When a government **census** counted the people living in Egypt, they recorded the results. Some scribes calculated and collected taxes. Legal scribes recorded court cases and helped enforce laws. Military scribes kept track of the army's soldiers and food supply, and the number of enemies killed in battle.

Every scribe used the same tools. For pens, a scribe used finely sharpened reeds. For paper, he used a sheet of papyrus laid out on a writing tablet. The tablets were made of wood or stone. Each tablet contained two wells, one for black ink and one for red ink. A small container held water that was used to wet the ink.

A scribe carried his tools with him wherever he traveled. His tablet hung from a cord slung over his shoulder. Leather bags and cases attached to the tablet held his other tools.

Scribes also carried rolls of papyrus. This paper was a remarkable invention of the Egyptians. To make it, they first cut the inner part of the papyrus plant into strips and soaked the strips in water for several days until they were soft. Then they laid the strips out in a crisscross pattern between two sheets of cloth. The papyrus strips were pressed together until the cloth had absorbed all the water. Finally, the papyrus strips were pressed one more time to form a sheet of paper.

census an official count of the population or number of people living in an area

This relief shows two scribes. Only men were allowed to be scribes, although women were sometimes taught to read and write.

Stone carvers were some of the most skilled workers in the artisan class.

9.6 Artisans

Below the scribes on the social pyramid were the artisans. Egypt's artisans were highly skilled laborers who created some of the most beautiful art objects in the ancient world. Yet, unlike scribes, they rarely got the respect they deserved. Only the select few who became master craftsmen were sometimes honored for their work.

Types of Artisans

Artisans specialized in any one of a number of crafts. Workers in this class included carpenters, jewelers, leatherworkers, metalworkers, painters, potters, sculptors, and weavers. Artisans made many beautiful objects, including stunning jewelry and elegant furniture. Painters portrayed scenes of Egyptian daily life. Most artisans were men, but some women wove fabric, beaded clothing, and made perfume.

The most skilled artisans were the stone carvers. They produced the statues, engravings, and reliefs found in Egyptian temples, tombs, and monuments.

Stone carvers played an important role in tomb building. The belief in an afterlife inspired wealthy Egyptians to order elaborate tombs for themselves. Stone carvers helped equip the tombs with artwork to honor and preserve the dead. They created statues of the deceased, highly detailed wall engravings, and stone coffins.

Stone carving was hard, time-consuming work. The carvers often worked with very hard rock, such as granite. They used a hard type of rock called *dolerite* to pound out the object's initial shape. Next, they refined the shape and carved in details using stone tools and copper chisels. Then they smoothed and polished the object using quartz sand. Painters often added color to the finished product.

This painting shows different kinds of artisans at work. Look carefully. What do you see?

The Daily Life and Work of Artisans

Artisans were a class in the middle of Egyptian society. They and their families lived in modest homes. Their houses were usually rectangular and barely 10 yards long. Three rooms stretched from front to back. The first room was used either as a workroom or to house animals. The living room came next. The final room was divided into a kitchen and a bedroom. The roof was sometimes used as a place to work or sleep.

Artisans typically worked side by side in large workshops. They usually worked for 10 days at a stretch before taking time off. The workers depended entirely on their employers for food. In hard times when food was in short supply, artisans often went hungry.

Pharaohs called upon hundreds of artisans at a time to work on royal projects. Artisans created the fine artwork that often covered temples, royal tombs, and other monuments. They worked in large groups to complete engravings, paintings, and hieroglyphics.

Despite artisans' skill and creativity, the upper classes often viewed them as little more than common laborers. Even the most talented artists were almost never allowed to sign their work. But some artists did receive recognition. Employers sometimes threw a banquet for their favorite artist. Occasionally they honored an artist by letting him portray himself in a painting or an engraving.

This painting shows two peasant farmers sowing their land. Peasants worked hard to supply Egyptians with food.

9.7 Peasants

Peasants made up the lowest and largest class in Egypt's social pyramid. They were generally considered unskilled laborers. Yet Egyptian society depended on their work. Peasants grew the crops that supplied everyone with food. When they weren't busy working the fields, they helped build monuments like the pyramids.

The Three Seasons of the Nile

Peasant life revolved around the Nile River and its three seasons: the flooding season, the planting season, and the harvest season.

The flooding season lasted from June to September. During this time, the Nile overran its banks and fertilized the fields. Farmers had to wait for the waters to go down before they could work the fields. In the meantime, they labored on royal projects, such as building pyramids and temples.

In October, the planting season began and farmers sowed their fields with seeds. The biggest crops were wheat and barley, which were used to make bread and beer.

Peasants worked in pairs to sow the fields. The farmer softened the earth with a plow pulled by cattle. A second person, often the farmer's wife, followed behind to scatter the seeds. Throughout the season, farmers carefully irrigated the land.

The harvest season began in March. Usually the farmer's entire family helped with the harvest. The men cut down the plants with sickles (metal blades with short wooden handles). Then the women and children gathered the tall stalks of grain.

During harvesttime, everyone worked from dawn to dusk. Peasants often sang songs to make the long hours of labor go more quickly. Sometimes musicians played in the fields while the workers sang.

The Daily Lives of Peasants

Peasants had the fewest comforts of any of the social classes. They lived in simple houses made of mud bricks. Their furniture was usually limited to woven mats.

The peasants' diet was simple. A typical meal might include onions, cucumbers, fish, homemade bread, and water or beer. Peas and lentils were also common. Unlike the upper classes, peasants rarely ate meat. In times of **famine,** they often had to boil tough papyrus plants for food.

Peasants spent most of their lives working, but they did have some time for fun. Men enjoyed a river game that involved knocking each other off papyrus rafts. Holidays were celebrated before planting and after the harvest. Peasants also took part in festivals honoring the Egyptian gods.

An important time of year for peasants was the end of the harvest season. As a reward for their hard work, they were allowed to gather up as much leftover grain as they could and keep it for food. But they could also be punished for a poor harvest.

Farmers had to pay taxes in the form of crops. If a farmer's harvest came up short and he couldn't pay the required tax, he was brutally beaten.

famine a severe shortage of food

This painting shows peasants cutting and gathering the wheat harvest.

9.8 Chapter Summary

In this chapter, you learned about Egypt's social pyramid. Each social class had its own role to play in society. You learned about the work and daily lives of government officials, priests, scribes, artisans, and peasants. In the next chapter, you will travel south along the Nile and explore the civilization of Kush.

CHAPTER 10

A painted fragment of a tomb wall shows Kushites bearing gifts for the pharaoh.

The Kingdom of Kush

10.1 Introduction

In the last chapter, you learned about daily life in Egypt during the New Kingdom. In this chapter, you will learn about Egypt's neighbor to the south, the African kingdom of **Kush**.

The civilization of Kush thrived from about 2000 B.C.E. to 350 C.E. Kush and Egypt had a close relationship throughout much of Kush's long history. Signs of their close ties can be found in pictures on the walls of some Egyptian tombs and temples.

A good example is the tomb of Hatshepsut, Egypt's first female pharaoh. If you entered the tomb, you would see many painted scenes of Egyptian life. But step a little closer, and you might notice that not all the people in the paintings are Egyptian. Some look a little different. They have darker skin and curly hair. These people are Kushites. In some scenes, the Kushites appear to be bearing gifts. In others, they look as if they are armed with bows and arrows. As these images suggest, Egypt and Kush had a complicated relationship. Sometimes it was peaceful. Often it was not.

In this chapter, you will learn more about the **relationship between Egypt and Kush**. You will discover how each culture influenced the other. You will also learn how Kush created its own unique civilization.

Use this illustration as a graphic organizer to explore the history of the kingdom of Kush.

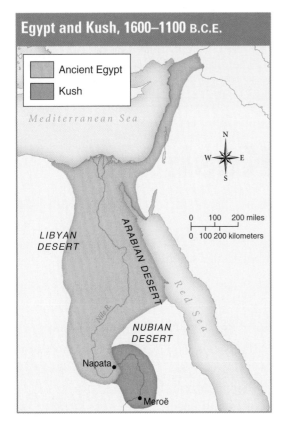

Egypt and Kush, 1600–1100 B.C.E.

Ancient Egypt

Kush

Mediterranean Sea

LIBYAN
DESERT

ARABIAN DESERT

Red Sea

Nile R.

NUBIAN
DESERT

Napata

Meroë

0   100   200 miles
0   100 200 kilometers

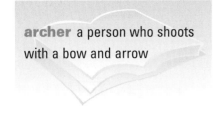

archer a person who shoots with a bow and arrow

While Egypt controlled Kush, the Kushites brought gifts to Egypt's governor as tribute. Sometimes the gifts included exotic animals such as giraffes and monkeys.

10.2 The Egyptianization of Kush

Next to Egypt, Kush was the greatest ancient civilization in Africa. Like its neighbor to the north, Kush grew up around the fertile banks of the Nile River. Kush was known for its rich gold mines. In fact, another word for Kush is Nubia, which comes from *nub*, the Egyptian word for gold.

Kush's location and natural resources made it an important trading hub, or center. Kush linked central and southern Africa to Egypt. Pharaohs sent expeditions on ships south along the Nile to buy, or sometimes steal, goods. The Egyptians traded grain, beer, and linen for Kush's gold, ivory, leather, and timber. They also bought slaves.

Several times Egypt raided Kush or took control of parts of its territory. During the New Kingdom period (about 1600–1100 B.C.E.), Egypt's power was at its height. Egypt used its power to conquer Kush. Kush was forced to pay tribute to Egypt in the form of gifts. The pharaoh appointed a governor to make sure the tribute was paid every year. The Kushites gave the governor gold, cattle, ivory, ebony, ostrich feathers, and slaves.

While Kush was under Egypt's control, its society became "Egyptianized." Kushites spoke and wrote in Egyptian. They worshiped Egyptian gods and wore Egyptian-style clothes. Kush's famed **archers** were hired to fight in Egypt's army. Princes from Kush's royal families were sent to Egypt to be educated.

Around 1100 B.C.E., Egypt's New Kingdom collapsed. After this, Kush regained its independence. However, Egyptian culture persisted. About 900 B.C.E., a new line of Kush kings was established. But even these kings continued to follow Egyptian traditions.

10.3 Kush Conquers Egypt

After the collapse of the New Kingdom, Egypt fell into political chaos. At least 10 Egyptian kingdoms fought each other for power. The constant fighting made Egypt weak and unstable.

In the mid 700s B.C.E., Kush took advantage of Egypt's weakness. Kushite armies invaded Egypt. In about 730 B.C.E., the kings in northern Egypt surrendered to Kush's King Piye.

After conquering Egypt, Piye declared himself pharaoh. One of his titles was "Uniter of the Two Lands." The kingdom of Kush now extended 1,500 miles. It reached from the Kushite city of Meroë, on the southern Nile, to the Mediterranean Sea.

In Egypt, Piye and his family became the 25th **dynasty,** or line of rulers. Kushite pharaohs ruled Egypt for nearly a century. Historians have traditionally called them the "black pharaohs."

The Kushite pharaohs did not want to tear Egypt down. Instead, they wanted to revive Egypt's past glory. They built magnificent new temples and pyramids in both Egypt and Kush. One of the most beautiful was the temple at Jebel Barkal. It was modeled after the temple of Ramses II at Abu Simbel. (You visited Ramses' temple in Chapter 8.)

By the 670s B.C.E., Egypt was being threatened by the Assyrians. As you read in Chapter 6, the Assyrians created a powerful empire in Mesopotamia. In 671 B.C.E., an Assyrian king invaded Egypt. For many years the Kushites tried to fight off the Assyrians. But the Assyrians used their advanced iron weapons to drive the Kushites out of Egypt. By the mid 650s B.C.E., the last of the Kushite pharaohs had returned to Kush.

dynasty a family or group that rules for several generations

This painting shows Egyptian royalty bowing and offering gifts to King Piye. In the past, Kush had been forced to pay tribute to Egypt. Now Egypt had to pay tribute to Kush.

10.4 The Kush Capital of Meroë

A new dynasty followed the Kushite pharaohs in Egypt. About 590 B.C.E., Egypt invaded Kush and destroyed its capital city, Napata. The Kushites decided to make Meroë their new capital. Meroë was 300 miles south of Napata, safely out of Egypt's reach.

Meroë's location helped Kush remain an important center of trade. Traders used the Nile, the Red Sea, and overland routes to transport their goods. These routes all took them through Kush. As a result, Kushites traded with many lands. Some, like other African kingdoms and Arabia, were nearby. But Kush also traded with such distant lands as Rome (on the peninsula of Italy), India, and possibly even China.

Meroë was a large and wealthy city. It became the center of a Kushite civilization that lasted for nearly 1,000 years. At its height, the city thrived as a great center of industry as well as culture. It became especially well known for producing iron. The Assyrians had triumphed over the Kushites in Egypt because of their superior knowledge of iron technology. The Kushites were determined to equal the Assyrians.

Meroë had everything need-ed to produce iron. It had a rich supply of iron deposits. It also had plenty of forests, which provided the wood needed to make charcoal. The charcoal was used to heat the iron deposits. Once the hot iron separated from the rock, it was cooled in the Nile's waters.

Ironworkers in Kush made a variety of things. They craft-ed weapons such as spears, arrows, and swords. They also created tools to make farming faster and easier. These tools included axes for quickly clearing forests and hoes for loosening soil.

Kushites used iron to make many useful objects. Here we see Kushite ironworkers crafting spearheads.

10.5 Kush Returns to Its African Roots

After splitting away from Egypt, Kush returned to its African roots. Artwork, clothing, and buildings no longer imitated Egyptian styles. Kushites worshiped an African lion-god instead of Egyptian gods. They wrote and spoke a native language, called Meroitic (after Meroë), which had its own alphabet.

Kush art and architecture flourished. Artisans made beautiful pottery, cloth, and gold and silver jewelry. Rulers built grand palaces, temples, and pyramids.

Kush also revived the African practice of female leadership. Powerful **kandakes,** or queen mothers, ruled Meroë. The kandakes usually co-ruled with their sons or husbands. They were considered goddesses and were very powerful.

One of the greatest kandakes was Queen Amanirenas. She defended Kush against the powerful Romans in 24 B.C.E. (You will learn about the Romans later in this book.) The Romans had taken over Egypt. Now they were demanding tribute from Kush. Amanirenas and her son, Prince Akinidad, led an attack that destroyed several Roman forts on Kush's borders.

After three years of fierce fighting, Rome signed a peace **treaty** with Kush. Kush no longer had to pay tribute to Rome.

Under Amanirenas, Kush had defeated the most powerful empire in the world. The kingdom of Kush survived for nearly 400 more years. In 350 C.E., Kush fell to invaders from the African country of Ethiopia.

kandake a powerful female leader who co-ruled Kush with her husband and sons

treaty a written agreement by which two or more states agree to be peaceful

Amanirenas and her son, Akinidad, watch a Roman fort burn. Amanirenas fought side by side with her soldiers, even losing an eye in battle.

10.6 Chapter Summary

In this chapter, you learned about the African kingdom of Kush. Egypt and Kush had close ties for centuries. Each country invaded and conquered the other. Kushite pharaohs ruled Egypt for nearly a century. After the Kushites left Egypt, Kush created its own, more African, culture. In the next chapter, you will learn about Egypt's northeastern neighbors, the ancient Hebrews.

CHAPTER 11

◀ Moses presents the Ten Commandments, setting forth the laws of Judaism.

The Ancient Hebrews and the Origins of Judaism

11.1 Introduction

In Chapter 10, you learned about Egypt's southern neighbor, the African kingdom of Kush. In this chapter, you will learn about a group of people who lived northeast of Egypt: the **Hebrews**.

The Hebrew civilization developed gradually after 1800 B.C.E. and flourished until 70 C.E. The people who became the Hebrews originally lived in Mesopotamia. Around 1950 B.C.E., they moved to the land of Canaan (modern-day Israel).

The Hebrews were the founders of **Judaism,** one of the world's major religions. As you will learn in the next chapter, the Hebrews eventually became known as the Jews. Judaism is the Jewish religion.

The origins of Judaism and its basic laws are recorded in its most sacred text, the **Torah**. The word Torah means "God's teaching." The Torah consists of the first five books of the Hebrew Bible. (Christians refer to the Hebrew Bible as the Old Testament.)

In this chapter, you will read about some of the early history of the Jewish people told in the Bible. You will meet four Hebrew leaders —**Abraham, Moses,** and kings **David** and **Solomon**—and learn about their contributions to the development of Judaism.

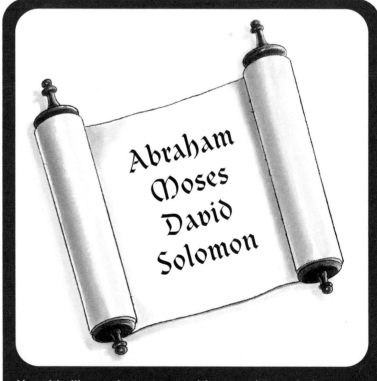

Abraham
Moses
David
Solomon

Use this illustration as a graphic organizer to help you remember important figures in the history of the ancient Hebrews and the development of Judaism.

11.2 What We Know About the Ancient Hebrews

Historians rely on many artifacts to learn about the ancient Hebrews and their time, including the Torah.

The Torah

Historians use the Torah to understand the history of the Jewish people and the development of Judaism. As often happened in ancient times, this history was handed down orally from generation to generation. Later it was written down.

In addition to the Torah, historians look for a variety of other sources of information about early Jewish history. To help them understand the events and ideas of the time period, they examine archaeological artifacts, as well as other written records.

The Early History of the Hebrews

According to the Torah, the ancestor of the Hebrews, a man named Abraham, lived near Ur in Mesopotamia. Around 1950 B.C.E., Abraham and his clan migrated to the land of Canaan. Settling in Canaan, the Hebrews herded flocks of sheep and goats.

About 1800 B.C.E., many Hebrews moved to Egypt. According to the first book of the Torah, they fled Canaan because of a famine. For a time they prospered in Egypt, but eventually they were made slaves. In time, one of their leaders, Moses, led the Hebrews in their escape from Egypt.

For 40 years, says the Torah, the Hebrews wandered in the wilderness, until they settled once again in Canaan. By 1000 B.C.E., the Hebrews had set up the kingdom of Israel in Canaan under King David and his son, King Solomon. David forged the Hebrews into one united nation. Solomon built a magnificent temple in the capital city of Jerusalem.

One wall of Solomon's temple in Jerusalem remains standing. Today, Jewish people travel from around the world to pray at the Western Wall. This rabbi is reading the Torah at the wall.

11.3 Important Hebrew Leaders

The Hebrew Bible tells about events in the lives of early Jewish leaders. Four key leaders were Abraham, Moses, David, and Solomon.

Abraham

Abraham is called the "father of the Hebrews." One central idea of Judaism is the belief in a single God. According to the Torah, it was Abraham who introduced this belief to the Hebrews. This was a new idea in the ancient world. At the time, most people worshiped many gods and goddesses.

According to the Torah, God told Abraham to move his family from Mesopotamia to Canaan. God also promised Abraham that He would make him the father of a great nation and that He would bless this nation. Abraham did as he was told, and his descendants became known to us as the Jewish people.

The ancient Hebrew leaders Abraham, Moses, and David were honored more than 2,000 years later in these statues, carved in the 13th century for Chartres Cathedral in France.

Moses

The greatest leader of the Hebrews was Moses. The Torah tells how he led his people out of slavery in Egypt. Moses told the Hebrews that God would lead them to Canaan, the "promised land," in exchange for their faithful obedience.

Moses also gave Judaism its fundamental laws. The Torah tells how God gave Moses 10 important laws engraved on two stone tablets. These laws became the foundation of Judaism.

Kings David and Solomon

After escaping from Egypt and wandering in the wilderness, the Hebrews came once more to Canaan. It was here that they created a united kingdom under King David and his son, Solomon.

King David established Jerusalem as a holy city. King Solomon built Jerusalem's first great temple. The city of Jerusalem and its temple became powerful symbols to the Hebrews of their faith in God.

Let's learn more about each of these four important leaders by looking at some history from the Hebrew Bible.

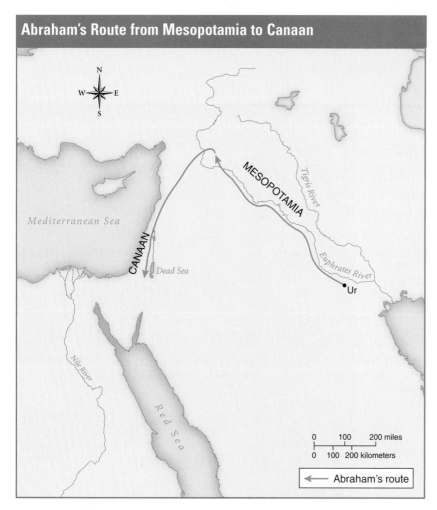

11.4 The Life of Abraham: Father of the Hebrews

The father of the Hebrews was a man named Abraham. Originally called Abram, he was born about 2,000 B.C.E. in the city of Ur in Mesopotamia. The people of Ur worshiped many gods. But Abram came to believe there was only one true God. This belief in one God would set Judaism apart from other ancient religions. And Abram's special relationship to God would become the foundation of the Hebrew faith.

Abraham's Covenant with God

According to the Torah, the faith that would become Judaism began with a sacred agreement, or **covenant,** between God and Abram. The Torah says that God visited Abram when he was an old man. God told him, "Leave your own country and your father's house, and go to a country that I will show you." God promised to make Abram the father of a great nation of people.

Abram obeyed. Around 1950 B.C.E. he gathered his many relatives and went west into the land of Canaan.

When Abram was 99 years old, the Torah says, God spoke to him again: "I will make a covenant between myself and you." God promised to favor and protect Abram's **descendants,** meaning his children and the generations that would follow. In return, Abram agreed that he and his people would always devote themselves to God.

As a mark of their covenant, God gave Abram a new name, Abraham, which means "father of many." God also promised the land of Canaan to Abraham's people. For Jews, Canaan became the "promised land." According to the Torah, the covenant meant that Jews would set an example for how God wanted people to live.

covenant an agreement or promise

descendant a daughter or son, granddaughter or grandson, and so on

Abraham's Sacrifice

According to the Torah, God tested Abraham's faith and obedience many times. The final test was the hardest.

It was common at that time to offer animals as a **sacrifice** to the gods. An animal such as a sheep would be killed and then burned on an altar. In his old age, Abraham had finally fathered a son, Isaac. The Torah says that one day God tested Abraham by telling him to make a sacrifice of his son.

Abraham dearly loved his son. Yet his devotion to God was so complete that he brought Isaac to a mountain to be sacrificed. At the last minute, God sent an angel to stop Abraham from killing his son. Abraham had proved his faith and obedience, and God renewed the promise to him. God said, "I will make your descendants as many as the stars of heaven."

According to the Torah, God kept the promise. The Hebrews flourished. The nation was made up of 12 tribes that were descended from Abraham's grandson, Jacob, whom an angel from God had named Israel.

Abraham made many contributions to the development of Judaism. He was the ancestor of the Jewish people. He introduced the belief in a single God. Because of his covenant with God, Jews believed they should set an example of how to live. Their reward was the promised land. These beliefs became a central part of Judaism.

sacrifice a gift of an animal for slaughter as a way to honor gods

This fresco painting was created in 1726 by the artist Giovanni Battista. It is titled *The Sacrifice of Isaac*.

The Torah tells the story of Moses parting the waters of the Red Sea. For Hebrews, this miracle proved that God was watching over them.

11.5 The Life of Moses: Leader and Prophet

The greatest leader of the Hebrews was the **prophet** Moses. The Torah tells the story of how Moses led the Hebrews out of slavery in Egypt and gave them God's laws to live by.

The Exodus from Egypt

By the time of Moses, around 1250 B.C.E., a large group of Abraham's descendants were living in Egypt. There, the Torah says, the Hebrews "increased in number and became very powerful." Fearful of their growing strength, the pharaoh turned them into slaves. But God heard the cries of the enslaved Hebrews. According to the Torah, God told Moses, "I will send you to the pharaoh, and you shall free my people."

Moses went before the pharaoh and told him to let the Hebrews go free. When the pharaoh refused, God punished Egypt with 10 terrible **plagues**. In one plague, insects called *locusts* devoured the crops. In another, the waters of the Nile turned to blood. Finally, God sent an angel to kill the firstborn son in every Egyptian family.

Weeping over his own dead son, the pharaoh gave in. Moses began to lead the Hebrews out of Egypt.

But the pharaoh soon changed his mind. The Egyptian army chased after the Hebrews and nearly caught up with them at the edge of the Red Sea. Calmly, Moses raised his staff (walking stick), and the waters of the sea parted. The Hebrews crossed safely to the other side. When the Egyptians tried to follow, the waters flooded over the army, drowning the soldiers. The Hebrews escaped.

The Torah calls the flight from Egypt the **Exodus,** which means "departure." It became a central event in the history of the Hebrew people.

prophet a person who speaks or interprets for God to other people

plague a terrible disaster affecting many people and thought to be sent by God as a punishment

Exodus the escape of the Hebrews from Egyptian slavery

The Ten Commandments

After leaving Egypt, the Torah says, the Hebrews wandered through a wilderness for 40 years. During this time, God gave Moses the laws that became the foundation of Judaism. These laws are called the **Ten Commandments**.

Moses received the Ten Commandments on Mount Sinai, the "Mountain of God." Moses had gone up the mountain alone to pray. When he returned, he was carrying two tablets of stone. Engraved on the tablets were the Ten Commandments.

Some of the commandments spelled out the Hebrews' duties to God. For example, the first commandment was, "You shall have no other God before me." During their wanderings, some of the Hebrews had begun to worship other gods. This commandment reminded them of their promise to worship only one God. Another commandment told them to set aside one day a week, the **Sabbath,** for rest and worship.

Other commandments laid down basic moral laws (laws about the right way to live). For example, one said, "You shall honor your father and mother." Other commandments forbid stealing, lying, and murdering.

The Ten Commandments state Judaism's basic laws. By obeying the commandments, Hebrews would fulfill their part of the covenant with God. That responsibility was to make God's moral laws known to the world. In turn, God would protect them.

Moses made several key contributions to the development of Judaism. First, he led the Exodus out of Egypt. Jews have celebrated this event ever since as proof that God would watch over them. Second, Moses gave Judaism its fundamental laws, the Ten Commandments. Third, he forged the Hebrews into a united people devoted to a single God.

Ten Commandments the ten laws said to be given to Moses by God

Sabbath the seventh day of the week to be used for rest and worship, according to one of the Ten Commandments

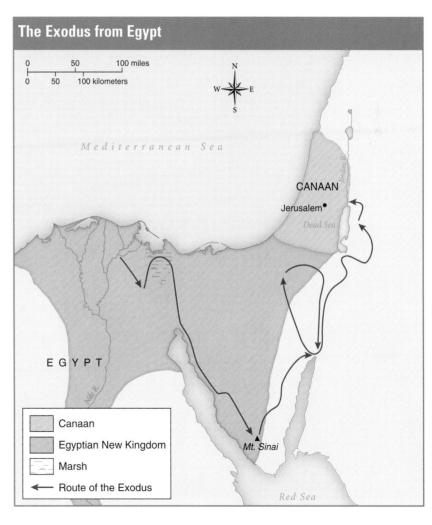

The Exodus from Egypt

0   50   100 miles
0   50   100 kilometers

N
W   E
S

Mediterranean Sea

CANAAN

Jerusalem •

Dead Sea

Jordan R.

EGYPT

Nile R.

Mt. Sinai

Red Sea

Canaan
Egyptian New Kingdom
Marsh
← Route of the Exodus

Ark of the Covenant
the chest containing the Ten
Commandments, written on
stone tablets, that the Hebrews
carried with them during their
wanderings after their flight
from Egypt

11.6 The Lives of David and Solomon: Kings of Israel

After their wanderings in the wilderness, the Hebrews settled once more in Canaan. The Hebrew Bible tells how they built a kingdom and a great temple under two kings, David and Solomon.

David Founds the Kingdom of Israel

In David's time, about 1000 B.C.E., the Hebrews were at war with a rival tribe, the Philistines. According to the Hebrew Bible, the Philistines promised to be the Hebrews' slaves if someone could beat their fiercest warrior, the giant Goliath.

David was not yet a grown man, but he was outraged at Goliath's mockery of the Hebrew God. Bravely he stepped forward. His only weapon was a slingshot. With one mighty throw, he felled Goliath with a stone.

David's courage and faith were rewarded later, when God made him king. According to the Hebrew Bible, God said, "The Hebrew kingdom will remain with him and with his children and his children's children forever."

As king, David completed the defeat of the Philistines as well as other enemies. He united the two parts of the Hebrews' land, Israel and Judah, into a single kingdom known as Israel. He created a strong central government. He gave the new kingdom its own army, courts, and government officials. David himself served as the nation's chief priest.

David chose the city of Jerusalem for his capital. Under David, Jerusalem became the center of Israel's political and religious life. David brought the Hebrews' most sacred object, the **Ark of the Covenant,** to Jerusalem. The Ark was a wood and gold chest that held the Ten Commandments. As the home of the Ark, Jerusalem became a holy city.

In this painting, Kind David leads a procession to bring the sacred Ark into Jerusalem.

Solomon Builds the Great Temple of Jerusalem

After David's death, his son, Solomon, became king. Solomon built a magnificent temple in Jerusalem to house the Ark of the Covenant and to be the center of Jewish worship. According to the Hebrew Bible, he told God, "Thus all the peoples of the earth will know Your name."

Building the temple was a huge undertaking and cost the Hebrews greatly. Solomon forced his people to work on the construction of the temple. More than 3,000 officials were needed to oversee the project. And Solomon taxed his people heavily to buy gold, cedar wood, copper, and other materials.

Solomon's methods angered many Hebrews. Near his death, their resentment exploded. In 931 B.C.E., the northern tribes broke away and became a separate kingdom of Israel. David and Solomon's descendants ruled the southern kingdom of Judah.

David and Solomon had made important contributions to Judaism. They laid the foundation for the Jewish people to be governed by kings for more than 400 years. David established Jerusalem as a holy city. And Solomon built the first great Temple of Jerusalem. After David and Solomon, Jerusalem would always be a holy city to the Jews and a powerful symbol of their faith.

Solomon built a magnificent temple in Jerusalem. Today the site of the Temple is the holiest place in the world to Jews.

11.7 Chapter Summary

In this chapter, you read about the ancient Hebrews and the origins of Judaism. Through the stories of Abraham, Moses, David, and Solomon, you learned how Judaism developed. In the next chapter, you will learn how the Hebrews became known as Jews and how they kept their ancient religion alive outside of Judah and Israel.

CHAPTER 12

The Struggle to Preserve Judaism

12.1 Introduction

In the last chapter, you read about the origins of Judaism. In this chapter, you will discover how Judaism was preserved even after the Hebrews lost their homeland.

As you have learned, the Hebrew kingdom split in two after the death of King Solomon. Weakened by this division, the Hebrews were less able to fight off invaders.

The northern kingdom of Israel was the first to fall. In 722 B.C.E., the Assyrians conquered Israel. The kingdom's leaders were carried off to Mesopotamia.

In 597 B.C.E., the kingdom of Judah was invaded by another Mesopotamian power, Babylon. King Nebuchadrezzar of Babylon laid siege to the city of Jerusalem. The Hebrews fought off the siege until their food ran out. With the people starving, the Babylonians broke through the walls and captured the city. In 586 B.C.E., Nebuchadrezzar burned down Solomon's great Temple of Jerusalem and all the houses in the city. Most of the people of Judah were taken as captives to Babylon.

The captivity in Babylon was the beginning of the **Jewish Diaspora**. The word *diaspora* means "a scattering." Never again would most of the followers of Judaism be together in a single homeland.

Yet the Jews, as they came to be known, were able to keep Judaism alive. In this chapter, you will first learn about four important **Jewish beliefs**. Then you will read about the Jews' **struggle to preserve Judaism** after they had been forced to settle in many lands.

The Classroom Activity | The History of Judaism

Use this T-chart as a graphic organizer to explore the struggle to preserve Judaism.

monotheism the belief that
there is only one God

12.2 The Central Beliefs and Teachings of Judaism

The religious and moral ideas of Judaism have left a lasting mark on Western civilization. Let's look at four central beliefs and teachings of Judaism that remain very influential today.

Monotheism

Most people in ancient times believed in many gods. The Hebrews were different. They believed that there is only one God, a belief called **monotheism**. Judaism is the world's oldest monotheistic religion.

Judaism teaches that God is all-powerful and all-knowing. God is also the source of morality (standards of right and wrong). Jews believe in a solemn duty to honor and obey God. Many Jews feel they have a personal relationship with God. They speak to God through prayer and feel that God is close to them in their daily lives.

Following God's Law

Following God's law is central to Jewish life. The Torah instructs Jews how to lead a life that pleases God.

As you have learned, Judaism's oldest laws are the Ten Commandments. The commandments tell how to honor God. For example, one commandment tells Jews to set aside a holy day, the Sabbath, every week. The Sabbath is a day of rest and prayer. The commandments also lay down laws of right and wrong, such as "You shall not steal" and "You shall not murder."

Over time, Jewish religious leaders developed a much larger set of laws. For example, there were rules about how to prepare food and what foods should be avoided. Many religious practices developed, such as the celebration of Passover. These holy days honor God's rescue of the Hebrews from Egypt. Jews strive to be faithful to these rules and practices.

In this painting, Moses holds the stone tablets on which are written the Ten Commandments. Following the law of God is a central part of Judaism.

Equality and Social Justice

Beginning with the Ten Commandments, Judaism has always been concerned with moral values of right and wrong. Two important values are equality and social justice.

Unlike some other ancient peoples, the Hebrews did not view their leaders as gods. They believed that there is only one God, and even kings had to obey God's laws. Judaism teaches that all people who keep the laws are equal in God's sight.

Belief in equality goes hand in hand with a concern for social justice. Many stories and sayings in the Torah teach about treating everyone fairly. For example, in one passage Jews are told, "You shall open wide your hand to your brother, to the needy and to the poor." Caring for the less fortunate people in society is a basic value in Judaism.

The Importance of Study

Study of the Torah is very important in Judaism. Jews also study interpretations of the Torah made by scholars and **rabbis**.

At first, decisions interpreting the Torah were passed down orally. In the 200s C.E., Jewish scholars began writing the **Talmud,** which contains this oral tradition along with learned commentaries. The Talmud became a basic source of Jewish law. Later rabbis wrote their own commentaries on both the Torah and the Talmud.

Throughout history, Jews have kept their reverence for study and learning. Many Jews stay in touch with Jewish history, law, and traditions through reading and discussion. They also pass on their knowledge to other members of the faith.

rabbi a religious teacher who studies and teaches others about Jewish law

Talmud the collection of ancient Jewish writings that interpret the law of the Torah

Jewish scholars today study and discuss the Torah as one way of understanding and practicing their religious beliefs.

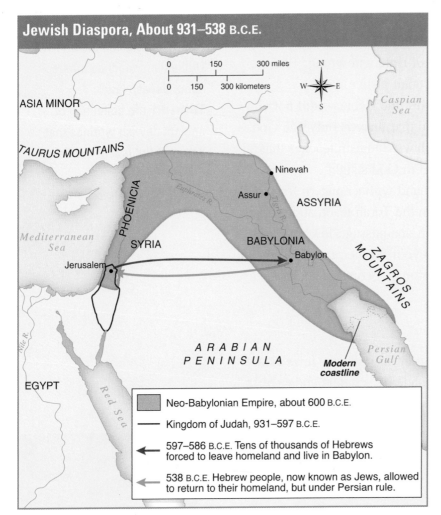

Jewish Diaspora, About 931–538 B.C.E.

0   150   300 miles
0   150   300 kilometers

ASIA MINOR

TAURUS MOUNTAINS

Caspian Sea

Ninevah

Assur

ASSYRIA

Euphrates R.

Tigris R.

PHOENICIA

SYRIA

BABYLONIA

Babylon

Mediterranean Sea

Jerusalem

ZAGROS MOUNTAINS

Nile R.

ARABIAN PENINSULA

Persian Gulf

Modern coastline

EGYPT

Red Sea

　Neo-Babylonian Empire, about 600 B.C.E.

——— Kingdom of Judah, 931–597 B.C.E.

⟵ 597–586 B.C.E. Tens of thousands of Hebrews forced to leave homeland and live in Babylon.

⟵ 538 B.C.E. Hebrew people, now known as Jews, allowed to return to their homeland, but under Persian rule.

12.3 Foreign Domination and the Jewish Diaspora

The fall of Judah in 597 B.C.E. and the destruction of Jerusalem and its temple in 586 B.C.E. threatened the survival of Jewish beliefs. Thousands of Hebrews entered captivity in Babylon. The Jewish Diaspora had begun. From this time on, the followers of Judaism would be scattered in many lands. Those who did return home found their land dominated by foreign rulers. It would not be easy to keep Judaism alive.

Rule by the Babylonians, Persians, and Greeks

The Hebrew captives in Babylon lived there for half a century. In this time of sorrow, great prophets rose up to encourage the people to remain faithful to Judaism.

It was after this time that the Hebrews came to be known as Jews. The Babylonians called their captives "Judaeans," after their homeland of Judah. The name was later shortened to "Jews."

In 539 B.C.E., the Babylonians were conquered by the Persians. The Persian king, Cyrus, released the Jews from captivity. Many Jews returned to Judah, where they immediately set to work building a new temple. Others stayed behind in Babylon. Since then, Jews outside their homeland never stopped praying to return.

For nearly 400 years, Judah was ruled by foreigners, first the Persians and later the Greeks. Sometimes the foreign rulers were kind. More often they were harsh.

The Greek rulers tried to force the Jews to worship idols of Greek gods in the temple. In 168 B.C.E., the Jews rebelled and started a war that lasted 27 years. In 164 B.C.E., they drove the Greeks from Jerusalem and reclaimed and repurified the temple. Jews today celebrate Hanukkah to honor this victory.

Rule by the Romans

For 88 years after the war with the Greeks, the Jews living in Judah had an independent kingdom. Then, in 63 B.C.E., they were conquered by the Romans.

The Romans were building a great empire, and they were quick to stamp out any sign of rebellion. More than 50,000 Jews were brutally **executed** under their rule. But the Romans did allow the Jews to practice their religion and to govern some of their own affairs. In 22 B.C.E., King Herod, who was allowed to rule in Judah, announced a huge project to rebuild the temple in Jerusalem so that it would be even more magnificent than Solomon's temple. The work took 46 years to complete.

In 66 C.E., the Jews rose up against the Romans. For three years, they managed to keep the Romans out of Jerusalem. Then, in 70 C.E., a Roman military leader named Titus led an army of 60,000 soldiers against the Jews. The Jews fought back fiercely, but they were hopelessly outnumbered. They watched in horror as the Romans destroyed Jerusalem and its great temple. All that remained of the temple was its western wall. To this day, Jews consider this wall sacred.

The Roman victory began the final scattering of the Jewish people from their homeland. The Romans seized Jewish land and forbade the Jews from entering Jerusalem. Although some Jews always remained in the land of Israel, thousands were sent to other parts of the Roman Empire.

The Jews had lost their homeland and their holy city. Yet Judaism not only survived, it flourished. Next you will learn how the Jews preserved their faith and way of life.

execute to kill

The Western Wall in modern-day Jerusalem was part of a network of supporting walls that surrounded the temple destroyed by the Romans.

12.4 Preserving and Passing On the Teachings of Judaism

After losing their homeland, their holy city, and the great temple that was the heart of their faith, the Jews faced a great struggle to preserve their religion. Jews were scattered among many **gentile,** or non-Jewish, lands. With creativity and dedication, they found a variety of ways to keep Judaism alive.

gentile non-Jewish

Rabbi Yohanan ben Zaccai

One individual who helped to preserve Judaism was a rabbi, or religious teacher, named Yohanan ben Zaccai. When the revolt against Rome broke out in 66 C.E., ben Zaccai was afraid Judaism would not survive. He worried that the Jewish rabbis would die in the fighting. If they were lost and the temple was destroyed, Judaism would be left with nothing.

Ben Zaccai begged the Jews to surrender in order to save Judaism. When they refused, he decided to approach the Romans for help.

Ben Zaccai faked his death and was smuggled out of Jerusalem in a coffin. He met with Vespasian, a Roman general, and pleaded for the chance to start a Jewish school in the small town of Yavneh. Together with other rabbis, ben Zaccai was allowed to start his school.

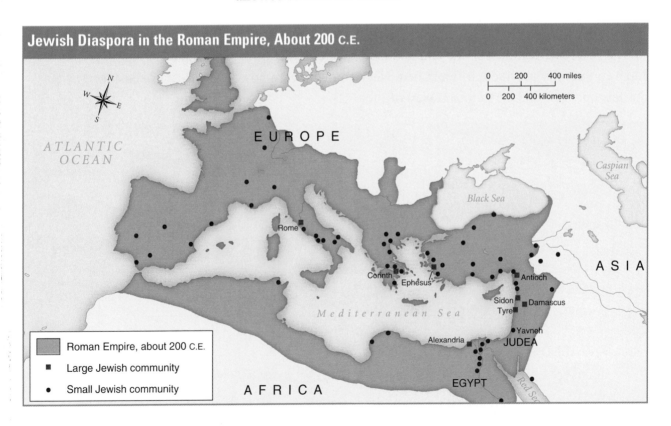

Jewish Diaspora in the Roman Empire, About 200 C.E.

ATLANTIC OCEAN

EUROPE

Caspian Sea

Black Sea

Rome

Corinth
Ephesus

Antioch

Sidon Damascus
Tyre

Mediterranean Sea

Alexandria

Yavneh
JUDEA

ASIA

AFRICA

EGYPT

Red Sea

0   200   400 miles
0   200   400 kilometers

Roman Empire, about 200 C.E.
■ Large Jewish community
• Small Jewish community

When Jerusalem fell, Yavneh became the center of Jewish life. Ben Zaccai and 71 other rabbis created a new religious lawmaking body. They also made Yavneh a training ground for other rabbis. Teachers from around the world came to Yavneh to study. Then they returned to their communities to share what they had learned. In this way, the rabbis at Yavneh made sure that Jews still had leaders to guide them.

New Teachers and Practices

In addition to training other rabbis, the rabbis at Yavneh introduced new practices to ensure that the teachings of Judaism would be passed on.

Traditionally, only religious leaders were allowed to read from the Torah. The Yavneh rabbis decided that any adult male could read from the sacred text. As a result, Jews no longer needed a trained leader to learn about Jewish history and law.

The rabbis also made the **synagogue** more important in Jewish life. A synagogue is a house of worship. But it is also a place to study and to hold meetings and social gatherings. The rabbis told Jews to build a synagogue wherever there were at least 10 adult male Jews. By building synagogues, Jews could strengthen their communities and their faith.

These new practices helped Jews preserve their religion in communities around the world. Over the centuries, rabbis studied and commented on Judaism's sacred texts, and developed other new practices. Jews often faced prejudice and persecution but kept their faith.

In 1948, a new Jewish state, Israel, was created in part of the lands once ruled by David and Solomon. Jews from many countries settled in Israel. For others, the traditions established over many centuries allowed their religion to thrive in many non-Jewish lands.

In the tradition of Rabbi ben Zaccai's first school, Jews today continue to learn and to share their understandings in Torah study groups.

synagogue a place of Jewish worship

12.5 Chapter Summary

In this chapter, you learned about Jewish beliefs and the Diaspora. After losing their homeland, Jews struggled to preserve and pass on their religion. With creativity and dedication, they found ways to keep Judaism alive. In the next unit, you will learn about ancient India, a fascinating civilization that gave birth to two major religions of its own.

Ancient Egypt and the Near East Timeline

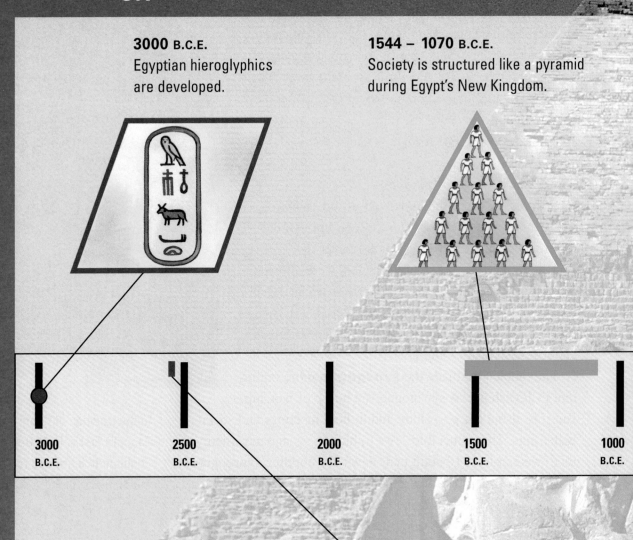

3000 B.C.E.
Egyptian hieroglyphics
are developed.

1544 – 1070 B.C.E.
Society is structured like a pyramid
during Egypt's New Kingdom.

| 3000 B.C.E. | 2500 B.C.E. | 2000 B.C.E. | 1500 B.C.E. | 1000 B.C.E. |

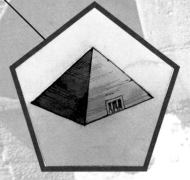

2551 – 2528 B.C.E.
The Great Pyramid
is built in Egypt.

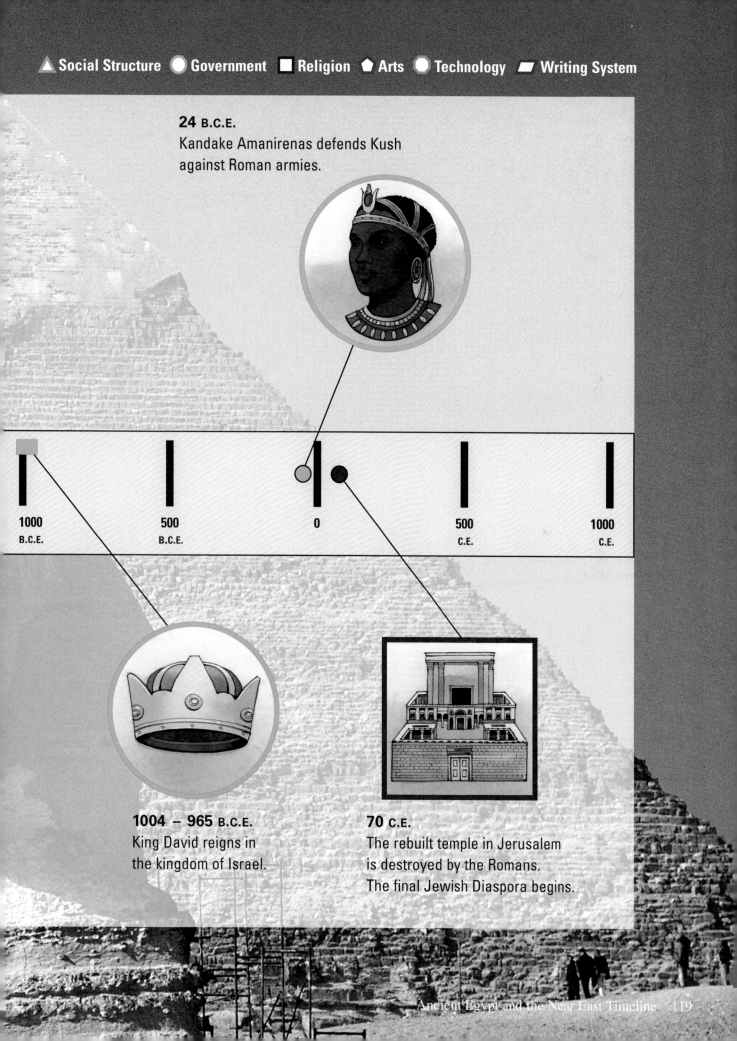

24 B.C.E.
Kandake Amanirenas defends Kush
against Roman armies.

| 1000 | 500 | 0 | 500 | 1000 |
| B.C.E. | B.C.E. | | C.E. | C.E. |

1004 – 965 B.C.E.
King David reigns in
the kingdom of Israel.

70 C.E.
The rebuilt temple in Jerusalem
is destroyed by the Romans.
The final Jewish Diaspora begins.

UNIT 3

Ancient India

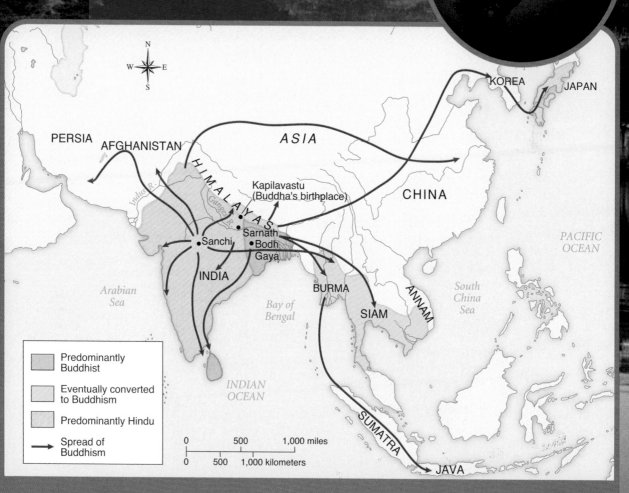

Hinduism and Buddhism in India, 600 C.E.

CHAPTER 13

◀ Boatmen glide along the Ganges River, which flows across northern India.

Geography and the Early Settlement of India

13.1 Introduction

In Unit 2, you explored the world of the ancient Egyptians, the Hebrews, and the people of Kush. In this unit, you will learn about the civilization of ancient India.

India is a **subcontinent** of Asia. If you look at a map of India, you can see that it is attached to the continent of Asia, but surrounded on three sides by water.

Early walled towns appeared on the Indian subcontinent in about 2500 B.C.E. Over the next 2,000 years, a unique civilization developed in India.

According to an ancient Indian story, a river god and goddess once lived in the snow-covered Himalayas, a mountain range north of the valleys. One day, they decided to race down the mountains to the plains below. The goddess sped straight down and won the race. But her joy soon turned to worry. Where was the river god?

The river god had slowed down to admire the snowcapped mountains and the rich brown earth in the valleys. In time, he flowed down to meet his beloved goddess. The two rivers became one, joined forever on India's plains. The rivers made the land good for farming.

In this chapter, you will learn about India's rivers and other **physical features**. You'll explore eight key features and their effects on the settlement of India.

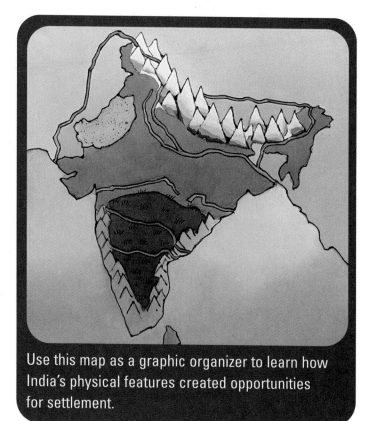

Use this map as a graphic organizer to learn how India's physical features created opportunities for settlement.

13.2 Brahmaputra River

Our exploration of India begins with the Brahmaputra River. This river starts high up in the Himalayas. From there, it winds through snowcapped mountains and narrow canyons. The water is clear and cold as it rushes over the sharp rocks.

The river becomes slower and deeper as it moves into its valley. Each summer, heavy monsoon rains add water to this part of the river. A **monsoon** is a large wind that often brings lots of rain. The heavy rains cause the river to overflow its banks. As it overflows, the river leaves the rich minerals it has carried down from the Himalayas in the earth of the valley.

Eventually, the river joins another river, the Ganges, on the plains. Where the two rivers meet, the land is very fertile (good for farming).

monsoon a strong wind that brings heavy rain to southern Asia in the summer

A typical southern town along the Brahmaputra River receives between 70 and 150 inches of rain a year. The heaviest rainfall occurs during the southwest monsoon between June and October. Temperatures along the river range from 45°F to 85°F.

The map shows India with the Deccan Plateau marked, bordered by the Arabian Sea, Bay of Bengal, and Indian Ocean.

13.3 Deccan Plateau

The Deccan Plateau is a triangle-shaped area between two mountain ranges in southern India. A **plateau** is an elevated, or raised, area of land that is flatter than a mountain. The Deccan Plateau has different kinds of land. In the flatter parts, large granite rocks formed by volcanoes cover the land. These rocks are among the world's oldest, dating back more than 600 million years. The hillier parts of the plateau have thin forests and low, scrubby bushes.

The plateau is fairly dry. There are a few rivers, but the monsoon rains provide most of the water. The soil on the plateau is black, yellow, or red. The black soil is rich in iron and good for growing cotton. The yellow and red soils are missing important minerals. Farmers have a hard time growing plants in them.

A typical town in the Deccan Plateau receives about 30 inches of rain a year. The heaviest rainfall occurs during the southwest monsoon between June and October. Temperatures on the plateau range from 65°F to 100°F.

plateau a flat area of land that is elevated, or raised, above the land around it

13.4 Eastern and Western Ghats

The Eastern and Western Ghats are long mountain chains near the coasts of India. When seen from above, they form a large V. The Deccan Plateau stretches between these two mountain ranges.

The Western Ghats are higher than the Eastern Ghats. They have steep slopes, narrow valleys, thick hardwood forests, and extremely heavy rains. The wet climate encourages the growth of tropical plants.

The Eastern Ghats are not as wet as the Western Ghats. Several rivers flow through these green mountains, which are sprinkled with hardwood trees. The rivers rarely flood, but they are not safe for travel. They move very fast, contain many rocks, and often plunge suddenly over cliffs.

Parts of the Ghats receive 100 or more inches of rain a year. Temperatures range from 60°F to 90°F.

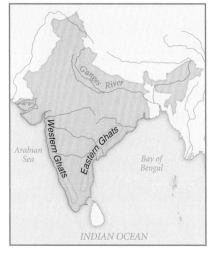

13.5 Ganges River

The Ganges River flows across most of northern India. It starts in the Himalaya Mountains. The river traces its way south through ice, rocks, and magnificent mountains and valleys.

The river carries sediment (bits of earth and sand) from the Himalayas to the northern plains. As the river passes through the plains, it leaves the rich sediment behind. As a result, the northern plains contain some of the most fertile farmland in the world.

The Ganges River plains have a good water supply from melting ice carried down from the Himalayas. During the rainy season, the river can flood and destroy crops planted along its banks.

Towns along the Ganges receive 25 to 60 inches of rain a year. Temperatures in the Ganges plains range from 55°F to 90°F.

13.6 Himalaya Mountains

The Himalayas are located along India's northern border. They are the highest mountain range in the world. Mount Everest, the world's tallest mountain, is part of the Himalayas. It reaches five and a half miles into the sky. The mountains form a natural border between the Indian subcontinent and most of the rest of Asia.

The Himalayas live up to their name, which means "home of snows." The highest peaks are always covered in snow and ice. Fierce storms can dump 10 feet of snow on the area at one time. The water from the range's **glaciers** (ice fields) feed northern India's major rivers.

Underneath the Himalaya Mountains, the earth is always moving. This movement causes Mount Everest to rise slightly every year. It also makes earthquakes and landslides common in the area.

glacier a huge mass of ice that slowly slides over a land area

The upper peaks of the Himalayas receive about 20 inches of snow a year. The heaviest snowfall occurs during the southwest monsoon between June and October. Temperatures on the highest peaks never rise above freezing (32°F) and can go as low as −76°F.

HIMALAYA MOUNTAINS

Arabian Sea

Bay of Bengal

INDIAN OCEAN

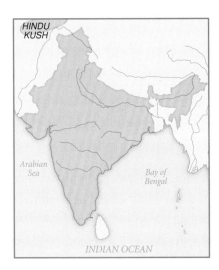

The Hindu Kush mountain range receives about 15 inches of rain and snow a year. Weather and seasons vary greatly across the range. Temperatures in the Hindu Kush vary from about 25°F to 75°F.

13.7 Hindu Kush Mountains

The Hindu Kush mountains form a fierce barrier between India and present-day Afghanistan. This mountain range is not as tall as the Himalayas, but it is still one of the highest in the world. Some of its peaks are almost 5 miles high. Many parts of the mountain range are unlivable. Snow and ice permanently cover the steep slopes and peaks.

The Khyber Pass is a 28-mile-long gap between the mountains. It connects central Asia to the Indian subcontinent. For thousands of years, traders used the pass to enter the Indus River valley. Invaders also used the pass, although many died in the mountains' unforgiving landscape.

13.8 Indus River

The Indus River begins in the Himalaya Mountains. It gets water from melting snow from the Hindu Kush mountains and other mountain ranges. The melting snow and ice from the mountains keep the river's water level high. Eventually, the river flows through what is now the country of Pakistan and empties into the Arabian Sea.

In addition, the Indus River valley contains some of the best farmland in the world. Like the Ganges, the Indus carries sediment from the mountains to the plains. The sediment leaves the surrounding soil rich and fertile.

The Indus River has often been compared to Egypt's Nile River. Like the Nile, the Indus is an important source of water for the farmland that lies along its banks.

Towns along the Indus River receive from 5 to 20 inches of rain a year. The heaviest rainfall occurs during the southwest monsoon between June and October. Temperatures in the Indus River valley range from 65°F to 90°F.

The Thar Desert receives about 4 to 20 inches of rain a year. The heaviest rainfall occurs during the southwest monsoon between June and October. Temperatures in the desert range from 45°F to 120°F.

13.9 Thar Desert

The massive Thar Desert in northern India is mostly sand and stone. Huge, rolling sand dunes stretch for hundreds of miles. The landscape is littered with rocks. There is very little plant life except for grass and low, hardy shrubs. Most of the time, the heat is unbearable.

Water is a precious resource in the desert. There is evidence of dried-up riverbeds near the desert's borders, but there are no rivers now. Rain is rare, although the monsoons occasionally bring a soothing storm. The dry conditions make dust storms common.

A variety of animals and birds make their home in the desert. There are more than 45 kinds of lizards and snakes. Gazelles lope across the sand. Birds include quail, ducks, and geese.

13.10 Early Settlements in India

Like many ancient peoples, the first people in India settled by rivers. The rivers provided plenty of water. The fertile soil was ideal for farming. The rivers could also be used for travel and trade.

India's early townspeople lived along the Indus River and the ancient Sarasvati River. The Sarasvati used to run through what is now the Thar Desert. Scientists believe the river dried up around 1900 B.C.E. Over time, the area became a hot, dry desert.

Farming settlements sprang up in the Indus-Sarasvati region as early as 6500 B.C.E. By 5000 B.C.E., people had also settled near the Ganges River. When the Sarasvati River dried up, the ancient Indians continued to settle along the Ganges.

By 2500 B.C.E., there were walled settlements near the Indus and Sarasvati Rivers. You'll learn more about this ancient civilization in the next chapter.

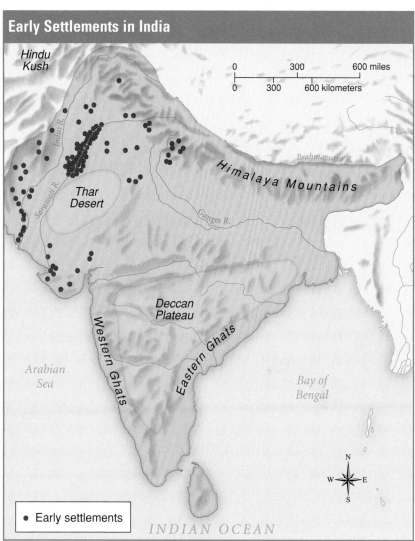

Early Settlements in India

Hindu Kush

Indus R.

Sarasvati R.

Thar Desert

Himalaya Mountains

Brahmaputra R.

Ganges R.

Deccan Plateau

Western Ghats

Eastern Ghats

Arabian Sea

Bay of Bengal

● Early settlements

INDIAN OCEAN

13.11 Chapter Summary

In this chapter, you explored eight physical features of the Indian subcontinent. You learned that India has a varied landscape. It contains high mountains, a large plateau, a desert, and many rivers.

India's early settlers farmed in the fertile river valleys. In time, walled settlements were built. This was the start of civilization in India.

What was life like for people in ancient India? In the next chapter, you will go on an archeological dig to unearth the ancient Indian city of Mohenjodaro.

CHAPTER 14

◀ The ruins of Mohenjodaro provide clues
about an ancient Indus River civilization.

Unlocking the Secrets of Mohenjodaro

14.1 Introduction

In Chapter 13, you explored the geography of the Indian subcontinent. You learned that early settlements in India were located in fertile river valleys. In this chapter, you will visit one of those settlements, the city of **Mohenjodaro**.

Mohenjodaro was located in the Indus River valley, in northern India. Many other towns also were clustered near the Sarasvati River. These settlements became known as the **Indus-Sarasvati civilization**. It is also called the Harappan civilization, after another city, Harappa. The civilization flourished for 800 years, from about 2700 B.C.E. to 1900 B.C.E.

The cities of Harappa and Mohenjodaro were the two great centers of this civilization. Mohenjodaro means "place or hill of the dead." Archeologists found its ruins in 1922. Carefully, they excavated (dug up) the ruins. They discovered that the city had two main parts.

The first part was a raised area that was used as a citadel, or fort. The citadel was surrounded by a wall. In times of trouble, people probably gathered in this area.

The second part of Mohenjodaro was below the citadel. The lower city had many houses and workshops. This area was probably where people lived in times of peace.

What was daily life like in Mohenjodaro? In this chapter, you will unlock the secrets of this ancient city. You'll explore its ruins and study its artifacts. What can these clues reveal about the city's people and their civilization?

Use this illustration as a graphic organizer to help you explore the ruins of Mohenjodaro.

The photo above is a view of the Mohenjodaro ruins from the top of the citadel. Use this map to locate Mohenjodaro on the Indian sub-continent.

citadel a fortress built to protect a city

14.2 The Mystery of Mohenjodaro

Mohenjodaro was built on the banks of the Indus River. From the city's ruins, we can see that the city was carefully planned. To the west, the **citadel** rose up on a platform of mud and brick. Below the citadel, nine streets divided the lower city into blocks, like those of a modern city. The streets were lined with houses and workshops made of mud bricks.

Mohenjodaro was a large city. At one time, as many as 50,000 people may have lived there. Like the other people of the Indus-Sarasvati civilization, they had an advanced culture. But one great mystery remains. What happened to this civilization?

No one knows for sure. After about 1900 B.C.E., the great cities of the Indus River valley disappeared. Some scientists believe that hostile invaders were to blame. According to this idea, fierce warriors swept in from central Asia and destroyed the local civilization.

Other scientists think natural events caused the decline of the Indus-Sarasvati civilization. Some point to floods and earth-quakes that struck the region around 1900 B.C.E. Others suggest that the Indus River changed course and people moved to the Ganges River valley in search of a steady water supply.

All that remains today of the Indus-Sarasvati people are the buildings and artifacts they left behind. These clues can tell us a great deal about how they lived. Let's explore the ruins of Mohenjodaro and see what we can find out.

14.3 Weights and Scale

Inside the walls of Mohenjodaro's citadel, several stone weights and a scale were found near a large building. When archeologists searched the ruins of this building, they found bits of grain such as barley and wheat. They decided the building must have been a **granary**. Workers may have crushed the grain into flour. The flour may have been used for trading with other cities.

granary a place to store grain

The scale and weights found near the granary are interesting clues. They suggest that ancient Indians might have used grain like money. They may have weighed the grain and used different amounts to trade for various goods. Farmers also had their own granaries outside the city, so perhaps the grain in the citadel's granary was collected as taxes.

These stone weights were found in Mohenjodaro.

This is the Great Bath as it looks today.

14.4 The Great Bath

The most dramatic feature of Mohenjodaro's citadel was the Great Bath. The Great Bath was a pool built of waterproofed brick. It was 39 feet long and 8 feet deep. Small dressing rooms circled the pool. One of the rooms contained a well that supplied the bath with water. Dirty water was removed through a drain that ran along one side of the bath.

It seems certain that the people of Mohenjodaro used the pool to bathe. On a hot, clear day, they probably enjoyed washing themselves in the bath's cooling waters. Some archeologists think the Great Bath was also used for religious rituals. They point out that bathing rituals are important in India's major religion, Hinduism. Ancient Hindu temples often featured bathing pools.

14.5 Statue and Beads

In the lower city, archeologists found a stone statue seven inches high. It shows how men in Mohenjodaro might have looked and dressed. The figure has a short, tidy beard and a clean upper lip. His hair is tied with a band. He is wearing a patterned robe draped over his left shoulder. He has a calm and noble expression. Archeologists are not sure who the statue represents. Some think he may have been a priest and a king.

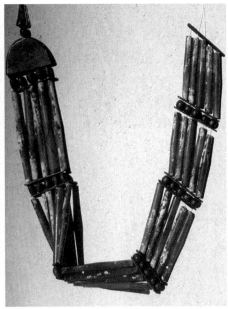

What do these artifacts reveal about the culture of the people who made them?

Beautiful stone beads in many shapes and colors have been found throughout Mohenjodaro. Women probably wore them in necklaces, bracelets, earrings, and rings. Indian bead makers also made beads of clay and baked them in hot ovens called *kilns*. They drilled holes in the beads and strung them into necklaces.

14.6 Seals

Small stone seals are among the most mysterious of Mohenjodaro's artifacts. They have been found in large numbers throughout the ruins. The seals are carved with pictographs, pictures used to stand for objects, sounds, or ideas. More than 400 pictographs have been discovered, but archeologists don't know what most of them stand for. Many seals show animals such as buffalo, bulls, tigers, elephants, rhinoceroses, fish, and crocodiles.

No one knows how the seals were used, but scientists have made some educated guesses. Many of the seals have a small loop on the back. Perhaps people wore them as charms to keep away evil. The seals may also have been pressed into wax to make a kind of tag. Merchants might have placed the wax tags on their goods to show who owned them.

What do you think the images on these seals represent?

14.7 Sewer System

A great achievement of Mohenjodaro was its sewer system. A **sewer system** carries waste away from houses. Mohenjodaro's complex system of drains, pipes, wells, and bathrooms set the city apart from other settlements of its time. Two thousand years would pass before the world would see another system like it, in ancient Rome.

A network of clay pipes connected Mohenjodaro's buildings and homes to the main sewer system. Dirty, used water and waste flowed in channels along the streets. This sewage then emptied into the Indus River. The sewer system made it possible for both rich and poor to have bathrooms in their homes.

Deep wells made of brick were located throughout the city. People stored water, including rainfall, in the wells.

sewer system a network of pipes that disposes of sewage, or waste water

Pieces of Mohenjodaro's sewer system can still be seen in the city's ruins.

14.8 Homes

Most of Mohenjodaro's people lived in the lower city, which was three times the size of the citadel. Rows of houses lined the streets. The houses had flat roofs and were two stories high. Like most of the city's buildings, they were made of mud bricks.

The houses faced narrow alleys. The backs of the houses opened onto courtyards where families could gather. The houses had narrow windows on the second floor with screens made of hard clay called *terra-cotta* or a see-through mineral called *alabaster*.

Homes had from one to a dozen rooms. Scientists believe that poorer people lived in the smaller homes, while richer citizens lived in the larger ones.

This narrow alley in the ruins of Mohenjodaro is lined with houses. Notice that there are no windows on the ground floor.

What game pieces can you identify in this picture?

14.9 Games

The people of Mohenjodaro enjoyed playing games. They crafted many objects for toys and parts of game sets. Archeologists have uncovered dice, stone balls, grooved clay tracks, and stone game boards.

The game of chess was probably invented in India. An ancient Indian book describes a war game played with dice and pieces called *pawns*. Although modern chess is not played with dice, historians believe the war game is an early form of chess. The small carved game pieces found at Mohenjodaro may have been used to play this game.

The children of Mohenjodaro played simpler games. Some of the objects found by archeologists seem to be children's toys. For example, children probably rolled stone balls along clay mazes and tracks.

14.10 Clay Models

Archeologists have found small clay models all around Mohenjodaro. Most of the models are made of terra cotta. In one model, two bulls are attached to a yoke (wooden harness). The bulls are pulling a person in a two-wheeled cart.

The model may be a toy, but archeologists believe it also shows how farm goods were transported to the city's market. On market day, farmers loaded their crops into carts. The crops

Children in Mohenjodaro may have played with clay models like this one.

probably included barley, cotton, dates, melons, peas, rice, sesame seeds, and wheat. Then the farmers hitched their bulls to the carts and headed to the market. There they sold or traded their goods with other farmers.

14.11 Chapter Summary

In this chapter, you learned about the Indus-Sarasvati civilization by exploring the city of Mohenjodaro. Mohenjodaro was a large and well-planned city. Its people enjoyed a high quality of life. They had private homes with indoor bathrooms. A complex sewer system carried away waste. People had time, after meeting their basic needs for food and shelter, to express themselves through arts and crafts. As the discovery of game pieces suggest, they even had time to play.

Historians and archeologists continue to investigate what happened to this remarkable civilization. Perhaps one day you can help solve the mystery.

In the next chapter, you will learn about one of the world's major religions, Hinduism. This religion began in ancient India. It continues to influence the lives of millions of people today.

The ruins at Mohenjodaro can be clearly seen from the air.

A Brahmin, or Hindu priest, prays at dawn beside the sacred Ganges River.

CHAPTER 15

Learning About Hindu Beliefs

15.1 Introduction

In Chapter 14, you visited the ruins of Mohenjodaro to learn about the Indus-Sarasvati civilization of ancient India. In this chapter, you will learn about the origins and beliefs of **Hinduism,** India's first major religion.

Hinduism has shaped Indian life in countless ways. It has affected how people worship, what jobs they do, and even what they eat. It has inspired great art and literature. And it has helped to determine the status of people in Indian society.

One of the basic beliefs of Hinduism is **dharma**. Dharma stands for law, obligation, and duty. To follow one's dharma means to perform one's duties and so to live as one should.

One of the most famous Hindu sacred texts is the *Ramayana*. The *Ramayana* tells about life in ancient India and offers models in dharma.

The central figure of the *Ramayana*, Rama, lives by the rules of dharma. When Rama is a young boy, he is a loyal son. When he grows up, he is a loving husband and a responsible ruler.

In this chapter, you will explore the origins of Hinduism. Then, you'll learn about dharma and the other basic Hindu beliefs: **Brahman, deities, karma,** and **samsara.**

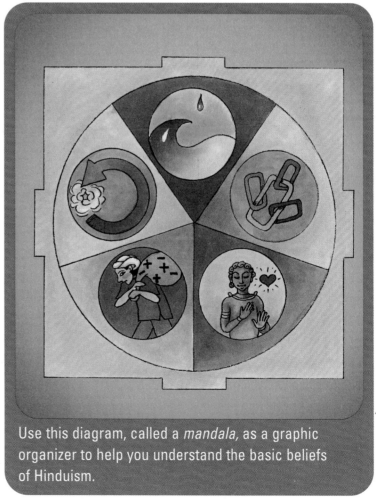

Use this diagram, called a *mandala,* as a graphic organizer to help you understand the basic beliefs of Hinduism.

15.2 The Origins of Hinduism

Hinduism is a very old religion, so old that it began before recorded history. No single person founded it. It developed slowly, over a long period of time.

In the second millennium B.C.E., people called Aryans migrated into northern India. Some historians credit the Aryans with bringing elements of what later became Hinduism to India. Others believe that traces of Hinduism can be found in ancient artifacts left by India's original settlers. These artifacts include items like those found at Mohenjodaro. Pools, hearths, and pictures on stone seals may be early evidence of practices that are features of Hinduism. Such practices include ritual bathing, lighting sacred (holy) fires, and worshiping certain deities.

Early Hindu religion is called Vedism, after the **Vedas**. The Vedas are a collection of sacred texts, including verses, hymns, prayers, and teachings composed in **Sanskrit**. (Veda is Sanskrit for "knowledge.") The Vedas were taught orally for hundreds of years before India had a written form of Sanskrit.

The sacred Vedas were composed in the ancient language of Sanskrit.

Vedic rituals and sacrifices honored a number of deities associated with nature and social order. Over time, these rituals became more and more complex. A class of priests and religious scholars, called Brahmins, grew increasingly important because only they knew how to interpret the Vedas and correctly perform the rituals. Brahmins became the dominant class in India. Later Vedism is often called **Brahmanism**.

Modern-day Hinduism is very complex. Many beliefs, many forms of worship, and many deities exist side by side. But all Hindus share certain beliefs. The Vedas remain sacred to Hindus today. Along with later sacred texts, the Vedas lay out the basic beliefs of Hinduism. As you will see, these beliefs have influenced every part of life in India.

Vedas a collection of Hindu sacred writings

Sanskrit an ancient language of India

Brahmanism an ancient Indian religion in which the Brahmins (priests and religious scholars) are the dominant class

15.3 Hinduism and the Caste System

Hinduism was not just a religion in ancient India. It was a way of life. It affected how Indians lived, what they believed, and even the way they organized their society.

Brahmanism taught that a well-organized society was divided into social classes. Europeans later called this the **caste** system. The Vedas describe four main social classes:

- *Brahmins* (priests and religious scholars)
- *Kshatriyas* (rulers and warriors)
- *Vaishyas* (herders and merchants)
- *Shudras* (servants)

According to the Vedas, each class, or *varna*, had its own duties. For example, Brahmins had a duty to study and teach the Vedas. Warriors had a duty to become skilled with weapons. But the caste system meant that some people were much more favored than others. Brahmins held the top place, while Shudras held the lowest.

Over the centuries a fifth class developed, called the *untouchables*. These were people whose jobs or ways of life involved activities that Hindus considered lowly or "dirty," such as handling garbage and dead animals. Untouchables often had to live in their own villages or neighborhoods. They could not enter many temples or attend most schools. Other Hindus avoided touching them and, in many cases, even looking at them.

The caste system affected all aspects of people's lives. Indians were born into a certain caste, and they could not change it. In addition, people could only marry within their own caste.

The class system is just one example of how Hinduism affected the fabric of daily life in India. Let's look now at the five basic beliefs of Hinduism and how they helped to shape Indian life and culture.

caste a class, or group, in Hindu society

Even today, the highest caste in India is the Brahmins. They are identified by the sacred thread worn over their shoulders.

15.4 Hindu Beliefs About Brahman

Brahman is the Hindu name for a supreme power, or a divine force, that is greater than all the other deities. To Hindus, only Brahman exists forever. Everything else in the world changes, from the passing seasons to living things that eventually die.

Hinduism sees time going around in a circle, like a great wheel. The same events return, just as the sun rises each morning and spring follows winter. Hindus believe Brahman is constantly creating, destroying, and re-creating the universe. This cycle never ends.

According to Hindu belief, everything in the world is a part of Brahman, including the human soul. Hindus call the soul *atman*. It is a part of Brahman, just as a drop of water is part of the ocean. Through their own souls, peo-

Modern Hindus can visit portable, or mobile, shrines set up at convenient locations.

ple are connected to Brahman. The other deities in Hinduism also are various forms of Brahman.

To connect with their deities, ancient Hindus began to build great temples in the sixth century C.E. They wrote exact instructions about where and how to build temples. Modern Hindu temples are still built using these ancient directions.

Many Hindu temples are magnificent in size and design. Their doors always face east, toward the rising sun. The buildings are covered with beautiful carvings and sculptures. These works of art usually show deities from Hindu sacred texts. Inside, temples usually contain a tower and a small shrine.

Modern Hindus continue to visit temples to express their love of the deities. Visitors often sit quietly and meditate. At other times they give thanks, make requests, and take part in rituals.

15.5 Hindu Beliefs About Deities

There are many deities in Hindu sacred texts and worship. Over time, Hindus came to believe that all the deities were different faces of Brahman. Each of them represented a power or quality of Brahman.

In ancient times, the most popular and powerful deity was Indra. Indra was the deity of thunder. He was fiercely warlike. He used lightning bolts as weapons. The Vedas describe him as driving a blazing gold chariot across the sky and riding a magnificent white elephant.

Today, the most important Hindu deities are Brahma, Vishnu, and Shiva. Each deity controls one aspect of the universe. Brahma creates it, Vishnu preserves it, and Shiva destroys it. The deity Devi is also important. She embodies the female powers of the universe. Hindu deities are often quite fantastic in appearance. For example, Vishnu is sometimes pictured as having blue skin and six arms. The deity's "extra" arms are a symbol of strength. Shiva has been pictured as having three eyes. This symbolizes being able to see events from a distance.

Ancient Hindu sacred texts often described heroic deities battling evil. One of the most famous stories is the *Ramayana*. It tells of Rama's fierce battle with Ravana, a demon (evil spirit). This sacred text also presents some of Hinduism's basic beliefs in an entertaining way. Many Hindu children have learned about their religion by listening to the *Ramayana*.

Sacred texts like the *Ramayana* have inspired many Hindu holidays and festivals. The Hindu New Year is celebrated during the Divali festival. Divali means "row of lamps." The lamps are symbols of good (light) winning over evil (darkness). They represent Rama's triumph over the evil Ravana, and the beginning of the Hindu New Year.

Hindu families light candles and sparklers to celebrate Divali, the festival of lights.

A Hindu wedding ceremony in Malaysia. Marriage is one form of dharma.

15.6 Hindu Beliefs About Dharma

Dharma is a very important idea in Hinduism. Dharma stands for law, obligation, and duty. To follow one's dharma means to perform one's duties and so to live as one should.

As you have already read, in the Vedas each social class, or varna, had its own duties. These duties usually involved a certain type of work, such as serving as a warrior or herding animals. Each class, then, had its own dharma. In fact, Hindus called their system of social classes *varna dharma*. This means "the way of one's kind." Hindus believed that when everyone followed the dharma of their varna, society would be in harmony.

Brahmins, for example, were society's priests and religious scholars. Their duties included performing rituals and teaching the Vedas. This was quite an accomplishment, since the Vedas were not written down for over 1,000 years. To recite them orally, the Brahmins had to memorize more than 100,000 verses!

In addition to the dharma of their varna, Hindus are expected to follow a common dharma, or set of values. For example, Hinduism values marriage, sharing food with others, and caring for one's soul.

Another basic value is nonviolence. Hindus believe that all life forms have a soul, so Hindus respect all forms of life and avoid doing them harm. This reverence for life came to be symbolized by the cow. Perhaps this was because cows were especially important in Indian life. Cows gave people milk and butter. After they died, their skins could be turned into clothing. People were taught not to kill them.

15.7 Hindu Beliefs About Karma

The belief of dharma expresses much of what Hindus believe about the right way to live. Another belief, *karma,* explains the importance of living according to dharma.

In Hindu belief, the law of karma governs what happens to people's souls after death. From ancient times, Hindus believed that souls had many lives. When a person died, his or her soul was reborn in a new body. But what type of body would the reborn soul get? The answer depended on the soul's karma.

Karma was made up of all the good and evil that a person had done in past lives. If people lived well, they might be born into a higher class in their next life. If they lived badly, they could expect to be reborn into a lower class. They might even be reborn as animals.

This Hindu man sits in prayer, or meditation.

For Hindus, the law of karma meant that the universe was just, or fair. Souls were rewarded or punished for the good and evil they had done. Karma also explained why people had a certain status in society. Recall that in the caste system, people could not escape the social class of their birth. According to karma, this was fair, because people's social class reflected what they had done in their past lives.

Over the centuries, many Hindu teachers criticized the caste system. They taught that all people, including the untouchables, should be treated equally. In the 20th century, the Indian leader Mahatma Gandhi called the untouchables "children of God." Today, Indian law protects the rights of all people, and the caste system is much less strict. But the ideas of karma and rebirth remain a central part of Hinduism.

Hindus from all over the world travel to the Ganges River to bathe in its waters.

15.8 Hindu Beliefs About Samsara

As you have learned, Hindus believe in a continuous cycle of birth, death, and rebirth. They call this cycle *samsara*. As long as people are part of samsara, they will know pain and death. Samsara ends when the soul escapes from the cycle of rebirth and is united with Brahman, the supreme force in the universe.

It takes many lifetimes before a person can be released from samsara. People escape the cycle of rebirth, or **reincarnation,** by following the basic beliefs of Hinduism. They balance their karma with good actions. They follow their dharma by behaving correctly and performing their social duties. They worship Brahman, including the deities that represent different aspects of Brahman, faithfully. They also strive for direct, personal connections with Brahman.

The Indians of ancient times connected with Brahman by going on holy journeys called **pilgrimages**. People would travel to sacred places like the Ganges and Sarasvati Rivers. Such pilgrims believed that the difficulty of the journey would cleanse them of their sins.

Faithful Hindus still make pilgrimages today. Pilgrims travel for days over difficult land, including mountains. They often lie facedown in worship at each holy site and temple they encounter. The Ganges River is still one of the most holy places in India. Like the ancient Indians, modern Hindus bathe in its waters as an act of devotion and purification.

reincarnation the belief that a person's soul is reborn into a new body after death
pilgrimage a journey to a holy place

Hindu monks, known as *sannyasins,* devote their entire lives to attaining divine enlightenment. There have been sannyasins since ancient times. They use a number of techniques to focus on Brahman. They meditate, perform breathing exercises, recite prayers, and sing sacred songs. They also practice the ancient art of yoga. Yoga is a type of meditation. It combines special body positions with deep, slow breathing.

15.9 Chapter Summary

In this chapter you learned about Hinduism, India's first major religion. You studied the five basic beliefs of Hinduism. They are belief in Brahman, deities, dharma, karma, and samsara. As you have learned, these beliefs helped to shape ancient Indian society. They inspired Indian art, sacred texts, and temple architecture. They were reflected in the caste system and in the treatment of people and animals.

Hinduism is an important link between ancient and modern India. Hindu beliefs continue to affect daily life in India. Hindus still worship in temples, make pilgrimages, and celebrate religious festivals. They practice meditation and other ways of connecting with Brahman. In addition, reverence for life and nonviolence remain important ideals in India. Many modern Hindus avoid eating meat because they believe in not doing harm to animals.

India's second great religion, Buddhism, grew out of Hinduism. You will learn about Buddhism in the next chapter.

Fire sacrifice accompanied by reading from the Vedas.

CHAPTER 16

This stone carving represents the Buddha, founder of the Buddhist religion.

The Story of Buddhism

16.1 Introduction

In Chapter 15, you read about Hinduism, India's first great religion. In this chapter, you will learn about another great religion that began in India, **Buddhism**.

Buddhism is based on the teachings of the **Buddha,** which means "Awakened One." The Buddha was a man who lived in India from about 563 to 483 B.C.E. Before earning the title of Buddha, he was a young prince named Siddhartha Gautama.

At the age of 29, Prince Siddhartha walked away from his royal life and went in search of spiritual peace. During his journeys, he learned great truths that changed his life. By sharing these truths with others, he began the great religion of Buddhism.

Buddhism was different from Hinduism in several ways. It was not based on complicated rituals and beliefs in many gods, as Hinduism was. Instead, it was a way of life based on simple teachings. Unlike ancient Hinduism, Buddhism embraced all people regardless of their caste. It taught people how to reach enlightenment, or happiness that comes from the knowledge of deep truth. Buddhists believed that once they reached enlightenment, they would no longer be reborn again and again.

In this chapter, you will learn about Buddhism through legends that are told about the Buddha's life. You'll find out what Prince Siddhartha discovered and how his teachings became the basis of Buddhism.

Use this illustration as a graphic organizer to help you follow the path the Buddha took to enlightenment.

16.2 Prince Siddhartha's Birth

Prince Siddhartha was born about 563 B.C.E. in the northern part of India, near the Himalaya Mountains. His father, Suddhodana, was a powerful king. His mother was the beautiful Queen Maya.

One night, before her son was born, the queen had a dream. In the dream, she was carried high over the Himalayas to a silver mountain and set on a silver couch. A white elephant with six tusks walked around her and then struck her right side.

The king and queen asked the Brahmins (Hindu priests) to explain her dream. "You are carrying a child who will be a great man," they told the queen. The Brahmins declared that the prince's future held two possible paths. As a prince, he could rule the universe. But if he left royal life to see the suffering in the world, he would become a Buddha, one who is enlightened.

The queen gave birth to Prince Siddhartha in a garden. Stories say that after the prince's birth, a soft, warm rain of heavenly flowers fell on the baby and his mother. The infant prince looked a few years old and could already walk and talk. Siddhartha began his remarkable life by taking a few steps and declaring, "I am the leader of the world and the guide to the world."

According to legend, the people around Siddhartha knew he was very special from the moment he was born.

16.3 The Prince's Royal Life

Prince Siddhartha's father wanted his son to be a great and powerful ruler. He was worried about the Brahmins' predictions. If the prince saw the world's suffering, he might give up his royal duties to seek a spiritual path.

The king decided to protect his son from all the horrors of the world. He raised the prince in a world of perfect wealth and beauty. He provided his son with only the finest gardens, houses, education, and food. Servants took care of the prince's every need, from washing his clothes to playing music for his amusement.

The prince enjoyed his easy life, yet he always felt curious about the world outside the palace walls. Some days he would sit under a rose apple tree and think about the world beyond his reach.

At the age of 16, Prince Siddhartha married a beautiful young noblewoman. The wedding feast lasted seven days and seven nights. For 12 years the couple lived together in perfect peace, enjoying the prince's many palaces. When Siddhartha turned 29, they had a son.

Prince Siddhartha enjoyed a life of wealth and pleasure in his father's palace.

Outside the palace, Siddhartha learned about three forms of suffering: aging, sickness, and death.

16.4 The Prince Discovers Three Forms of Suffering

After Siddhartha became a father, the king gave him more freedom to travel outside the royal palaces. During his trips, the prince discovered three forms of suffering.

On his first trip, the prince and his chariot driver saw a thin man who walked with the aid of a stick. "Why does that man look so terrible?" the prince asked. His driver replied that the man was old. He told the prince that everyone's body weakens as it ages.

On the second trip, the prince and his driver saw a man crying out in pain on the ground. "What is the matter with that poor man?" the prince asked. The driver explained that the man was sick.

On the third trip, the prince saw a group of people walking slowly down the road. The group carried a figure wrapped in white cloth. "Death came for that man," Siddhartha's driver said quietly. "One day it will come for you, too."

The prince was deeply troubled by his discovery of aging, sickness, and death. Unable to sit at home with his thoughts, he set out a fourth time. This time he met a man who glowed with inner peace and calm. The man was an ascetic. An **ascetic** is someone who gives up worldly pleasures such as possessions, fine clothes, money, and even shelter.

"How can you sit so peacefully when there is so much suffering around you?" the prince asked the man. The ascetic replied, "To be free of suffering, one must give up the desires, pleasures, and comforts of the world. I find peace by helping others find peace."

ascetic a person who gives up worldly pleasures

16.5 The Prince Becomes an Ascetic

Prince Siddhartha's experiences with suffering changed him forever. Suddenly, his royal life seemed empty. He wanted to find the happiness and peace the ascetic had found.

Siddhartha decided to give up his old life and find enlightenment. Becoming enlightened meant finding deep truth and being free of suffering.

One night the prince asked his faithful driver to take him to the forest. At the edge of the dark woods, Siddhartha removed his royal robes, sandals, and jewels. He cut off his hair with a knife. He put on a simple robe and kept only a small bowl for **alms,** or gifts of food. Wishing his driver farewell, Siddhartha began his life as an ascetic.

Siddhartha met other ascetics as he wandered the forests and fields. Like him, they wanted to understand the nature of the world. They believed they could reach enlightenment through meditation. While meditating, the ascetics sat quietly and focused their minds on spiritual questions. Siddhartha quickly became an expert at meditation.

The ascetics also denied their bodies many basic needs. For example, they stayed up all night without sleeping. They sat in the hot sun without shelter. They held their breath for long periods of time. They also fasted, or stopped eating, for many days at a time. They hoped to find spiritual truth through self-denial.

Siddhartha followed the way of the ascetics until he was pitifully thin from lack of food. Legends say that he became so skinny that he could touch his stomach and feel his backbone. Eventually, he became unhappy with this extreme way of living. And he had not yet found the key to enlightenment.

alms goods given to the poor

Siddhartha's search for enlightenment led him to give up riches and live the simple life of an ascetic.

16.6 The Prince Becomes the Buddha

During a night of deep meditation under the Bodhi tree, Siddhartha achieved enlightenment.

Siddhartha had learned that giving up bodily pleasures did not bring enlightenment. He decided to balance himself between the extremes of pleasure and pain. He would be neither a prince nor an ascetic. Instead, he would seek a "middle way" as a path to enlightenment.

The prince's new way of thinking caused the other ascetics to leave him. But he was content to be alone. He was not yet enlightened, but he was on the right path.

A full moon rose on Siddhartha's 35th birthday. He bathed in the river and rested quietly in a grove of trees. When he awoke, he had a strong feeling that he would soon become enlightened. Then a grass cutter gave him eight handfuls of soft grass as a present. Siddhartha walked until he reached a tree that became known as the Bodhi (Enlightenment) tree. He placed the grass at the foot of the tree and sat down. He vowed to meditate under the tree until he reached enlightenment.

While Siddhartha meditated, a wicked god, Mara, tried to frighten him. Then Mara tried to tempt him by sending his three daughters, Discontent (Unhappiness), Delight, and Desire. Siddhartha resisted them all. He meditated through the night about the nature of reality and how to reach **nirvana,** or true happiness and peace. As the night went on, his mind filled with the truths he had been seeking. He saw his past lives and the great cycle of rebirth. He saw the importance of karma. Eventually he saw how to gain freedom from the endless cycle and so end all suffering.

By morning, the young prince had become the Buddha, the Awakened One. He had reached enlightenment.

The truths that the Buddha discovered under the Bodhi tree are the basis of Buddhism. They are often called the Four Noble Truths. The Buddha would spend the rest of his life sharing these truths with the people of India.

nirvana an ideal state of happiness and peace

16.7 The Buddha's Teachings

Behind Buddhism's Four Noble Truths is the idea that all things change. The Buddha saw that even when one finds pleasure, it does not last forever, and one suffers when it is lost. To end suffering, he taught, people should travel the Eightfold Path. This path follows the "middle way."

The Buddha could have selfishly escaped into enlightenment. Instead, he chose to teach others the path that he had found. In time, his followers spread his teachings throughout India and other parts of Asia.

The Four Noble Truths

1. Suffering is present in all things, and nothing lasts forever.
2. Suffering is caused by cravings (desires and wants).
3. The way to end suffering is to give up all cravings.
4. The way to give up all cravings is to live life according to the Eightfold Path.

The Eightfold Path	
Right understanding	Develop a deep understanding of the Four Noble Truths.
Right purpose	Live a life of selflessness (not selfishness), love, and nonviolence.
Right speech	Be careful and truthful in what you say. Do not lie or gossip.
Right action	Do not kill, steal, or lie. Be honest.
Right way to earn a living	Do not work at a job that causes harm to people or living creatures.
Right effort	Promote good actions and prevent evil actions.
Right mindfulness	Be aware of but not attached to your emotions, thoughts, and feelings.
Right concentration	Focus your mind with practices such as meditation.

16.8 Chapter Summary

In this chapter, you learned about Buddhism. Buddhism was India's second great religion. It is based on the teachings of Siddhartha Gautama. Siddhartha became the Buddha by reaching enlightenment. In the next chapter, you will discover how a powerful Indian leader used Buddhism to help unify ancient India.

CHAPTER 17

Buddhism and the First Unification of India

17.1 Introduction

In Chapter 16, you learned about the origins of Buddhism. In this chapter, you will learn how one Indian leader, King **Ashoka,** used Buddhist values to **unify** India.

King Ashoka was part of the Maurya family. They united India for the first time under the **Mauryan Empire,** which flourished from about 322 to 187 B.C.E. The Mauryas, including Ashoka, fought wars of conquest to build their empire. Then a great change came over Ashoka, and he turned to peaceful ways of keeping India united.

The change came about in this way. One day when he was a young man, King Ashoka sat on his horse and looked out over a bloody battlefield. Men and animals lay dying under the hot Indian sun. Ashoka could hear the wounded groaning in pain. With growing horror, he thought of the thousands of people who had been killed or enslaved in his family's war for land. In that moment, he swore to give up violence.

Ashoka's promise led him to the Buddhist religion. He gave up making war and instead created an empire based on Buddhist values. He spread Buddhist beliefs through **edicts,** official messages carved on walls, rocks, and tall pillars.

In this chapter, you will read about how the Mauryan family unified India. Then you'll see how King Ashoka used Buddhist values to rule his empire.

Everywhere, I, Ashoka, King Priyadarsi, Beloved of the Gods, have arranged for....

Use this image of an engraved pillar as a graphic organizer to help you understand how King Ashoka unified India.

Buddhism and the First Unification of India   161

17.2 The Mauryas Unify India

The Maurya family were the first leaders to unify India. This was a major accomplishment because India was so huge and diverse. The Indian subcontinent covers more than one million square miles. Before the Mauryas united this vast land, it was divided into many small kingdoms.

Chandragupta Maurya began building the Mauryan Empire in the 320s B.C.E. He saw that the kingdoms of northern India were weak. They had wasted a great deal of money and men fighting among themselves. Chandragupta used his great army of 700,000 soldiers and 9,000 elephants to overthrow the rulers of these kingdoms. He conquered and united all of northern India.

Chandragupta kept his empire strong by using force whenever necessary. He was deathly afraid of enemies. He used his powerful army, a network of spies, and torture to keep his subjects in line.

Chandragupta's rule was harsh, but it was successful in some ways. He created a strong central government. He wrote laws. He made sure farmers had water for their crops. To help connect the parts of his empire, he built a royal road over 1,000 miles long.

Toward the end of his life, Chandragupta gave up his power. Tradition says that he became an ascetic (a person who has given up worldly pleasures). He lived in poverty and traveled with **monks** (simple holy men). Meanwhile, the empire grew even larger. Under Chandragupta's grandson, King Ashoka, it included nearly all of the Indian subcontinent.

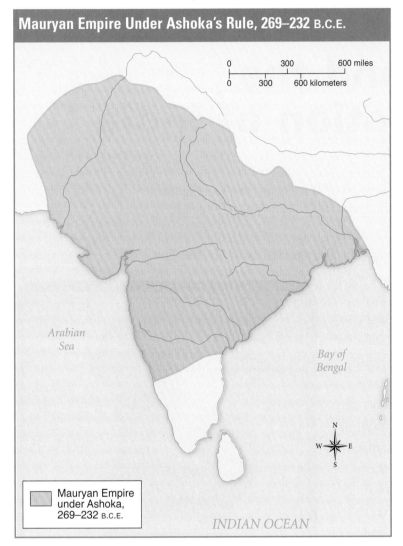

Mauryan Empire Under Ashoka's Rule, 269–232 B.C.E.

0   300   600 miles
0   300   600 kilometers

Arabian Sea

Bay of Bengal

N
W   E
S

Mauryan Empire under Ashoka, 269–232 B.C.E.

INDIAN OCEAN

monk a holy man who devotes his life to religious practice

17.3 Ashoka's Rule

The Mauryan Empire reached its height during the reign of King Ashoka. He ruled the empire from about 269 to 232 B.C.E.

During the early part of his reign, Ashoka expanded the empire to the south and east through a series of wars. Then, after one especially brutal battle, he made his decision to reject violence.

Ashoka decided to embrace Buddhism. He supported the Buddhist values of love, peace, and nonviolence. As a Buddhist, he respected all living things. He gave up hunting and became a strict vegetarian. (A vegetarian is someone who does not eat meat). He visited holy Buddhist sites. Perhaps most amazingly, Ashoka gave up wars of conquest. Never again would he fight another kingdom for its land.

Ashoka wanted his people to follow the Buddhist path. He urged them to be kind, respectful, and moral (behave in right ways). He told them to respect their elders, to tolerate people of different religions, and to treat their servants well. Ashoka saw himself as a wise and loving father figure. He often referred to the people he ruled as his children.

Ashoka also spread Buddhism beyond India. According to tradition, he sent his son, Mahinda, to Ceylon, a large island off India's southern tip. (Today it is called Sri Lanka.) Mahinda converted the king to Buddhism, which became the official faith of the kingdom.

Not all of Ashoka's actions reflected Buddhist values. He was a practical ruler. He allowed slavery and permitted people to be executed for serious crimes. He still kept a strong army. Although he gave up conquest, he did not return any of the lands the Mauryas had already conquered.

King Ashoka built this dome, called a *stupa,* to hold sacred objects associated with Buddhism.

One of Ashoka's edicts is inscribed on this pillar in the city of Delhi. Ashoka's pillars were 40 to 50 feet high and weighed over 100,000 pounds. They usually had a statue of an animal at the top. The pillars were polished until they shone like glass.

17.4 Ashoka's Edicts

Ashoka wanted a strong, united empire guided by Buddhist values. To spread those values to his people, he had **edicts** carved into walls, rocks, and tall pillars in public places so the greatest number of people could see them.

Ashoka's edicts were designed to promote four main goals:

Buddhist Values   These edicts promoted the Buddha's teachings. They asked people to be loving and respectful, and to practice nonviolence. They said people should not get too attached to worldly things, such as money. They also told people to act morally (do right rather than wrong).

General Welfare   These edicts promoted people's well-being. They were intended to make sure people had good health, shelter, clean water, and enough food.

Justice   These edicts were concerned with fair laws. They also described the way people were to be treated in court and jail.

Security   These edicts were concerned with enemies of the Mauryan Empire and people who were not citizens. They often dealt with issues of peace and conquest.

Ashoka's four goals were intended to give his empire a strong foundation. His reign is still remembered in India as a time of great achievements and progress. But his dream of a united empire did not last. About 45 years after his death, the empire broke apart into separate kingdoms.

A more lasting legacy was Ashoka's support of Buddhism. As you have read, Ashoka introduced Buddhism to Ceylon. Later, around the start of the Common Era, Buddhism spread from northwestern India to Central Asia. From there it traveled to China, Korea, and Japan. (See map on page 121.)

17.5 Chapter Summary

In this chapter, you learned how India was unified for the first time under the Mauryan Empire. The Mauryas created their empire through a series of wars and conquests. This changed when King Ashoka turned away from violence. Ashoka adopted Buddhist values. He kept India united through wise edicts. These edicts promoted Buddhism, general welfare, justice, and security.

In the next chapter, you will learn about the next great Indian empire, the Gupta Empire. In some ways, the Guptas were similar to the Mauryas. In others, they were quite different. As you will see, their rule led to many remarkable achievements.

The symbol seen on this pillar of Ashoka and on the flag of India is called the Ashoka Chakra or the Wheel of the Law. It symbolizes the perpetual movement and change that is part of all life.

CHAPTER 18

◀ ◀ ◀ An artist of the Gupta Empire painted this delicate image of the Buddha.

The Achievements of the Gupta Empire

18.1 Introduction

In Chapter 17, you learned how India was unified for the first time under the Mauryan Empire. In this chapter, you will explore the next great Indian empire, the **Gupta Empire**.

The Guptas were a line of rulers who ruled much of India from 320 to 550 C.E. Many historians have called this period a **golden age,** a time of great prosperity and achievement. Peaceful times allow people to spend time thinking and being creative. During nonpeaceful times, people are usually too busy keeping themselves alive to spend time on inventions and artwork. For this reason, a number of advances in the arts and sciences came out during the peaceful golden age of the Gupta Empire. These achievements have left a lasting mark on the world.

Archeologists have made some amazing discoveries that have helped us learn about the accomplishments of the Gupta Empire. For example, they have unearthed palm-leaf books that were created about 550 C.E. Sacred texts often appeared in palm-leaf books. These sacred texts are just one of many kinds of literature that Indians created under the Guptas.

Literature was one of several areas of great accomplishment during India's Golden Age. In this chapter, you'll learn more about the rise of the Gupta Empire. Then you'll take a close look at seven **achievements** that came out of this rich period in India's history.

Use this illustration of a palm-leaf book as a graphic organizer to help you learn more about Indian achievements during the Gupta Empire.

18.2 The Rise of the Gupta Empire

After the Mauryan Empire fell in about 187 B.C.E., India broke apart into separate kingdoms. For the next 500 years, these smaller kingdoms fought each other for land and power. Beginning around 320 C.E., a second great empire arose in India: the Gupta Empire.

The empire began under Chandragupta I. He and his family, the Guptas, united the northern kingdoms by conquering them through war. They also formed alliances by arranging marriages with the sons and daughters of other rulers.

The Gupta line of kings lasted until 550 C.E. At the height of their power, the Guptas ruled most of northern India. Their empire was the largest India had known since the days of the Mauryas.

In some ways, the Gupta Empire was similar to the Mauryan Empire. The Guptas set up a central government to oversee the empire. A council helped the king make decisions. The council was made up of advisors and members of the royal family.

province a territory that is part of a country or an empire

Unlike the Mauryas, the Guptas gave local areas a great deal of independence. The empire was divided into large areas called **provinces**. The provinces were ruled by royal governors. Within the provinces, town leaders could make many of their own decisions.

The Guptas' ruling strategy helped them to stay in power for nearly 230 years. Generally peaceful times and the empire's stability encouraged growth in the arts and sciences. The result was a "golden age" that produced some of the greatest advances in Indian history. Let's look at seven areas of great achievement under the Guptas.

During their reign, Gupta kings were often shown on coins.

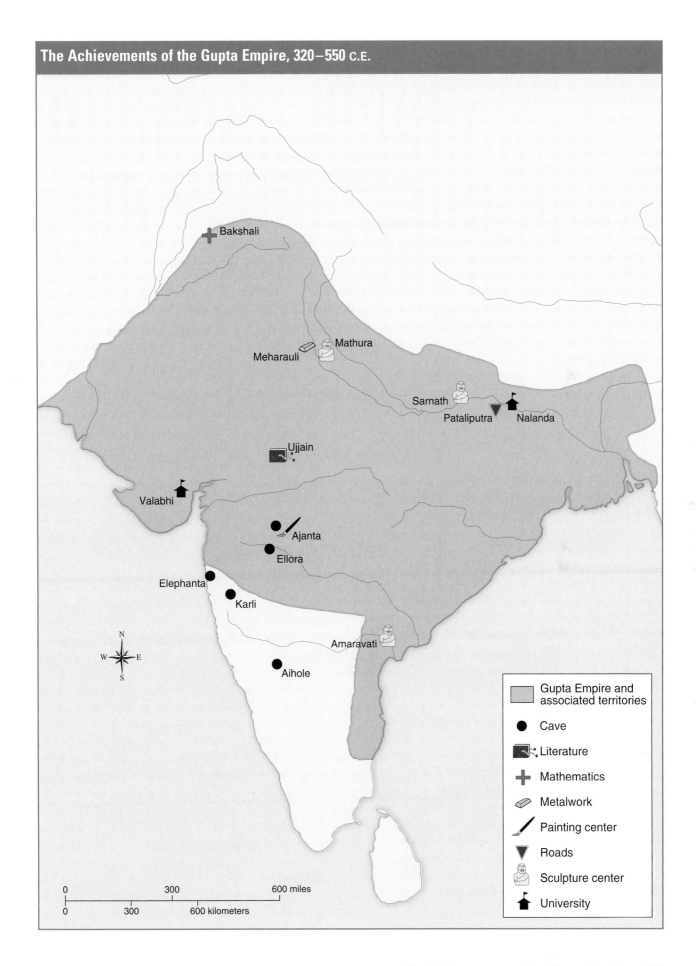

Bakshali

Meharauli Mathura

Sarnath

Pataliputra Nalanda

Ujjain

Valabhi

Ajanta

Ellora

Elephanta

Karli

Amaravati

Aihole

N
W E
S

0   300   600 miles

0   300   600 kilometers

Gupta Empire and associated territories

● Cave

Literature

Mathematics

Metalwork

Painting center

▼ Roads

Sculpture center

University

18.3 Universities

The period of the Gupta Empire was a time of great learning. The Guptas built many colleges and universities throughout the empire. Some universities were Hindu, and some were Buddhist. The schools were open primarily only to males. However, teachers' daughters were allowed to attend.

Hindu universities provided the upper classes with religious training. Students attended classes in religion, mathematics, astronomy, chemistry, and Sanskrit. They could also learn sculpture, painting, music, and dancing.

The most famous university was the Buddhist school at Nalanda. The school had eight colleges and three libraries. It also had a hospital and a **monastery**. Students were instructed in Buddhist and Hindu philosophy. They also studied logic, grammar, and medicine.

Students of medicine learned the practices of the day. They were trained how to question patients about their physical problems. They learned how to make cures from bark, roots, leaves, and minerals. They used the front claws of giant ants to stitch up wounds. Hindu doctors were especially skilled at surgery.

monastery a home for monks

The ruins of the University of Nalanda are still impressive in size.

18.4 Literature

Gupta writers created many kinds of literary works. They wrote poetry, fables, and folktales. They also wrote plays, including both comedies and dramas. Some of the plays were about historical and political subjects. Large audiences gathered to watch the performances.

There were other forms of writing as well. Scholars and lawyers wrote about Hindu law and religion. Some of the great Sanskrit literature took shape during this time. The *Puranas* ("Ancient Lore") described many Hindu legends. These sacred texts had been passed down orally for generations. They were first gathered together and recorded under the Guptas. The *Mahabharata* ("Great Work"), a poem composed over hundreds of years, reached its final form during the Gupta era. Its themes relate to Hindu values and the battle between good and evil.

The *Bhagavad Gita* ("Song of the Lord") is part of the *Mahabharata.* It is one of the most beautiful and beloved works of Hinduism. In this poem, Prince Arjuna is taught basic truths of Hinduism by Krishna, an earthly form of the deity Vishnu.

Some Gupta literature spread far beyond India. Gupta sacred texts influenced cultures as far away as Greece and Persia (present-day Iran). The famous Arabian tale about Aladdin and his magic lamp was inspired by a Gupta folktale.

Manuscripts were written in Sanskrit and often illustrated. This manuscript page is from the *Bhagavata Purana*.

This detail of an Ajanta cave mural pictures a procession of elephants.

18.5 Painting

The Gupta Empire is famous for its beautiful paintings. For noble (wealthy) families, painting was an important part of life. No home was complete without a painting board or easel. Popular subjects included deities and other religious topics. Nobles also hired artists to paint pictures of their families and of royalty. Some paintings highlighted the wealth and luxury of noble life. The paintings were often done on long **scrolls**.

Perhaps the greatest ancient Indian paintings are those known as the Ajanta cave **murals**. The murals cover the walls of the 30 caves that make up an ancient Buddhist monastery in central India. The paintings are done in rich, bright colors like red, purple, and green. Artists made the paints from minerals and clay.

Some of the Ajanta murals show scenes from the Buddha's life. Some portray stories that reflect Buddhist values, such as love and understanding. Many of the paintings are graceful images of kings, queens, musicians, and dancers. Others show animals and hunters in the forest. The woodland scenes are decorated with flowers, trees, and fancy patterns. Gupta artists painted all these subjects with a sure and delicate hand.

18.6 Sculpture

Another area of great artistic achievement in the Gupta Empire was sculpture. Sculptors created statues out of stone, wood, bronze, and terra-cotta clay. Many of these statues portrayed the Buddha or Hindu deities. Some showed scenes from important people's lives. Many sculptures were created to stand on their own. Others were carved into the walls of temples and caves.

Gupta sculptures portrayed the human form simply and gracefully. One fine example is a sculpture of the river deity, Ganga. She is riding on the back of a sea monster. In her left hand she holds a water jug. The statue's lines are rounded and elegant. Her dress, jewelry, and hair are carved in beautiful detail. Her expression is quiet and thoughtful.

A temple statue of the Buddha reflects the same attention to beauty and detail. The Buddha is seated on a highly decorated seat. His hands and legs are smoothly crossed. His expression is calm and peaceful. The sculptor used lowered eyes and a calm face to portray the Buddha's wisdom.

These sculptures of the river deity, Ganga, (below) and the Buddha (left) are typical of Gupta sculptures.

18.7 Metalwork

One of the most amazing accomplishments of the Gupta Empire was its metalwork. Gupta kings controlled huge mines of gold, copper, and iron. Metalworkers made gold and copper coins. They engraved the coins with pictures honoring Gupta rulers. The coins often highlighted the rulers' wealth and their achievements in art, politics, and war.

Gupta metalworkers were also famous for their ironwork. An iron pillar at a place called Meharauli is an impressive and mysterious example of their skill. The pillar is made of solid iron. It stands 25 feet tall and weighs about 13,000 pounds. The sides are engraved with a story that describes the accomplishments of a Gupta emperor. The iron is almost rust-free after 1,600 years in the rain and sun. No one knows how Gupta ironworkers acquired such advanced metalworking skills.

Gupta metalworkers made gold coins to honor the kings who owned the mines.

18.8 Mathematics

Earlier Hindu mathematicians had created a way of writing whole numbers using the numerals 1 through 9. Gupta mathematicians made further advances. For example, they used the decimal system to write numbers. The decimal system uses 10 basic numerals that have different values depending on their "place." In the number 105, for instance, 1 is in the "hundreds place" and means 100. The system also works for fractions. In the decimal 0.10, 1 means one tenth. Note the zeros in these examples. Hindu mathematicians were the first to treat zero as a number. Many calculations are impossible without the zero.

In later centuries, Arabs learned the Indian system of numbers and spread it to Europe. As a result, Europeans called this way of writing numbers "Arabic numerals." A better name is "Hindu-Arabic numerals," because the system began with the ancient Indians. We still use this system today.

One of the most famous Gupta mathematicians was a man named Aryabhata. He combined mathematics and astronomy to make important discoveries. He figured out that a year was exactly 365.258 days long. He calculated the approximate size of Earth. He proposed that planets were spheres (shaped like balls). And he was one of the earliest scientists to suggest that Earth spins on its axis (an imaginary line through Earth's center).

Mathematics had immediate practical uses as well. For example, Gupta builders used mathematics to design more complex structures.

The use of mathematics allowed ancient Indians to build complex structures such as this temple.

18.9 Roads

Gupta rulers encouraged trade by creating a huge system of well-built roads. The roads were built with care and precision. Engineers first cleared the pathway of plants, trees, and rocks. Then they filled in any holes. Finally, they smoothed the ground until it was level. The finished roads were made of hard-packed dirt.

The roadways were designed for safety and comfort. They were built a few feet off the ground. Ditches, or canals, ran along either side. These features helped prevent flooding during the rainy monsoon season. Water would simply run off the road and into the ditches.

Signs along the roadway told travelers where they were. They also marked off the distances so people could figure out how far they had traveled. Rest houses gave travelers a place to relax or spend the night. Wells provided water for drinking and cooking.

The empire's roads greatly benefited trade. They allowed traders to move easily from city to city within the empire. Traders could also move goods from the middle of the country to important waterways. From there, the goods could be shipped and sold to other countries. The roads also connected India to China and the lands east of the Mediterranean Sea.

The Karakoram Highway connects northern Pakistan with China.

18.10 Chapter Summary

In this chapter, you learned about India's Golden Age during the time of the Gupta Empire. Like the Mauryas, the Guptas created a strong central government to rule their empire. At the same time, they granted significant independence to local leaders. This strategy helped to create an era of stability and prosperity. The result was a great surge of learning and artistic growth.

Under the Guptas, India made achievements in a number of areas. The Guptas encouraged learning by building universities. Writing, painting, sculpture, and metalwork flourished. Gupta mathematicians made important advances. Engineers designed and built a vast system of roads. Many of these achievements, especially in mathematics and literature, continue to affect the world today.

This chapter on the Gupta Empire ends our study of ancient India. In the next unit, you will travel east to learn about another great civilization, ancient China.

Each person in this mural from the Ajanta caves is shown displaying a different mudra, or hand position. These Buddhist gestures symbolize beliefs about the gods and communicate such things as compassion and fearlessness.

Ancient India Timeline

2700 – 1900 B.C.E.
Advanced sewer system is designed in Mohenjodaro.

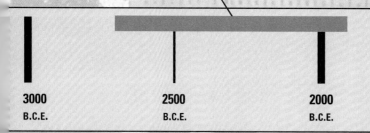

3000	2500	2000	1500	1000
B.C.E.	B.C.E.	B.C.E.	B.C.E.	B.C.E.

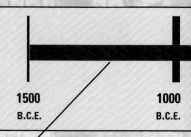

About 1500–900 B.C.E.
The Vedas, oral teachings that outline the basic beliefs of Hinduism, are composed.

About 500 B.C.E.
Sanskrit language is first
written down.

563 – 483 B.C.E.
Life of Prince Siddhartha,
founder of Buddhism.

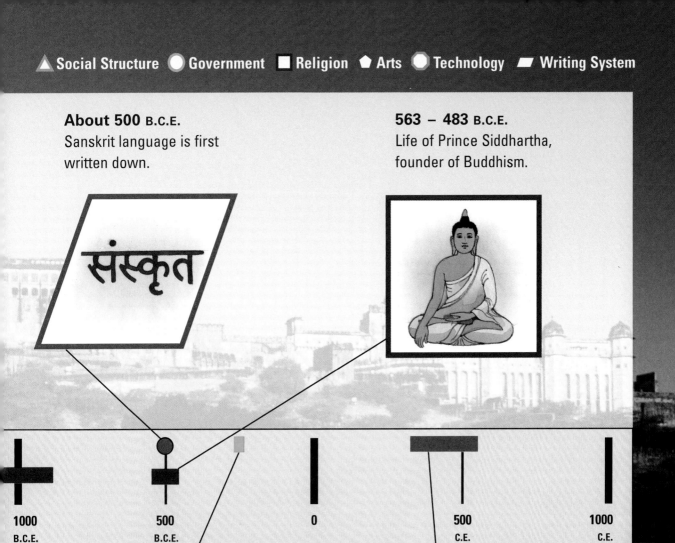

| 1000 | | 500 | | 0 | | 500 | | 1000 |
| B.C.E. | | B.C.E. | | | | C.E. | | C.E. |

269 – 232 B.C.E.
Ashoka rules Mauryan Empire using
edicts to promote four main goals.

320 – 550 C.E.
Gupta Empire, during which Ajanta
cave murals and *Mahabharata* poem
are completed.

Ancient China

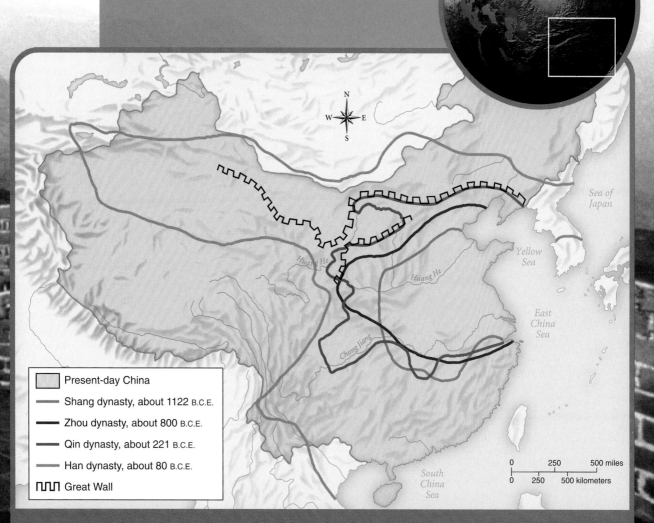

Present-day China

Shang dynasty, about 1122 B.C.E.

Zhou dynasty, about 800 B.C.E.

Qin dynasty, about 221 B.C.E.

Han dynasty, about 80 B.C.E.

ⅬⅬⅬⅬ Great Wall

Sea of Japan

Yellow Sea

East China Sea

South China Sea

Huang He

Chang Jiang

0   250   500 miles
0   250   500 kilometers

Areas Controlled by the Four Dynasties of Ancient China

CHAPTER 19

◀ ◀ ◀ The Huang He (Yellow River) flows
through the "Land of the Yellow Earth."

Geography and the Early Settlement of China

19.1 Introduction

In the last unit, you learned about the people and empires of ancient India. In this unit, you will explore the civilization of ancient China. This civilization flourished from about 1700 B.C.E. to 220 C.E.

China is a large country in eastern Asia. It's easy to use words like *highest, largest,* and *longest* when talking about China's geography. The world's highest mountains, the Himalayas, are in China. So is one of the world's largest deserts, the Taklimakan Desert. China also boasts some of the longest rivers in the world.

China's climate is just as extreme as its physical features. The weather can vary from ice storms in the high mountains to the dreaded sandstorms of the Taklimakan Desert. During a sandstorm, the sky darkens until it feels like night. Hot, howling winds drive sand and gravel against you. The only way to survive is to wrap yourself in clothes or blankets and lie down until the storm passes. That could be hours or even days.

As you can see, China is a land of contrasts. In this chapter, you will compare five **geographic regions** in China. You'll learn about the **climate, physical features,** and **vegetation** of each region. You'll also discover how geography affected where the first Chinese settled, the way they lived, and their ability to communicate with other civilizations.

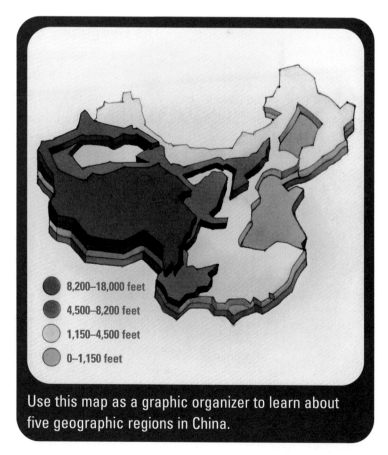

8,200–18,000 feet

4,500–8,200 feet

1,150–4,500 feet

0–1,150 feet

Use this map as a graphic organizer to learn about five geographic regions in China.

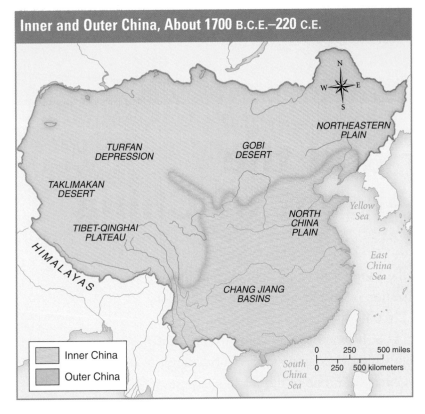

Inner and Outer China, About 1700 B.C.E.–220 C.E.

NORTHEASTERN PLAIN

TURFAN DEPRESSION

GOBI DESERT

TAKLIMAKAN DESERT

Yellow Sea

NORTH CHINA PLAIN

TIBET-QINGHAI PLATEAU

East China Sea

HIMALAYAS

CHANG JIANG BASINS

0   250   500 miles
0   250   500 kilometers

South China Sea

Inner China

Outer China

19.2 An Overview of China's Geography

Modern China is the third-largest country in the world, after Russia and Canada. It covers about 3.7 million square miles (9.6 million square kilometers). About 1.2 billion people live in China, more than in any other country.

China was much smaller in ancient times. To understand Chinese history, it's helpful to divide China into two main areas: Outer China and Inner China. Most of ancient Chinese history involves only Inner China. The two areas did not become one country until the 1600s C.E.

But the geography of both areas affected the early settlement and history of China.

The Geography of Outer China

Outer China includes the western and northern parts of present-day China. It is an area of great extremes.

In the southwest, China is bounded by the Himalaya Mountains. The major geographical region in this area is the Tibet-Qinghai Plateau. It is the world's largest plateau. This region is a bitterly cold place to live. There are only about 50 days a year without frost. Snowstorms are common, even in July.

In the northwest, the major region is the Northwestern Deserts. This area includes the second-lowest place in China. Called the Turfan Depression, it is 505 feet below sea level. It can grow so hot that raindrops evaporate before reaching the ground.

In ancient times, areas near water were the only livable places in the Taklimakan Desert, one of China's Northwestern Deserts.

In the northeast, the major region is the Northeastern Plain. This is a land of low hills and plains. It has short, hot summers. Winters are long and dry, with five months of freezing temperatures.

The Geography of Inner China

Inner China includes the southeastern part of present-day China. Compared to the west, this part of China is closer to sea level. It is a land of rolling hills, river valleys, and plains. Rivers flow through the area from the west. The rivers often enrich the soil by flooding. They also provide water for irrigation. These physical features made Inner China more attractive to early settlers than Outer China.

Inner China has two main regions. The northern region is the North China Plain. To the south are the low river plains of the middle and lower Chang Jiang Basins. These regions have very different climates. The Chang Jiang Basins are warm and wet. The North China Plain is drier and often cooler.

Each of China's major regions has its own climate, physical features, and vegetation. Let's take a closer look at each region, starting with those in Outer China.

The wet, warm Chang Jiang Basins are a major region for growing rice.

The Tibetan Plateau is cold and dry. Summer temperatures average only 45 degrees Fahrenheit. Winters average 18 degrees. The annual precipitation is only 10 inches.

19.3 The Tibet-Qinghai Plateau

The southwestern part of Outer China is dominated by the high Tibet-Qinghai Plateau. Also known as the Tibetan Plateau, this area is often called the "Roof of the World." Its average elevation is more than two miles (13,500 feet) above sea level. It is a very large area, covering almost a quarter of the land in China.

The Tibetan Plateau is a rocky land surrounded by towering mountains. The Himalayas are on the southern edge of the plateau. The tallest mountain in the world, Mount Everest, is part of this mountain range. Its peak is more than five miles (29,000 feet) high.

Since the Tibetan Plateau is so high, the climate is very cold. The air is thin and dry. Snow falls even in the summer.

Two of China's major rivers begin in this area, the Huang He (Yellow River) and the Chang Jiang (Yangtze River). In spite of the rivers, the plateau is rather dry. The natural vegetation consists of sparse scrubs and grasses. Antelopes and yaks, a type of ox, roam the area. Sometimes they are hunted by wolves and wildcats.

For the people of ancient times, the Tibetan Plateau was a challenging place to live. It was too cold and dry to grow crops. But the grasses did provide food for yaks and other livestock. The cold, rocky plateau and the high mountains made travel through this area to Inner China very difficult.

19.4 The Northwestern Deserts

The northwestern part of Outer China is known for its great deserts, including the Taklimakan and Gobi Deserts. The deserts are harsh places to live and difficult for travelers to cross. The climate varies from sizzling hot in the summer to below freezing in winter. The only places to grow crops or raise animals such as sheep are the **oases,** where water can be found. In ancient times, shelters made of mud were sometimes built near oases.

Temperatures vary greatly in the Northwestern Deserts. Summer temperatures can be 100 degrees Fahrenheit. Winter temperatures might be a chilly 15 degrees. The annual precipitation is about 5 inches.

The Taklimakan Desert

The Taklimakan Desert is about 105,000 square miles. It is considered one of the most dangerous deserts in the world. In fact, its name means, "Once you go in, you will not come out." The desert's huge sand dunes shift and change as the wind blows the sand around. Sandstorms arise with stunning speed. Legend says that two armies and 300 cities are buried 600 feet beneath the sand dunes.

As you might expect, the desert is too dry to have much vegetation. Bushes, weeds, and trees grow only near oases and along rivers.

The Gobi Desert

Stretching over 500,000 square miles, the Gobi Desert is one of the world's largest deserts. It covers part of China and present-day Mongolia. Unlike the Taklimakan Desert, the Gobi has very few sand dunes. Most of the desert is stony. Its surface is made up of small pebbles and tiny bits of sand. Vegetation is sparse. Plants tend to be small and widely spaced.

The Northeastern Plain is generally rather cold and dry. During the
short summer, temperatures climb
to 75 degrees Fahrenheit. In winter, they fall to 10 degrees. The
annual precipitation is about
20 inches.

19.5 The Northeastern Plain

The Northeastern Plain is located east of present-day
Mongolia. Today this area is sometimes called Inner Mongolia
and sometimes Manchuria. It is a land of low hills and plains.
The natural vegetation is mostly prairie grass. In ancient times,
the grass provided food for horses, sheep, and other animals
raised by herders.

The major rivers running through the Northeastern Plain are
the Liao and Sungari. The Liao is a shallow river. Only small
boats can navigate it. The Sungari is deeper. It can carry larger
boats. The rivers freeze in the winter, and people use them as
roads.

The Northeastern Plain is an area of great contrasts in climate.
It has short, warm summers. The northern and eastern parts of the
plain are dry and cold in winter. The southern half, especially the
valley of the Liao, has milder weather and more water. In general,
though, the plain is too cold and dry to be a good place for growing crops.

In the south, a narrow coastal plain links this area to the rest of
China. This plain was the route several groups of invaders took
into Inner China.

19.6 The North China Plain

The North China Plain is a flat region of grassland in Inner China. Temperatures range from very warm in the summer to quite cold in the winter.

This region is sometimes called the "Land of the Yellow Earth" because the ground is covered by yellow limestone **silt**. The silt comes from the Gobi Desert. It is carried by the wind to the North China Plain. The river that runs through the plain is also full of yellow silt. The silt gives the river its name, Huang He (Yellow River).

The Huang He is one of the longest rivers in the world. It may also be the world's muddiest river. The mud makes it look more like soup than river water. The river starts in the high western mountains and winds its way down to the eastern plains. The silt it carries helps fertilize the surrounding lands, making the North China Plain a good place to settle down and grow crops.

While the Huang He helps farmers, it has also been the source of many disasters for the Chinese. In the past 3,000 years, the river is said to have flooded more that 1,500 times, causing much damage and loss of life.

silt fine particles of rock

The North China Plain, near the Huang He, is grassy, fertile land. In the summer, the average temperature is 82 degrees Fahrenheit. In the winter, the average temperature is 28 degrees. The annual precipitation is about 23 inches.

19.7 The Middle and Lower Chang Jiang Basins

The middle and lower Chang Jiang Basins are areas of low, wet coastal plains. The basins are located along the river called the Chang Jiang.

The Chang Jiang is even longer than the Huang He. In fact, its name means "Long River." It has hundreds of **tributaries**. People use the river to move goods between eastern and western areas of the region.

Like the Huang He, the Chang Jiang starts in the high western mountains. It flows through three plains and then to a rich delta. Its deposits help to make the surrounding lands very fertile. The river floods less often than the Huang He, making it much less dangerous.

The climate in the Chang Jiang Basins is warm and wet. In ancient times, the vegetation may have been thick rainforest. There was limited space for farming, and the area was not suitable for grazing animals. But the basins were very good for growing rice, which needs lots of warmth and moisture.

tributary a stream that feeds into a larger river

The Chang Jiang Basins have a mild, wet climate. Temperatures range from about 68 degrees Fahrenheit in summer to about 39 degrees in winter. The annual precipitation is about 41 inches.

19.8 Early Settlement in Ancient China

Archeologists believe that the first inhabitants of China lived in caves more than 500,000 years ago. Remains of these people, known as Peking (or Beijing) Man, were found in the 1920s in the northeastern part of China. They lived by hunting, gathering, and fishing. They made tools and probably used fire.

When people in China began farming, they settled mostly on the North China Plain in Inner China. They grew crops and lived in villages near the Huang He. This marked the beginnings of settled Chinese society.

It's not surprising that early farmers chose this area to live in. The North China Plain had plenty of water, fertile soil, and a moderate climate. In contrast, the Tibetan Plateau and Northeastern Plain were too cold and dry to grow crops. The Northwestern Deserts were also too dry. The Chang Jiang Basins were wet and fertile, but heavy rains may have made farming difficult.

19.9 Ancient China's Isolation

China's geography kept the early settlements in Inner China isolated. Only a narrow coastal plain linked the Northeastern Plain to Inner China. In the southwest, the towering mountains, rocky plateau, and cold climate formed a natural barrier. In the northwest, the large deserts were another barrier.

Later in Chinese history, the same geographic features that kept China isolated also made it difficult to govern China as one unified state.

Traveling was difficult during China's early history. This 18th-century painting shows a traveler and camel making their way through towering sand dunes in a desert.

19.10 Different Regions, Different Ways of Life

Although most early inhabitants settled on the North China Plain, people did live in the other geographic regions. People in these regions had quite different ways of life.

Life in Outer China

Fewer people settled in Outer China than in Inner China, which was much more suitable for farming. The Tibetan Plateau is not suitable for growing crops, but herders could raise livestock, especially yaks. The people who lived on the plateau had to move frequently to find new grazing land. Yaks provided meat, and their milk was made into butter and yogurt. Yak wool was turned into the heavy clothing people needed in the cold climate. Yak hair was woven into material for tents.

In the Northwestern Deserts, the only settled communities were on the oases. There, people built homes out of mud. They grew cotton, winter wheat, and **maize**. Their main foods were wheat noodles, bread, and **mutton**.

The Northeastern Plain is too cold and dry for much farming, but its prairie grass supported livestock. Early settlers in this region were nomads who raised sheep, goats, cattle, and horses. Their main food was meat. They were constantly moving to find grass for their animals, so they lived in tents. The nomads often invaded the North China Plain to get needed supplies. Eventually, the people of Inner China built the Great Wall to keep them out. You'll learn more about the Great Wall later in this unit.

maize a type of corn
mutton meat from sheep

In some parts of Outer China, people lived as nomads.

Life in Inner China

The fertile land of Inner China supported larger and more settled populations. Most people settled on the fertile North China Plain. There they grew mainly wheat and **millet**. They raised cattle, sheep, oxen, pigs, and chickens. They herded cattle, water buffalo, and horses. People built permanent homes out of rammed earth (soil tightly packed to make solid walls).

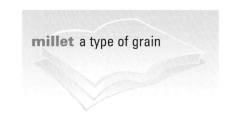

millet a type of grain

The Chang Jiang Basins had limited areas for farming, and they lacked grazing land for raising animals such as cattle. But rice thrived in this warm, wet area. Settlers began growing rice in the river valley as early as 10,000 B.C.E. They also raised pigs and poultry, and they ate seafood. They built permanent houses so they could stay in one place and tend their animals and crops.

In Inner China, most people lived in one place and raised crops such as millet and rice.

19.11 Chapter Summary

In this chapter, you explored five geographic regions in China. Three of these regions are in Outer China: the Tibetan Plateau, the Northwestern Deserts, and the Northeastern Plain. The two regions of Inner China are the North China Plain and the Chang Jiang Basins. You learned about each region's physical features, climate, and vegetation. You also discovered how differences in geography led to different ways of life.

Many early farmers settled on Inner China's northern plain. Outer China's physical features isolated Inner China. These features included high mountains, a cold and rocky plateau, and large deserts.

The ancient Chinese traced their history through several dynasties, or ruling families. In the next chapter, you will explore one of the earliest of these dynasties, the Shang dynasty.

○ CHAPTER 20

◄ ◄ ◀ A chariot buried in a Shang ruler's tomb was to serve the king in the afterlife.

The Shang Dynasty

20.1 Introduction

In Chapter 19, you explored five geographic regions of China. You learned that most of China's early farmers settled on the North China Plain, near the Huang He (Yellow River). In this chapter, you will explore one of China's earliest dynasties, the **Shang dynasty**. This dynasty ruled the area around the Huang He from 1700 to 1122 B.C.E.

Ancient China was not one country, but a number of clans, or extended families, led by warrior kings. Rival clans often fought each other. Occasionally, one clan became powerful enough to control all of ancient China and start a dynasty. The Shang (pronounced *shung*) was one such clan.

For hundreds of years, the Shang dynasty was considered to be a myth by western scholars. Stories about mysterious markings on animal bones hinted that the Shang might have been the first Chinese to learn to write. But there was no solid archeological evidence that they had existed.

Then, in 1899, a Chinese scholar found some bones with writing on them. He thought they might be Shang oracle bones. Oracle bones are animal bones and turtle shells with inscriptions carved by engravers. They were thought to tell the future.

Later, in the 1920s, the ruins of a Shang city were found at Anyang. Archeologists unearthed many artifacts from these ruins that revealed an ancient civilization. Let's see what they learned about Shang **government, social structure, religion, writing, art,** and **technology**.

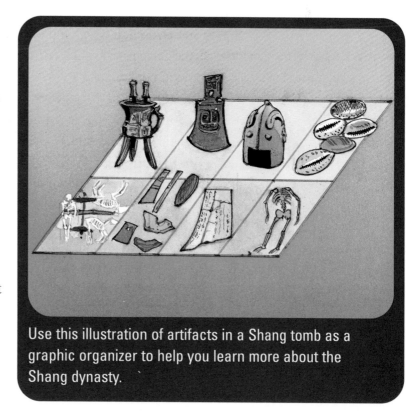

Use this illustration of artifacts in a Shang tomb as a graphic organizer to help you learn more about the Shang dynasty.

Nobles lived in homes made of wood and earth near the king's palace. People of the lower classes lived in smaller earthen houses that were farther from the palace.

human sacrifice a person who is killed as part of a religious ritual

20.2 A Shang Capital City

Archeologists learned a lot about the Shang when they began excavating the ruins at Anyang in 1928. The ruins were the remains of one of the royal cities of the Shang. The city included a palace, a temple, and houses. There were also workshops for artisans who worked with bronze, pottery, stone, and jade.

The king's palace sat on a platform. The palace was made of mud-plastered walls held up by wooden posts. Under its foundations, archeologists found human bones. The bones suggest that the Shang performed **human sacrifices** when they built a new royal house.

Human sacrifices were also part of Shang burials. While excavating at Anyang, archeologists found at least 9 royal tombs. Each tomb was a large pit with ramps leading down to it from the north and south. When a king was buried, slaves, servants, and animals were led down the ramps into the pit. There they were sacrificed so that, the Shang believed, they could serve the needs of the king in the afterlife.

Because of their belief in an afterlife, Shang kings were also buried with or near bronze vessels and containers of food. The treasures found in royal tombs include bronze weapons, carved jade ornaments, bone carvings, pottery, stone sculptures, and even chariots.

The artifacts unearthed at Anyang reveal some interesting facts about Shang beliefs and ways of life. Let's see what else scholars have learned about the Shang, beginning with their government.

20.3 Shang Government

The Shang government was led by a powerful king who controlled the land. To expand his power, the king set up smaller kingdoms under his younger brothers and nephews. Power sometimes passed to a younger brother when a king died. Sometimes a son inherited the kingdom.

Shang kings depended on strong armies to maintain their rule. The kings engaged in almost constant war with their enemies. They fought to keep other **clans** under control and to defend and expand their kingdoms. They also captured prisoners in war to use as laborers and in human sacrifices.

clan a large group of friends and family

The king's armies were especially powerful because Shang nobles had weapons made of bronze. The Shang were among the first people in the world to discover how to make bronze from a mixture of copper and tin.

Shang armies were made up of large numbers of foot soldiers, archers, cavalry riding horses and elephants, and fighters in chariots. The chariots were two-wheeled boxes drawn by horses. Three soldiers rode in each chariot. The driver stood in the middle with a spear carrier on his left and an archer on his right. The Shang army must have been a terrifying sight to their enemies.

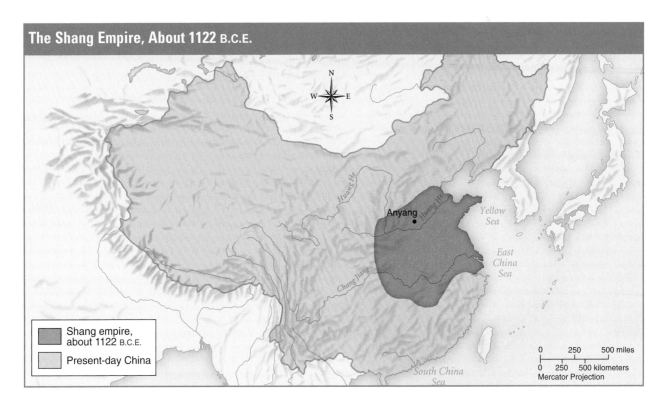

The Shang Empire, About 1122 B.C.E.

Anyang

Huang He

Huang Ho

Yellow Sea

East China Sea

Chang Jiang

South China Sea

Shang empire, about 1122 B.C.E.

Present-day China

0   250   500 miles
0   250   500 kilometers
Mercator Projection

20.4 Shang Social Classes

Shang society can be divided into six social classes. The king and his relatives were at the top. Below them were the nobles, craftspeople, traders, farmers, and slaves.

Nobles

The nobles made up the highest-ranking social class after the ruling family. Nobles fought in the king's army. They also provided weapons, foot soldiers, and chariots. In exchange for their military help, the king did not interfere with their control over the land.

Shang nobles enjoyed a life of luxury. They lived in great palaces and spent time hunting. We know the Shang were great hunters because of the large number of wild animal bones found at excavation sites. In addition, writings on oracle bones show that the king went hunting and invited nobles to hunt foxes, badgers, and other wild animals.

The king often gave nobles symbols of power, such as jade discs. The discs might show a "lucky" creature such as a dragon or tiger. Nobles often mounted the discs on posts in their homes.

Shang kings gave nobles jade discs to symbolize power. This disc is made in the shape of a dragon.

Craftspeople

Craftspeople formed a small social class. This class included bronze and jade workers, potters, and stonemasons. These skilled workers had lower status than nobles but higher status than farmers. Bronze workers were especially valued. They made the weapons used by Shang warriors. They also made and decorated containers for the king and nobles to use in religious ceremonies or simply as symbols of their wealth.

Traders

Like craftspeople, traders ranked below nobles but above farmers in Shang society. Scholars believe that the Shang traded extensively, because the modern Chinese word for merchant is *shang ren,* which

From stone sculptures like this one of an ox, archeologists have learned the kinds of animals raised by Shang farmers.

could also mean "Shang man." During the Shang dynasty, people mostly traded goods. But they also used cowrie shells, a type of seashell, as money. The shells were valuable because they came from far away. The Shang had to trade with neighboring regions to get them.

Farmers

Farmers were the largest social class in Shang society. They worked small plots of land, growing millet, wheat, barley, rice, fruit, vegetables, and nuts. They did not own the land they farmed. The land was under the control of either the king or the nobles. The farmers did not even get to keep most of their crops. They kept only enough to feed themselves and their families. They gave the rest to the nobles, who sent some to the king.

Even after the Chinese became good at making bronze and iron weapons, many farmers used simple wooden and stone tools. They dug with wooden sticks, weeded with stone-tipped hoes, and harvested grain with stone knives and scythes.

In addition to growing crops, farmers may have raised pigs and chickens. They also learned to keep and raise cattle.

Slaves

At the very bottom of Shang society were slaves, who had often been captured in wars. They spent their lives building tombs and palaces. When their masters died, slaves were sometimes sacrificed so they could serve their masters in the afterlife.

20.5 Religion Under the Shang

The religion of the Shang centered on **ancestor worship**. As the treasures buried in kings' tombs show, the Shang believed in a life after death. They also believed that dead ancestors had power to help or harm the living. For this reason, they believed it was important for people to honor their ancestors. They did this through offerings of wine and food, and sometimes through human sacrifices.

The king's relationship to ancestral spirits was especially important to the Shang. In Shang belief, kings had the power to rule because they were descended from powerful ancestors. But kings also had responsibilities, including a duty to follow the wishes of their ancestors.

Kings used oracle bones to ask their ancestors' advice on such important matters as when to hunt, where to build new cities, and whether to go to war. The oracle bones were made from turtle shells or the shoulder blade of a cow. To ask a question, a holy man made a statement such as "Tomorrow is a good day for the hunt." Then the holy man pressed a hot needle against the back of the bone. The heat would make the bone crack. The pattern of the crack was believed to be a message, which the holy man or king translated. He might then carve the message on the oracle bone. Today these inscriptions reveal valuable information about life under the Shang dynasty.

The artifacts found buried in Shang tombs, such as this one, included animals, soldiers, servants, and various objects.

20.6 Writing Under the Shang

The inscriptions on oracle bones are among the earliest known examples of Chinese writing. In Shang writing, as in modern Chinese, characters stand for words rather than sounds. At first, Chinese writing contained only pictographs, images that stand for objects. By the Shang dynasty, people also used **logographs,** characters that stand for words. For example, the character for "good" is a combination of the characters for "woman" and "child."

Having a written language helped to unify the Chinese people. Although spoken language varied from place to place, people of the upper classes used the same written language.

Shang writing is the ancestor of modern Chinese writing. Inscriptions have been found inside objects like the rhinoceros statue above.

20.7 Art Under the Shang

Shang artists showed great skill in working with bronze. Craftspeople made beautiful vessels and other objects. Some bronze vessels had geometric designs and pictures of mythical creatures. The most common picture was an animal mask, later known as a *taotie*. It might have had the horns of an ox, the ears of an elephant, the talons of a bird, the eye of a man, and the crest of a dragon. Some scholars say it was a symbol of all the beings in the world.

The Shang also produced outstanding jade pieces. Jade is a very hard stone. Jade workers made objects by sawing, filing, and sanding the stone.

The Chinese may have believed that the qualities of jade represented the qualities of a superior person. The hardness of jade stood for wisdom. Jade was also smooth and shiny. These qualities stood for kindness.

Shang craftspeople made fine jewelry from jade. The jade pendant below is shaped like a fish.

20.8 Technology Under the Shang

Working with bronze was an important technology for the
Shang. Craftspeople used bronze to make many tools of war,
including arrowheads, spearheads, ax heads, and helmets. The
bronze-making skill of the Shang is one of the reasons they were
able to remain in power for more than 500 years.

20.9 The End of the Shang Dynasty

The Shang excelled in war, and the ruling classes built up
great wealth. But in time these very strengths helped to bring
about the end of the dynasty.

Fighting so many wars eventually weakened the military
power of the Shang.

The Shang king and his nobles spent enormous amounts of
money on their palaces, furnishings, clothing, and even their
tombs. In time, this lavish spending may have weakened the
economy.

A later king would say the final blow was the corruption of the
last Shang king. Instead of looking after his people, he spent all
his time on pleasurable activities like hunting. But no one knows
if this was true.

Around 1045 B.C.E., a frontier state called Zhou (pronounced
joh) rose up against the dynasty. Zhou armies under King Wu
caught the Shang unaware, defeating and overthrowing them.
One story says that the last Shang king ran from the battlefield,
put on all his jewelry, and threw himself into the flames of a fire
as Zhou rebels stormed his capital city.

economy a system of managing the wealth of a country
or region

20.10 Chapter Summary

In this chapter, you learned about one of China's earliest dynasties, the Shang dynasty. The ruins and artifacts found at Anyang showed that the Shang believed in an afterlife. Kings were buried with goods that would be useful to them in their life after death.

Shang kings were powerful rulers who kept their power through military might. Shang society can be divided into six social classes. These were the king's clan, nobles, craftspeople, traders, farmers, and slaves.

The Shang practiced ancestor worship and, sometimes, human sacrifice. Their writing used logographs as well as pictographs. Shang craftspeople excelled in working with bronze and jade.

The Shang ruled in the valley of the Huang He for some 500 years. China's next line of rulers was the Zhou dynasty. In the next chapter, you'll learn more about the Zhou. You'll also explore three important philosophies (schools of thought) that developed toward the end of their reign.

Archeologists unearthed this Shang tomb, which is more than 300 feet long and 60 feet deep.

CHAPTER 21

◀ ◀ In this Chinese scroll painting, scholars study the Daoist symbol for *yin* and *yang*.

Three Chinese Philosophies

21.1 Introduction

In the last chapter, you read about one of China's earliest dynasties, the Shang dynasty. In this chapter, you will learn about China's next line of rulers, the **Zhou dynasty**. Then you'll explore three Chinese **philosophies** that arose during the time of the Zhou.

The Zhou dynasty lasted from about 1045 to 256 B.C.E. During its later years, different leaders fought for control in China. The country was thrown into disorder. These troubles led Chinese thinkers to ask questions about the best way to have peace and order in society. Three very different answers emerged. They were the philosophies of **Confucianism, Daoism** (also spelled Taoism), and **Legalism**.

The following scene illustrates the differences between these schools of thought. Imagine that it is 360 B.C.E. The ruler of a small kingdom has sent three advisors to learn about the three philosophies. Upon their return, he asks them, "What shall I do to rule well?"

The first advisor has learned about Confucianism. He tells the king, "Lead by example." The second advisor has studied Daoism. He says, "If you must rule, rule as little as possible." The third advisor has learned about Legalism. He says, "Set clear laws and harshly punish those who disobey them."

In this chapter, you will learn why the advisors gave such different answers. You'll explore Confucianism, Daoism, and Legalism and how each philosophy influenced China.

Use this illustrated map as a graphic organizer to help you remember how Confucianism, Daoism, and Legalism proposed to bring peace to China.

Mandate of Heaven
a power or law believed to be
granted by a god
feudalism a system of government based on landowners
and tenants

21.2 The Zhou Dynasty

Around 1045 B.C.E., the Zhou, a group of people in northwestern China moved into the central plains. They rebelled and established a new dynasty. For several centuries, the Zhou ruled over
a group of states in China. But in the later years of the dynasty,
wars between states plunged China into disorder.

The Early Years: Stability and Feudalism

After overthrowing the Shang, the Zhou established their rule
over China. To justify their conquest, they claimed they had been
given the **Mandate of Heaven,** a divine
right to rule China.

According to this belief, Heaven was
a power that controlled human destiny.
The king was the son of Heaven. As long
as the king governed his people well,
Heaven gave him the right to rule. If the
king did not govern well, Heaven would
send signs of its displeasure, such as
earthquakes and floods. When the king
lost the support of Heaven, others had
the right to overthrow him.

The Zhou increased the stability of
their rule through a system of relationships
called **feudalism.** Under feudalism, the
king owned all the land. But he gave large
pieces of the land to loyal supporters,
called *lords.* In exchange, lords sent
soldiers to fight if the king was attacked.
The lords were rulers of their own lands,
or states. They had absolute power over
the peasant farmers who worked the land.
Peasants had the lord's protection, but in
return they gave a portion of their crops
to the lord.

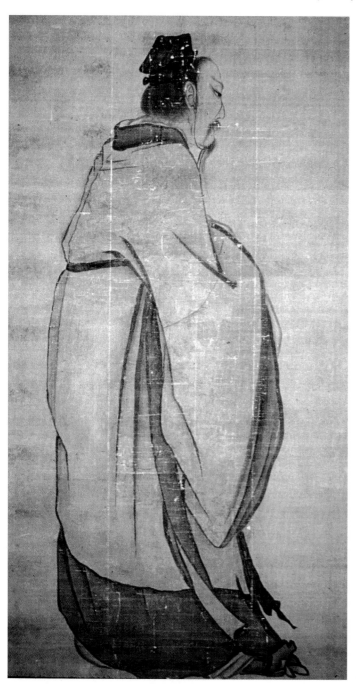

King Wu was the first ruler of the Zhou
dynasty. He was considered a just and
able leader.

The Later Years: Conflict and Creative Thought

Feudalism worked for a time to keep China stable. But by the 700s B.C.E., the system was starting to break down. The lords of individual states became more powerful and ambitious. Eventually, the power of some lords rivaled that of the king.

Between about 770 and 453 B.C.E., a number of small states often quarreled with one another. They eventually grouped into six or seven larger states that warred for power. These wars brought some 250 years of disorder to China. This time is often called the Warring States period.

So much instability led the Chinese to ask important questions about human nature and the best way for rulers to govern. Ambitious rulers hired scholars to advise them on how to create order and increase their power.

So many ideas were offered that the Chinese later called them the "Hundred Schools of Thought." The three most influential schools of thought that emerged were Confucianism, Daoism, and Legalism. Each of these philosophies had a major influence on Chinese culture. Let's take a closer look at their origins, teachings, and influence, beginning with Confucianism.

The Zhou Empire, About 800 B.C.E.

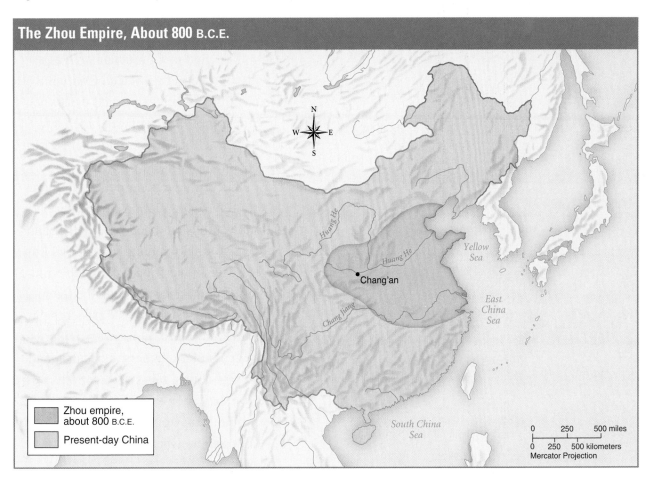

Zhou empire, about 800 B.C.E.

Present-day China

21.3 Confucianism

Confucianism is based on the teachings of Kongfuzi, who is called Confucius by westerners. This philosophy deeply influenced Chinese government and culture.

The Founder of Confucianism

Confucius is the most famous philosopher in Chinese history. Late in life, he said that he set his heart on learning at the age of 15.

Confucius lived from 551 to 479 B.C.E. He was born in the small state of Lu in eastern China. He experienced firsthand the disorder that erupted when lords fought for power. Between 722 and 481 B.C.E., his own state was invaded many times.

Confucius deeply respected Chinese traditions such as reverence for ancestors and the honor given to scholars. But he also saw that society and government had to change if there was to be peace and order. In particular, rulers needed to govern wisely. Confucius wanted to teach men of good character to work as honest and fair government officials.

The Teachings of Confucianism

The goal of Confucianism was a just and peaceful society. Confucius taught that society worked well when all people acted properly based upon their roles and their relationships with others.

According to Confucianism, there are five basic relationships: ruler and subject, husband and wife, father and son, older sibling and younger sibling, and friend and friend. All people must respect and obey those above them. In particular, they must respect their elders. In return, those with authority, such as rulers, fathers, husbands, and older siblings, must set a good example. They should be kind, honest, wise, and faithful. Confucius taught, "Do not do to others what you would not want done to you."

The Influence of Confucianism

Confucius attracted many students who spread his teachings. After his death, some of them collected his sayings in a book called *The Analects*. Later scholars further developed Confucianism.

Confucianism had a very practical effect on government under a later dynasty, the Han dynasty. People who do the work of government are called **civil servants**. In China, civil servants were traditionally the sons of nobles. They might or might not have the ability and wisdom to do their jobs well. Because of the influence of Confucianism, civil servants under the Han were hired on the basis of their ability. Before being hired, they were expected to know the Chinese classics in detail. For example, they had to know the proper behavior for people in various roles, from laborers to government officials. To prove they had this knowledge, they had to take exams that the emperor himself might grade.

The teachings of Confucius had a major influence on Chinese culture. Values such as respect for elders, proper behavior, and love of scholarship became deeply woven into Chinese society. Even today, the sayings of Confucius are wise and practical. Here are two examples from the *Analects*:

Confucius said to his follower:
The gentleman first practices what he preaches
and then preaches what he practices.

Confucius said to his student:
Shall I teach you what knowledge is?
When you know a thing, say that you know it;
when you do not know a thing,
admit that you do not know it.
That is knowledge.

Under the Han dynasty, candidates for government positions had to pass a lengthy exam. Here candidates wait for the posting of their exam results.

civil servant a person who works for a government

21.4 Daoism

The second great philosophy to come out of China's time of trouble was Daoism. Like Confucianism, it tried to give answers to the problems of right living and good government.

The Founder of Daoism

According to tradition, the great sage, or wise man, of Daoism was Laozi (also spelled Lao-tzu). He was said to be the author of the *Dao De Jing* (The Classic of the Way and Its Power).

Some modern scholars believe that Laozi was a real man who lived in the late 500s B.C.E. Others think he was only a legend. Scholars do agree that the *Dao De Jing* was actually written over time by many writers.

Old stories of Laozi's life tell how he came to write the *Dao De Jing*. These stories say that Laozi worked as an advisor to the Zhou court for many years. When he was 90 years old, he tired of government work and decided to leave China. When he came to the Chinese border, a guard recognized him. The guard was upset that the great teacher's wisdom would be lost to China. He asked Laozi to record his thoughts before leaving. So Laozi sat down and wrote a small manuscript of only 5,000 characters, the *Dao De Jing*.

The *Dao De Jing* preached a return to a simple and natural way of living. For example, one passage says:

According to Chinese tradition, Laozi was leaving China on a water buffalo when he met a border guard who asked him to write down his thoughts.

If you do not want your house
* to be molested by robbers,*
Do not fill it with gold
* and jade.*
Wealth, rank, and arrogance
* add up to ruin,*
As surely as two and two
* are four.*

The Teachings of Daoism

Daoism was based on the ancient Chinese idea of the Dao, or "the Way." Dao was the force that gave order to the natural universe. Daoism taught that people gained happiness and peace by living in harmony, or agreement, with the way of nature.

To the Daoists, nature is full of opposites, like life and death or light and darkness. True harmony comes from balancing the opposite forces of nature, called **yin** and **yang**. Yin means "shaded," and yang means "sunlit." In the same way, human life is a whole made up of opposites. It is impossible to have good without bad, beauty without ugliness, or pleasure without pain.

The Daoists taught that people followed the way of nature by living simple lives of quiet meditation. Notice, they said, how nothing in nature strives for fame, power, or knowledge. Similarly, people should avoid feeling self-important or striving for possessions or honors. Instead, they should accept whatever comes, like a blade of grass that bends when the breeze blows.

The Daoists believed that everyone must discover the Dao for themselves. Too many laws and social rules only got in the way of living naturally and following the Dao. Therefore, the best rulers were those who ruled the least. The *Dao De Jing* says, "Governing a large country is like frying a small fish. You spoil it with too much poking." It also tells rulers, "Be weak. Let things alone."

The Influence of Daoism

Daoism encouraged rulers to rule less harshly. But Daoism's more important influence was on Chinese thought, writing, and art. In time, Daoism developed into a popular religion.

Religious Daoists believed in immortality, or eternal life. This painted scroll shows a Daoist scholar sleeping in his thatched cottage. The scholar dreams that he has gained immortality. On the left side of the painting he is shown happily floating away over a mountain.

yin one half of the Daoist concept of opposing forces of nature; the opposite of yang

yang one half of the Daoist concept of opposing forces of nature; the opposite of yin

This illustration of the afterlife shows the type of punishment recommended by Legalists for those who disobey the laws.

21.5 Legalism

The third major philosophy that came out of China's time of trouble was Legalism. It gave very different answers to the problems of order and good government than either Confucianism or Daoism.

The Founder of Legalism

Legalism was based on the teachings of Hanfeizi (also spelled Han-fei-tzu). Hanfeizi lived from 280 to 233 B.C.E. He was a prince of the royal family of the state of Han. Hanfeizi lived to see the end of the Warring States period and of the Zhou dynasty.

Like Confucius, Hanfeizi was very concerned with creating peace and order in society. But he did not think the Confucian teachings about proper behavior were the answer. Many of his ideas survive today in a book named after him, *Hanfeizi*.

The Teachings of Legalism

Legalism was based on the idea that most people are naturally selfish. Left to themselves, Legalists said, people always pursue their own self-interest. They could not be relied upon to have a good influence on one another. Therefore, it was not enough for rulers to set a good example. Instead, they should establish strict laws and enforce them with rewards for good behavior and harsh punishments for bad behavior. Civil servants should be watched carefully and punished for doing a poor job. People caught criticizing the government should be banished to China's far northern frontier.

In Hanfeizi's time, rulers were frequently overthrown. To solve this problem, Hanfeizi said that rulers must have absolute power backed up by military might. Rulers should trust no one, not even their own families. Hanfeizi wrote, "He who trusts will be controlled by others."

The Influence of Legalism

Legalist philosophy had an almost immediate influence on government in China. At the end of the Warring Sates period, the Qin dynasty seized control of China. Qin rulers read and admired Hanfeizi's writings. They wanted to build a strong central government and a well-organized society. To achieve these goals, they adopted strict Legalist ideas. People were forbidden to criticize the government. Anyone caught doing so was severely punished. Many people were put to death for disloyalty and other crimes. You'll learn more about Legalism under the Qin in the next chapter.

21.6 Chapter Summary

In this chapter, you read about three Chinese philosophies, Confucianism, Daoism, and Legalism. All three schools of thought developed in the later years of the Zhou dynasty.

For a time, feudalism helped to stabilize China under the Zhou. But during the dynasty's later years, China collapsed into disorder. Political instability led many scholars to debate the proper way to rule.

Confucius taught that peace and order depended upon proper behavior. Those in authority must lead by example. Those below them must obey. Daoists believed that people should live simply and in harmony with nature. They said the best rulers were those who ruled the least. Finally, Legalists like Hanfeizi believed that people were driven by their own self-interest. They taught that rulers could create order only through strict laws and harsh punishments.

In the next chapter, you will meet China's first emperor, Qin Shihuangdi. You'll discover how he used Legalist ideas to unite China's warring states.

This silk scroll shows women instructing other women in the teachings of Confucianism.

CHAPTER 22

China's first emperor, Qin Shihuangdi, was both a strong and a cruel ruler.

The First Emperor of China

22.1 Introduction

In Chapter 21, you learned about three Chinese philosophies and how China fell into disorder at the end of the Zhou dynasty. In this chapter, you will learn about the **unification of China** under **Qin Shihuangdi**.

The Emperor of Qin (pronounced *chin*) ruled over a united China from 221 to 210 B.C.E. His reign was marked by great contrasts. He executed hundreds of enemies, and his building projects killed thousands of his own people. But he also unified Chinese government and culture. And his construction projects were among the most spectacular in the world.

The emperor's most ambitious project was the building of the Great Wall along China's northern border. The purpose of the wall was to protect the north China border from invasion. The Emperor of Qin set about building the wall like a general trying to win a war. Supply camps were set up to bring food and materials to the mountains and deserts of the northern frontier. Soldiers were posted to fight off bandits and to stop workers from running away. Thousands of Chinese were marched from their homes and forced to work on the wall. It is said that many of them never returned.

Clearly, the Emperor of Qin was both a strong leader and a cruel one. It's little wonder that later Chinese historians had very differing opinions of him.

In this chapter, you'll find out more about the Emperor of Qin's reign. Then you can form your own opinion of China's first emperor.

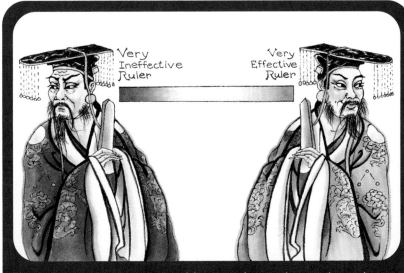

Use this spectrum as a graphic organizer to learn about the reign of Emperor Qin Shihuangdi.

22.2 Creating an Empire

China's first emperor began life as Prince Zheng of the royal family of the state of Qin. He was born in 259 B.C.E., near the end of the Warring States period. In 256 B.C.E., Qin took over the state of Zhou, ending the Zhou dynasty. Ten years later, 13-year-old Prince Zheng became king.

Sometimes called the Tiger of Qin, Zheng was an extremely ambitious man. He used military might, spies, bribery, and alliances to conquer the remaining rival states. His empire became far larger than the kingdoms of earlier dynasties. In 221 B.C.E., he gained control of all of China. He decided then to take a new title, Qin Shihuangdi, or First Emperor of Qin.

As a ruler, the Emperor of Qin was greatly influenced by Legalism. Recall that Legalists believed in strict laws, harsh punishments, and a strong central authority. The emperor adopted these ideas. So that he would not be threatened by powerful lords, he replaced the old system of feudalism with a government he controlled personally. He divided his vast territory into 36 districts. Three officials were appointed to govern each district. One was responsible for the army. Another took care of the laws and agriculture. The third reported what was going on to the emperor.

The Emperor of Qin used harsh measures to maintain his power. When he discovered plots against his life, he had the leaders of the plots and their families killed. He even exiled his own mother from court when he feared she was plotting against him.

The Emperor of Qin's wars of conquests cost many millions of lives.

22.3 Standardizing the Culture

The Emperor of Qin wanted to unify China. One way he did this was by **standardizing** cultural practices that differed from place to place.

One key step was to create a unified system of laws. Many of the emperor's new laws were aimed at government officials. For example, officials were punished if the grain in storehouses spoiled or if a wall built under their supervision collapsed. Other laws governed everyday life. For example, widows were not allowed to remarry.

The emperor's laws were based on Legalist beliefs. They were very detailed, and they spelled out exact punishments for bad behavior. Rich and poor were punished equally. Typical punishments included fines paid in suits of armor, shields, or gold. But there were also physical punishments, including forced labor, whippings, and beheadings.

To make it easier to trade, the emperor standardized money, weights, and measures. Throughout China, people had used various types of items as money, including shells, pearls, silver, tin objects, and coins. Under the Emperor of Qin, the only acceptable form of money became metal coins made of gold or bronze. The coins had holes in the center so that people could carry several of them together on a cord. The emperor also ordered measuring cups to be made so they held the same amount. To standardize weights, he had metalworkers create bell-shaped weights out of bronze or iron in a variety of standard sizes.

The emperor also simplified the writing system. He got rid of many of the written characters that were in use across China. A later dictionary listed 9,000 approved characters.

The Emperor of Qin frequently went on inspection tours to make sure his orders were being obeyed. During his tours, he performed sacrifices and erected stone tablets that told of his achievements.

22.4 Protecting the Northern Border

To protect his empire from invaders, the Emperor of Qin ordered a long wall to be built along China's northern border. Earlier kingdoms had already built smaller walls of their own. The emperor had long sections built to connect these walls. He also extended the wall to the west. It was called the "10,000 Li Long Wall." (One *li* is about three tenths of a mile.) Later it became known as the Great Wall.

Few traces of this Great Wall survive. (The Great Wall as we know it today was built by later rulers.) Most likely, it was made of layers of earth pounded into wooden frames that held everything together.

Construction of the wall took 10 years. A workforce of 300,000 men was assembled to build it. Some were soldiers. Many were peasants who were forced to leave their fields to work on the project. Still others were musicians, teachers, writers, and artists that the emperor sent into **exile** in the north.

The workers who built the wall labored under difficult conditions. The wall crossed high mountains, desert, swampland, and quicksand. The weather was bitterly cold in the winter and blazing hot in the summer. According to later accounts, tens of thousands of men died while working on the project. Their bodies were buried in the wall.

When the Chinese armies to the south were strong, the Great Wall proved very effective at stopping invasions. The nomads living to the north could not move sheep or cattle over it, and horses could not jump over it. So invaders were left without supplies or a cavalry.

exile living away from one's native country

Later Chinese rulers rebuilt and added to the Great Wall. Soldiers guarded the frontier from the watchtowers you see here. They lit fires to warn of approaching invaders.

22.5 Ending Opposition

The changes introduced by the Emperor of Qin to unify and protect China aroused a great deal of opposition. They were especially unpopular with Confucian scholars. The Confucians believed in proper behavior and good example, not harsh laws.

The emperor was determined to end opposition to his rule. It is said that he executed 460 Confucian scholars for plotting against him.

The conflict between the emperor and the scholars came to a head during a royal banquet in 213 B.C.E. During the banquet, a Confucian scholar criticized the emperor. He warned that the Qin dynasty would not last unless the emperor followed the ways of the past.

Later emperors said the Emperor of Qin crushed opposition to his rule by executing Confucian scholars. According to legend, some scholars were buried alive. Others were buried up to their necks and then beheaded.

The scholar's comments angered the emperor's trusted advisor, Li Siu. Li told the emperor that the scholars' criticisms were causing trouble and must be stopped. No one, he said, should be allowed to learn about Confucianism. All Confucian books should be brought to the capital city and burned. Only books dealing with medicine, farming, and the history of the Qin kingdom should be spared.

The Emperor of Qin agreed to order the book burning. He said that scholars who disobeyed the order would be marked with a tattoo on their faces and sent to do forced labor. Anyone who discussed ancient teachings to criticize the government would be executed.

The emperor's brutal action shocked China. Some scholars chose to die rather than give up their books. Even the emperor's son became a victim of the campaign to end opposition. When he criticized the killing of the scholars, he was sent to oversee work on the Great Wall.

22.6 The Emperor's Death and the End of the Qin Dynasty

immortal able to live forever

Despite the Emperor of Qin's many achievements, ancient Chinese writings say that he was unable to find happiness. Above all, the emperor was afraid to die. He called magicians to his court, asking them how he could become **immortal**. Some magicians said that he must find a magic potion. The emperor searched far and near for the potion. Once he sent an expedition to islands in the sea east of China, but the potion was never found.

The Death and Burial of the Emperor of Qin

In 210 B.C.E., after just over 10 years as ruler of China, the Emperor of Qin died. He had been searching for the magic potion and was 600 miles from the capital city. No one knows the cause of his death. He may have been poisoned.

The Emperor of Qin's body was taken back to the capital and buried in a gigantic tomb in a man-made mound. The tomb complex, or group of structures, covered many square miles. Ancient Chinese writings say that more than 700,000 workers helped build it. Some of them were buried with the emperor to prevent grave robbers from learning about the tomb's fabulous treasures.

The treasures in the Emperor of Qin's tomb were not discovered until 1974 C.E. Among them were tools, precious jewels, and rare objects. Most amazing of all, there was an entire army made of a kind of clay called *terra-cotta*. The army included more than 6,000 life-size figures such as archers, foot soldiers, chariot drivers, and horses. So far, archeologists have not found any two figures that are exactly alike. Each seems to be unique.

The terra-cotta army found in the Emperor of Qin's tomb faces east to lead the emperor into the next world.

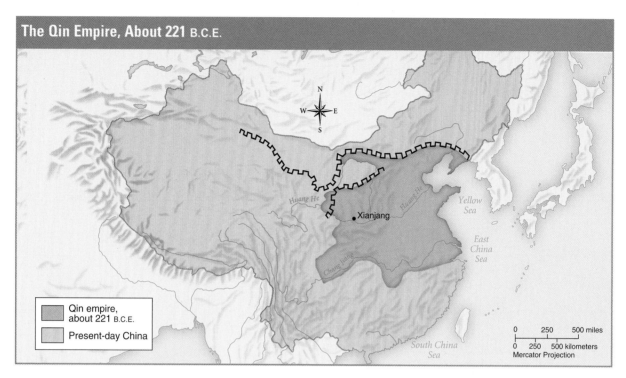

The Qin Empire, About 221 B.C.E.

Legend:
- Qin empire, about 221 B.C.E.
- Present-day China

Xianjang

Huang He, Huang He, Chang Jiang

Yellow Sea, East China Sea, South China Sea

0 250 500 miles
0 250 500 kilometers
Mercator Projection

The End of the Qin Dynasty

When he took the title of Shihuangdi, the Emperor of Qin said his dynasty would last 10,000 years. In fact, it fell apart shortly after his death.

The harshness of the emperor's rule had caused a great deal of unhappiness. Soon after he died, rebellions broke out in the countryside. Members of the royal families of conquered states joined in the revolt. Civil war followed as various leaders struggled for control. Finally, in 206 B.C.E., Liu Bang, a peasant leader, defeated his rivals and established the Han dynasty.

22.7 Chapter Summary

In this chapter, you learned about Qin Shihuangdi, China's first emperor. The Emperor of Qin had a major influence on China. He unified China and greatly expanded its borders. He centralized the government. He standardized Chinese laws, money, weights, measures, and writing. Among his many construction projects was the Great Wall.

Later Chinese rulers built on what the Emperor of Qin left behind, including government institutions and the Great Wall itself. The office of emperor that he created lasted for 2,000 years. Even China's name in the western world comes from the word Qin. But the harshness of the Emperor of Qin's rule led to an early end for his dynasty. In the next chapter, you will learn about the dynasty that followed, the Han dynasty.

CHAPTER 23

◀ ◀ ◀ With a large army, the first emperor of the
Han dynasty marches toward his capital.

The Han Dynasty

23.1 Introduction

In Chapter 22, you learned about Qin Shihuangdi, China's first emperor. The Qin dynasty lasted only about 14 years. In this chapter, you'll learn about China's next dynasty, the **Han dynasty**. It lasted over 400 years, from about 206 B.C.E. to 220 C.E.

The Han (pronounced *hahn*) dynasty arose during a time of unrest. The Chinese people were unhappy with the harsh, Legalist government of the Qin. After the first emperor's death, they rebelled against their Qin rulers. The Han dynasty began when Liu Bang, a rebel who had gained control of the Han kingdom, conquered the Qin army and established his own empire.

Over time, Han emperors began to change the way China was ruled. Han leaders came to believe that they could not rule people with force alone. Gradually, they incorporated Confucian ideals of moral behavior into the government.

Under the Han, China enjoyed a golden age, a long period of stability and wealth. Education, literature, and art flourished. Many important practices, inventions, and discoveries improved people's lives.

The Han dynasty was also known for its military achievements. Han emperors expanded the empire as far as present-day Korea and Vietnam. Once Central Asia was under its control, the Han established trade relationships with the West.

In this chapter, you'll explore **warfare, government, agriculture, industry, art, medicine,** and **science** under the Han dynasty.

Use this Han wall of achievements as a graphic organizer to help you learn about the Han dynasty.

The Han Dynasty   223

23.2 Warfare

The Han excelled in warfare. Their military tactics and new weapons helped them expand their empire. At its height, the empire reached west into central Asia, east to present-day Korea, and south to present-day Vietnam.

The Han had a large and well-organized army. All men from about ages 25 to 60 had to serve two years in the army. Historians estimate that Han armies had 130,000 to 300,000 men.

The army was helped by new technologies. Advances in iron making improved the strength and quality of armor. Han iron-workers produced a kind of fish-scale armor that flexed and moved with the body. The Han were among the first people to make iron swords. The strength of iron allowed them to fashion longer swords. With a long sword, a soldier could swing at an enemy from a safer distance.

Another favorite weapon of the Han was the crossbow. A crossbow is made of two pieces of wood in the shape of a cross. A string is attached to each end of the vertical piece. That string is pulled back in order to shoot an arrow from the crossbow.

The Han invented the kite and used it in clever ways for military purposes. According to one legend, a Han general once used a kite to measure the width of a heavily guarded wall. Kites were used to send messages from one part of an army to another. They were also used to frighten the enemy. Kites with bamboo pipes were flown over enemy camps at night. Enemy soldiers would hear a ghostly noise coming from the darkness above them. It sounded like *"fu, fu"* ("beware, beware"). The frightened soldiers often ran away.

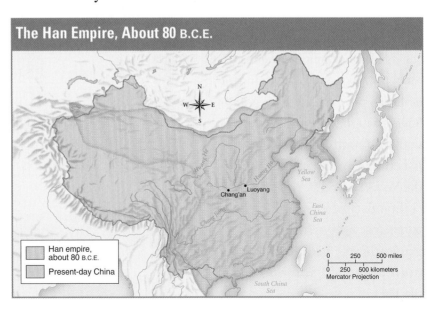

The Han Empire, About 80 B.C.E.

Han empire, about 80 B.C.E.

Present-day China

23.3 Government

The Han made significant improvements in Chinese government. They adopted the centralized government established by Emperor Qin Shihuangdi. But they softened the harsh ruling style of the emperor and brought Confucian ideas back into government.

The emperor used many government officials to help him run his vast empire. The government of China during this time was a **bureaucracy**. A bureaucracy is structured like a pyramid, with a few people at the top and many at the bottom. At each level, people direct those who are below them.

This bronze statue shows a Han official riding in a chariot with an escort walking behind.

The top Han officials lived in the capital and gave advice to the emperor. Lower-level officials lived throughout the empire. Their responsibilities included checking roads and canals. They also had to make sure that enough grain was produced and stored in case of famine.

One key improvement made by the Han concerned the way civil servants were hired. Before the Han dynasty, government officials were chosen based on their social status. Under the Han, they were chosen based on their ability and knowledge. To become officials, young men had to pass a long and difficult civil service exam. The exam was based on the classic writings. Candidates had to learn five books by heart. Legend says they spent several days in tiny rooms taking the exam. All the while, they were watched by guards to prevent them from cheating.

Once civil servants were hired, they were not allowed to serve in their home district. This rule was intended to prevent them from giving special favors to friends and relatives. Every three years, their work was evaluated. Based on their evaluation, they could be promoted or demoted.

bureaucracy a form of government that is structured like a pyramid, with a few people at the top and many at the bottom

In this painting, a thatched roof shades men from the sun as they work the pedals of a chain pump, bringing water to their fields.

23.4 Agriculture

Ancient Chinese farmers faced many difficulties. Important advances in agriculture under the Han dynasty improved their lives.

Han farmers were expected to grow enough food to feed their own families and help stock the shared granaries, or grain storehouses. In addition to growing crops, farmers had to make their clothing, build their homes, and give one month of unpaid labor to the government for building projects such as canals and roads. All this was hard enough, but floods and drought often destroyed crops, presenting farmers with yet another challenge.

One invention that helped farmers was the chain pump. The chain pump made it easier to move water from low irrigation ditches and canals up to the fields. Workers used pedals to turn a wheel, which pulled a series of wooden planks. The planks moved water uphill to the fields.

The Han skill in ironwork also came to the farmers' aid. The Chinese were the first to learn how to pour melted iron into molds. This process made it easier to make strong iron plows. Han plows were designed to push the dirt away from the row being plowed so that it did not pile up in front of the plow.

Finally, the Han invented the wheelbarrow. The Chinese wheelbarrow had one large wheel in the center. Goods were carried on either side of the wheel. It was much easier for farmers to push a heavy load in a wheelbarrow than to carry it on their backs or in buckets suspended from a pole across their shoulders.

23.5 Industry

Like agriculture, industry benefited from advances made under the Han dynasty. The Han government controlled the two most important industries in China, silk and salt. Both industries were helped by new inventions.

Silk is a material produced from the fibers of a silkworm cocoon. For the ancient Chinese, making silk was difficult and time-consuming. During the Han dynasty, the Chinese developed a foot-powered machine that wound fibers onto a large reel, ready for use. Making silk production more efficient was important because silk was very valuable in trade with people outside of China. The silk trade began under the Han. You'll learn more about it in the next chapter.

Salt was an equally important trade item. Salt was valuable to people in ancient times because they used it to help preserve meat and vegetables. At first, people only knew how to get salt from the sea. During the Han dynasty, the Chinese learned how to mine salt from under the ground.

Salt water, or brine, exists deep beneath Earth's surface. The Chinese dug deep wells using iron-tipped bamboo drills. When they reached salt water (sometimes 1,000 feet below the surface), a hollow bamboo pole was dropped into the well. The pole had a valve that allowed the salt water to enter the pole. The valve was then closed, and the pole was brought back to the surface with the salt water inside. Workers placed the water in large iron pots. The pots were heated until the water evaporated, leaving just the salt. In this way, the Chinese could get salt even if they were far from the sea.

The production of silk was an important industry under the Han. This foot-powered reeling machine threaded silk fibers through a series of guides and onto a large reel.

23.6 Art

A key advance in art under the Han was the invention of paper. Paper was the ideal material for **calligraphy**. Calligraphy was an important art form to the Chinese. They particularly valued a style of writing that flowed naturally, as if inspired by nature.

Chinese scribes used some of the same tools and techniques as painters did. They wrote their characters by painting them with a brush and ink. Characters were created by one or more strokes, drawn in a particular order. The ideal stroke was done quickly and created both delicate and bold lines. Paper was perfect for this art because it absorbed the ink well.

Before the invention of paper, the Chinese wrote on silk. Silk could easily be rolled into scrolls, but it was very expensive. People also wrote on bamboo. They wrote their symbols vertically on bamboo strips. To make books, they tied a series of strips together in a bundle. Bamboo was cheaper than silk, but it was bulky and awkward to use.

The invention of paper in about the first century C.E. not only helped calligraphers but also changed the way people communicated. Paper was cheaper than bamboo or silk, so people could afford to write more. Paper was also easier to bind together into books.

A variety of materials were used to make paper, including silk fibers, hemp, bamboo, straw, and seaweed. Materials were boiled into a soupy pulp. Then a screen was dipped into the pulp and brought out again. When the pulp dried on the screen, the result was paper.

calligraphy the art of fine handwriting

This 19th-century woodblock print shows papermakers hanging sheets of paper on a wall.

23.7 Medicine

The practice of medicine under the Han involved ideas and treatments that are still used in traditional Chinese healing today. The ancient Chinese believed that illnesses happened when the forces of yin and yang in the body were out of balance. Healers tried to restore the natural balance of these opposite forces.

One technique for this purpose is acupuncture. In acupuncture, thin needles are inserted into specific parts of the body. This is thought to rebalance the forces of yin and yang. Acupuncture is thought to be useful for curing illnesses that strike quickly, like headaches.

A second healing technique is moxibustion. In moxibustion, a small cone of powdered leaves or sticks called a *moxa* is placed on the skin and set on fire. The heat is believed to reduce pain and promote healing. This technique is used to treat long-term diseases, such as arthritis.

These doctors are performing the healing technique of moxibustion. This technique is still used today, often in combination with acupuncture.

anesthetic something that takes away the feeling of pain

The ancient Chinese also made discoveries about how the human body works. For example, they learned to judge health by listening to a person's heartbeat or feeling his or her pulse. The pulse is the little throb in your blood vessels caused by the contraction of your heart as it pumps blood through the body. The Chinese also discovered that blood circulates from the heart through the body and back to the heart. Western science did not make this discovery until the 1600s C.E.

Finally, Han doctors discovered a type of wine that could be used as an **anesthetic**.

23.8 Science

The Chinese under the Han made a number of scientific advances. Chinese astronomers closely observed the heavens. They recorded the appearance of comets, which they called "broom stars." They discovered that the moon shines because it reflects the light of the sun. They also learned that solar eclipses happen when the moon blocks our view of the sun.

The Chinese of this period also invented two useful instruments, the seismograph and the magnetic compass. A **seismograph** is an instrument for detecting earthquakes. The first Chinese seismograph was a circular machine made of bronze. The machine had a pendulum in the center and was surrounded by eight sculpted animal heads. During an earthquake, the pendulum vibrated. The vibration triggered the release of one of eight balls. The ball would then fall in the direction of the earthquake. Using this ingenious machine, the Han were able to detect earthquakes up to several hundred miles away.

A magnetic **compass** is an instrument for determining direction, such as which way is north or south. The Chinese believed that it was important to place temples, graves, and homes in the correct position for luck. By the 200s C.E., they understood that a **lodestone** tends to align itself in a north-south direction because of Earth's magnetism. With this knowledge, they used lodestones to make compasses. The lodestone was carved into the shape of a spoon with a handle that would always point south.

seismograph an instrument for detecting earthquakes
compass an instrument for determining direction
lodestone a type of iron ore

The Chinese "south-pointing spoon" is the oldest known compass.

23.9 Chapter Summary

In this chapter, you read about the Han dynasty. The Han ruled China for more than 400 years. Most of this period was a time of peace, wealth, and achievement for China.

Under the Han, the Chinese made advances in many areas. New weapons helped Han emperors succeed in war and expand their empire. The government was organized into a bureaucracy staffed by civil servants who were chosen for their ability. A number of inventions improved agriculture and the important silk and salt industries. The invention of paper advanced the art of calligraphy. Healers used techniques and practices that are still used today. Finally, Chinese scientists made important observations and invented the seismograph and the compass.

The many achievements of the Han left a deep impact on Chinese culture. In fact, in Chinese the word *Han* is still used today to describe the culture of the people of China.

In earlier chapters, you learned that at one time China was isolated from other cultures. In the next chapter, you'll learn how the silk trade encouraged an exchange of wealth and ideas between China and the cultures of the West.

Emperor Wudi, the figure in the center, improved government by setting up a university to prepare students for the civil service exam.

CHAPTER 24

◀ ◀ ◀ Traders formed camel caravans to cross the desert sands along the Silk Road.

The Silk Road

24.1 Introduction

In the last chapter, you learned about the achievements of the Han dynasty. Under the Han, **trade routes** were opened that allowed the Chinese to trade with other ancient cultures. In this chapter, you'll explore the great trade route known as the **Silk Road**.

The Silk Road was actually a network of smaller trade routes that stretched more than 4,000 miles across Asia. It reached from Luoyang and the Han capital of Chang'an in China to Mediterranean ports such as Antioch in Syria. By the first century C.E., the Mediterranean region was dominated by the Roman Empire, whose capital city was Rome (in present-day Italy). The Silk Road connected the great empires of the Han and the Romans. (You will learn about the Roman Empire later in this book.)

Both goods and ideas traveled along the Silk Road. The Chinese traded such things as silk and jade. In return, they acquired new products such as spices from India and glassware from Rome. New ideas, including Buddhism, also entered China as a result of this trade.

The Silk Road linked the peoples of the East and the West for more than 1,000 years. In this chapter, you will learn about the opening of the Silk Road. You'll discover what traveling the Silk Road was like in the time of the Han. You'll also learn about the goods and ideas that were exchanged between the cultures of Asia and the West.

Use this image as a graphic organizer to learn about the goods and ideas traded between the East and the West along the Silk Road.

24.2 The Opening of the Silk Road

The Silk Road was made possible by the expansion of the Han empire. The military campaigns of the Han beat back nomadic peoples in northwestern China, allowing trade routes to the west to be opened.

The Father of the Silk Road

A Chinese explorer named Zhang Qian is often called the Father of the Silk Road. His travels opened the way for trade between China and its western neighbors.

In 138 B.C.E., a Han emperor sent Zhang Qian west with 100 men. His mission was to form an alliance with western peoples against China's northern enemy, the Huns. Zhang Qian traveled across central Asia to what is now the country of Iran. Twice he was taken prisoner by the Huns. Both times he managed to escape.

Zhang Qian was not able to form an alliance. But his trip was a success in other ways as it helped the Chinese learn about cultures to the west. He brought back word of such places as Persia, Syria, India, and Rome.

Some years later, Zhang Qian went on a second journey to the west. This time, he discovered a more powerful type of horse that was better suited for war than the smaller Chinese horse. He also discovered grapes, which were unknown in China. Most importantly, he was able to establish trade relationships with some central Asian peoples.

Over time, Chinese traders traveled farther west. Smaller trade routes connected to form larger networks. The most famous of these became known as the Silk Road after the product that traders valued most of all: Chinese silk.

This wine cup is carved to show Zhang Qian floating down the Huang He in a hollow log.

Silk as a Trade Good

Silk is a fiber used to make cloth. Silk cloth is strong, but also warm, light, and soft.

Silk was a valuable good for trade because at first only the Chinese knew how to make it. As you learned in the last chapter, the Chinese discovered how to make silk from fibers taken from the cocoon of the silkworm. To protect the trade value of silk, the Chinese tried to keep the process for producing it a secret. Under the Han dynasty, revealing the secret was a crime punishable by death.

24.3 Rome Trades Glassware for Silk

When people of other cultures learned about silk, it became a highly prized material. The Romans, in particular, eagerly traded valuable goods for silk.

The first time the Romans saw silk was during a battle near the Euphrates River in Mesopotamia. At a key moment, the enemy unfurled many colorful silk banners. The Romans lost the battle, but this experience led them to want to acquire this wonderful new material.

Chinese silk was a luxury item. It was rare and expensive. Even the richest Romans could afford to wear only a strip or a patch of silk stitched to their white **togas**. But silk was so highly prized that traders willingly went on the dangerous journey eastward to trade for it.

The Romans had gold to trade and something else the Chinese prized: glassware. The Romans knew how to blow glass into wonderful, delicate shapes. Just as the Romans had never seen silk, the Chinese were unfamiliar with glass production. The Romans were happy to trade glassware for silk.

These women are making silk. The Chinese closely guarded the secret of how silk was made.

toga a loose robe worn by men in Rome

Traders often formed long caravans to cross the Taklimakan Desert. Some caravans had as many as 1,000 camels.

24.4 The Eastern Silk Road

The Silk Road was not one continuous route. Instead it was a network of shorter trade routes between various stops. Most traders traveled between these stops rather than over the entire route. Goods changed hands many times before reaching their final destination.

The two major parts of the route were the Eastern Silk Road and the Western Silk Road. The Eastern Silk Road connected Luoyang to Kashgar, in the western part of the Taklimakan Desert. The Western Silk Road ran from Kashgar to Antioch and other Mediterranean ports.

Traveling the Eastern Silk Road

From Luoyang, the Silk Road led west along the Gobi Desert to Dunhuang, in northwestern China. This part of the route was protected to the north by the Great Wall.

From Dunhuang, travelers could choose either a northern or a southern route across the desert to Kashgar. Many chose the northern route, where the distances between oases like Loulan and Kucha were shorter.

Several dangers faced traders crossing the Taklimakan. Bandits often attacked travelers on the northern route between Dunhuang and Kucha. Throughout the desert, sudden sandstorms sometimes buried travelers in sand. Travelers may have been lured off the main path to their deaths by **mirages**.

Before entering the desert, travelers formed long camel **caravans** for protection. One type of camel was especially suited for desert travel. Bactrian camels have double eyelids and nostrils that can close to keep out blowing sand. They could carry enough food and water for a traveler to make it to the next oasis.

mirage an image of something that isn't really there, such as water

caravan a group of people traveling together

Goods Exchanged Along the Eastern Silk Road

It was very expensive to carry goods over the Silk Road. For traders to make a profit, goods had to be valuable and easy to carry. That way a merchant could take more goods on fewer animals.

Silk was the perfect trading good, because it was both light and valuable. Huge quantities of silk traveled from China along the Eastern Silk Road. After being traded for other goods, the silk eventually reached the shores of the Mediterranean Sea. Then it was taken by boat to Rome and other Mediterranean cities.

Besides silk, the Chinese also traded fine dishware (which became known as *china*), ornaments, jewelry, cast-iron products, and decorative boxes. In return, they received a variety of goods from other traders. They particularly valued horses from Central Asia. Other goods from Central Asia included jade, furs, and gold. India sent various goods north to Kashgar, including cotton, spices, pearls (from oysters), and ivory (from elephant tusks). From Kashgar, the goods made their way east to China.

Strong horses from Central Asia were traded and highly valued. This bronze statue depicts a spirited horse such as those the Han Chinese admired.

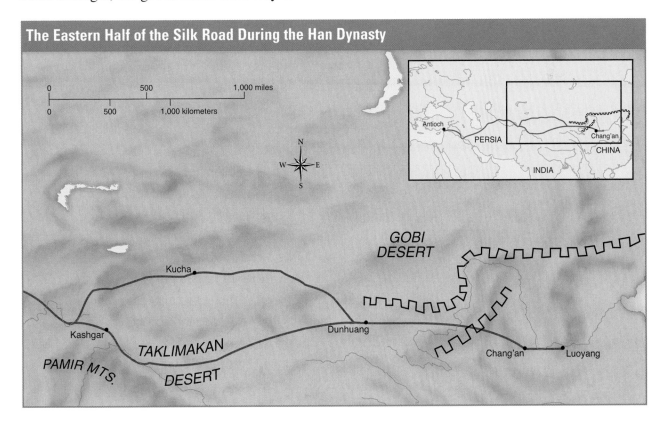

The Eastern Half of the Silk Road During the Han Dynasty

GOBI DESERT

Kucha

Kashgar

PAMIR MTS.

TAKLIMAKAN DESERT

Dunhuang

Chang'an   Luoyang

Antioch

PERSIA   Chang'an

CHINA

INDIA

Crossing the Pamir Mountains presented many challenges. In winter, travelers could be caught in snowstorms and freeze to death.

24.5 The Western Silk Road

Kashgar was the central trading point where the Eastern and Western Silk Roads met. Goods from various areas were exchanged there and sent in both directions along the trade route. Goods traveling westward went by yak rather than camel. The Western Silk Road ended in Mediterranean ports like Antioch.

Traveling the Western Silk Road

The journey west from Kashgar began with a difficult trek across the Pamir Mountains. Some peaks rose over 20,000 feet. Travelers often experienced headaches, dizziness, and ringing in the ears caused by lack of oxygen in the thin air of the high mountains.

Many of the mountain passes were narrow and dangerous. This part of the route was sometimes called the "trail of bones" because of the many animals and people who died there. Pack animals such as donkeys could slip off the narrow trails and tumble over cliffs. Sometimes traders unloaded their animals and carried the goods through the passes themselves.

After the Pamir Mountains, the route took travelers through a fertile valley in what is now Afghanistan. Then it headed across the Iranian Plateau, passed south of the Caspian Sea, and crossed Mesopotamia. A major stop along this part of the route was Ctesiphon (in modern-day Iraq). Ctesiphon was located on the eastern bank of the Tigris River, north of ancient Babylon.

From Ctesiphon, the Silk Road turned north and crossed the Syrian Desert. Travelers across the desert faced many difficulties. They were threatened by tigers, lions, and scorpions, and they were tormented by flies.

The goods finally reached Antioch and other Mediterranean ports. From there, they were transported by ship throughout the Mediterranean world.

Goods Exchanged Along the Western Silk Road

Many goods traveled along the Western Silk Road and eventually ended up in China. Traders from Egypt, Arabia, and Persia brought perfumes, cosmetics, and carpets. Central Asian traders brought metal items and dyes. They also sometimes traded slaves.

Rome sent a number of products to be exchanged for Chinese silk. The Chinese highly valued Roman glass products, including trays, vases, necklaces, and small bottles. They also prized asbestos, which they used for making fireproof cloth, and coral. Chinese doctors used coral to help them locate illness, as it was said that coral lost its color when placed on the skin of someone who was sick.

The Romans also sent massive amounts of gold to trade for silk. In fact, so much gold was shipped out of Rome that in the first century C.E. the Roman emperor Tiberius passed a law forbidding men to wear silk. Legend says the emperor was afraid that wearing so much finery would make the Romans soft and weak. More likely, he wanted to reduce the amount of gold that was flowing out of his empire.

Carpets like this one from Persia were traded along the Silk Road.

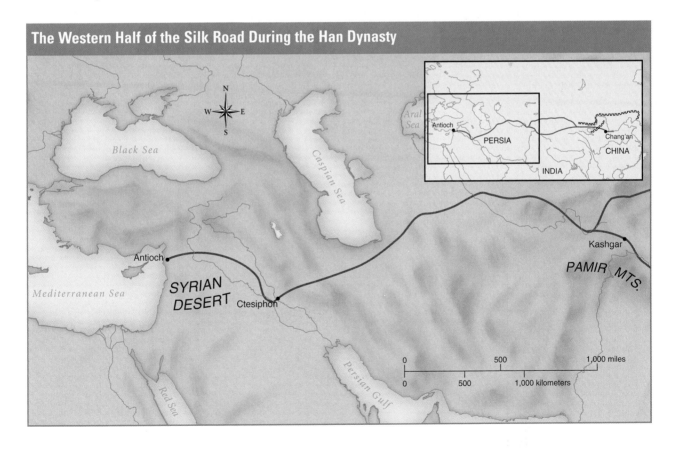

The Western Half of the Silk Road During the Han Dynasty

24.6 Cultural Exchanges Along the Silk Road

Goods weren't the only things to travel along the Silk Road. The trade between East and West also resulted in cultural exchanges.

For example, China and Rome didn't just learn about new products from each other. In time, they learned how to make these products for themselves. By 500 C.E., the Chinese had learned how to make glass. About the same time, the West learned how to produce silk.

Buddhism entered China by way of the Silk Road. This is the earliest Chinese statue of Buddha that has been found.

Diets, gardening, and agriculture also changed as new plants were introduced into different areas. China imported many new foods and spices. Among them were grapes, alfalfa, cucumbers, figs, pomegranates, walnuts, chives, sesame, and coriander. The West imported roses, azaleas, chrysanthemums, peonies, camellias, oranges, peaches, and pears.

The Silk Road also helped to spread Buddhism. As you have learned, Buddhism began in India. Because the Silk Road passed through many different nations, religious travelers used the route to spread their beliefs.

Buddhism was introduced to China around the middle of the first century. Some Chinese Buddhists journeyed on foot across Central Asia to India to learn more about their new religion. They returned to China with copies of sacred Buddhist texts. Buddhism would eventually become a major religion in China.

24.7 Chapter Summary

In this chapter, you explored the Silk Road, the network of trade routes between China and the West. The Silk Road was opened under the Han and remained a major route of trade for more than 1,000 years.

The eastern and western parts of the Silk Road presented many dangers and difficulties to travelers. The Eastern Silk Road connected the capital of China to Dunhuang, on the edge of the Taklimakan Desert. From there, the northern route took travelers across the desert through Kucha to Kashgar. From Kashgar, the Western Silk Road crossed the Pamir Mountains and passed through Ctesiphon on its way to Mediterranean ports like Antioch.

Many goods were exchanged along the Silk Road, including silk from China and glassware from Rome. In addition to new products, trade brought cultural changes to both East and West. One of the most important changes was the introduction of Buddhism to China.

In the next unit, you'll return to the Mediterranean world. You'll explore ancient Greece, a civilization that has had a deep and lasting influence on our own culture.

This fragment of ancient Chinese silk was probably part of a valuable garment or piece of cloth.

Ancient China Timeline

1700 – 1122 B.C.E.
Bronze masterpieces are produced
during the Shang dynasty.

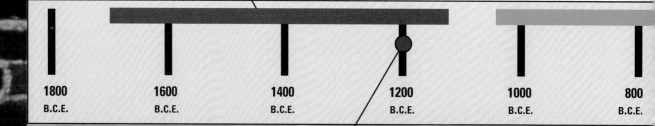

| 1800 | 1600 | 1400 | 1200 | 1000 | 800 |
| B.C.E. | B.C.E. | B.C.E. | B.C.E. | B.C.E. | B.C.E. |

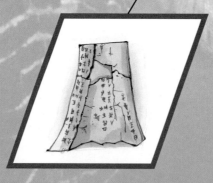

1200 B.C.E.
Writing appears on oracle bones.

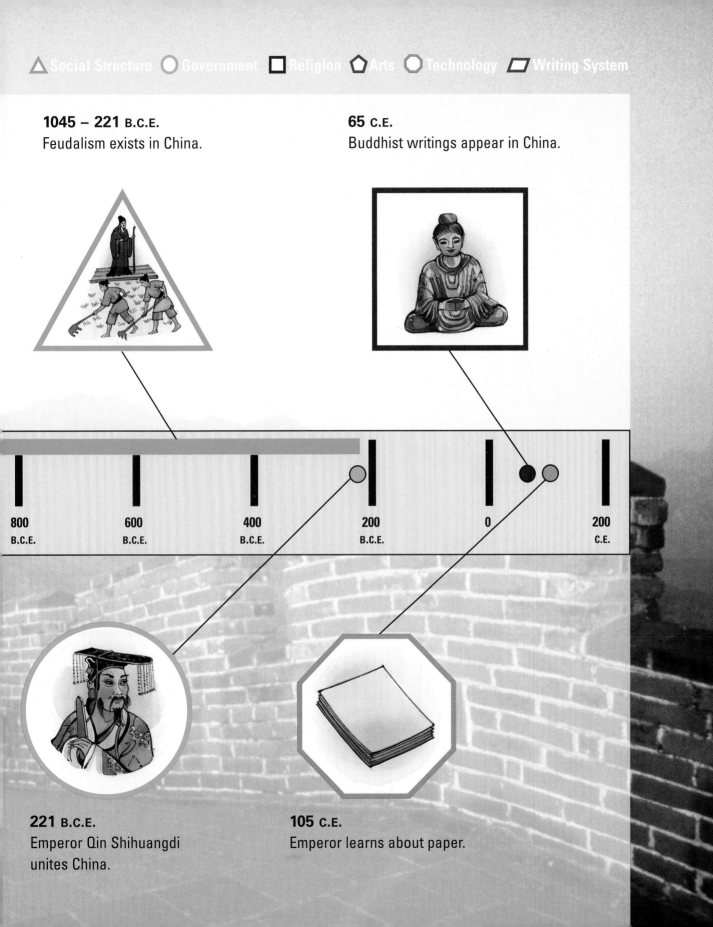

△ Social Structure ◯ Government ▢ Religion ⬠ Arts ⬡ Technology ▱ Writing System

1045 – 221 B.C.E.
Feudalism exists in China.

65 C.E.
Buddhist writings appear in China.

| 800 B.C.E. | 600 B.C.E. | 400 B.C.E. | 200 B.C.E. | 0 | 200 C.E. |

221 B.C.E.
Emperor Qin Shihuangdi
unites China.

105 C.E.
Emperor learns about paper.

UNIT 5

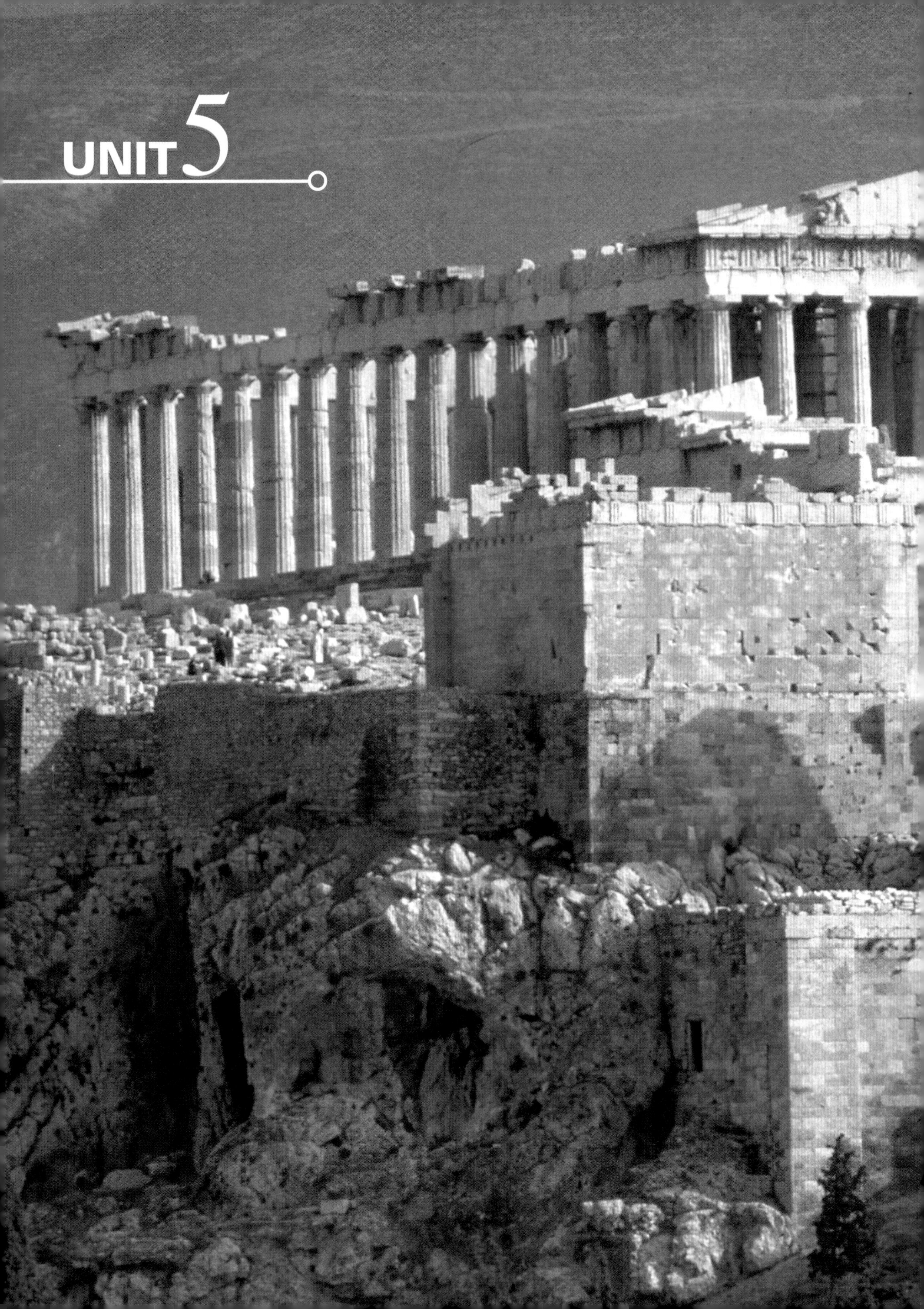

Ancient Greece

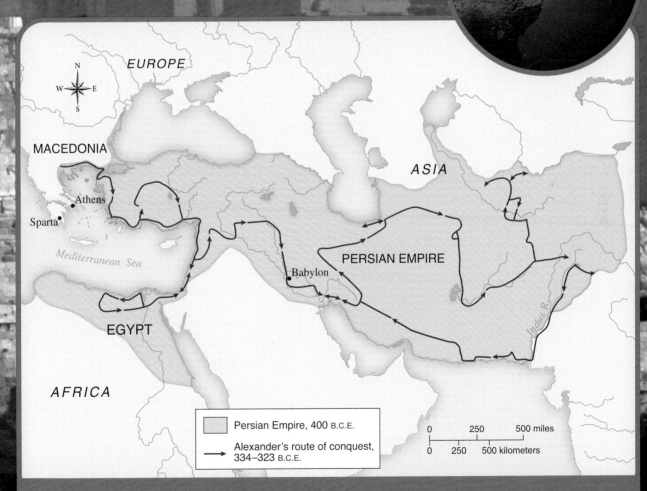

Greece and the Persian Empire, 400 B.C.E.

Greece has little farmland, but olive trees and grapes grow on the rocky hillsides.

Geography and the Settlement of Greece

25.1 Introduction

In Unit 4, you explored the fascinating culture of ancient China. In this unit, you will learn about the civilization of ancient Greece. This remarkable culture flourished between 750 and 338 B.C.E. Ancient Greek art, ideas, and writings continue to influence us today.

Greece is a small country in southern Europe. It is shaped a little like a hand, with fingers that reach into the Mediterranean Sea. The mainland of Greece is a peninsula. A *peninsula* is land that is surrounded on three sides by water. Greece also includes many islands throughout the Mediterranean and Aegean Seas.

Mainland Greece is a land of steep, rocky mountains, almost entirely surrounded by turquoise-blue seas. The ancient Greeks lived on farms or in small villages scattered throughout the country. These farms and villages were isolated, or separated, from one another by the high mountains.

In this chapter, you will explore how Greece's **geography** influenced the way the ancient Greeks lived. You will learn why they lived and farmed in **isolated communities**. You will also discover how they used the sea to establish **colonies** and **trade** with people from other lands.

Use this graphic organizer to help you remember the map of Greece and to understand how travel, farming, colonization, and trade affected life in ancient Greece.

25.2 Isolated Communities and the Difficulties of Travel

In ancient Greece, communities were isolated from one another because of the high mountains. It was hard to travel over the mountains, so there was little communication between people in different settlements.

Communities in Ancient Greece, About 340 B.C.E.

Travel by land was especially difficult. People walked, or rode in carts pulled by oxen or mules. Roads were unpaved. Sharp rocks frequently shattered wooden wheels, and wagons could become stuck in mud. Only the wealthy could afford to ride horses.

Travelers could stop at inns on the main roads, but many inns provided only shelter. People had to bring their own food and other supplies with them. Slaves or pack animals carried bedding, food, and other necessities. With all these things to carry, the Greeks had to travel in groups that moved more slowly than someone traveling alone. And there was always the danger of being attacked by bandits.

Traveling by boat was easier, but it was still uncomfortable and dangerous. Travelers might be attacked by pirates or robbed by dishonest sailors. The greatest danger was from the sea itself. Sudden storms sometimes drove ships off course or sent them smashing into the rocky shoreline. Even in open waters, ships could sink.

The Greeks treated the sea with great respect. Whenever possible, sailors kept their ships close to shore. They sailed only during daylight and stopped each night to anchor. And a wise captain always made a sacrifice to the sea god Poseidon before sailing.

This ancient Greek vase shows women gathering fruit.

25.3 Farming in Ancient Greece

Most people in ancient Greece survived by farming. But farming wasn't easy in that mountainous land. Even in the plains and valleys, the land was rocky and water was scarce. No major rivers flow through Greece, and it rains mostly during the winter months.

With so little flat land available, Greek farmers had to think of the best ways to use the land they had. Some farmers built wide earth steps into the hills to create more flat land for planting. A few farmers were able to grow wheat and barley, but most grew crops that needed less land, especially grapes and olives. Greek farmers produced a lot of olive oil, which was used for cooking, soap, and fuel for lamps.

Ancient Greek farmers grew food for their own families. In addition to small vegetable gardens, many farmers planted hill-side orchards of fruit and nut trees. Some Greek families kept bees to make honey. Honey was the best known sweetener in the ancient world.

Greek farmers also raised animals. Instead of cattle, which need lots of flat land for grazing, they raised sheep and goats, which can graze on the sides of mountains. Sheep supplied wool for clothing, while goats provided milk and cheese. Farmers kept a few oxen, mules, and donkeys for plowing and transportation. Many Greek families also kept pigs and chickens.

The shortage of good farmland sometimes led to wars between Greek settlements, with each one claiming land for itself. As you will see, some settlements were also forced to look beyond the mainland for new sources of food and other goods.

25.4 Starting Colonies

As the populations of Greek communities grew, some communities did not have enough farmland to feed their people. One solution to this problem was to start colonies. *Colonies* are settlements in distant places. Many Greek communities sent people over the sea, hoping they could grow food in new lands and send it home. These people were called **colonists**.

Colonists had many preparations to make before starting their journey. Often they began by asking the Greek gods if their efforts would be successful. To do this, they consulted an oracle. An *oracle* was a holy person whom they believed could communicate with the gods.

Next, the colonists gathered food and supplies. They made sure to take a flame from their town's sacred fire so they could start a sacred fire in their new home.

Starting a colony wasn't easy. First, there was a long sea voyage to survive. Then settlers had to find a place for their colony. They looked for areas that had natural harbors and good farmland. They also tried to avoid places where the local people might be strong enough to prevent them from settling. Finally, they had to establish their new community and work hard to make it survive.

The Greeks established colonies over a period of more than 300 years, from 1000 to 650 B.C.E. The first group of settlers created a colony called Ionia in Asia Minor, in what is today Turkey. Later, Greeks started colonies in Spain, France, Italy, and Africa, and along the coast of the Black Sea.

The colonies helped to spread Greek culture. Some of the colonies became quite wealthy through farming and trade. Colonists continued to enjoy the rights of citizens back home, including the right to participate in Greek athletic games.

colonist a person who lives in a colony

Routes Used by Ancient Greek Traders, About 500 B.C.E.

From BRITAIN

From SPAIN

0   250   500 miles
0   250   500 kilometers

Greek settlements
Import route to Greece

TYRAS
Black Sea

ITALY

SARDIS

MILETUS

CARTHAGE

CRETE
Mediterranean Sea

CYPRUS

From PERSIA

CYRENE

EGYPT

Copper   Oil
Gold   Pottery
Grain   Silver
Hides   Timber
Iron   Wool

N
W   E
S

25.5 Trading for Needed Goods

Besides starting new colonies, many Greek settlements on the mainland used trade to get goods they needed. Some settlements had enough farmland to take care of their own needs, so they traded very little. But others relied on trade because they had too little land to grow everything they required.

The Greeks traded among the city-states, with Greek colonies, and in the wider Mediterranean region. Olive oil, pottery, and wine from the mainland were traded for such goods as grain, timber, and metal.

Most goods traveled on ships owned by **merchants**. Merchant ships were built of wood, with large rectangular cloth sails. Merchants built their ships for space to hold goods rather than for speed. Because ships traveled about three to five miles per hour, journeys were long. A one-way trip from the mainland could take two months.

Navigating the ships was difficult. The Greeks had no compasses or charts. They had only the stars to guide them. The stars could tell sailors where they were, but they could not tell them what hazards lay nearby. No lighthouses warned sailors of dangerous coastlines.

In spite of these dangers, adventurous sailors carried more and more goods, and trade flourished along the Mediterranean coast.

merchant a person who makes money by selling goods

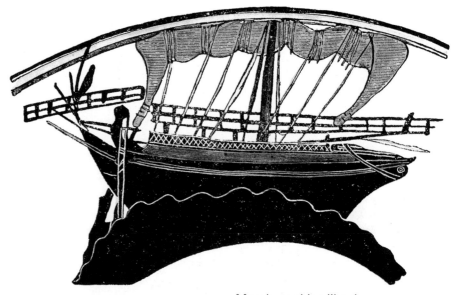

Merchant ships like the one shown here sailed the Mediterranean Sea around 500 B.C.E.

25.6 Chapter Summary

In this chapter, you learned how the Greeks settled in isolated communities because of their country's mountainous geography. Most Greeks survived by farming, but good farmland was scarce. So the Greeks took to the seas, creating new colonies and trading with other peoples.

In the next chapter, you will see how the isolated communities of ancient Greece developed their own customs, including different forms of government.

CHAPTER 26

One typical Greek city-state, Olympia, was built among wooded hills.

The Rise of Democracy

26.1 Introduction

In Chapter 25, you learned how the steep mountains of Greece led people to settle in isolated communities. Because settlements were separated from each other, they developed in different ways. One important difference was how they governed themselves. In this chapter, you will learn how ancient Greek communities tried different forms of government.

The ancient Greeks knew they had many things in common. For example, they all spoke the same language. But they did not think of themselves as one country. Instead, every Greek identified with a hometown that he or she called "the city." The city included both a settlement and its surrounding farmland.

Most Greeks were fiercely proud of their cities. Each city had its own laws, its own army, and its own money. Most important, each city had its own form of government. For this reason, ancient Greek cities are called **city-states**.

In this chapter, you will explore the four forms of government that developed in the Greek city-states: **monarchy, oligarchy, tyranny,** and **democracy**. You'll discover why unhappiness with one form of rule led the Greeks to try another.

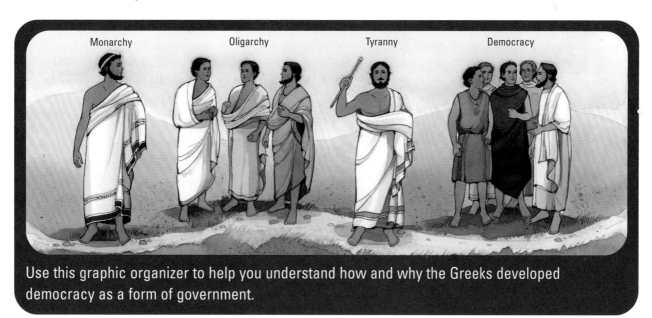

Monarchy   Oligarchy   Tyranny   Democracy

Use this graphic organizer to help you understand how and why the Greeks developed democracy as a form of government.

monarch a single ruler, such
as a king, queen, or emperor,
who holds all the power in a
country or empire

26.2 Monarchy: One Person Inherits Power

aristocrat a member of the
most powerful class in ancient
Greek society

From about 2000 to 800 B.C.E., most Greek city-states were ruled by a monarch, or king. In a monarchy, the ruling power is in the hands of one person, usually a king. Greek settlements did not have queens.

At first, Greek kings were chosen by the people of a city-state. When the king died, another leader was selected to take his place. Eventually, though, kings demanded that their power go to their children after their death, usually their oldest son. In a monarchy, then, rulers inherit their power.

The kings of ancient Greece had many powers. They made laws and acted as judges. They conducted religious ceremonies. They even led the army during wars. They used armed soldiers to punish people who disobeyed the laws or didn't pay their taxes.

Agesilaus II was king of the city-state of Sparta.

Kings had councils of aristocrats to advise them. The word *aristocrat* is formed from a Greek word that means "best." To the Greeks, the "best" people were wealthy men who had inherited large pieces of land.

At first, councils of aristocrats had no real power. But kings depended upon aristocrats for help during wars, since only the wealthy could afford horses and armor. The aristocrats soon realized that, as a group, they were stronger than the king. They wanted a share in the king's power.

In some city-states, aristocrats insisted that the king should be elected instead of inheriting his crown. Then they said the king could rule only for a certain number of years. Eventually, aristocrats in most city-states overthrew the monarchy and took the power for themselves. By 800 B.C.E., kings no longer ruled most Greek city-states.

26.3 Oligarchy: A Few People Share Power

By 800 B.C.E., most Greek city-states were ruled by a small group of wealthy men. These men were called **oligarchs,** from a Greek word that means "few." In an oligarchy, the ruling power is in the hands of a few people.

Most Greek oligarchs were aristocrats, men who had inherited land from their families. A few were wealthy merchants.

Compared to the poor, oligarchs had very comfortable lives. They spent their days hunting and taking part in chariot races. In the evenings, they lay on couches and drank wine. They had parties where slaves and hired professionals entertained guests with music, dance, and acrobatics.

Meanwhile, the poor had to work all day in the fields. The hardworking poor saw the difference between their lives and the easy lives of the wealthy, and they thought it was very unfair.

To make matters worse, the oligarchs ignored the needs of most of the people. They passed laws that the poor did not like, and they used the army to force people to obey them. Many of their laws protected and increased their own wealth. In some city-states, oligarchs passed laws forcing farmers to sell themselves into slavery if they could not pay their debts.

Under the oligarchs, the rich became richer and the poor became poorer. Many people who weren't wealthy came to hate the oligarchs. Eventually, the poor turned to leaders who promised to improve their lives. These leaders were usually in the army. Backed by the people, they used their soldiers to throw the oligarchs out of power.

> **oligarch** one of several people who rule a country or empire together, sharing the power

This ancient Greek vase shows scenes of boar hunting and chariot racing. These activities were favorite pastimes of ancient Greek aristocrats.

26.4 Tyranny: One Person Takes Power by Force

During the mid 600s B.C.E., people in many Greek city-states turned to men who promised to change the government. The men who forced the oligarchs from power were called **tyrants**. In a tyranny, the ruling power is in the hands of one person who is not a lawful king.

A tyranny is different from a monarchy in two ways. First, a tyrant cannot claim that he has a legal right to rule. Second, a tyrant's son does not usually inherit his father's power.

Tyrants usually took and kept control by force. But that doesn't mean they were always unpopular. Most Greek tyrants were military leaders who gained the support of the people by promising them more rights. And once they were in control, many Greek tyrants ruled well. They made changes that helped the poor. Some canceled the debts of poor farmers. Others were hostile to aristocrats and may have taken away their land.

Other tyrants, though, did not use their power to help the people. Hippias, the last tyrant in the city-state of Athens, is one example. Along with his brother, Hipparchus, Hippias ruled well at first. Then two enemies of the brothers murdered Hipparchus. After that, Hippias ruled more harshly.

tyrant a person who seizes power illegally

Most tyrants were forced out of power by the people. The artwork on this vase shows the killing of the Greek tyrant Hipparchus.

He paid spies to report anyone who criticized him. As his rule became more and more unbearable, he was finally forced to leave power. Soon Athens would try another form of government, one that shared power among all citizens.

26.5 Democracy: All Citizens Share Power

Around 500 B.C.E., the people of Athens decided to try governing themselves. They developed democracy, or "rule by the people." In a democracy, all **citizens** share in the ruling power.

Ancient Greek democracy was different from democracy today. The government of Athens was a *direct democracy*. In this type of government, every citizen can vote on every issue. Unlike Athens, the United States is a *representative democracy*. In this type of government, people vote for representatives who decide issues in their name.

How did direct democracy work in Athens? The city had an **assembly,** or lawmaking group. Any free man could speak in the Assembly and vote on a new law or a proposal to go to war. Free men also ran the city's day-to-day business.

The painting on this piece of pottery shows Greek citizens casting votes in an election.

Not all Greeks believed that democracy was a good type of government. Powerful speakers sometimes persuaded ordinary citizens to vote unwisely. Often, the assembly reversed important decisions after just a few weeks. Because of problems like these, most city-states returned to earlier forms of government, such as dictatorships and oligarchies.

But the idea that people should rule themselves would survive. In time, the ideal of democracy would become one of the great gifts of ancient Greece to the modern world.

26.6 Chapter Summary

In this chapter, you read how the city-states of ancient Greece developed four very different forms of government. Early monarchies gave way to oligarchies. In turn, many oligarchies were replaced by tyrannies. Finally, Athens developed democracy.

The next chapter compares Athens with its great rival, Sparta. Unlike Athens, Sparta remained an oligarchy. You'll see how two different forms of government led to two very different ways of life.

CHAPTER 27

◄ ◄ ◄ The city-states of Sparta (above)
and Athens (below) were bitter rivals.

Life in Two City-States: Athens and Sparta

27.1 Introduction

In Chapter 26, you learned that ancient Greece was a collection of city-states, each with its own government. In this chapter, you will learn about two of the most important Greek city-states, Athens and Sparta. They not only had different forms of government, but very different ways of life.

Athens was a walled city near the sea. Nearby, ships came and went from a busy port. Inside the city walls, master potters and sculptors labored in workshops. Wealthy people and their slaves strolled through the marketplace. Often the city's citizens (free men) gathered to loudly debate the issues of the day.

Sparta was located in a farming area on a plain. No walls surrounded the city. Its buildings were simple and plain compared to those of Athens. Even the clothing of the people in the streets was drab. Columns of soldiers tramped through the streets, with fierce expressions behind their bronze helmets.

Even a casual visitor could see that Athens and Sparta were very different. Let's take a closer look at the way people lived in these two city-states. We'll examine each city's **government, economy, education,** and treatment of women and slaves.

Use this graphic organizer to help you compare various aspects of life in Athens and Sparta.

27.2 Comparing Two City-States

Athens and Sparta were both Greek cities, and they were only about 150 miles apart. Yet they were as different as they could be. Why?

Part of the answer is geography. Athens is in central Greece, only four miles from the Aegean Sea. Its location encouraged Athenians to look outward toward the world beyond the city. Athenians liked to travel. They were eager to spread their own ideas and to learn from others. They encouraged artists from other parts of Greece to come and share their knowledge of art and architecture. Athens developed strong relationships with other city-states, and it grew large and powerful through trade. A great fleet made it the leading naval power in Greece.

In contrast, Sparta was more isolated. It was located on a plain between the mountains and the sea in the part of Greece known as the **Peloponnesus**. Spartans were suspicious of outsiders and their ideas. They grew much of what they needed in the fertile soil around Sparta. What they couldn't grow, they often took from their neighbors through the power of their armies. While Athenians boasted of their art and culture, Spartans valued strength and simplicity. They taught their sons and daughters to fight, and they produced soldiers rather than artists and thinkers.

For most of their histories, the two city-states were bitter rivals. As you will see, their differences were reflected in every part of life.

Athens and Sparta, About 500 B.C.E.

Map showing Athens and Sparta, About 500 B.C.E. Locations include: Mt. Olympus, Thessaly, Iolcus, Delphi, Thebes, Ithaca, Achaea, Athens, Corinth, Attica, Mycenae, Argos, Olympia, Tiryns, Troezen, Arcadia, Peloponnesus, Sparta, Aegean Sea, Crete, Mediterranean Sea. Inset maps of Athens (Agora, Marble Shop, Acropolis, Parthenon, Theater of Dionysus) and Sparta (Temple of Athene Chalkioikos, Acropolis, Theater, Portico, Agora, Sanctuary of Artemis Orthia, Altar of Lykouros, Heroon, Temple).

27.3 Athenian Government

As you learned in the last chapter, Athens became a democracy around 500 B.C.E. But unlike modern democracies, Athens allowed only free men to be citizens. All men over the age of 18 who were born in Athens were Athenian citizens. Women and slaves were not citizens.

Every citizen could take part in the city's government. A group called the Council of 500 met every day. Each year, the names of all citizens 30 years of age or older were collected, and 500 of those names were chosen. The council ran the day-to-day business of government and suggested new laws.

Proposed laws had to be approved by a much larger group, the Assembly. The Assembly met on a hill every 10 days. At least 6,000 citizens had to be present for a meeting to take place. If not enough people showed up, slaves would round up more citizens with ropes dipped in red paint. Men were embarrassed to appear at the meeting with their clothes stained with red marks.

The Assembly debated and voted on laws proposed by the council. Every citizen

Desmosthenes, an Athenian leader, speaks to the Assembly.

had the right to speak at Assembly meetings. Some speakers were more skilled than others. Some spoke longer than others. Sometimes a water clock was used to time the speaker. One cup of water was set above another. The first cup had a small hole drilled into the bottom. The speaker could talk only until all the water ran out of the top cup and into the bottom cup.

Most Athenian men enjoyed taking part in the city's democracy. They liked to gather and debate the issues. They were proud of their freedom as Athenian citizens.

agora a marketplace in
ancient Greece

27.4 Athenian Economy

An important part of life in any community is its economy. An *economy* is the way a community or region organizes the manufacture and exchange of money, food, products, and services.

The Athenian economy was based on trade. The land around Athens did not provide enough food for all the city's people. But Athens was near the sea, and it had a good harbor. So Athenians traded with other city-states and some foreign lands to get the goods and natural resources they needed. They acquired wood from Italy and grain from Egypt. In exchange, Athenians traded honey, olive oil, silver, and beautifully painted pottery.

Athenians bought and sold goods at a huge marketplace called

Athenians shopped for food and household goods in the agora. On this vase, a shopper is shown inspecting a piece of pottery.

the **agora**. There, merchants sold their goods from small stands. People bought lettuce, onions, olive oil, wine, and other foods. They could also buy household items like pottery, furniture, and clay oil lamps. Most Athenians made their clothes at home, but leather sandals and jewelry were popular items at the market. In addition, Athenians bought and sold slaves at the agora.

Like most city-states, Athens developed its own coins to make trade easier. Coins were made of such metals as gold, silver, and bronze. Athenians decorated the flat sides of their coins. One of their coins had an image of the goddess Athena on one side. The other side pictured Athena's favorite bird, the owl.

27.5 Education in Athens

Athenian democracy depended on having good citizens. Athenians believed that producing good citizens was the main purpose of education. Since only boys grew up to be citizens, boys and girls were educated quite differently.

Athenians believed that a good citizen had a sharp mind and a healthy body. So education meant physical training as well as book learning. Until age 6 or 7, boys were taught at home by their mothers or male slaves. From age 6 to 14, boys went to school. Teachers taught reading, writing, arithmetic, and literature. Books were rare and very expensive, so subjects were read out loud and the boys had to memorize everything. To help them learn, they used writing tablets. Coaches taught sports such as wrestling and gymnastics to strengthen students' muscles. Boys also studied music. They learned to sing and to play the lyre.

At 18, Athenian men began their military training. After their service, wealthy young men might study with private teachers. These teachers charged high fees for lessons in debate and public speaking that would help young men become political leaders.

Unlike boys, most girls did not learn to read or write. Girls grew up helping their mothers around the house. They were taught to cook, clean, spin thread, and weave cloth. Some also learned ancient secret songs and dances for religious festivals. Girls usually married around the age of 15. Those from wealthy families married men chosen by their fathers. Girls from poor families often had more choice.

Athenian boys learned poetry and music as well as reading and writing. The stringed instrument near the top of this ancient Greek painting is a lyre.

The women of Athens had their greatest influence in the home.

27.6 Women and Slaves in Athens

As you have already learned, only men were considered citizens in Athens. Women and slaves were not. As a result, they had far fewer rights than free men did.

Athenian women could not inherit or own much property. They could not vote or attend the Assembly. Most could not even choose their own husbands.

priestess a female priest

A few women had jobs. Some women sold goods in the market. A few very important women were **priestesses**. But most Athenian women had their greatest influence in the home. They spent their days managing the household and bringing up their children. An Athenian wife had separate rooms at home and never went out alone. She would spin, weave, and supervise the slaves. She educated her sons until they were 6 or 7 and ready for school. She taught her daughters until they were 15 and ready to be married.

There were many slaves in ancient Athens. Most people who weren't poor owned at least one slave. Some slaves were born into slavery. Others became slaves when they were captured in wars.

Slaves performed a wide variety of jobs in Athens, including tasks that required a great deal of skill. Some slaves ran households and tutored Athenian children. A number of slaves were trained as craftsmen. Others worked in farms or factories. Some slaves worked for the city as clerks.

The unluckiest slaves worked in the silver mines. They might work 10 hours a day in cramped tunnels 300 feet below the surface. They had little air to breathe and were often whipped if they stopped to rest.

Some Athenian slaves labored in silver mines.

27.7 Spartan Government

Sparta was different from Athens in almost every way, beginning with its government. While Athens was a democracy, Sparta was an oligarchy. As you learned in Chapter 26, in an oligarchy the ruling power is in the hands of a few people. Like Athens, Sparta had an assembly. But the important decisions were really made by a much smaller group called the Council of Elders.

The Council of Elders consisted of two kings and 28 other men. The two kings inherited their position and shared equal powers. The other 28 members of the council were elected by the Assembly.

To be elected to the Council of Elders, men had to be at least 60 years old and from a noble family. Some scholars believe that Assembly members shouted for the man they wanted most. The candidates who received the loudest support were elected. Once they were elected, they served for life.

The Council of Elders held the real power in Sparta. It prepared laws for the Assembly to vote on, and it had the power to stop any laws passed by the Assembly that the council members didn't like.

The Assembly in Sparta was made up of male citizens. Because the Assembly was large, it met in a large outdoor area away from the center of the city. The Assembly had very little power. Unlike the Assembly in Athens, it did not debate issues. Members of the Assembly could only vote yes or no on laws suggested by the Council of Elders.

The agora in Sparta was a place where people could gather. Spartan men often debated government issues there.

Sparta's economy depended more on farming, as shown in this cup from ancient Greece, than on trade.

27.8 Spartan Economy

While the Athenian economy depended on trade, Sparta's economy relied on farming and on conquering other people. Sparta didn't have enough land to feed all its people, so Spartans took the land they needed from their neighbors. Because Spartan men spent their lives as warriors, Sparta used slaves and noncitizens to produce needed goods.

The Spartans turned the neighbors they conquered into slaves, called *helots*. The helots continued to live in their own villages, but they had to give much of the food they grew to the Spartan citizens.

The Spartans also made use of noncitizens, called *perioikoi*. Perioikoi were free men, not slaves. They might serve in the army when needed, but they could not take part in Sparta's government. The perioikoi made such necessary items as shoes, red cloaks for the soldiers, iron tools like knives and spears, and pottery. They also conducted some trade with other city-states for goods that Sparta could not provide for itself.

In general, though, Sparta discouraged trade. The Spartans feared that contact with other city-states would lead to new ideas and weaken their government. Trading with Sparta was also difficult because of its system of money. Sparta didn't have coins. Instead, it used heavy iron bars as money. Legend says that an ancient Spartan leader decided to use iron as money to make it hard to steal. A thief would need a wagon to carry enough iron bars to be valuable. As you can imagine, other city-states were not anxious to receive iron as payment for goods.

These iron rods were used as money in Sparta.

Boys in Sparta often exercised in outdoor areas.

27.9 Education in Sparta

In Sparta, the purpose of education was to produce men and women who could protect the city-state. If a baby did not appear healthy and strong, it might be left to die on a hillside.

Spartans valued discipline and strength. From the age of 7, all Spartan children were trained to fight. Even girls received some military training. They learned wrestling, boxing, footracing, and gymnastics. Spartan boys lived and trained in buildings called *barracks*. They were taught to read and write, but Spartans did not consider those skills as important.

What was important was to be a brave soldier. Spartan boys were taught to suffer any amount of physical pain without complaining. They marched without shoes. They were not fed well, and they were encouraged to steal food as long as they did not get caught. One Spartan legend tells of a boy who stole a fox because he was starving. When he saw his teacher coming, the boy quickly hid the fox under his cloak. Rather than confess, he let the fox bite his stomach.

At the age of 20 or so, Spartan men were given a difficult test of fitness, military ability, and leadership skills. If they passed, they became Spartan soldiers and full citizens. Even then, they continued to live in soldiers' barracks, where they ate, slept, and trained with their classmates. A man could not live at home with his wife and family until he was 30 years old. And his military service continued long after that.

27.10 Women and Slaves in Sparta

Unlike women in Athens, Spartan women could speak with men in public.

Spartan women lived the same simple life as Spartan men. They wore plain clothing with little decoration. They did not wear jewelry or use cosmetics or perfume. Like Spartan men, women were expected to be strong and healthy—and ready to fight. A woman was expected to look after her husband's property in times of war. She also had to guard it against invaders and revolts from slaves.

Spartan women had many rights that other Greek women did not have. They were free to speak with their husbands' friends. They could own and control their own property. They could even marry another man if their first husband had been away at war too long.

Spartan slaves, the helots, were people who had been conquered by the Spartans. There were many more helots than citizens in Sparta. The Spartans were afraid the helots would revolt, so they treated them very harshly.

The government sometimes declared war on the helots so that it could legally kill any slaves it thought might rebel. Once the Spartan government asked the helots to choose their best fighters. The Spartans said these men would be set free as thanks for fighting for Sparta. Two thousand helots were chosen. Immediately, the Spartans killed every one of them to eliminate any future helot leaders.

Despite this treatment, helots actually had some rights. They could marry whomever and whenever they wanted. They could pass their names on to their children. They could sell any extra crops they had after giving their master his share. If they saved enough money, they could even buy their freedom.

An architect shows the Athenian leader Pericles plans for the building of the Parthenon, a temple in Athens.

This statue is of a Spartan warrior.

27.11 Chapter Summary

In this chapter, you learned about Athens and Sparta, two very different city-states in ancient Greece. Athens was a democracy, though only free men could take part in its government. Its economy depended on trade. Boys were educated to be good citizens. Girls learned skills for managing the household. Women and slaves had far fewer rights than men had.

Sparta was more isolated than Athens. It was primarily a military state. Its government was an oligarchy in which a few men held most of the power. The Spartan economy depended on farming and conquest. Boys and girls alike were educated to protect the city-state. Spartan women had more rights than other Greek women. The city depended on slaves and other noncitizens to provide for many of its needs.

Athens and Sparta were bitter rivals. But in the next chapter, you'll see how they came together with other Greek city-states to fight a terrible threat to their freedom and independence.

This painted pottery bowl portrays the defeat of a Persian soldier by a Greek soldier.

Fighting the Persian Wars

28.1 Introduction

In Chapter 27, you learned about two very different city-states, Athens and Sparta. Sometimes their differences led these city-states to distrust each other. But between 499 and 479 B.C.E., they had a common enemy—the **Persian Empire**.

At the time, Persia was the largest empire the world had ever seen. Its powerful kings ruled over land in Africa, the Middle East, and Asia. During the 400s B.C.E., the Persians invaded Greece, and the **Persian wars** began.

To fight the Persians, the Greek city-states eventually banded together as allies. **Allies** are states that agree to help each other against a common enemy.

Throughout history, soldiers have written home before battle. We can image the kind of letter an Athenian might have written to his family. "The Persians are fierce fighters. But I will stand shoulder to shoulder with the brave men of Greece—Spartans as well as fellow Athenians—and fight to the death, if that is what it takes to stop these murderous invaders."

The tiny Greek city-states had much less land and far fewer people than Persia. How could they possibly turn back the powerful invaders? In this chapter, you will learn about important battles during the Persian wars and discover who won them.

Persian soldier

Greek soldier

Use this graphic organizer to help you understand how the Greek city-states banded together to fight the powerful Persian Empire.

28.2 The Persian Empire and the Ionian Revolt

The Persians started out as a small tribe in present-day Iran. They built a large empire by conquering their neighbors. Persian archers won many battles by unleashing a storm of arrows before their enemies were close enough to use their lances, or spears.

At its height, the Persian Empire was the largest empire the world had ever known. It was ruled by powerful kings who conquered Mesopotamia, Asia Minor, Syria, Egypt, and parts of India and Europe.

To rule such a large area, King Darius, one of the greatest of the Persian kings, divided the empire into 20 provinces known as satrapies. He established a tax-collection system and appointed officials to rule local areas. But he allowed conquered people to keep their own customs and religions.

The Ionian Revolt, which began in 499 B.C.E., marked the beginning of the Greek-Persian wars. In 546 B.C.E., the Persians had conquered the wealthy Greek settlements in Ionia, in Asia Minor. The Persians took the Ionians' farmland and harbors. They forced the Ionians to pay tributes, or the regular payments of goods. The Ionians also had to serve in the Persian army.

The Ionians knew they could not defeat the Persians by themselves, so they asked mainland

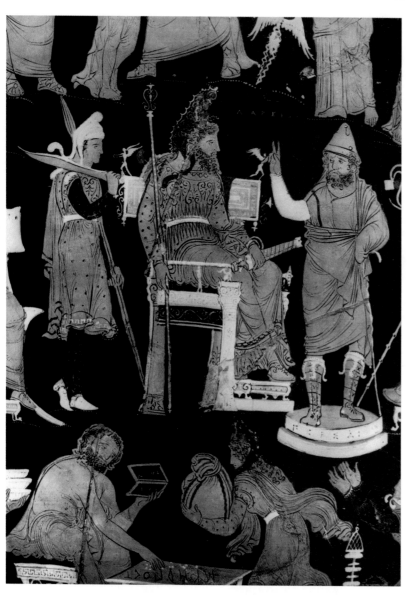

King Darius of Persia holding a council of war.

Greece for help. Athens sent soldiers and a small fleet of ships. Unfortunately for the Ionians, the Athenians went home after their initial success, leaving the small Ionian army to fight alone.

In 493 B.C.E., the Persian army defeated the Ionians. To punish the Ionians for rebelling, the Persians destroyed the city of Miletus. They may have sold some of its people into slavery.

28.3 The Battle of Marathon: A Stunning Victory

After the Ionian Revolt, King Darius decided to conquer the city-states of mainland Greece. He sent messengers to ask for presents of Greek earth and water. The presents would be a sign that the Greeks agreed to accept Persian rule. But the Greeks refused to hand over the tribute. Instead, they threw the messengers into pits and wells. Legend has it that they shouted, "If you want Greek earth and water, help yourselves!"

Darius was furious. In 490 B.C.E., he sent a large army of foot soldiers and **cavalry** across the Aegean Sea by boat to Greece. The army assembled on the plain of Marathon. (See the map on page 277.)

The Battle of Marathon was the first of many battles between the Greeks and Persians.

A brilliant general named Miltiades convinced the other Greek commanders to fight the Persians at Marathon. Desperate for help, the Athenians sent a runner named Pheidippides to Sparta. Pheidippides ran for two days and two nights. When he arrived, he found the Spartans celebrating a religious festival. They told him that they could not leave Sparta until the next full moon.

The Athenians and their allies had to face the Persians alone. Miltiades stretched his men across a narrow valley. For several days, both sides hesitated to attack.

Finally, Miltiades decided to attack. He ordered the center portion of his army to advance. When the Persians came forward to meet them, he then ordered the left and right sides of his army to sweep down and attack the Persians from the sides as well.

Soon the Persian soldiers were running for their ships. Then the Greeks marched back to Athens in time to defend the city against the Persian cavalry.

The Greeks had won a stunning victory. But their fight with the Persians was only beginning.

Hellespont the long, narrow body of water between Europe and Asia in present-day Turkey

The Persians were delayed by the fierce fighting in the narrow pass at Thermopylae.

28.4 The Battle of Thermopylae: The Bravery of the 300

After King Darius died, his son, King Xerxes, organized another attack on Greece. Xerxes put together a huge army of more than 180,000 soldiers. To get his army to Greece, Xerxes chose to cross the **Hellespont,** a narrow sea channel between Europe and Asia. There he made two bridges by roping hundreds of boats together, with wooden boards across their bows. Then he walked his army across the channel into Europe. (See the map on page 277.)

In 480 B.C.E., Xerxes marched west from the Hellespont and then south. Several Greek city-states were overwhelmed. Athens and Sparta decided to work together to fight the enemy. The Athenian navy would try to stop the Persian navy. Meanwhile, the Spartan king, Leonidas, would try to stop the Persian army.

The Spartans chose to make their stand at a place called Thermopylae, where the Persian army would have to go through a narrow pass between the mountains and the sea. Leonidas had only 6,000 to 7,000 soldiers to stop 180,000 Persians. Still, when the Persians tried to get through the pass, the Greeks drove them back. Then a Greek traitor offered to show the Persians a secret path through the mountains. The path would allow them to attack the Greeks from the front and the rear at the same time.

Leonidas knew that he could only delay the Persians. To keep his army from being destroyed, he ordered most of his troops to escape. With a much smaller army, including 300 Spartans, he prepared to fight.

The Spartans were obedient to the end. Legend says they fought until their weapons broke. Then they fought with their hands. In the end, all 300 were killed. But the Greeks would never forget their bravery.

28.5 The Battle of Salamis: The Navy to the Rescue

When news of the slaughter at Thermopylae reached Athens, its citizens panicked. They boarded ships and sailed for nearby islands. They left in such a hurry that they had to leave their pets behind. Legend has it that one loyal dog swam alongside a ship, following its master all the way to shore, where it died.

Only a small army was left to defend the city. Within two weeks, Xerxes had burned Athens to the ground.

An Athenian navy leader, Themistocles, thought he knew a way to defeat the Persians. He wanted to fight their navy in the narrow channels between the islands and the mainland. The Persians would find it hard to move their ships around to attack the Greek navy.

For his plan to work, Themistocles had to get the Persian ships into a channel near a place called Salamis. So he set a trap. He sent a loyal slave to Xerxes' camp with a message. The message said that Themistocles wanted to change sides and join the Persians. If Xerxes attacked now, it said, half the Greek sailors would surrender.

Xerxes fell for the trick. He ordered his ships to enter the narrow waterway between Salamis and the mainland to attack.

As the Persians approached, the Greek ships seemed to retreat. But this was just another trick to draw the Persians farther into the channel. Soon the Greeks had them surrounded. The Greek ships had wooden rams at the front. They rammed into the Persian boats, crushing their hulls and sending 300 of the ships to the bottom of the sea. The Greeks lost only 40 ships. Once again, the Greeks had beaten the mighty Persian Empire.

At the Battle of Salamis, the Greeks tricked the Persians into entering a narrow channel, where the Greeks rammed the Persian ships.

The Spartans led the fight against the Persians in a fierce battle outside the city of Plataea.

28.6 The Battle of Plataea: The End of the Persian Wars

After the defeat at Salamis, Xerxes fled with some of his soldiers. He was afraid the Greeks would get to the Hellespont first and destroy the bridges he had built. As it turned out, the bridges had already been wrecked by a fierce storm. Xerxes had to ferry his men across the water by boat.

Xerxes left the rest of his army in Greece with orders to attack again in the spring. When spring arrived, the Persians approached Athens once more. The Spartans feared that the Athenians, with their city destroyed, would agree to make peace with Persia. But the Athenians proudly declared their "common brotherhood with the Greeks." They would fight.

The decisive battle took place outside the town of Plataea in 479 B.C.E. Led by the Spartans, a force of 80,000 Greek troops destroyed the Persian army. The threat from the Persian Empire was finally over.

This important victory preserved the Greeks' independence and kept Persia from conquering all of Europe. The Greeks paid a high price for their victory. Thousands of Greeks were dead, and the city of Athens was in ruins. But the Athenians would soon rebuild their city and raise it to even greater glory.

28.7 Chapter Summary

In this chapter, you learned how Athens and Sparta joined forces to defeat the Persian Empire. The Persian wars began with the Ionian Revolt and ended 20 years later with the Greek victory at the Battle of Plataea.

After the wars, Athens would become the center of Greek culture and expand its own empire. In the next chapter, you will tour the city at the height of its power and learn more about Greek culture.

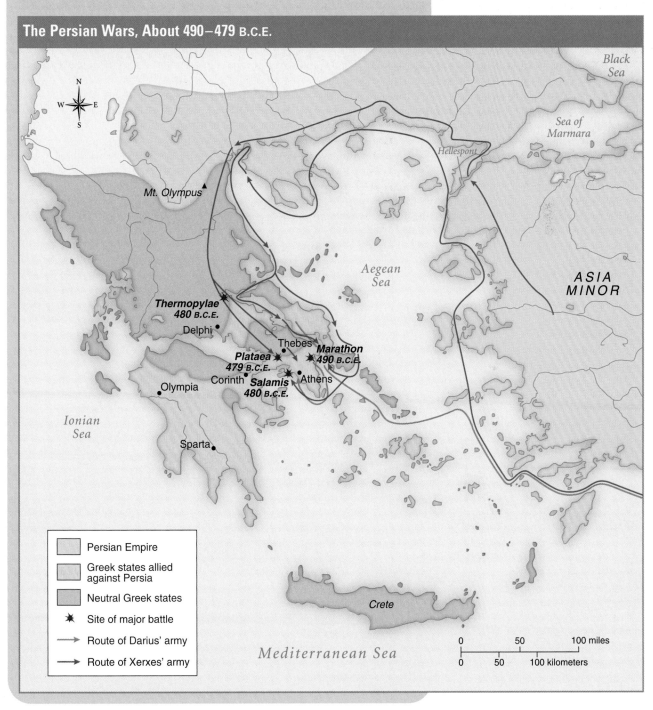

The Persian Wars, About 490–479 B.C.E.

Black Sea

Sea of Marmara

Hellespont

ASIA MINOR

Mt. Olympus

Aegean Sea

Thermopylae
480 B.C.E.

Delphi

Thebes

Marathon
490 B.C.E.

Plataea
479 B.C.E.

Corinth

Salamis
480 B.C.E.

Athens

Olympia

Ionian Sea

Sparta

Crete

Mediterranean Sea

Persian Empire

Greek states allied against Persia

Neutral Greek states

★ Site of major battle

→ Route of Darius' army

→ Route of Xerxes' army

0   50   100 miles
0   50   100 kilometers

CHAPTER 29

◀ ◀ ◀ Temples and statues crown the acropolis,
the hill above the city of Athens.

The Golden Age of Athens

29.1 Introduction

In Chapter 28, you read about how Athens and Sparta came together to defeat the Persian Empire. At the end of the Persian wars, Athens was in ruins. The Athenians were inspired to rebuild by a great leader named Pericles. Under his leadership, Athens entered a **golden age,** a period of great peace and wealth. Between 479 and 431 B.C.E., Athens was the artistic and cultural center of Greece.

Imagine that you could visit Athens during its Golden Age. Passing through the city's gates, you wind your way through narrow streets to the agora, the public meeting place in the center of the city. The agora is a great square. On two sides there are large, stately public buildings. The other two sides have covered walkways where people meet and talk with friends. In the center are market stalls with things to buy from all over Greece and beyond. A high, craggy hill known as the *acropolis* rises above the city, crowned with great temples.

In this chapter, you will explore several sites in ancient Athens. At each stop, you'll learn more about **Greek culture**. You'll find out about Greek religion, architecture, sculpture, drama, philosophy, and sports.

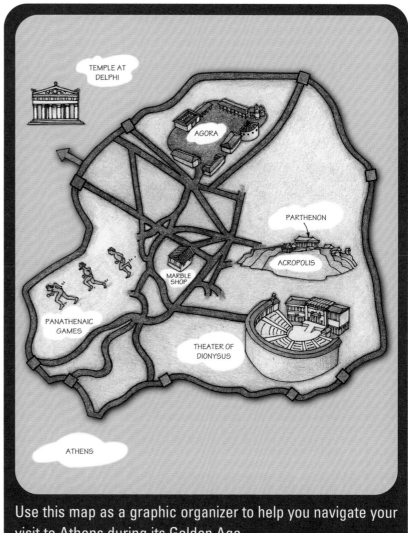

Use this map as a graphic organizer to help you navigate your visit to Athens during its Golden Age.

29.2 A City of Contrasts

acropolis the hill above a Greek city on which temples were built

Parthenon the temple honoring the goddess Athena, built on the acropolis above Athens

Ancient Athens was a city of great contrasts, or differences. People lived in small, uncomfortable houses that lined narrow streets. Yet the city's public spaces and buildings were large and stately.

Most homes in Athens were one story high and made of mud bricks. The homes of poor families were very simple. Wealthier people had larger houses with rooms built around a central courtyard. But even the homes of the rich were plain and often uncomfortable. Athenian houses had few windows, and they were lit by oil lamps. They were smoky and cold in the winter, and smoky and hot in the summer. The streets between the houses were narrow, crooked, and dirty. People threw their garbage into the streets, so neighborhoods often smelled bad.

It was the public spaces and buildings that were the pride of Athens. The Athenians built large government buildings around the agora. These buildings were made of stone. On the **acropolis,** the hill above the city, the Athenians built magnificent temples as earthly homes for their gods and goddesses.

The most famous temple standing on the acropolis was the **Parthenon**. It was built to honor the goddess Athena. As you remember from the last chapter, Athens was burned to the ground during the Persian wars. According to legend, when the Athenians returned to their city, even the sacred olive tree, a gift from Athena, had been burned and seemed to be dead. Then someone noticed a tiny leaf growing from the burnt trunk. The Athenians took this as a sign that Athena had not abandoned the city, and they decided to rebuild.

Athenians were proud of their city's public buildings and spaces.

29.3 Religion: The Temple at Delphi

The temples of Athens show how important religion was to the Greeks. The Greeks worshiped many gods and goddesses who, they believed, looked and often acted like humans but did not grow old or die.

Each god or goddess had power over a particular area of life. Sometimes the Greeks asked them for advice. For example, a famous temple in the town of Delphi was dedicated to the god Apollo. People could ask Apollo questions through a priestess who was called the oracle of Delphi. To answer a question, the priestess went into a trance. The words she spoke were thought to come from Apollo himself.

The Greeks told colorful stories about the gods, called **myths**. According to these stories, the home of the gods was Mount Olympus, a real mountain in Greece. Twelve of the gods and goddesses were particularly important. They are often called the Olympian gods.

The Olympian gods were part of the everyday life of the ancient Greeks. People asked the gods for help when setting out on journeys by land or sea. They dedicated festivals and sporting events to them. They decorated their temples with images of the gods.

The oracle of Delphi sat on a three-legged stool as she listened for the voice of the god Apollo.

The Olympian Gods and Goddesses

Zeus Ruler of the gods

Hera Wife of Zeus; goddess of marriage

Poseidon Brother of Zeus; god of the sea

Hestia Sister of Zeus; goddess of the hearth (the family fire)

Demeter Sister of Zeus; goddess of agriculture

Ares Son of Zeus; god of war

Athena Daughter of Zeus; goddess of wisdom and war

Apollo Son of Zeus; god of the sun, poetry, and music

Artemis Daughter of Zeus; goddess of the moon and the hunt

Hephaestus Son of Zeus; god of fire and metalworkers

Aphrodite Daughter of Zeus; goddess of love and beauty

Hermes Son of Zeus; messenger of the gods and god of travel

myth a traditional story that helps to explain a culture's beliefs

In this painting of the Parthenon, you can see the triangle-shaped pediment and the sculpted figures in the frieze.

29.4 Architecture: The Acropolis

Temples are good examples of the Greeks' talent for **architecture**. The Greeks built their temples as beautiful dwelling places for the gods and goddesses rather than as places to worship. Religious ceremonies were conducted outside.

The temples show the importance of balance and order in the Greeks' idea of beauty. Temples were built with rows of tall columns. The Greeks used three kinds of columns. The Doric column was the simplest. It had no base and got slimmer toward the top. The Ionic column was thinner. It sat on a base and had spirals carved into the top. The Corinthian column was the most complex, with carvings that looked like leaves at the top.

Athenians built three temples on the acropolis to honor Athena. One of these was the Parthenon. One of the most beautiful temples in Greece, the Parthenon was built on a long rectangular platform. There were 8 columns across both the front and back and 17 along each side. The roof slanted, creating triangles called *pediments* at the front and back of the building. At the top of the temple was a band of sculptures called a *frieze*. The sculptures themselves are called *metopes*.

Greek temples were many different sizes, but their basic shape was similar. Most had a main room with a statue of the temple's god or goddess. The Parthenon had a magnificent statue of Athena that stood 30 feet high. Made of wood, the statue was covered with ivory to look like flesh. Then it was dressed in clothes and decorated with gold. Like the temple itself, the statue expressed both the Greeks' love of beauty and their awe of the gods.

architecture the art of designing buildings

Greek buildings use three different styles of columns. Doric columns, the oldest style, have no base. Ionic columns are more graceful than Doric columns. Corinthian columns are the most decorative.

Doric   Ionic   Corinthian

29.5 Sculpture: A Marble Workshop

The statue of Athena in the Parthenon was a wonderful example of another important Greek art: **sculpture**. Sculptors in Athens often set up a workshop near the site where the finished statue would go. Sculptor apprentices first made a life-size clay model supported by wooden or metal frames. The general outline of the statue was then roughed out in marble. A master sculptor added details and finishing touches.

Greek statues were colorful. Metalworkers attached any bronze pieces that went with the statue, like spears and shields. Painters applied wax and bright colors to the statue's hair, lips, clothes, and headdress.

Creating lifelike statues was one of the great achievements of Greek sculptors. The earliest Greek statues had been influenced by Egyptian styles. Like the Egyptians, the Greeks created larger-than-life figures that faced front, with their arms held stiffly at their sides. Later Greek sculptors created much more realistic statues in natural poses with more detailed muscles, hair, and clothing.

One of the most famous sculptors in Athens was a man named Phidias. He designed the figures that line the top of the Parthenon. He also sculpted the statue of Athena that stood inside the temple. The statue carried a shield of gold, with carvings of two faces—those of the great Athenian leader Pericles and of Phidias himself.

Some people thought Phidias had gone too far by carving his own likeness on Athena's shield. Still, the Greeks greatly admired his marvelous statues. They said that Phidias was the one person who had seen the true image of the gods and revealed it to humans.

sculpture the art of creating three-dimensional figures from such materials as wood, stone, and clay

The sculptor Phidias created the huge statue of Athena that stood inside the Parthenon.

A Greek theater was shaped like a bowl, with seats that rose in a semicircle around the stage.

drama the art of writing, acting in, and producing plays

29.6 Drama: The Theater of Dionysus

In addition to architecture and sculpture, the ancient Greeks excelled in **drama,** the art of the theater. Going to the theater was a regular part of Athenian life. The Theater of Dionysus in the city could hold thousands of people.

Dionysus was the god of theater and wine. Greek plays grew out of the songs and dances that the Greeks performed at harvest time to honor him. As Greek playwrights developed their art, they began to write plays that told stories. The plays included a few main characters and a chorus. The chorus was a group of men who recited lines that commented on the actions of the characters. The words spoken by the chorus helped to explain and expand on the story.

There were no women actors in ancient Greece. Men played all the characters, both male and female. That was one reason actors wore masks. The masks also showed the audience whether a character was happy or sad.

Plays were staged in open-air theaters. The Greeks would build a theater into the side of a hill. The theater was shaped like a bowl so that everyone could hear what was said. The seats rose in a semicircle around a stage at the bottom of the bowl. Scenery was painted on canvas and hung behind the actors.

Plays were often part of competitions that could last for days. Judges chose winners in four categories: tragic playwrights, comic playwrights, leading tragic actor, and leading comic actor. The winning writers and actors were crowned with olive leaves and given prizes such as figs and wine.

29.7 Philosophy: The Agora

Like other Greeks, Athenians loved to talk and argue. In the sheltered spaces on the side of the agora, men gathered to discuss the world around them. They talked about nature, trading ideas about what the natural world was made of and how it worked. They also talked about things they couldn't see, such as the meaning of life, justice, truth, and beauty. They called this kind of thinking **philosophy,** which means "the love of wisdom."

One of the greatest philosophers in Athens was a man named Socrates. Socrates was always encouraging people to question the things they thought they knew. He taught others by asking them questions that forced them to think about their beliefs. He asked such questions as, What is the good life for a man? What is truth? How do you know?

Even in Athens, where people loved new ideas, this constant questioning got Socrates into trouble. His enemies accused him of not honoring the gods and of leading young people into error and disloyalty. In 399 B.C.E., Socrates was brought to trial. In defending himself, Socrates said he was the wisest man in Greece because he knew that he did not know anything!

The jury found Socrates guilty and sentenced him to death. Friends encouraged him to escape from Athens, but Socrates said he would honor the law. He died by drinking hemlock, the juice of a poisonous plant.

The example of Socrates inspired many other Greek thinkers, especially his student Plato. In turn, Plato taught another great philosopher, Aristotle. You will meet Aristotle in the next chapter.

philosophy the search for wisdom or knowledge

Socrates calmly drank poison after being sentenced to death by the Athenian jury.

A piece of pottery like this may have been awarded to the winner of a footrace at the Panathenaic Games.

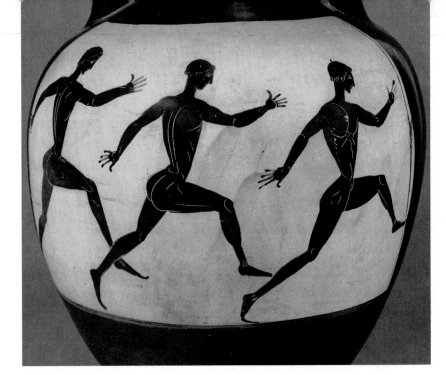

29.8 Sports: The Panathenaic Games

The Greeks' interest in philosophy shows how much they valued the mind. Their love of sports shows that they also prized a healthy body.

The Greeks often held athletic events to honor gods and goddesses. In Athens, games were held as part of the Panathenaea, a festival that honored the goddess Athena. The high point of the festival was the procession, or solemn parade. The Athenians attached a new robe for the statue of Athena to the mast of a ship and pulled it through the city to the temple.

The Panathenaic Games included many events. There were horse and chariot races, including one event in which men jumped on and off a moving chariot. Men also competed in footraces. In one race, men ran in their armor. The race was fun to watch because the heavy armor led the men to swerve and crash into each other.

The games also included combat sports, like boxing and wrestling. In an event called the *pancratium,* men were allowed to punch, kick, and even choke each other. The event ended when one fighter surrendered, lost consciousness, or died.

The winning athletes in these games were crowned with wreaths of laurel leaves and given pots filled with olive oil.

Another set of games was played every four years at Olympia to honor the god Zeus. Called the Olympics, these games were so important that the Greeks would call a truce from all wars so that athletes could travel safely to the games.

29.9 Chapter Summary

In this chapter, you explored Greek culture by visiting Athens during the 400s B.C.E. The temple at Delphi illustrated the role of religion in Greek life. Within Athens, the temples on the acropolis showed the Greek talent for architecture. The life-like statues made in marble workshops displayed the art of sculpture. The Theater of Dionysus introduced Greek drama, while Socrates provided an example of Greek philosophy. Finally, you learned about Greek sports through the Panathenaic Games.

At this time, Athens was at the height of its power and glory. Its power soon faded, but Greek culture lived on. In the next chapter, you will learn how Alexander the Great helped to spread Greek ideas far beyond the country's borders.

This plaster model shows what the acropolis looked like in ancient times.

◀ ◀ ◀ A damaged Roman mosaic re-creates a battle featuring Alexander the Great (at left).

Alexander the Great and His Empire

30.1 Introduction

In Chapter 29, you read about Athens during its golden age. As the power of Athens grew, other city-states, especially Sparta, became jealous and fearful. Athens and Sparta had mistrusted each other for a long time. After coming together to defeat the Persians, they soon began to quarrel.

In 431 B.C.E., Sparta declared war on Athens. Many of the smaller city-states were dragged into the fight. This conflict is called the **Peloponnesian War**. It lasted for 27 years. Even after Sparta won the war, the Greeks continued to fight one another.

Meanwhile, a new danger was growing to the north, in **Macedonia**. A Macedonian king, Philip II, saw that constant wars had left the Greeks divided and weak. He seized the chance and brought Greece under his control.

Philip's son, Alexander, was even more ambitious. Today he is known as **Alexander the Great**. Alexander extended Macedonian rule over a vast area. In time, his power reached from Macedonia and Greece through central Asia all the way to parts of India.

In this chapter, you will learn how Alexander tried to rule this vast **empire**. How did he plan to unite so many different peoples under his rule? Did his plan succeed? Let's find out.

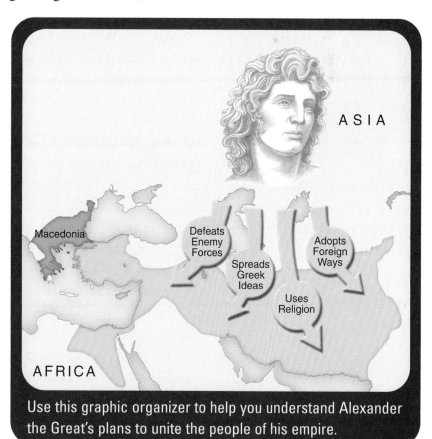

ASIA

Macedonia

Defeats Enemy Forces

Spreads Greek Ideas

Adopts Foreign Ways

Uses Religion

AFRICA

Use this graphic organizer to help you understand Alexander the Great's plans to unite the people of his empire.

30.2 The Peloponnesian War and the Rise of Macedonia

In 431 B.C.E., the quarrel between Athens and Sparta boiled over into war. This conflict is called the Peloponnesian War, after the area of Greece where Sparta was located (the Peloponnesus). Other city-states were drawn into the war as **allies** of either Athens or Sparta.

The war lasted for 27 years, from 431 B.C.E. to 404 B.C.E. In the end, Sparta won. For a time it was the most powerful city-state in Greece. Then Sparta, in turn, was defeated by Thebes.

While the Greek city-states fought one another, Macedonia was growing stronger. For a long while, the Macedonians had been a collection of scattered tribes. Then a bold leader, King Philip II, took the throne. In a short time, he unified the warlike tribes of the north and created a well-trained army.

Philip then looked south. Years of war had left the Greeks divided and weak. Philip thought he could take advantage of their weakness.

30.3 Philip Unites Greece

By 338 B.C.E., King Philip had conquered most of mainland Greece. He allowed the Greek city-states to keep many of their freedoms. But they were now under his control. Never again would a Greek city-state become a great power.

Philip wanted to attack Persia next, but in 336 B.C.E. he was murdered. His son, Alexander, became the new Macedonian king.

30.4 Alexander Creates an Empire

Alexander was only 20 when he became king. But the young man was well prepared for his new duties. As a youth, he had studied under Aristotle, the famous Greek philosopher. Aristotle taught him public speaking, science, and philosophy. He also taught Alexander to appreciate Greek culture.

As king, Alexander put down a rebellion by some of the Greek city-states. Then he turned to the east. Alexander wanted to carry out his father's plan to invade Persia. Fighting Persia would help to unite the Greeks by giving them a common enemy. And a victory over Persia would add greatly to Alexander's wealth.

In 334 B.C.E., Alexander invaded Asia Minor with a united Greek and Macedonian army. Alexander planned to use terror and kindness to conquer an empire. The towns and cities that resisted him would be burned to the ground and their people sold into

ally a country or group that joins with another for a common purpose

Coins in ancient Greece often had portraits of important leaders on them. This coin shows King Philip on horseback.

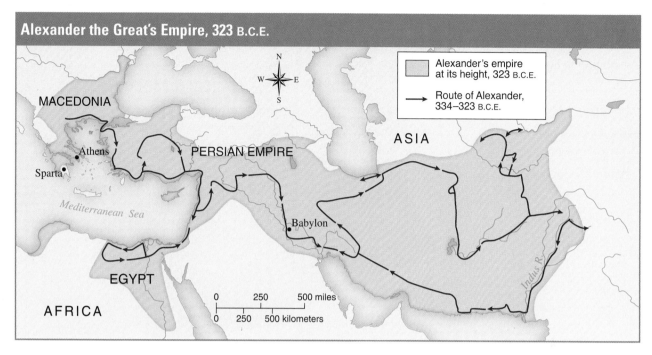

Alexander the Great's Empire, 323 B.C.E.

Legend:
- Alexander's empire at its height, 323 B.C.E.
- Route of Alexander, 334–323 B.C.E.

MACEDONIA

Athens

Sparta

Mediterranean Sea

PERSIAN EMPIRE

ASIA

Babylon

EGYPT

AFRICA

Indus R.

0   250   500 miles
0   250   500 kilometers

slavery. The towns and cities that surrendered would keep their government officials, and Alexander would help them rebuild damaged property.

30.5 Alexander's Plan to Unite His Empire

In a short time, Alexander extended his rule over Asia Minor, Egypt, and central Asia. Still he pushed on. He marched to the farthest limit of the Persian Empire. His armies even reached western India.

Many leaders in history have dreamed of ruling the world. Alexander the Great came as close as anyone to fulfilling that dream. He brought most of the world that was known to him under his rule.

Alexander was a bold and brilliant general, but his conquests created new challenges. How could he control such a large territory? And how could he unite so many different peoples and cultures?

Alexander wanted all the people he conquered to accept him as their ruler. He also wanted to spread Greek culture. At the same time, he did not want to destroy every local custom in his empire. His goal was to bring people of very different cultures together under a single government.

Alexander created a plan to achieve his goals. The plan had three key parts. First, he would spread Greek culture and ideas. Second, he would use religion to inspire loyalty. Third, he would show respect for the cultures he conquered and even adopt some of their customs. Let's look at each part of his plan.

This mosaic, or tile art, from a church floor is of the city of Alexandria in Egypt.

30.6 How Alexander Spread Greek Ideas

Alexander deeply admired Greek culture. He wanted to spread Greek ideas to the far corners of his empire. He hoped Greek culture would blend with the cultures of the people he conquered.

One way Alexander tried to accomplish his goal was by building Greek-style cities. He established many cities in different parts of the empire. Like Greek cities, they had marketplaces, temples, and theaters.

Settlers from Greece flocked to Alexander's cities. They brought with them Greek laws, art, and literature. Alexander wanted local soldiers and government officials to speak only Greek.

The most famous of the new cities was called Alexandria. It was located in Egypt near the sea. Alexander may have marked out the city boundaries himself.

Alexandria was designed with wide major streets crossed by narrower streets. It had many Greek features. It had a marketplace, a university, a gymnasium, and a theater. The city also boasted law courts and a library. There was even a temple dedicated to Poseidon, the Greek god of the sea.

In time, Alexandria became one of the ancient world's most important centers of trade and learning. Its library contained more than half a million books. It was one of the largest libraries in the world.

Because of Alexander, Greek ideas spread to Egypt, the Near East, and beyond.

30.7 How Alexander Used Religion

The second part of Alexander's plan involved religion. Alexander used religion in two ways to inspire loyalty among his followers and the people he conquered.

First, he honored the Egyptian and Persian gods. He treated them as equal to Greek gods. He visited oracle sites, made sacrifices, and had temples built in their honor. On one occasion, he visited the oracle site of the Egyptian god Ammon. When he arrived, a priest welcomed him as "God's son." The priest's words helped Alexander gain the loyalty of the Egyptians.

Second, Alexander encouraged the idea that he himself was a god. After his visit to the Egyptian oracle, he began wearing a crown of two rams' horns. This crown was the sacred headdress of Ammon. Seeing Alexander wearing the crown encouraged the Egyptians to accept him as a god.

Alexander also made sure to spread the story of the priest's greeting throughout the empire. Later, he required all Greeks to accept him as the son of Zeus.

Was Alexander sincere in his religious beliefs? It is hard to say for sure.

Alexander the Great (kneeling) and a Jewish high priest meet to show their mutual respect for each other.

30.8 How Alexander Adopted the Ways of Conquered Cultures

The third part of Alexander's plan was to show respect for the cultural practices of the people he conquered. He did this by adopting some of these practices himself.

For example, in Persia he adopted the Persian system of government. He allowed Persian governors to run the day-to-day business of their lands. Still, he was careful to **appoint** Macedonians to head the army. He also made sure his own people controlled the taxes that were collected.

Alexander also borrowed Persian customs. He began wearing decorative Persian-style clothes. He received official visitors as a Persian king would, in a luxurious tent. The tent was supported by 30-foot columns. The columns were covered in gold and silver and decorated with precious stones.

Alexander demanded that his visitors greet him in the Persian style. A visitor had to kneel in front of the throne and bend over until his head touched the ground. Alexander then raised his visitor to his feet, kissed him, and called him "Kinsman."

Finally, Alexander encouraged marriage between Macedonians and Persians. He himself married the eldest daughter of Darius, the Persian king he had defeated.

As with religion, historians aren't sure why Alexander acted this way. Some think he was simply trying to be a more acceptable ruler to his former enemies by adopting their customs. Others think that he truly considered the people he conquered to be equal to Greeks and Macedonians.

appoint to choose someone to fill an office or a position

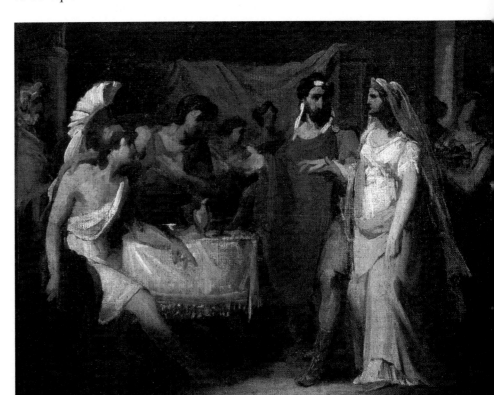

Alexander's marriage to the daughter of King Darius of Persia was a symbol of the blending of cultures in his empire.

30.9 The Empire Crumbles

By 324 B.C.E., Alexander's armies were in northern India. After 10 years of fighting, the exhausted soldiers refused to go on. Reluctantly, Alexander returned to Babylon, in Persia.

The next year, Alexander caught a swamp fever, perhaps malaria. He died in his soldiers' tent at the age of 33.

After his death, Alexander's empire crumbled. Settlers left the cities he had constructed, and they fell into ruin. His generals fought each other for control of the empire. In the end, Alexander's vast realm was divided into three separate kingdoms. Egypt became one kingdom. There was a second kingdom in Asia. Macedonia and Greece made a third kingdom.

Alexander's plan failed when his empire died, but a part of his dream lived on. He had spread Greek ideas throughout a vast area. In the centuries to come, Greek power would slowly fade away. But Greek culture would continue to influence the lands that Alexander had once ruled.

Alexander the Great died at the age of 33, leaving behind an empire that soon crumbled.

30.10 Chapter Summary

In this chapter, you learned about Alexander the Great. Alexander became king of Macedonia after his father's murder. By that time, Macedonia already controlled most of Greece.

A skilled general, Alexander conquered a vast empire. To unify this huge territory, he spread Greek ideas, used religion, and showed respect for the cultures of the people he conquered.

Alexander's empire soon died, but Greek ideas lived on. In the next chapter, you'll explore how these ideas continue to influence us today.

CHAPTER 31

◄ ◄ ◄ Plato and Aristotle gather in Athens with other great philosophers and scientists.

The Legacy of Ancient Greece

31.1 Introduction

In the last chapter, you learned how Alexander the Great helped to spread Greek civilization. In this chapter, you'll explore how ancient Greek culture continues to affect our lives today.

One day long ago, a Greek thinker named Archimedes climbed into a bath, filled to the top. As water overflowed onto the floor, he realized something. The volume of his body could be measured by the amount of water that left the tub. "Eureka!" he shouted. By being curious and observing events closely, Archimedes had discovered an interesting fact about the natural world.

Curiosity and careful observation are important parts of science. This way of thinking is just one of the gifts we have received from the ancient Greeks. The Greeks left us valuable ideas in many other fields as well.

And it's not just ideas that have come from the Greeks. So do many of the words we use to describe those ideas. The world of the ancient Greeks may seem far away, but it is as close as the thoughts we think and the words we speak. Let's look at **Greek contributions** to our lives in the areas of language, government, medicine, mathematics and science, architecture, entertainment, and sports.

Use this illustration as a graphic organizer to help you discover contributions the ancient Greeks made to our modern world.

Thucydides wrote about the wars between Athens and Sparta. He is considered one of the greatest historians of the ancient world.

31.2 Greek Contributions to Modern Language and Literature

Did you know that the word *alphabet* comes from the first two letters of the Greek alphabet, alpha and beta? This is just one of many connections between modern English and ancient Greek. Our alphabet grew out of the one the Greeks used. In addition, many English words have Greek roots. For example, the word *telephone* is made up of the Greek words for "far off" (*tel*) and "voice" (*phone*).

Even the way we write sentences comes from the Greek language. English grammar, punctuation, and paragraphing are all based on Greek writing. And don't forget literature. The Greeks invented drama, including both tragedy and comedy. They also developed historical writing. Modern historians are following in the footsteps of Greek writers like Herodotus and Thucydides. Herodotus is known as the "father of history."

31.3 Greek Contributions to Modern Government

As you learned in an earlier chapter, our form of government was a Greek idea. Democracy, or rule by the people, began in Athens. The practice of having citizens serve on juries also began in Greece.

There are important differences between modern democracy and ancient Greek democracy. In Athens, all citizens debated and voted on every issue. Today we elect representatives to speak for us and make laws. Another difference is that only native-born men could be citizens in Athens. Today women are citizens, and people from other countries can become U.S. citizens too.

Still, the basic principles of democracy come from the ancient Greeks. Athenians were proud that their government allowed citizens to control their own destiny. This idea is the basis of democracy today.

31.4 Greek Contributions to Modern Medicine

For centuries, the Greeks believed that the gods and goddesses controlled natural events, including health and sickness. The earliest Greeks thought that illnesses and accidents were punishments sent by the gods. They didn't know about the natural causes of disease and healing.

A Greek man named Hippocrates changed the way people thought about health and medicine. Hippocrates brought a scientific way of thinking to his work as a doctor. Hippocrates believed that diseases had natural causes. He taught his students to carefully observe their patients and write down what they saw.

Hippocrates is often called the "father of modern medicine." Today, people who become doctors take the Hippocratic Oath. They promise to be honest, to preserve life, and to keep information about their patients private.

All doctors try to do what they think is best for their patients. This vase painting shows a doctor from ancient Greece "bleeding" a patient. Some ancient Greek doctors thought that drawing blood would aid healing.

31.5 Greek Contributions to the Modern Understanding of the Body

As you know, the Greeks loved sports. Their interest in athletics gave them some knowledge about the way people's bodies move. But their understanding of the body was limited. That was partly because they couldn't look inside to see how the body works. The early Greeks believed that cutting people open would offend the gods. As these beliefs changed over time, the Greeks made new discoveries.

Several centuries after Hippocrates, medical students were able to name and describe organs inside the body. They discovered that the heart was a pump that sent blood flowing throughout the body. And they learned that the brain was the center of the nervous system.

geometry the branch of mathematics involving points, lines, planes, and figures

31.6 Greek Contributions to Modern Mathematics

The Greeks loved reasoning. They looked for logical answers to nature's mysteries. Greek scientists often found those answers in mathematics.

One such scientist, Pythagoras, believed that numbers were the key to understanding nature. He started a school where students developed mathematical theories.

Like many Greeks, Pythagoras was especially fascinated by geometry. *Geometry* comes from a Greek word that means "to measure land." Geometry began as a system for measuring areas of land. The Egyptians could also measure shapes and spaces, but the Greeks created new and improved methods. Using geometry, they could figure out how much seed to buy for planting a field or how to lay out a city.

Another famous Greek mathematician was Euclid. His geometry textbook became the basis for the teaching of geometry for more than 2,000 years.

Greek culture produced the first woman to earn fame as a mathematician, Hypatia. Born in Egypt in about 370 C.E., she taught Greek philosophy and mathematics in the city of Alexandria.

31.7 Greek Contributions to Modern Astronomy

Astronomy comes from the Greek word for "star." The Greeks were pioneers in this field as well.

People in all civilizations observed the sun, moon, and stars. But a Greek scientist named Aristarchus was the first person to suggest that Earth moves around the sun. This idea upset many Greeks who believed that Earth was the center of the universe.

Another Greek, Hipparchus, is often called the greatest astronomer of the ancient world. He studied and named more than 850 stars. He also figured out how to estimate the distances from Earth to the sun and the moon. His theories allowed later scientists to accurately predict eclipses of the moon.

Hypatia was a highly respected mathematician and philosopher in Alexandria, Egypt.

31.8 Greek Contributions to Modern Geography

The work of Greek astronomers also contributed to geography, the study of Earth's surfaces. *Geography* comes from Greek words meaning "writing about the Earth." As astronomers recorded the positions of stars, mapmakers began to locate places on Earth relative to the stars. To describe where places were, they developed a system of **longitude** and **latitude**.

A great geographer of ancient times was the Greek scientist Ptolemy. He wrote a book called *Geography* that listed over 8,000 places. His book also contained maps that showed how to represent the curved Earth on a flat surface.

31.9 Greek Contributions to the Modern Understanding of Plants and Animals

The Greeks' curiosity led them to study plants and animals. By studying the anatomy, or body structure, of animals, the Greeks also learned about the human body. This knowledge helped doctors in their medical studies.

The Greeks identified many types of plants and named their parts. They learned how plants reproduce by spreading seeds. They also discovered that some plants are useful as medicines. Greek doctors used many plants, especially herbs, to reduce pain and help people heal.

The philosopher Aristotle was fascinated by living things. He collected information about many types of animals and plants. Then he organized animals into groups such as "those with backbones" and "those without backbones." He also divided plants into groups such as herbs, shrubs, and trees. The way we classify, or group, animals and plants today reflects Aristotle's work.

longitude a measure of how far a place on Earth is from an imaginary line that runs between the North and South Poles on the globe

latitude a measure of how far a place on Earth is from the equator

In this famous painting by Eugene Delacroix, Aristotle is making drawings of animals as part of his study of them.

31.10 Greek Contributions to Modern Architecture

The word *architecture* comes from a Greek word that means "master builder." You read about Greek architecture in the chapter about ancient Athens. You learned how the Greeks used columns to make their temples balanced and stately. You saw examples of *pediments,* the triangular shapes where roof lines come together. And you studied the decorated bands called *friezes.*

Greek styles are still used in many buildings today. They are especially common in public structures like government buildings, schools, churches, libraries, and museums. But you can also see Greek styles in homes and stores. For example, many houses have covered porches. These porches come from the Greek *stoa,* a covered line of columns.

31.11 Greek Contributions to the Modern Theater

When you toured Athens, you learned about Greek theater. The word *theater* comes from a Greek word that means "a viewing place." Greek theaters were built as semicircles. The rows of seats rose steeply from the stage so that everyone in the audience could see and hear. These ideas influence the way theaters are built today.

The Greeks even invented special effects. For example, they used hoists to lift actors off the stage and make it seem as if they were flying. They also created scenery that revolved, or turned. Revolving the scenery let them quickly change where the action in a play was taking place.

But perhaps the greatest Greek contributions to the theater are their stories and plays. Writers throughout the ages have been inspired by Greek myths and stories. And Greek dramas are still performed today all over the world.

Greek actors wore masks that showed the characters they were playing.

31.12 Greek Contributions to Modern Sports

Many modern sports have their roots in ancient Greece. The most famous example is the Olympic Games.

The first Olympics were held in 776 B.C.E. to honor the Greek god Zeus. Today's Olympics reflect ancient Greek customs. During the opening ceremony, an athlete lights the Olympic flame. This custom comes from the time when the first Olympic athletes lit a fire on the altar of Zeus.

Many modern Olympic events grew out of Greek contests. One example is the pentathlon. *Pentathlon* is a Greek word that means "five contests." The Greek pentathlon included the footrace, discus throw, long jump, javelin throw, and wrestling. The Greeks invented this event as a test of all-around athletic skill. Although the five contests are different today, the pentathlon is still an Olympic event.

In ancient Greece, the opening ceremonies for the Olympic Games included the sacrifice of an animal to the gods.

31.13 Chapter Summary

In this chapter, you learned how ancient Greek civilization influences our lives today. We still use Greek words and ideas. Our form of government was invented by the Greeks. So were many ideas used in modern medicine, mathematics, and science. You can see traces of Greek culture in our buildings, theaters, and sporting events.

The Greeks were fiercely proud of their independence as a people. But their freedom did not last. In the next unit, you will learn about the rise of a great power, the Roman Empire. As you will see, the Romans admired and imitated Greek art and customs. They spread Greek culture across their vast empire. As a result, Greek ideas lived on long after the Greeks had lost their independence.

Ancient Greece Timeline

776 B.C.E.
First Olympic Games are held, in honor of Zeus.

507 B.C.E.
Athenian constitution gives political rights to free men. Women and slaves are denied political rights.

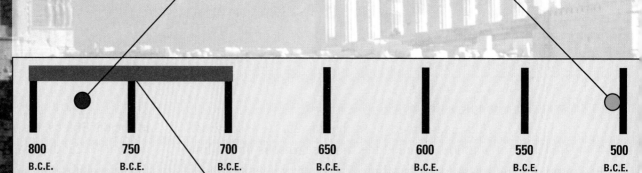

800 B.C.E.	750 B.C.E.	700 B.C.E.	650 B.C.E.	600 B.C.E.	550 B.C.E.	500 B.C.E.

800 – 700 B.C.E.
Greeks adopt Phoenician writing.

△ Social Structure ● Government ■ Religion ◆ Arts ● Technology ▰ Writing System

499 – 479 B.C.E.
Persian wars are fought.

| 500 B.C.E. | 450 B.C.E. | 400 B.C.E. | 350 B.C.E. | 300 B.C.E. | 250 B.C.E. | 200 B.C.E. |

447 – 438 B.C.E.
Parthenon is built.

377 B.C.E.
Hippocrates, the father of medicine, dies.

UNIT 6

Ancient Rome

BRITAIN

ATLANTIC OCEAN

Rhine R.

CARPATHIAN MTS.

Danube R.

GAUL

ALPS

Rubicon R.

ETRURIA

APENNINES

Black Sea

LATIUM PLAIN

Rome

PALATINE

SPAIN

ASIA MINOR

ASSYRIA

GREECE

SYRIA

Carthage

Mediterranean Sea

JUDEA

The Roman Empire, about 117 C.E.

0   200   400 miles

0   200   400 kilometers

SAHARA

EGYPT

The Roman Empire, About 117 C.E.

◀ ◀ ◀ This painting touches on the myth of Romulus and Remus, said to be founders of Rome.

CHAPTER 32

Geography and the Early Development of Rome

32.1 Introduction

In Unit 5, you learned about the civilization of ancient Greece. In this unit, you will explore the Roman civilization, which flourished from about 700 B.C.E. to about 476 C.E. It began in the ancient city of **Rome**.

Rome is located in Italy, which includes islands and a peninsula in southern Europe. The Italian peninsula is shaped a lot like a boot. It reaches into the Mediterranean Sea—ready to kick the island of Sicily.

The Romans have a **myth** about the founding of their city. Long ago, the story goes, a princess gave birth to twin sons, Romulus and Remus. The boys' father was Mars, the Roman god of war. The princess's uncle—the king—was afraid the boys would grow up to take his throne, so he ordered his men to drown them in the Tiber River. But before the twins drowned, a wolf rescued them.

When Romulus and Remus grew up, they decided to build a town on the banks of the Tiber River where the wolf had found them. But they quarreled over who would rule their settlement. Romulus killed his brother. He became king of the city, which he named Rome.

The tale of Romulus and Remus is a colorful myth. In this chapter, you will learn about the real founding of Rome. You will also learn how two important groups, the **Etruscans** and the **Greeks,** influenced the development of Roman culture.

Use this illustration as a graphic organizer to explore how the Etruscans and the Greeks influenced Roman culture.

32.2 The Early Romans and Their Neighbors

Over the years, historians have tried to discover the truth about the founding of Rome. No one really knows who Rome's first king was. We do know that the first Romans were **Latins**. The Latins were one of several groups who had invaded Italy sometime before 1000 B.C.E.

Perhaps around 700 B.C.E., a Latin tribe built the village that eventually became Rome. They built their village on the **Palatine,** a hill in central Italy. The Palatine overlooks the Tiber River, about 12 miles inland from the sea. In time, the village of thatched huts grew into a mighty city that spread over seven hills.

As Rome grew, Roman culture was greatly influenced by two of Rome's neighbors, the Etruscans and the Greeks. The Romans borrowed many ideas and skills from these two groups, beginning with the Etruscans.

The Etruscans had dominated Etruria, a land just north of the Palatine, about 800 B.C.E. No one knows exactly where they came from. They built some city-states and conquered others. By 600 B.C.E., they ruled much of northern and central Italy, including the town of Rome.

The Greeks also had a major influence on Roman culture. The Romans learned about Greek culture when Greek colonists established towns in southern Italy and on the island of Sicily. Romans also learned about Greek ways from traders and the many Greeks who came to Rome.

Let's look at the some of the ideas and customs the Romans learned from these two groups.

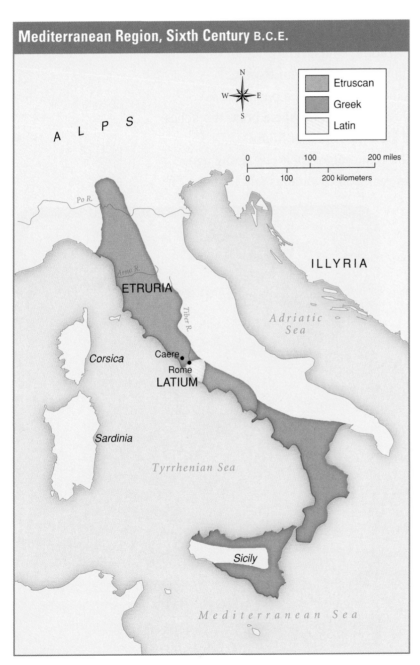

Mediterranean Region, Sixth Century B.C.E.

Etruscan
Greek
Latin

0   100   200 miles
0   100   200 kilometers

ALPS
Po R.
Arno R.
ETRURIA
Tiber R.
ILLYRIA
Adriatic Sea
Corsica
Caere
Rome
LATIUM
Sardinia
Tyrrhenian Sea
Sicily
Mediterranean Sea

32.3 The Influence of Etruscan Engineering

The Romans became great builders. They learned many techniques about engineering, or the science of building, from the Etruscans. Two important Etruscan structures the Romans borrowed were the arch and the cuniculus.

Etruscan arches rested on two pillars. The pillars supported a half-circle of wedge-shaped stones. A keystone in the center held the stones in place.

The **cuniculus** was a long underground trench. Vertical shafts connected it to the ground above. Etruscans used these trenches to irrigate land. They also used them to drain swamps and to carry water to their cities.

The Romans adopted both of these structures. In time, they became even better engineers than the Etruscans. They used arches to build huge public works, including bridges, stadiums, and aqueducts.

This arched city gate was built by the Etruscans. The arch is held in place by the pressure of the stones against each other.

32.4 The Influence of Etruscan Sporting Events

Romans also adopted two bloody Etruscan sporting events. The first was slave fighting. The Etruscan custom was to stage slave fights during funerals. Two slaves of the dead master fought to the death with swords and small shields. After being congratulated, the winner was executed.

The Etruscans also enjoyed watching chariot races. The drivers, or charioteers, were strapped to their chariots. If a chariot overturned, a driver could be dragged under the chariot's wheels or trampled by the horses. These fierce competitions often resulted in injury or death.

These Etruscan sports became popular amusements in Rome. In Roman stadiums, thousands of slaves died fighting as **gladiators**. The gladiators fought against each other or wild animals. And Romans flocked to see charioteers risk their lives racing four-horse teams.

cuniculus an irrigation system invented by the Etruscans
gladiator a person trained to fight another person to the death for public entertainment

Etruscan charioteers risked their lives racing around the turns in the track of a chariot race.

In the ruins of the Parthenon from ancient Greece, we can see the architectural details that have influenced future building designs.

32.5 The Influence of Greek Architecture

The Romans borrowed and adapted ideas from the Greeks as well as the Etruscans. Greek architecture was one important influence on the Romans. As you remember, the Greeks built marble temples as homes for their gods. Temples like the Parthenon had stately columns that added to their beauty.

The Romans used Greek designs in their own public buildings. In time, they learned to use concrete to make even larger structures, such as the Pantheon in Rome.

The Romans also used concrete to build huge stadiums like the Colosseum, where gladiators fought. The Circus Maximus, where people watched chariot racing, could seat more than 200,000 spectators.

32.6 The Influence of Greek Writing

Sometimes the Greek influence on Roman culture was indirect. For example, the Greek alphabet was adopted and then changed by the Etruscans. The Romans then borrowed and altered the Etruscan alphabet.

The Greeks' use of their alphabet had a more direct influence on Roman life. Like the Greeks, the Romans wrote in all capital letters. The Greeks carved important documents, such as laws and treaties, into bronze or stone plaques. The plaques were posted in the public squares. The Romans also carved inscriptions in walls and columns for all to see.

Many Roman writers were inspired by Greek poetry and myths. The Roman poet Virgil built on Greek tales of a long-ago conflict, the Trojan War. His poem told how Aeneas, a Trojan prince, fled to Italy after the war. According to Virgil's story, Aeneas was the ancestor of the first Romans.

Greeks and Romans wrote in all capital letters. This example of Greek writing is on a voting token called an *ostrakon*.

32.7 The Influence of Greek Art

Both the Etruscans and the Romans admired Greek pottery, painting, and sculpture. The Romans got some Greek ideas from Etruscan art. They borrowed others directly from the Greeks.

Greek pottery was valued throughout the Mediterranean world for its usefulness and beauty. Greek potters created large clay vessels for storing food, water, and wine. They often painted black figures on the red clay. Some of their designs showed pictures of gods and heroes. Others showed people in their daily lives. The Romans eagerly took the work of Greek potters into their homes. Roman artists imitated the technique but had their own style.

The Greek influence on Roman painting and sculpture was so great that historians speak of "Greco-Roman art." Wealthy Romans often collected Greek art. They had monuments built in a Greek style. Roman sculptors and painters used Greek art as models for their own work.

Roman artists also created a lively and realistic style of their own. Greek artists often tried to show an ideal, or perfect, human being or god. As Rome's power grew, much of Roman art celebrated great leaders and events. Roman sculptors became especially skilled in creating lifelike portraits. They made realistic busts, or statues showing the subject's head and shoulders. They also carved life-size statues of famous generals. The statues often seemed just as powerful as the generals themselves.

These vases show the two most common painting styles that the Greeks and Romans used on their pottery. On the left, the figures are painted black on red clay. On the right, they are the red color of the clay.

32.8 The Influence of Greek Mythology

The religion of the Romans was a blend of many influences. For example, they followed Etruscan religious rituals in founding their cities. But it was Greek mythology that especially influenced Roman ideas about the gods.

As you learned in Chapter 29, the Greeks worshiped a number of gods and goddesses. The gods governed every part of Greek life. The Greeks performed rituals and sacrifices to gain the gods' favor for everything from a good harvest to curing the sick.

The early Romans had their own gods and rituals. But their ideas about the gods changed as they came in contact with other cultures. When the Romans encountered a similar god from another culture, they blended that god's characteristics with those of their god.

The Romans adopted many of the Greek gods as their own, but they gave them Roman names. The greatest Greek god, Zeus, became Jupiter. Aphrodite, the goddess of love, became Venus. And Aries, the god of war, became Mars.

The Romans were much less interested in telling stories about the gods than the Greeks were. They were more concerned with performing exactly the right ritual for a particular occasion.

The Greek gods and goddesses of Mount Olympus, shown in this painting, were adopted into Roman mythology as well.

32.9 Chapter Summary

In this chapter, you learned about the beginnings of Rome. The city of Rome was founded by Latins who settled near the Tiber River. Over time, the Romans borrowed many ideas and skills from their neighbors.

Two groups who greatly influenced Roman culture were the Etruscans and the Greeks. Romans learned a great deal about engineering from the Etruscans. They also adopted some Etruscan sporting events.

Greek civilization had a huge influence on Roman culture. You can see the influence of Greek ideas in Roman architecture, writing, art, and mythology.

The birth of Rome is only the start of the story. In the next chapter, you will learn about the struggles that created a new form of government in Rome.

Examples of both Etruscan and Greek influence are seen in the magnificent Baths of Carcalla in Rome.

CHAPTER 33

In the Roman republic, elected senators debated and interpreted the laws.

The Rise of the Roman Republic

33.1 Introduction

In the last chapter, you learned about Etruscan and Greek influences on Rome. Early Rome was ruled by Etruscan kings from northern Italy. In this chapter, you will learn how the Romans overthrew the Etruscans and created a republic around 509 B.C.E. A **republic** is a form of government with elected leaders.

Ancient Romans told an interesting story about the overthrow of their Etruscan masters. One day, two Etruscan princes went to see the famous oracle at Delphi, in Greece. A Roman named Lucius Junius Brutus traveled with them.

At Delphi, the princes asked the oracle which of them would be the next king of Rome. The oracle answered, "The next man to have authority in Rome will be the man who first kisses his mother." Hearing these words, Brutus pretended to trip. He fell on his face, and his lips touched the Earth, "the mother of all living things."

Back in Rome, Brutus led the revolt that drove out the Etruscan kings. He became one of the first leaders of the new republic. In this way, the oracle's mysterious words came true. The Romans were now free to govern themselves. But not all Romans were equal. Power in the early republic belonged to rich men called **patricians**. The majority of Romans, the **plebeians,** had no say in the government. In this chapter, you will see how a long struggle between patricians and plebeians shaped the government of Rome.

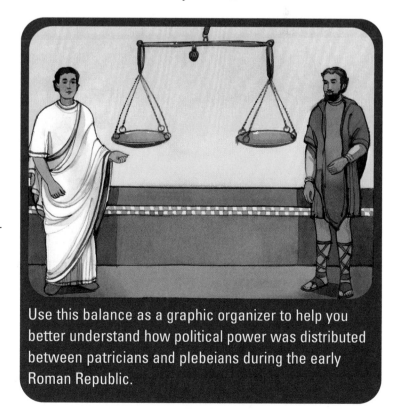

Use this balance as a graphic organizer to help you better understand how political power was distributed between patricians and plebeians during the early Roman Republic.

33.2 Patricians and Plebeians Under Etruscan Rule

Between 616 and 509 B.C.E., the Etruscans ruled Rome. During this time, Roman society was divided into two classes, patricians and plebeians.

Upper-class citizens, called *patricians,* came from a small group of wealthy landowners. *Patricians* comes from the Latin word *patres,* which means "father." The patricians chose the "fathers of the state," the men who advised the Etruscan king. Patricians controlled the most valuable land. They also held the important military and religious offices.

Lower-class citizens, called *plebeians,* were mostly peasants, laborers, craftspeople, and shopkeepers. The word *plebeians* comes from *plebs,* which means "many." Plebeians made up about 95 percent of Rome's population. They could not be priests or government officials. They had little say in the government. Yet they still were forced to serve in the army.

Senate a group of 300 men elected to govern Rome in the Roman Republic

consul one of two chief leaders in the Roman Republic

One of the heroes of the early Roman Republic was Lucius Junius Brutus. Here, Brutus is promising to support the new republic.

33.3 The Patricians Create a Republic

Over time, the patricians came to resent Etruscan rule. In 509 B.C.E., a group of patricians rebelled. They drove out the last Etruscan king. In place of a king, they created a republic. In a republic, elected officials work for the interests of the people.

To the patricians, "the people" meant the patricians themselves, not the plebeians. They put most of the power in the hands of the Senate. The **Senate** was a group of 300 men that the patricians elected. The senators served for life. They also appointed other government officials and served as judges.

Two elected leaders called **consuls** shared command of the army. The Senate was supposed to advise the consuls. In fact, the Senate's decisions were treated as law.

The creation of the republic gave Rome a more democratic government. But only the patricians could participate in that government.

33.4 The Plebeians Rebel

Rome was now a republic, but the patricians held all the power. They made sure that only they could be part of the government. Only they could become senators or consuls. Plebeians had to obey their decisions. Because laws were not written down, patricians often changed or interpreted the laws to benefit themselves. As a result, a small group of families held all the power in Rome.

The plebeians had to fight for what they wanted. They began to demand more political rights. The struggle between the plebeians and the patricians was known as the Conflict of the Orders, or conflict between the classes.

The conflict grew especially heated during times of war. The new republic frequently fought wars against neighboring tribes. Plebeians had to fight in the army even though the patricians decided whether to go to war. Plebeians resented this.

For many years, plebeians struggled to gain a share of the political power enjoyed by patricians.

The struggle took a dramatic turn in 494 B.C.E. By then, Rome was a city of between 25,000 and 40,000 people. Most of the population were plebeians. Angry over their lack of power, the plebeians marched out of the city and camped on a nearby hill. They refused to come back until the patricians met their demands.

Rome was in crisis. Work in the city and on the farms came to a halt. Without the plebeians, patricians feared that the army would be helpless if an enemy struck at Rome. "A great panic seized the city," wrote Livy, a famous Roman historian. The patricians had little choice but to compromise.

veto to refuse to approve proposals of government made by the Senate

tribune an official of the Roman Republic elected by plebeians to protect their rights

Plebeians won a major victory when patricians agreed to post Rome's laws on the Twelve Tables.

33.5 The Plebeians Gain Political Equality

The plebeians' revolt led to a major change in Roman government. The patricians agreed to let the plebeians elect officials called Tribunes of the Plebs. The **tribunes** spoke for the plebeians to the Senate and the consuls. Later, they gained the power to **veto,** or overrule, actions by the Senate and government officials that they thought were unfair. Over time, the number of tribunes grew from 2 to 10.

Plebeians could also elect a lawmaking body, the Council of Plebs. However, the council made laws only for plebeians, not patricians.

The plebeians had gained some important rights. But they still

had less power than the patricians. Over the next 200 years, the plebeians used a series of protests to gradually win political equality.

First, they demanded that the laws be written down. That way, the patricians couldn't change them at will. Around 451 B.C.E., the patricians agreed. The laws were written down on tablets called the Twelve Tables.

Next, in 367 B.C.E., a new law said that one of the two Roman consuls had to be a plebeian. Former consuls held seats in the Senate, so this change also made it possible for plebeians to become senators.

Finally, in 287 B.C.E., the plebeians gained the right to pass laws for all Roman citizens. Now, assemblies of all Roman citizens could approve or reject laws. These plebeian assemblies also nominated the consuls, the tribunes, and the members of the Senate. More and more plebeians served alongside patricians in the Senate. After 200 years of struggle, the plebeians had won their fight for equality.

Rome's republican form of government inspired future ages in Europe and America. Rome set an example of a government ruled by a written *constitution* (set of basic laws). Future republicans also pointed to Roman ideals of elected assemblies, citizenship, and civic duty. They adopted the model of governmental bodies that could check each other's power. Above all, they were inspired by the spirit of republicanism. Cicero, a famous Roman statesman, captured this spirit when he wrote, "The people's good is the highest law."

33.6 Chapter Summary

In this chapter, you learned how the Romans overthrew the Etruscans and created a republic. Romans were proud of their republic. Sometimes, during times of war, they handed power over to a dictator. Dictators were men who were given special powers for a limited period of time. But for the most part, elected leaders ruled Rome for 500 years.

Because of the conflict between patricians and plebeians, the Roman Republic became more democratic over time. The plebeians eventually won more political power. In time, most of the important differences between patricians and plebeians disappeared.

In the next chapter, you will learn how Rome grew from a small republic into a mighty empire.

In the Senate, Roman senators debated important decisions facing the city.

As Rome grew into a huge empire, power fell into the hands of a single supreme ruler.

From Republic to Empire

34.1 Introduction

In the last chapter, you learned how Rome became a republic. In this chapter, you'll discover how the republic grew into a mighty **empire** that ruled the entire Mediterranean world.

The **expansion** of Roman power took place over about 500 years, from 509 B.C.E. to 14 C.E. At the start of this period, Rome was a tiny republic in central Italy. Five hundred years later, it was a thriving center of a vast empire. At its height, the Roman Empire included most of Europe together with North Africa, Egypt, Syria, and Asia Minor.

The growth in Rome's power happened gradually, and it came at a price. Romans had to fight countless wars to defend their growing territory and to conquer new lands. Along the way, Rome itself changed. Romans had once been proud to be governed by elected leaders. Their heroes were men who had helped to preserve the republic. By 14 C.E., the republic was just a memory. Power was in the hands of a single supreme ruler, the emperor. Romans even worshiped the emperor as a god.

In this chapter, you'll see how this dramatic change occurred. You'll trace the gradual expansion of Roman power. You'll also explore the costs of this expansion, both for Romans and for the people they conquered.

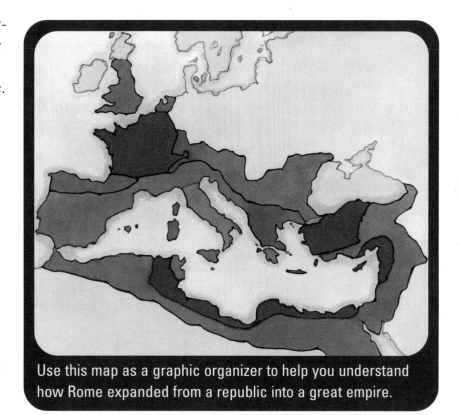

Use this map as a graphic organizer to help you understand how Rome expanded from a republic into a great empire.

34.2 From Republic to Empire: An Overview

The growth of Rome from a republic to an empire took place over 500 years. The story can be divided into four major periods.

The First Period of Expansion   The first period began in 509 B.C.E. when the Romans drove the last Etruscan king out of power. At that time, Rome became a republic.

The Romans wanted to protect their borders and to gain more land. This led to a series of wars. During the next 245 years, the Romans fought one enemy after another. They conquered their Latin neighbors in central Italy. They also defeated their old masters, the Etruscans.

Wisely, the Romans eventually made allies, or friends, of their former enemies. By 264 B.C.E., Rome and its allies controlled all of Italy.

The Second Period of Expansion   Rome's growth threatened another great power, the city of Carthage in North Africa. During the second period of expansion, from 264 to 146 B.C.E., Rome and Carthage fought three major wars. Through these wars, Rome gained control of North Africa, much of Spain, and the island of Sicily. Roman armies also conquered Macedonia and Greece.

Rome gained power over new lands through three savage wars with Carthage across the Mediterranean Sea.

Roman general Julius Caesar helped expand the Roman Empire by conquering Gaul and invading Britain.

The Third Period of Expansion   During the third period of expansion, from 145 to 44 B.C.E., Rome came to rule the entire Mediterranean world. In the east, Rome took control of Asia Minor, Syria, and Egypt. In the west, a general named Julius Caesar conquered much of Gaul (modern-day France).

Proud Romans now called the Mediterranean "our sea." But the republic was in trouble. **Civil wars** divided the city. Roman generals were becoming dictators. They set their armies against the power of the Senate. Caesar himself ruled as a dictator before he was murdered in 44 B.C.E.

The men who killed Caesar thought they were saving the power of the Senate. However, several more years of civil war followed. Then Caesar's grandnephew, Octavian, seized power. The Senate named him Augustus, or "honored one." Rome was now an empire governed by one supreme ruler.

The Fourth Period of Expansion   The fourth period of expansion began with the start of the empire. It lasted until 14 C.E. The first emperor, Augustus, added a great deal of new territory by pushing the borders of the empire all the way to natural boundaries, like rivers, to make it easier to defend. Later emperors added more territory. At its height, the Roman Empire stretched from the island of Britain in the west to the Black Sea in the east.

Each period of expansion involved cost and sacrifice. The next four sections give more details about each period of expansion. As you read, ask yourself what Romans of the time might have thought about these events.

civil war a war between regions of the same country

Julius Caesar's grandnephew, Octavian, became Caesar Augustus, the supreme ruler of the Roman Empire.

One of the heroes of the Roman republic was Lucius Quintius Cincinnatus. In 458 B.C.E., the Roman Senate made Cincinnatus dictator, or supreme ruler, so that he could rescue the city from an attack by a neighboring tribe. After defeating the enemy, Cincinnatus willingly gave up his power and returned to his farm.

34.3 Rome's Conquest of the Italian Peninsula, 509 to 264 B.C.E.

Rome's first period of expansion included more than 200 years of almost constant warfare. During this time, Rome gradually took control of the entire Italian peninsula.

After the last Etruscan king was overthrown in 509 B.C.E., the Romans began to expand their territory and influence. In 493 B.C.E., Roman leaders signed a treaty, or agreement, with their Latin neighbors to the south. The treaty said, "There shall be peace between the Romans and all the communities of Latins as long as heaven and earth endure." The new allies agreed to band together against their common enemies. During the next 100 years, the Romans fought a number of wars against the Etruscans as well as against tribes living in hills in the area around Rome.

Then, in 390 B.C.E., Rome nearly came to an end. A band of Gauls, a warlike people from the north, crushed a Roman army and surged into the city. Most of Rome's people fled into the countryside. The Gauls looted the city and burned most of it down.

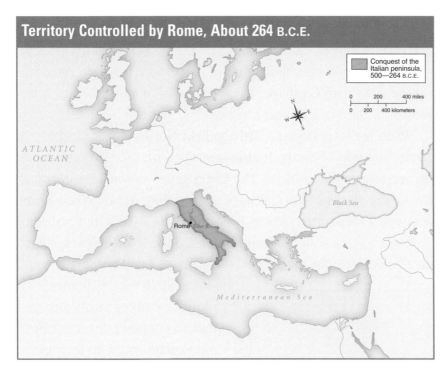

Territory Controlled by Rome, About 264 B.C.E.

Conquest of the Italian peninsula, 500—264 B.C.E.

0   200   400 miles
0   200   400 kilometers

ATLANTIC OCEAN

Black Sea

Rome Tiber R.

Mediterranean Sea

With the city in ruins, the Romans considered fleeing to some other place. Instead, they bravely decided to start over. They rebuilt their city and surrounded it with walls. They also built up their army. Before long, Roman soldiers were on the march again.

During the 300s B.C.E., Rome conquered the Etruscans and many neighboring tribes. To the south, they battled a people called the Samnites, as well as several Greek cities. By 275 B.C.E., Rome's conquest of the Italian peninsula was complete. Rome now controlled the Italian peninsula. But Rome's expansion came at great cost. Romans had been fighting wars for two centuries. And the Gauls had once destroyed their city.

As Rome's territory grew, the city had to keep a large, permanent army to defend it and the conquered lands. As a result, more and more Romans were forced to serve in the army. Most of the soldiers were plebeians. This was one reason for the struggle between the plebeians and the patricians.

Roman citizens were not the only ones who paid a cost for Rome's expansion. Rome allowed the people of some defeated cities to become Roman citizens. But other cities were not treated as well. Many received more limited privileges, such as the ability to trade with Rome. And Roman allies had to pay Roman taxes and supply soldiers for Roman armies.

By 264 B.C.E., Rome had more citizens and well-trained soldiers than any other power in the Mediterranean world. But very soon, the Romans would face their greatest challenge yet.

34.4 Overseas Expansion During the Punic Wars, 264 B.C.E. to 146 B.C.E.

During Rome's second period of expansion, it fought three savage wars with Carthage, a powerful city in North Africa, for control of the Mediterranean region.

When the wars began, Carthage held North Africa, most of Spain, and part of Sicily. It also controlled most of the trade in the western Mediterranean. The Greek cities in southern Italy had frequently clashed with Carthage over trading rights. When Rome conquered these cities, it was drawn into the fight with Carthage.

Rome's wars with Carthage are called the **Punic Wars,** after the Greek name for the people of Carthage. The First Punic War began in 264 B.C.E. It was fought mostly at sea. Carthage had a very powerful navy. But the Romans built up their own navy by copying and improving on the Carthaginians' ship designs. A decisive victory at sea in 241 B.C.E. won the war for the Romans. The triumphant Romans took over Sicily, as well as other islands.

The Second Punic War started 23 years later. This time, the Carthaginians decided to attack Italy itself. In 218 B.C.E., Hannibal, a brilliant Carthaginian general, surprised the Romans by marching his army from Spain across the Alps (a high mountain range) and into Italy. His troops rode elephants and braved snowstorms, landslides, and attacks by local tribes. For 15 years, Hannibal's men fought the Romans.

In 202 B.C.E., Hannibal returned home to defend Carthage against a Roman army. There he was defeated in the battle that ended the

In 218 B.C.E., the Carthaginian general Hannibal led his troops across the Alps to attack Rome.

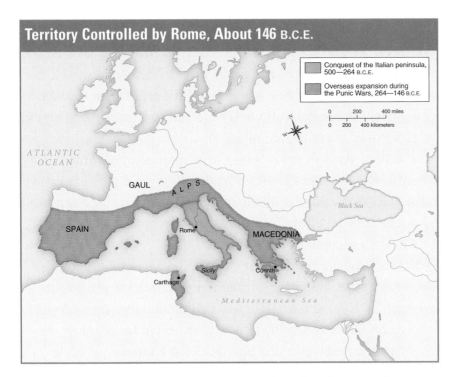

Territory Controlled by Rome, About 146 B.C.E.

Conquest of the Italian peninsula, 500—264 B.C.E.

Overseas expansion during the Punic Wars, 264—146 B.C.E.

0   200   400 miles

0   200   400 kilometers

ATLANTIC OCEAN

GAUL

ALPS

Black Sea

SPAIN

Rome

MACEDONIA

Sicily

Corinth

Carthage

Mediterranean Sea

Second Punic War. Carthage was forced to give Spain to Rome along with huge sums of money.

For about 50 years, there was peace between Rome and Carthage. Then, spurred on by Cato, a senator who demanded the destruction of Carthage, the Romans attacked once more.

The Third Punic War lasted three years. In 146 B.C.E., the Romans burned Carthage to the ground. They killed many people and sold others into slavery. Rome was now the greatest power in the Mediterranean region. It controlled North Africa, much of Spain, Macedonia, and Greece.

The Punic Wars expanded Roman power and territory, but Rome's victories came at a price. Families mourned for the countless soldiers who had died in the long wars. In addition, people living outside Rome suffered huge losses. Hannibal's army had destroyed thousands of farms. Other farms had been neglected while farmers went off to fight in Rome's armies. By the time the soldiers returned home, grain was flowing into Italy from Sicily and other places. Small farms were being replaced by large estates where the wealthy planted vineyards and raised live-stock. Unable to compete with the wealthy landowners, many poor farmers had to sell their land.

Although riches and slaves flowed into Rome from the con-quered lands, so did new customs. Many of the new ideas came from Greece. Wealthy Romans competed with one another to build Greek-style homes and beautiful temples.

34.5 Expansion During the Final Years of the Republic, 145 B.C.E. to 44 B.C.E.

By 145 B.C.E., Roman conquests had brought great wealth to the city of Rome. But they had also put the republican form of government under great strain. By the end of Rome's third period of expansion, the republic collapsed.

The final years of the republic were marked by still more wars. Many of Rome's allies resented having to pay Roman taxes and fight in Roman armies without enjoying the rights of citizens. In 91 B.C.E., they rebelled. To end the revolt, Rome agreed to let all free Italians become Roman citizens.

Rome also had to fight to put down slave revolts. As Romans conquered other lands, they brought hundreds of thousands of prisoners to Roman lands. They turned them into slaves who labored on farms and in the city. Romans often treated their slaves very harshly. A slave named Spartacus led a famous revolt in 73 B.C.E. After crushing his army and killing Spartacus in battle, the Romans hung thousands of the surviving rebels on crosses.

There was trouble in the city, too. With so many slaves to do the work, thousands of farmers and laborers had no jobs. They crowded into Rome, becoming a mob that an ambitious leader could turn into an army.

Rome's army was producing many such leaders. Generals used their armies to gain fame in far-off lands and then fight for power in Rome. In one civil war in the 80s B.C.E., 200,000 Romans were killed.

Forty years later, another civil war broke out between two ambitious generals, Pompey and Julius Caesar. Pompey had

Julius Caesar was stabbed 23 times and bled to death at the door of the Senate.

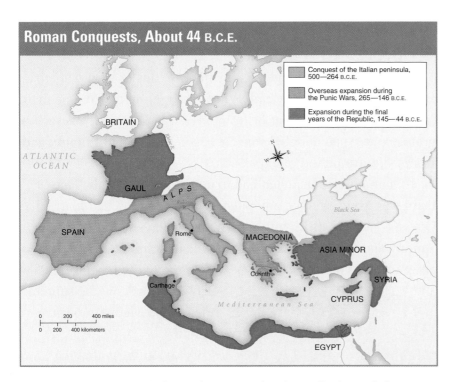

Roman Conquests, About 44 B.C.E.

Conquest of the Italian peninsula, 500—264 B.C.E.

Overseas expansion during the Punic Wars, 265—146 B.C.E.

Expansion during the final years of the Republic, 145—44 B.C.E.

BRITAIN

ATLANTIC OCEAN

GAUL

ALPS

SPAIN

Rome

MACEDONIA

Black Sea

ASIA MINOR

Corinth

SYRIA

Carthage

CYPRUS

Mediterranean Sea

EGYPT

0 200 400 miles

0 200 400 kilometers

expanded Roman rule in such eastern lands as Syria and the island of Cyprus. Caesar had conquered much of Gaul. By 49 B.C.E., Pompey was back in Rome, while Caesar commanded an army to the north of Italy, across the Rubicon River. Both men wanted to control Rome, but Pompey had the support of the Roman Senate.

Urged on by Pompey, the Senate forbade Caesar from entering Italy with his army. Caesar disobeyed. On January 11, 49 B.C.E., he crossed the Rubicon with his army. After three years of fighting, he defeated Pompey. The frightened Senate named Caesar dictator for life. With Caesar in control, the republican form of government was at an end.

As dictator, Julius Caesar introduced many reforms. He gave work to thousands of Romans by starting projects to make new roads and public buildings. To keep the poor happy, he staged gladiator contests they could watch for free. He also adopted a new calendar that is still used today.

Caesar had a vision of Rome as a great empire. He started new colonies and granted citizenship to the people of cities in Gaul and Spain. But he did not live to see his vision come true. On March 15, 44 B.C.E., a group of enemies stabbed Caesar to death as he was entering the Senate.

The plotters who killed Caesar thought they were saving the republic. But they were wrong. Instead, a true Roman emperor soon emerged to take Caesar's place.

34.6 Rome Becomes an Empire, 44 B.C.E. to 14 C.E.

Caesar's murder plunged Rome into a series of civil wars that lasted for more than 10 years. When the fighting ended, one man stood as the absolute ruler of Rome. He was Octavian, Caesar's grandnephew and adopted son. So began the Roman Empire, and Rome's fourth period of expansion.

To gain power, Octavian had to defeat jealous rivals. One of them was Marc Antony, a popular general. Antony had married Queen Cleopatra of Egypt. In 31 B.C.E., Octavian defeated Antony and Cleopatra in a sea battle near Actium, Greece. His army chased the lovers to Egypt, where they killed themselves.

As emperor, Augustus encouraged education and literature. Here he reads to a group of citizens. Augustus ruled for 41 years, until his death in 14 C.E.

Octavian was now the supreme ruler of the Mediterranean region.

Octavian knew that the Romans prized their republic. He told them he was restoring the authority of the Senate and the Roman people. But in fact he was in complete control. The Senate gave him the title Augustus, which means "revered" (honored). Historians call him Rome's first emperor.

As ruler of Rome, Augustus encouraged education, art, and literature. He completed grand construction projects, repairing more than 80 ruined temples. "I found Rome brick and left it marble," he boasted. He also gave Rome its first police force, firefighters, and library.

As emperor, Augustus ruled over 50 million people. He turned eastern kingdoms like Judea and Armenia into Roman provinces. To defend the empire, he pushed its borders to natural boundaries: the Rhine and Danube Rivers in the north, the Sahara Desert in the south, and the Atlantic Ocean in the west.

This vast empire needed a strong economy. The Romans improved trade routes by building harbors, canals, and roads. Goods flowed into Rome from throughout the empire and as far away as China. Roman coins made trade easier by providing a single system of currency (money).

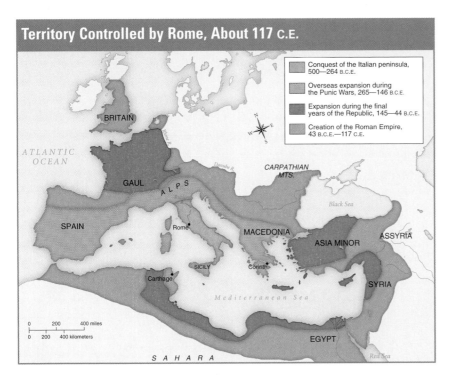

Territory Controlled by Rome, About 117 C.E.

Conquest of the Italian peninsula, 500—264 B.C.E.

Overseas expansion during the Punic Wars, 265—146 B.C.E.

Expansion during the final years of the Republic, 145—44 B.C.E.

Creation of the Roman Empire, 43 B.C.E.—117 C.E.

But Rome's final expansion brought new problems. To reform Roman morals, Augustus harshly punished people for being unfaithful to their husbands or wives. To protect the emperor, he established a private army, the Praetorian Guard. In later years, this same Guard sometimes murdered the emperors it was supposed to protect.

Under Roman rule, the Mediterranean world was mostly at peace for 200 years. This period is called the Pax Romana, or Roman Peace. But keeping the peace cost the Romans dearly. During Augustus's reign, one rebellion in the east took three years and 100,000 soldiers to put down. Before it was over, a Roman army was completely destroyed.

Later emperors added to the territory controlled by Rome. From Britain to the Red Sea, a single power ruled over the greatest empire the world had ever known. Defending this vast empire became increasingly challenging and costly as time went on.

34.7 Chapter Summary

In this chapter, you read about how Rome became a great empire. Roman power grew through four main periods of expansion. In each period, the costs of expansion were great. Yet, in the end, Rome ruled over an empire that lasted 500 years. In the next chapter, you will discover what daily life was like for Romans at the height of the empire's power.

CHAPTER 35

Daily Life in the Roman Empire

35.1 Introduction

In the last chapter, you learned how Rome became the center of a sprawling empire. In this chapter, you'll explore what **daily life** was like for people living in the empire at the height of Rome's power—around 100 C.E.

"All roads lead to Rome," boasted the Romans. For thousands of miles, road markers showed the distance to Rome. But more than roads connected the empire's 50 million people. They were also connected by Roman law, Roman customs, and Roman military might.

If Rome was the center of the empire, the Forum was the center of Rome. The word *forum* means "gathering place." The original forum in Rome was an open area used for merchants' stalls, races, games, and plays. In time, the Forum became a sprawling complex of government buildings, meeting halls, temples, theaters, and monuments. This collection of buildings and plazas was the heart of Rome's religious, business, and government life. If you wanted to find out what life was like for people in the Roman Empire, the Forum would be a good place to start.

In this chapter, you'll visit the bustling center of Rome's vast empire. You'll learn about eight areas of daily life in ancient Rome and discover how different life was there for the rich and the poor.

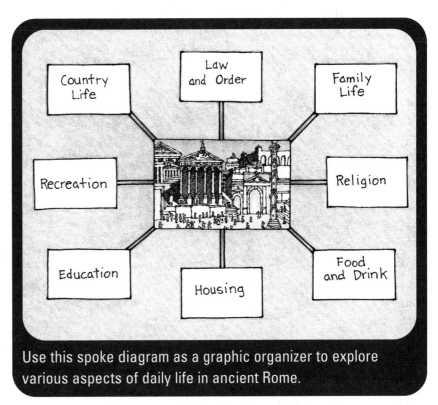

Use this spoke diagram as a graphic organizer to explore various aspects of daily life in ancient Rome.

Daily Life in the Roman Empire   335

The area known as the Forum was the heart of Rome's business, government, and religious life.

35.2 Daily Life in Ancient Rome

If you had visited Rome in the first century or two C.E., you would have seen a city of great contrasts. Nearly a million people lived in the empire's capital city. Rome was full of beautiful temples, stately palaces, and flowering gardens. Yet most of its people lived in tiny apartments crammed into narrow, dirty streets.

In the city's markets, wealthy Roman women shopped for goods, accompanied by their slaves. Proud senators strolled with their bodyguards while soldiers tramped through the streets. Merchants and craftspeople labored at their trades. Foreigners roamed the streets from such faraway places as Britain, Spain, and Egypt. And in the midst of it all were Rome's slaves—hundreds of thousands of them, many of them captured in war.

People and goods flowed into Rome from the four corners of the empire. Wealthy Romans spent fabulous sums of money on silk, perfumes, jeweled weapons, and musical instruments. They decorated their homes with statues, fountains, and fine pottery.

But the rich were only a small part of Rome's population. Most of the city's people lived in filthy neighborhoods filled with crime and disease. Their children were lucky to live past the age of 10. To keep the poor from becoming a dangerous mob, Roman emperors gave away food and provided entertainment like gladiator games and chariot races.

The empire had many large cities, but most people lived in the countryside. There, too, most of the people were poor. Some worked their own small farms. Others labored on huge estates owned by the rich.

Let's take a closer look at daily life in the empire.

35.3 Law and Order

Romans always believed in the rule of law. In the days of the republic, the Senate and the assemblies were important sources of law. In the empire, the ultimate source of law was the emperor. As one Roman judge said, "Whatever pleases the emperor is the law."

Even in the empire, however, Romans honored their old traditions. The Senate continued to meet, and senators had high status in society. They even had their own styles of clothing. They might wear special rings, pins, or togas (robes). Important senators had their own bodyguards. The guards carried fasces, bundles of sticks with an ax in the center. The fasces were symbols of the government's right to use physical punishment on lawbreakers.

Roman laws were strict, but crime was common in Rome. The most frequent crimes were stealing, assault, and murder. Roman police kept an eye on richer neighborhoods but rarely patrolled the poorer sections of the city. Some streets were so dangerous that they were closed at night.

Romans tried to protect themselves against crime. Rich men tried to hide their wealth by wearing old, dirty togas when they traveled at night. Women and children in rich families were told never to go outdoors alone, even during the day.

Any Roman, including the poor, could accuse someone else of a crime. A jury of citizens decided the case. Accused persons sometimes tried to win the jury's sympathy. They might wear rags or dirty clothes to court or have their wives and children sob in front of the jury.

Romans believed that one law should apply to all citizens. Still, under the empire Roman law was not applied equally. The poor faced harsher punishments than the rich and sometimes even torture.

In Rome's courts, lawyers represented both accused persons and their accusers.

Bulls were often offered as a sacrifice to Mars, the Roman god of war.

35.4 Religion

Religion was very important to the Romans. In an earlier chapter, you learned that the Romans adopted many Greek gods. They also adopted gods from other cultures to create their own group of Roman gods.

Romans wanted to please their gods because they believed that the gods controlled their daily lives. At Rome's many temples and shrines, people made offerings and promises to the gods. They often left gifts of food, such as honey cakes and fruit. They also sacrificed animals, including bulls, sheep, and oxen.

When someone was sick or injured, Romans would leave a small offering at a temple in the shape of the hurt part of the body. For instance, they might leave a clay foot to remind the god which part of the body to cure.

Special festivals and holidays, or holy days, were held throughout the year to honor the gods. But religion was also a part of daily life. Each home had an altar where the family worshiped its own household gods and spirits. The family hearth, or fireplace, was sacred to the goddess Vesta. During the main meal of the day, the family threw a small cake into the fire as an offering to Vesta.

In time, the Romans came to honor their emperors as gods. One emperor, Caligula, had a temple built to house a statue of himself made of gold. Every day the statue was dressed in the type of clothes that Caligula was wearing that day.

As the empire grew, foreigners brought new gods and forms of worship to Rome. The Romans welcomed these new religions as long as they didn't encourage disloyalty to the emperor.

35.5 Family Life

Family life in Rome was ruled by the *paterfamilias,* or "father of the family." A Roman father's word was law in his own home. Even his grown sons and daughters had to obey him.

Roman men were expected to provide for the family. In richer families, husbands often held well-paid political positions. In poor families, both husbands and wives often had to work in order to feed and care for their families.

Wealthy Roman women ran their households. They bought and trained the family's slaves. Many wanted money of their own and were active in business. Often they bought and sold property.

Roman babies were usually born at home. The Romans kept only strong, healthy babies. If the father didn't approve of a newborn, it was left outside to die. Romans found it strange that people like the Egyptians raised all their children.

Babies were named in a special ceremony when they were nine days old. A good-luck charm called a *bulla* was placed around the baby's neck. Children wore their bullas throughout childhood.

Between the ages of 14 and 18, a Roman boy celebrated becoming a man. In a special ceremony, he offered his bulla, along with his child-hood toys and clothes, to the gods.

Roman girls did not have a ceremony to celebrate the end of childhood. They became adults when they were married, usually between the ages of 12 and 18.

Weddings were held at a temple. The bride wore a white toga with a long veil. The groom also wore a white toga, along with leather shoes that he had shined with animal fat. But the new husband did not become a paterfamilias until his own father died.

Roman parents allowed only strong, healthy babies to live.

For young men and women in Rome, getting married was a step into adulthood.

In Rome's bustling marketplace, merchants sold many kinds of food and other goods.

35.6 Food and Drink

What Romans cooked and ate depended on whether they were rich or poor. Only the rich had kitchens in their homes. The poor cooked on small grills and depended on "fast food" places called *thermopolia,* where people could buy hot and cold foods that were ready to go. Even the rich often bought their daytime meals at thermopolia because the service was fast and convenient.

The main foods in ancient Rome were bread, beans, spices, a few vegetables, cheese, and meats. Favorite drinks included plain water, hot water with herbs and honey, and wine.

For breakfast, Romans usually ate a piece of bread and a bowl of beans or porridge. Porridge was an oatmeal-like cereal made from grains like barley or wheat. Lunch might include a small bit of cheese and bread, and perhaps some olives or celery.

For dinner, poor Romans might have chunks of fish along with some asparagus and a fig for dessert. Wealthy Romans ate much fancier dinners. Besides the main part of the meal, they had special appetizers. Some favorites were mice cooked in honey, roasted parrots stuffed with dates, salted jellyfish, and snails dipped in milk.

Roman markets offered many choices to those who could afford them. Wealthy Roman women or their slaves shopped for the perfect foods for fancy dinner parties. Merchants often kept playful monkeys or colorful birds on display to attract customers. Their shelves were packed with fruits, live rabbits, chickens, geese, baskets of snails, and cuts of meat. Large clay jars were filled with a salty fish sauce the Romans liked to pour over the main dish at dinner.

35.7 Housing

Like food, housing was very different in Rome for the rich and for the poor. The spacious, airy homes of the rich stood side by side with the small, dark apartments that housed the poor.

Wealthy Romans lived in grand houses built of stone and marble. The walls were thick to keep out the noise of the city.

Inside the front door was a hall called an *atrium* where the family received guests. An indoor pool helped to keep the atrium cool. An opening in the roof let in plenty of light.

Beyond the atrium, there were many rooms for the family and guests. The fanciest room was the dining room. Its walls were covered in pictures, both painted murals and mosaics made of tiles. Graceful statues stood in the corners. Some dining rooms had beautiful fountains in the center to provide guests with cool water.

During dinner parties, guests lay on couches and ate delicious meals prepared by slaves. While they ate, they listened to music played by slaves on flutes and stringed instruments like the lyre and the lute.

Nearby, many of the poor crowded into tall apartment buildings. Others lived in small apartments above the shops where they worked. Without proper kitchens, the poor cooked their meals on small portable grills, which filled the rooms with smoke.

The apartments were cramped, noisy, and dirty. Filth and disease-carrying rats allowed sickness to spread rapidly. Fire was another danger. Many of the buildings were made of wood, and the cooking grills caught fire easily. In 64 C.E., a disastrous fire broke out that burned down much of the city.

In this atrium of a wealthy Roman's home, you can see the opening in the roof that let in light and the indoor pool that helped to cool the house.

Unlike the rich, Rome's poor lived in crowded, dirty apartment buildings.

Children from wealthier Roman families were taught by tutors.

35.8 Education

If you had grown up in ancient Rome, your schooling would have depended on the type of family you were from. Many poor children in Rome were sent to work instead of to school. They learned trades like leatherworking and metalworking to help earn money for their families.

In wealthier families, boys and girls were tutored by their fathers, and often by slaves, until they were six or seven. Then they went off to school. Classes were held in public buildings and private homes. Many of the tutors were educated Greek slaves.

A typical school day in Rome began very early in the morning. Students walked through crowded streets, carrying their supplies in a leather shoulder bag. On the way, they stopped at local breakfast bars. There they bought beans, nuts, and freshly baked bread to munch on while they walked to class.

Inside the schoolroom, students sat on small stools around the tutor. They used a pointed pen called a **stylus** to copy down lessons on small wooden boards covered with wax. When the lesson was over, they rubbed out the writing with the flat end of the stylus so they could use the board over again. The school day lasted until two or three o'clock in the afternoon.

Roman students learned Latin, Greek, math, science, literature, music, and public speaking. Girls were trained to become dentists, real estate agents, tutors, or midwives (nurses who helped with childbirth). Boys typically became soldiers, doctors, politicians, or lawyers.

Students stayed in school until age 12 or 13. Boys from wealthy families often continued their studies until they were 16, when they began to manage their own properties.

stylus a pointed instrument used for writing

35.9 Recreation

There were many forms of recreation in Rome. Wealthy Romans had lots of leisure time, because slaves did so much of the work. The rich enjoyed going to plays in public theaters and musical performances in one another's homes.

At the Circus Maximus, dangerous chariot races thrilled thousands of spectators.

Both rich and poor often relaxed at Rome's public baths. There they could bathe, swim, exercise, and enjoy a steam bath or a massage. Besides places to bathe and swim, the baths had gardens, libraries, shops, and art galleries.

Roman emperors made sure to give the poor "bread and circuses"—food and entertainment to keep them busy and happy. Besides the many festivals throughout the year, rich and poor alike flocked to two spectacles: gladiator games and chariot races.

Gladiator games were held in large public arenas like the Colosseum. Both men and women were gladiators. Usually they were slaves or prisoners of war. The crowd shouted as the gladiators fought each other and wild animals to the death. Many thousands of gladiators died bloody and painful deaths for the entertainment of the spectators.

The Romans' favorite gathering place was the Circus Maximus, a huge racetrack with room for 200,000 spectators. There Romans watched and gambled on thrilling chariot races. Wealthy citizens sat on plush cushions close to the track, with shades protecting them from the sun. The poor sat on wooden benches high above the track.

Rome's gladiator games were bloody—and deadly.

Men and women sat in separate sections at the Colosseum, but at the Circus Maximus they could sit together. A Roman poet said the Circus Maximus was the best place to meet a new boyfriend or girlfriend because you never knew who would sit next to you.

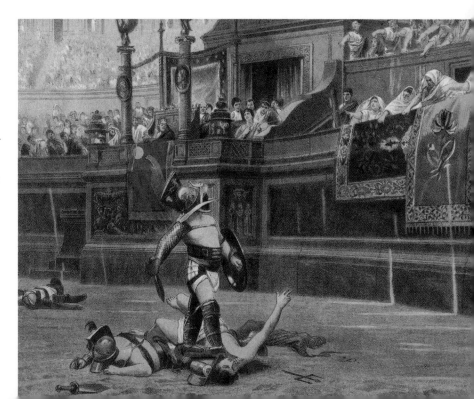

At a Roman villa, lush land-scaping surrounded a large house.

villa a large house in the country

35.10 Country Life

Rome was only one of many cities scattered throughout the Roman Empire. But 90 percent of the empire's people lived in the country. There, too, rich and poor had very different lives.

Wealthy Romans often owned country estates with large homes called **villas**. A country estate was a place for Romans to invest their money in crops and livestock. And the villa was a pleasant place to relax in the summer's heat.

When they went to the country, wealthy estate owners checked up on how their farms were being managed. But they had plenty of time left over for reading and writing as well as hunting, picnicking, and taking long walks in the fresh air.

The empire's farms provided much of the food for Rome and other cities. They produced grain for bread, grapes for wine, and olives for oil. Goats and sheep provided cheese, and their skins and wool were used to make clothing. Cattle and pigs were raised for their meat. Farmers also kept bees for making honey, the sweetener used by the Romans.

Slaves did much of the actual work of farming. Overseers, or supervisors, kept a close eye on the slaves and often treated them cruelly.

Many country folk were not slaves, but their lives were very hard all the same. They lived in huts and worked their own small farms, trying to earn enough to live. Or they labored on the great estates, tending the animals, helping with the crops, or working as servants. In the first century C.E., Saint Paul, a Christian writer, summed up the lives of the empire's poor. He wrote, "He who does not work shall not eat."

35.11 Chapter Summary

In this chapter, you learned about daily life in the Roman Empire. As the center of the vast empire, Rome became a thriving city. Yet Rome's magnificent temples and monuments were surrounded by narrow, dirty streets crowded with the city's poor.

Rich and poor did have some things in common. They worshiped the same gods, and they enjoyed some of the same spectacles. But in both the city and the countryside, rich and poor lived very different lives. While the wealthy enjoyed many pleasures, the poor struggled to survive.

To the proud Romans, Rome was the center of the world. Yet a great change was brewing in a poor and distant part of the empire. In a province called Judea, a man named Jesus was attracting followers. In the next chapter, you will learn how his teachings gave rise to a new religion, one that would shake the foundations of the mighty Roman Empire.

Many wealthy Roman women were attended by personal servants.

CHAPTER 36

◀ Early Christians were hunted down and persecuted by Roman soldiers.

The Origins and Spread of Christianity

36.1 Introduction

In the last chapter, you explored daily life in Rome at the height of the Roman Empire. In this chapter, you will discover how a new religion, called **Christianity,** spread through the empire. Christians are followers of **Jesus Christ,** who was put to death on a Roman cross in the first century C.E. Christians believe that Jesus was the Son of God and rose from the dead.

Many Romans saw Christianity as a threat to Roman order and traditions. Several emperors tried to stop the spread of the new religion through violent persecutions. Then, in 312 C.E., the emperor Constantine had a dream about Jesus the night before going into battle against a rival. The next day, he had a vision of a cross hanging in the sky in front of the sun. Around the cross were the words "In this sign, you will conquer."

Constantine's men went into battle with the first two letters of the word *Christ* on their shields. At the Milvian Bridge, near Rome, they won a great victory. From that time on, Constantine favored the Christian God over all others. Eighty years later, Christianity became the official religion of the Roman Empire.

How did this amazing change happen? Where did Christianity begin? How did it gradually spread throughout the empire? In this chapter, you'll find out.

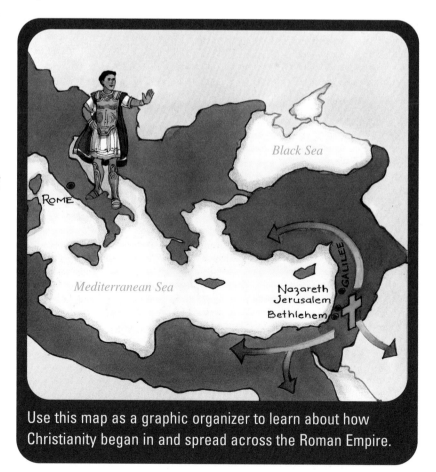

Use this map as a graphic organizer to learn about how Christianity began in and spread across the Roman Empire.

36.2 Judea: The Birthplace of Christianity

The birthplace of Christianity was a remote territory on the eastern end of the Mediterranean Sea where Jesus was born. The Romans called it Judea. Once it had been part of the ancient kingdom of Israel ruled by Kings David and Solomon.

The Jews were devoted to their homeland and to their belief in a single God. This belief, together with their religious customs, set them apart from their neighbors in the ancient world.

Once an independent kingdom, Judea came under Roman rule in 63 B.C.E. The Romans tried to govern the country by putting in charge Jewish rulers who agreed with Roman rule. But several times, groups of Jews rebelled against Roman control.

In 37 B.C.E., Rome appointed a man named Herod to be the king of Judea. Herod was not Jewish by birth, but he converted to the Jewish religion and rebuilt the Temple of Jerusalem. Still, many Jews distrusted him. They saw him as a puppet of, or controlled by, the Romans.

When Herod died in 4 B.C.E., his kingdom was divided among his three sons. Once again, unrest broke out. Finally, Rome sent soldiers to Judea to take control of the Jews. They replaced Herod's sons with a **prefect,** or military governor.

The prefect kept order and made sure Judea paid tribute (money) to Rome. But he usually left local affairs to the Jews themselves. For example, a council of Jewish leaders, led by a high (chief) priest, ruled the Jews' holy city of Jerusalem.

At the time of Jesus' birth, Judea was outwardly peaceful. But many Jews hated the Romans. In their sacred writings, they saw prophecies that one day God would send a savior to restore the glorious kingdom of David. This savior was called the **Messiah,** or "anointed one." ("Anointed" means blessed with oil. More generally, it means specially chosen by God.) When, the Jews asked, will the Messiah come?

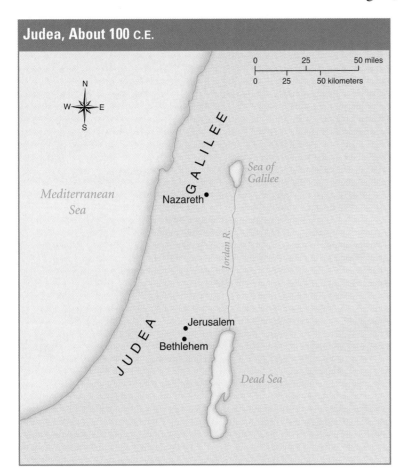

Judea, About 100 C.E.

36.3 Writings About the Life of Jesus

Historical records tell us a great deal about the days of the Roman Empire. The lives of the emperors, for example, were recorded in detail. But there were no historians to write about the life of Jesus, a little-known teacher in the tiny and far-off territory of Judea. Instead, most of the information about him comes from the writings of his followers.

These writings make up the New Testament of the Christian Bible. Among them are four gospels. The gospels are accounts of Jesus' life that were written in Greek by four of his followers. Their names have come down to us as Matthew, Mark, Luke, and John.

The word *gospel* means "good news." The gospels were written to spread the news of Jesus' life and teachings. They were statements of faith in Jesus as the promised Messiah. Often the gospels relate events in Jesus' life to prophecies about the Messiah. The Greek word for Messiah was "Christos" (Christ). In time Jesus became known as Jesus the Christ, or simply Jesus Christ.

The gospels were written down from oral and written sources 30 to 70 years after Jesus died. They tell of many incidents in the life of Jesus. They describe him as working miracles, healing the sick, and befriending the poor and the friendless. They also tell about his preaching (what he taught). He preached of God's mercy and love, and urged his followers to love one another.

> **gospel** an account of the life and teachings of Jesus Christ

The writers of the four gospels are called *evangelists,* from a Greek word that means "bringer of good news."

36.4 The Birth of Jesus

No one knows exactly when Jesus was born. Our modern calendar dates the start of the Common Era from the supposed year of Jesus' birth. But after careful study, later historians now believe that Jesus was probably born in about 6 B.C.E., during the reign of King Herod.

The gospel of Luke tells the story of Jesus' birth. According to the gospel, Jesus' mother, Mary, lived in a town called Nazareth, in the Roman territory of Galilee. There, the gospels claim, an angel appeared to her. The angel told Mary she would have a child and that she should name him Jesus.

Around this time, Luke's gospel says, the emperor Augustus ordered a census, or count, of all the people in the empire. Each man was supposed to go to the town of his birth to be counted. Mary's husband, a carpenter named Joseph, set out from Nazareth on the 90-mile journey to his hometown of Bethlehem, in the territory of Judea. Mary, already pregnant with Jesus, went with him.

According to the gospel of Luke, Jesus was born in a stable, where his mother laid him in a manger.

Bethlehem was called "the city of David," after the revered king who had once ruled Israel. According to the gospel, when Mary and Joseph arrived, the inn was already crowded, and they were forced to seek shelter in a stable. There Mary gave birth. She wrapped her baby in strips of cloth and laid him in a manger, or a feed box for animals. Only humble shepherds came to see the newborn baby.

According to the gospel of Luke, Jesus' family returned to Nazareth after his birth. The gospels say little about Jesus' childhood. It is likely that he grew up in Nazareth and learned carpentry, Joseph's trade. Like other boys, he probably spent long hours studying Jewish law and religious writings. According to Luke, at the age of 12 Jesus astonished the rabbis, or teachers, in the great Temple of Jerusalem with his wisdom and his knowledge of Jewish law.

When he was about 30, Jesus was **baptized** in the Jordan River by a preacher known as John the Baptist. John was urging people to change their way of life because, he said, the Messiah was coming soon.

The gospel says that when Jesus came to be baptized, John identified him as the savior the Jews had been waiting for. His baptism was a turning point in his life. After 40 days of praying in the wilderness, Jesus returned to Galilee and began to preach.

This star marks the spot where, according to tradition, Jesus was born. The star is located in a cave underneath the Church of the Nativity in Bethlehem.

baptize a ritual by which a person is welcomed into a religion

36.5 Jesus' Teachings

According to the gospels, Jesus began his ministry—or career of teaching, healings, and service to others—in the towns and villages of Galilee. At first he preached in synagogues, Jewish places of worship. As his reputation spread, larger and larger crowds came to hear him. So Jesus began teaching in open areas—in the street, on hillsides, and by the Sea of Galilee.

Early on, Jesus called a small number to be his followers, or **disciples**. The disciples were mostly simple, plain-spoken people—laborers and fishermen. Throughout his ministry, Jesus spent time with ordinary people, the poor, and the sick rather than those who were wealthy and important.

Jesus based his teaching on traditional Jewish beliefs. But the gospels say he put special emphasis on love and mercy. Of all the Jewish laws, he said, two were the most important. The first was, "You shall love your God with all your heart and all your soul." The second was, "You shall love your neighbor as yourself."

Jesus told his followers that the kingdom of God was coming soon. But for Jesus, God's kingdom was not an earthly kingdom of power and riches.

Large crowds gathered to hear Jesus preach and to ask him to cure the sick.

Instead, the kingdom of God meant a time when people would live according to God's will. Then, Jesus said, everyone would know God's love for all people, even those who suffer or who are looked down upon by others.

One of Jesus' favorite ways of teaching was through **parables,** simple stories with moral or religious messages. Jewish law says that you should love your neighbor as yourself. When asked, "Who is my neighbor?" Jesus told the parable of the good Samaritan. Once a traveler was beaten and robbed on the road. Two people passed by and ignored him. But a Samaritan stopped and helped the man. Because of the Samaritan's good deed, Jesus considered him to be a neighbor and worthy of love.

In another parable, Jesus described the happiness of a man who had found one lost sheep, even though he had 99 others. Like that man, Jesus said, God would rejoice more for one sinner who had changed his ways than for 99 righteous people who did not need to change.

Teachings like this shocked and angered some of Jesus' listeners. To some Jews, this way of thinking was wrong and dangerous. Others worried that Jesus' growing following would stir up trouble with the Romans.

Jesus did not preach revolt against the Romans. "Give to Caesar what belongs to Caesar, and to God what belongs to God," he said. Still, it was easy for some people to see him as a troublemaker.

parable a simple story that explains a moral or religious lesson

Jesus taught along these shores of the Sea of Galilee.

Jesus died the painful death of a common criminal.

36.6 The Crucifixion and Resurrection

After a year or two of traveling and preaching, Jesus went to Jerusalem for the Jewish festival of Passover. The festival celebrated God's rescue of the Jews from Egypt more than a thousand years before Jesus' time. Every year, many thousands of Jews came to Jerusalem to celebrate Passover. Roman soldiers kept a sharp eye out for anyone who might start a demonstration against Rome.

Shouting crowds welcomed Jesus into the city. At the Temple, Jesus saw the traders and money-changers who were allowed to do business in the outer court. In a fury, he drove them from the Temple. "This is a house of prayer," he cried, "but you have made it into a den of thieves!" Jesus' bold action enraged the temple's priests.

The gospels say that Jesus knew what would happen. According to the gospels, Jesus said that his enemies would come together to destroy him and that he would be killed.

Judas Iscariot, one of Jesus' handpicked disciples, had decided to betray him. After a final meal (the Last Supper) with his disciples, Jesus went to pray in a garden. Judas then reported where Jesus could be found. As Jesus was led away under guard, the other disciples ran away.

Jesus had gained a large following in Jerusalem. The city's Roman rulers feared that Jesus' supporters might stir up trouble. They were afraid that Jesus himself might lead such a revolt. To end this threat, they decided that he must die. Pontius Pilate, the Roman governor of Judea, found Jesus guilty and ordered that he die a rebel's death. To the Romans, proper punishment for enemies was to hang them from a cross.

According to the Christian Bible, the Romans took Jesus to a hill outside the city walls. There they nailed him to a cross and left him to die between two other condemned men.

After hours of agony, Jesus died. A few faithful followers took his body and buried it that Friday in a tomb carved out of rock.

On Sunday, the gospels say, Jesus rose from the dead. His followers call this event the Resurrection. Belief in the Resurrection convinced Jesus' disciples that he was the son of God. According to the gospels, Jesus left them again some time later to join his Father in heaven. His disciples then found the courage to begin spreading the news of his life and teaching.

This 15th-century painting by Piero della Francesca is called *The Resurrection of Christ*. It is the artist's interpretation of how Jesus may have risen from his tomb after his death.

36.7 The Missionary Work of Paul

When Jesus' followers began preaching that he was the Son of God, they ran into fierce opposition. One of their enemies was a man named Saul. Saul came from Tarsus, a town in modern-day Turkey. He was a Greek-speaking Jew and a Roman citizen. Saul thought the new religion was both wrong and dangerous. He did not believe the new teachings and argued against them.

According to the New Testament, one day he was riding on his horse to the town of Damascus in Syria. Suddenly he fell from his horse, blinded by a light from heaven. He heard a voice calling, "Saul, Saul, why do you persecute me?"

Blind and paralyzed, Saul was taken by some of his followers to Damascus, where a Christian healed him. Saul firmly believed

Even under arrest, Paul continued to teach and encourage communities of Christians through his letters. The letters became part of the Christian Bible.

In this enamel plaque from the 12th century, Paul speaks with Jews and Gentiles.

that he had heard the voice of the risen Jesus. From that time on, he was convinced that Jesus was the promised Messiah and the Son of God. Saul adopted the new faith himself and became a tireless Christian **missionary,** one who tries to convert others to his or her religion.

The early converts to Christianity were Jews, just as Jesus and his disciples had been. As an educated man who spoke Greek, Saul made it his special mission to convert non-Jews, called Gentiles, to the new religion. Known as Paul to the Greeks, he spent 17 years visiting cities throughout the Greek-speaking world. Wherever he went, he made new converts and started new churches.

In his preaching and letters, Paul stressed the need to believe in Jesus as the Son of God. He taught that all people, Jews and Gentiles alike, were God's children. Jesus, he said, was the Christ, God's chosen one. He was a Messiah for everyone, not just his fellow Jews. Paul made it easier for Gentiles to become Christians by teaching that they did not have to adopt such Jewish customs as not eating pork or shellfish.

Paul's journeys took him through much of the empire. He preached throughout Asia Minor, in Greece, and in Rome. Sometimes his visits caused riots when angry Jews protested what they considered blasphemous teaching.

For a time Paul was jailed in Rome, where he continued to write letters to other Christians. Tradition says that the Romans cut off his head in about 65 C.E. By that time, the Romans were beginning to persecute Christian believers.

missionary someone who tries to persuade others to believe in his or her religious teachings

Christian martyrs—people killed for their faith—faced terrible deaths with courage.

36.8 Persecution and Triumph

By the 60s C.E., Christians were beginning to attract the notice of the Romans. Christian preachers traveled along the roads of the empire, winning converts to their new religion. Both Paul and Peter, a close friend of Jesus, preached in Rome itself. At first, Rome was not unfriendly to Christians. What was another god, among so many?

But Christians refused to worship the other Roman gods. Worse, they would not admit that the emperor was a god. Their very way of life seemed to be an insult to Roman customs. Instead of wealth and luxury, they preferred simplicity. Recalling Jesus' message of peace and love, many of them refused to serve in the army.

As the number of Christians grew, many Romans saw them as a threat to Roman order and patriotism. Eventually the Christian religion was declared illegal.

Some emperors were determined to make an example of these disloyal citizens. For refusing to honor the Roman gods, Christians were sentenced to die in cruel and painful ways. Some were crucified. Some were burned to death. Others were hauled into arenas, where they were devoured by wild animals in front of cheering crowds.

But the persecutions failed to destroy the new religion. Instead, Christians won new admirers by facing death bravely, even singing hymns (religious songs) as lions or bears tore them apart. And Christianity offered many people in the empire a sense of purpose and hope. It taught that even the poor and slaves could look forward to a better life after death if they followed the way of Christ.

Gradually, people of all classes adopted the new faith. By 300 C.E., there were perhaps 5 million Christians in the Roman lands of Europe, North Africa, and western Asia.

In 313, Emperor Constantine gave Christians the freedom to practice their religion openly. Future emperors also accepted the new faith. In 392, Emperor Theodosius I banned all pagan sacrifices. By the time he died in 395, Christianity was the official religion of the Roman Empire.

Emperor Constantine supported Christianity and was baptized before he died.

36.9 Chapter Summary

In this chapter, you learned how Christianity was born in Judea. You read about Jesus and his followers. And you saw how the new religion survived harsh persecution and gradually spread throughout the Roman Empire. Eventually, it outlasted the mighty empire itself.

Although the Roman Empire fell more than 1,500 years ago, its influence has lasted to this day. The Christian religion became part of the legacy of ancient Rome.

In the next chapter, you will learn what caused the Roman Empire to fall. Then you will explore other ways in which the civilization of ancient Rome continues to influence us today.

CHAPTER 37

◀ ◀ ◀ The influence of Roman architecture is seen in the design of the U.S. Capitol.

The Legacy of Rome in the Modern World

37.1 Introduction

In Chapter 36, you learned about one **legacy** of ancient Rome, the Christian religion. In this chapter, you will learn about some other contributions the Romans made to the modern world.

In 1764 C.E., long after the Roman Empire was gone, a young Englishman named Edward Gibbon visited the city of Rome. Gibbon saw the ruins of ancient buildings like the Roman Colosseum. He marveled at Roman statues and the remains of aqueducts and bridges. He wondered, "How did such a great empire come to an end?"

Gibbon decided to write a book on the Roman Empire. More than 20 years later, Gibbon finally laid down his pen. His work filled six books. He called it *The History of the Decline and Fall of the Roman Empire.*

Why did Gibbon spend so many years learning and writing about ancient Rome? One reason is that Rome has had an enormous influence on western civilization. As one historian said, "Rome perished, yet it lived on."

In this chapter, you will discover how and why the Roman Empire fell. Then you will learn how Rome's influence lives on in modern **architecture, art, engineering, language, philosophy,** and **law**.

Use this drawing as a graphic organizer to help you explore Roman influences on modern life.

After years of attacks by invaders, the city of Rome itself was finally captured, marking the official collapse of the western part of the Roman Empire.

37.2 The End of the Empire in the West

At the height of Rome's power in the 100s C.E., proud Romans believed the empire would last forever. Yet by the year 500, the western half of the empire had collapsed. What happened to cause the fall of the mightiest empire the world had ever known?

Problems in the Late Empire

Most modern historians believe that a number of problems combined to bring about Rome's fall. Here are three of the main reasons.

Political Instability Rome never solved the problem of how to peacefully transfer political power to a new and capable leader. When an emperor died, ambitious rivals often fought each other for the emperor's crown. Real power fell into the hands of the armies, who could help leaders into power— or destroy them. Sometimes rivals didn't wait for an emperor to die; emperors were regularly murdered. After 180 C.E., Rome had a series of weak—and sometimes dishonest— emperors.

Economic and Social Issues Political instability contributed to other problems. To finance Rome's huge armies, its citizens had to pay heavy taxes. These taxes hurt the economy and drove many people into poverty. Trade also suffered. Across the empire, the spirit of citizenship declined.

Weakening Frontiers The huge size of the empire made it hard to defend. By the 300s, Germanic tribes were pressing hard on the western borders of the empire. Many of these people settled inside the empire and were recruited into the army. But these soldiers had little loyalty to Rome.

The Fall of Rome

In 330 C.E., the emperor Constantine took a step that changed the future of Rome. He moved his capital 850 miles to the east, to the ancient city of Byzantium. He renamed the city New Rome. Later it was called Constantinople. (Today it is known as Istanbul, Turkey.)

Before Constantine, emperors had tried sharing power over the vast empire between co-rulers. After Constantine's reign, power was usually divided between two emperors, one based in Rome and one in Constantinople. Rome became the capital of just the western part of the empire.

The emperors in Rome soon found themselves threatened by invading Germanic tribes. In 410 C.E., one of these tribes attacked and looted Rome itself. Finally, in 476, the last emperor in the west was driven from his throne. The western half of the empire began to dissolve into separate kingdoms ruled by different tribes.

In the east, the empire continued for another 1,000 years. Today we call this eastern empire the Byzantine Empire, after Byzantium, the original name of its capital city. The Byzantines wove the Roman heritage into their own rich civilization. But they were never able to put the old empire back together. For historians, the fall of Rome marks the end of the ancient world.

Yet the influence of Rome lived on. Let's look now at how Rome's legacy continues to affect our lives today.

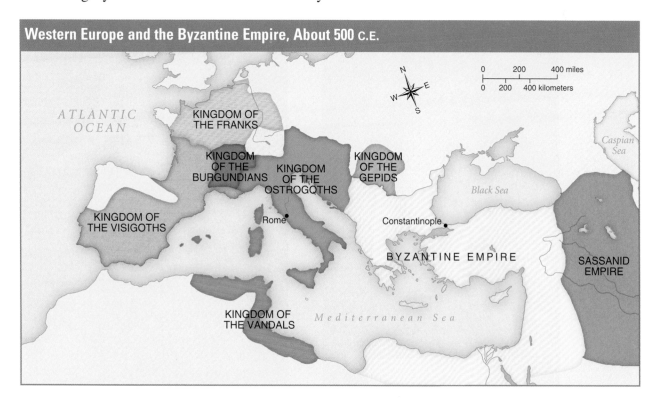

Western Europe and the Byzantine Empire, About 500 C.E.

37.3 Art

The Romans adopted aspects of other cultures. They modified and blended them into their own culture. This was true of Roman art. The Romans were especially influenced by the art of the Greeks. In fact, historians often speak of **Greco-Roman** art.

The Romans were skilled in creating realistic statues. They imitated Greek sculpture, but they were particularly good at making their sculpted images lifelike.

The homes of wealthy Romans were decorated with colorful murals and mosaics. Again, the Romans took existing art forms and made them their own. They painted beautiful frescoes, a type of mural. Frescoes are painted on moist plaster with water-based paints.

Roman frescoes often showed three-dimensional landscapes and other scenes. Looking at one of these frescoes was almost like looking through the wall at a scene outside. You've probably seen similar murals in restaurants, banks, and other buildings.

Romans were also great patrons (sponsors) of art. They paid thousands of painters, sculptors, and craftspeople to create their works. As a result, the Romans left behind many examples to inspire future generations.

Greco-Roman having the characteristics of Roman art with a strong Greek influence

American artists have often used a Roman style in sculptures and paintings of heroes. Here you see a Roman statue of the emperor Trajan and an American statue of George Washington. In what ways are they alike?

With their frescoes and mosaics, wealthy Roman homes were like art galleries.

A thousand years after the fall of the empire, Roman art was rediscovered during the period called the **Renaissance**. Great artists like Michelangelo revived the Greco-Roman style in their paintings and sculptures.

A good example is the famous ceiling of the Sistine Chapel in Rome. The ceiling shows scenes from the Bible painted by Michelangelo in the 1500s. A Roman would feel right at home looking up at this amazing creation.

Roman art has continued to influence painters and sculptors. Roman styles were especially popular during the early days of the United States. Americans imitated these styles to give their art dignity and nobility. You can still see statues in Washington, D.C., that reflect a strong Roman influence.

The Romans also brought a sense of style and luxury to everyday objects. They made highly decorative bottles of blown glass. A bottle for wine might be made in the shape of a cluster of grapes. Romans also developed the arts of gem cutting and metalworking. One popular art form was the cameo. A cameo is a gem that is carved to show a portrait of a person's head or a scene. The Romans wore cameos as jewelry and used them to decorate vases and other objects. You can find examples of all these art forms today.

Renaissance a period of European history around the 14th century in which there was a rebirth of interest and accomplishments in art, literature, and learning

37.4 Architecture and Engineering

The Romans' greatest contributions to science and technology came in the practical fields of architecture and engineering. Roman builders learned from the Greeks, Etruscans, and others. Then they added their own genius to take feats of construction to new heights.

Architecture

The Romans learned how to use the arch, the vault, and the dome to build huge structures. A **vault** is an arch used to support a ceiling or roof. A **dome** is a vault in the shape of a hemisphere that rests on a circular wall.

The Romans were the first to make widespread use of concrete. They made concrete by mixing broken stone with sand, cement, and water and then allowing the mixture to harden. With concrete, they were able to build much bigger arches than anyone had attempted before. Roman baths and other public buildings often had great arched vaults. The Pantheon, a magnificent temple that still stands in Rome, is famous for its huge dome.

The Romans also invented a new kind of building, the stadium. These were large, open-air structures. The Romans used concrete to build tunnels into the famous Colosseum in Rome. The tunnels made it easy for spectators to reach their seats. Modern football stadiums still use this feature.

vault an arched structure used to hold up a ceiling or roof

dome a half-round or hemisphere-shaped roof

The roof of the famous Pantheon in Rome is a huge dome.

The grand style of Roman buildings has inspired many architects through the centuries. One Roman innovation that was widely copied was the triumphal arch. This was a huge monument built to celebrate great victories or achievements. A famous modern example is the Arc de Triomphe (Arch of Triumph) in Paris, France. This monument celebrates the victories of the French emperor Napoleon in the early 1800s. Today it is the national war memorial of France.

You can see a Roman influence in the design of many modern churches, banks, and government buildings. A fine example is the Capitol building, the home of the U.S. Congress in Washington, D.C.

The Roman Colosseum has inspired stadium builders throughout history.

Engineering

The Romans changed engineering as well as architecture. They were the greatest builders of roads, bridges, and aqueducts in the ancient world.

Nearly 53,000 miles of road connected Rome with the frontiers of the empire. The Romans built their roads with layers of stone, sand, and gravel. Their techniques set the standard of road building for 2,000 years. Cars in some parts of Europe still drive on freeways built over old Roman roads.

The Romans also set a new standard for building aqueducts. They did not invent the aqueduct, but once again the Romans learned the technique and expanded on it. They created a system of aqueducts for Rome. The aqueducts brought water from about 60 miles away to the homes of the wealthiest citizens, as well as to the city's public baths and fountains. The Romans built aqueducts in other parts of the empire as well. The water system in Segovia, Spain, still uses part of an ancient Roman aqueduct. Roman arches from aqueducts can still be found in Europe, North Africa, and Asia Minor.

What features of Roman style can you spot in the U.S. Capitol building?

Romans wrote in all capital letters. This Latin inscription on the Arch of Constantine dedicates the arch to Constantine by the Senate and the people of Rome.

37.5 Language

One legacy of Rome that affects us every day is the Roman language, Latin. We still use the Latin alphabet (although Roman Latin used 23 letters and English uses 26). Many of our words come from Latin. Even Latin proverbs are still in use. For example, look at the reverse side of a U.S. dime. You'll see the United States motto *E pluribus unum* ("Out of many, one").

Several modern European languages developed from Latin, including Italian, Spanish, and French. English is a Germanic language, but it was strongly influenced by the French-speaking Normans, who conquered England in 1066 C.E. English has borrowed heavily from Latin, both directly and by way of French.

You can see the influence of Latin on many of the words we use today. For example, recall that our calendar comes from the one adopted by Julius Caesar. The names of several months come from Latin. *August* honors Caesar Augustus. *September* comes from Latin words meaning "the seventh month." (The Roman year started in March.) *October* means "the eighth

Latin Prefixes Used in English Words		
Latin Prefix	**Meaning**	**English Words**
in, im, il	not	inactive, impossible, illogical
inter	among, between	international
com, co	together, with	communicate, cooperate
pre	before	precede
post	after, behind	postpone
re	back, again	remember
semi	half	semicircle
sub	under, less than, inferior to	submarine
trans	across, through	transportation

month" in Latin. Can you guess the meanings of *November* and *December*?

Many English words start with Latin prefixes. A prefix is a set of letters at the beginning of a word that carries its own meaning. Attaching a prefix to a root word creates a new word with a new meaning. In fact, the word *prefix* is formed this way. It comes from *pre* ("in front of") and *fix* ("fasten" or "attach"). The table on the opposite page shows other examples.

As you can see from the table at the right, other English words come from Latin root words. For instance, *manual* is derived from *manus*, the Latin word for "hand."

Finally, we still often use Roman numerals. The Romans used a system of letters to write numbers. Look at the second table on this page. You may have seen Roman numerals used on clocks, sundials, and the first pages of books, like this one. You might also spot Roman numerals on buildings and in some movie credits to show the year in which they were made.

The Romans combined the seven letters shown in the table to express larger numbers. Putting letters *after* another adds the value of the additional letters. For example, VIII = 5 + 3 = 8 and XX = 10 + 10 = 20. Putting a letter *before* a letter with a greater value subtracts its value. For example, IV = 5 − 1 = 4 and IX = 10 − 1 = 9.

Latin Roots Used in English Words		
Latin Root	**Meaning**	**English Word**
anima	life, breath, soul	animal
civis	citizen, community	civic
lex, legalis	law, legal	legislature
manus	hand	manual
militare	to serve as a soldier	military
portare	to carry	portable
unus	one	united
urbs	city	urban
verbum	word	verbal

Roman Numerals			
Seven Basic Roman Numerals	**Meaning**	**Other Roman Numerals**	**Meaning**
I	1	II	2
V	5	III	3
X	10	IV	4
L	50	VI	6
C	100	VII	7
D	500	VIII	8
M	1,000	IX	9

37.6 Philosophy and Law

Like art and architecture, Roman philosophy and law were greatly influenced by the Greeks. But the Romans made contributions of their own that they passed on to future generations.

A Philosophy Called Stoicism

Stoicism was a philosophy that came from the Greeks. Many upper-class Romans made it their own.

Stoics believed that a divine (godly) intelligence ruled all of nature. A person's soul was a spark of that divine intelligence. "Living rightly" meant living in a way that agreed with nature.

The emperor Marcus Aurelius reigned from 161 to 180 C.E. His book *Meditations* still inspires people today.

To the Stoics, the one truly good thing in life was to have a good character. This meant having virtues such as self-control and courage. Stoics disagreed with those who said that happiness meant only avoiding pain and experiencing pleasure. They prized duty and the welfare of the community over their personal comfort. They said that true happiness was the peace of mind that came from living up to Stoic ideals.

The most famous Roman Stoic was the emperor Marcus Aurelius. Aurelius wrote down his private thoughts in a book he called "To Himself." Later it was given the title *Meditations*. In his writings, Aurelius constantly reminded himself of Stoic ideals. "Do not worry," he wrote, "if you encounter ungratefulness, insults, disloyalty, or selfishness. If you think and act rightly, none of these things can hurt you."

Stoics were famous for bearing pain and suffering bravely and quietly. To this day, we call someone who behaves this way "stoic."

Law and Justice

The Stoics' beliefs about justice and nature fit very well with Roman ideas about law. Roman law covered marriages, inheritances, contracts (agreements) between people, and countless other parts of daily life. Modern law codes in European countries like France and Italy are based in part on ancient Roman laws.

Another legacy of the Romans was the Roman idea of justice. The Romans believed that there was a universal law of justice that came from nature. By this natural law, every person had rights. Romans spread this idea by applying it to all citizens of the empire. Judges in Roman courts tried to make just, or fair, decisions that respected people's rights.

Like people everywhere, the Romans did not always live up to their ideals. Their courts did not treat the poor or slaves as equal to the rich. Emperors often made bad laws. But the ideals of justice and natural rights live on. Like judges in Roman courts, modern-day judges make decisions based on these ideals as well as on written law. Similarly, many people today believe that all humans have basic rights that no written law can take away.

Like the ancient Romans, modern judges are guided both by written law and by ideals of fairness and the rights of citizens.

37.7 Chapter Summary

In this chapter, you learned about the fall of the Roman Empire and explored the legacy of ancient Rome. Although the Roman Empire ended more than 1,500 years ago, the Romans greatly influenced our art, architecture, engineering, language, philosophy, and law.

Our exploration of the ancient world started near the very beginning of human history. And it ends here. Or does it? Throughout our journey, we've discovered that the human story is one of change, connection, and continuity. Because our lives have been so influenced by ancient cultures, in some way those great civilizations live on in us today.

Ancient Rome Timeline

616 – 509 B.C.E.
Two main classes of Roman society, patricians and plebeians, develop under Etruscan rule.

31 B.C.E.
Augustus Caesar becomes the first emperor of Rome.

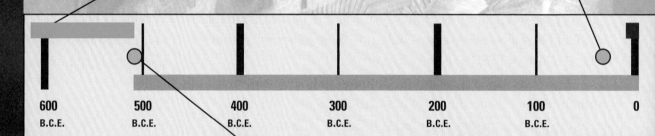

| 600 B.C.E. | 500 B.C.E. | 400 B.C.E. | 300 B.C.E. | 200 B.C.E. | 100 B.C.E. | 0 |

509 B.C.E.
The Roman Republic is created, giving political rights to patricians but not plebeians.

About 118 – 128 C.E.
The Pantheon, with its huge
dome, is built.

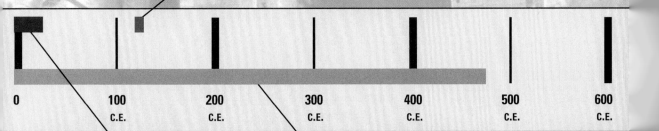

0	100 C.E.	200 C.E.	300 C.E.	400 C.E.	500 C.E.	600 C.E.

About 6 B.C.E. **– 27** C.E.
The life and teachings of Jesus lay
the foundation of Christianity.

About 509 B.C.E. **– 476** C.E.
Romans build 53,000 miles of
roads to connect their republic
and, later, empire.

RESOURCES

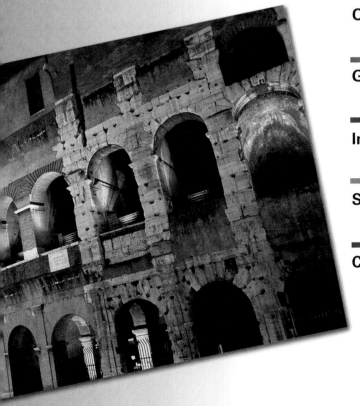

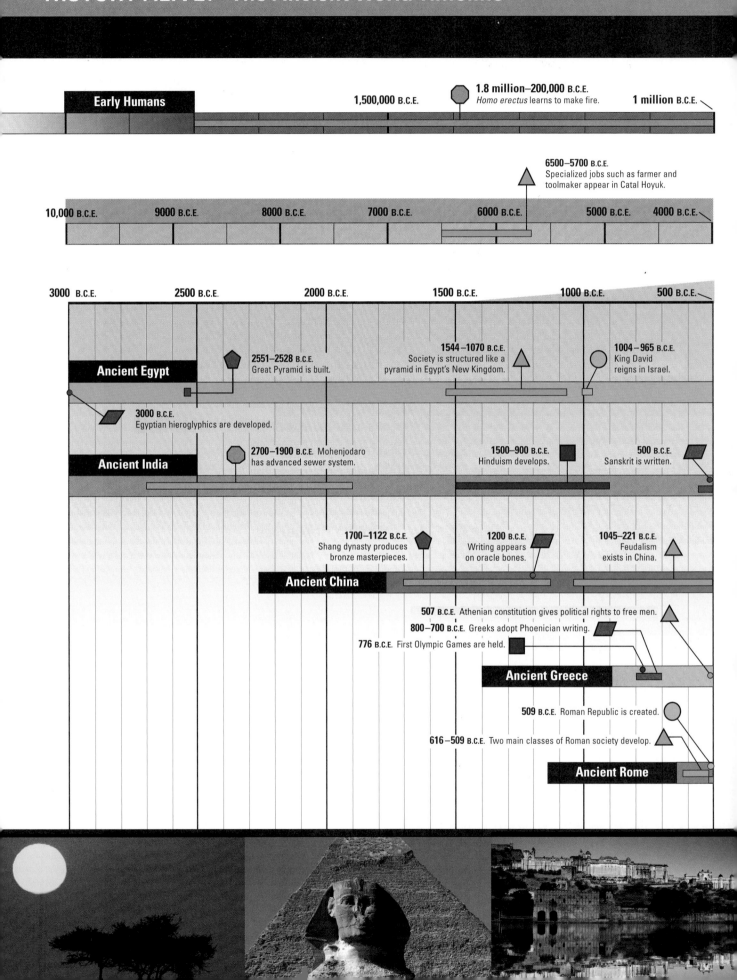

Early Humans

1,500,000 B.C.E.

1.8 million–200,000 B.C.E.
Homo erectus learns to make fire.

1 million B.C.E.

6500–5700 B.C.E.
Specialized jobs such as farmer and toolmaker appear in Catal Hoyuk.

10,000 B.C.E.   **9000** B.C.E.   **8000** B.C.E.   **7000** B.C.E.   **6000** B.C.E.   **5000** B.C.E.   **4000** B.C.E.

3000 B.C.E.   **2500** B.C.E.   **2000** B.C.E.   **1500** B.C.E.   **1000** B.C.E.   **500** B.C.E.

Ancient Egypt

2551–2528 B.C.E.
Great Pyramid is built.

1544–1070 B.C.E.
Society is structured like a pyramid in Egypt's New Kingdom.

1004–965 B.C.E.
King David reigns in Israel.

3000 B.C.E.
Egyptian hieroglyphics are developed.

Ancient India

2700–1900 B.C.E. Mohenjodaro has advanced sewer system.

1500–900 B.C.E.
Hinduism develops.

500 B.C.E.
Sanskrit is written.

1700–1122 B.C.E.
Shang dynasty produces bronze masterpieces.

1200 B.C.E.
Writing appears on oracle bones.

1045–221 B.C.E.
Feudalism exists in China.

Ancient China

507 B.C.E. Athenian constitution gives political rights to free men.
800–700 B.C.E. Greeks adopt Phoenician writing.
776 B.C.E. First Olympic Games are held.

Ancient Greece

509 B.C.E. Roman Republic is created.

616–509 B.C.E. Two main classes of Roman society develop.

Ancient Rome

1 million B.C.E.

500,000 B.C.E.

35,000–12,000 B.C.E. *Homo sapiens sapiens* create cave paintings.

10,000 to Today

3500 B.C.E.
Sumerians invent the wheel.

1792–1750 B.C.E.
Hammurabi creates a code of laws.

2500–500 B.C.E.
Sumerians and others develop cuneiform.

4000 B.C.E. **3000** B.C.E. **2000** B.C.E. **1000** B.C.E. **0** **1,000** C.E. **2000** C.E.

500 B.C.E. **0** **500** C.E. **1000** C.E. **1500** C.E. **2000** C.E.

24 B.C.E.
Amanirenas defends Kush against Romans.

70 C.E.
Final Jewish Diaspora begins.

563–483 B.C.E.
Life of Siddhartha, founder of Buddhism.

269–232 B.C.E.
Ashoka rules Mauryan Empire.

320–550 C.E.
Ajanta cave murals are created during Gupta Empire.

221 B.C.E.
Emperor Qin unites China.

65 C.E.
Buddhist writings appear in China.

105 C.E.
Emperor learns about paper.

499 – 479 B.C.E.
Persian Wars

447–438 B.C.E.
Parthenon is built.

377 B.C.E.
Hippocrates, the father of medicine, dies.

31 B.C.E.
Augustus Caesar becomes first Roman emperor.

About 6 B.C.E.**–27** C.E.
Jesus and his teachings lay the foundations of Christianity.

About 118–128 C.E.
Panthenon is built.

About 509 B.C.E.**–476** C.E.
Romans build 53,000 miles of roads.

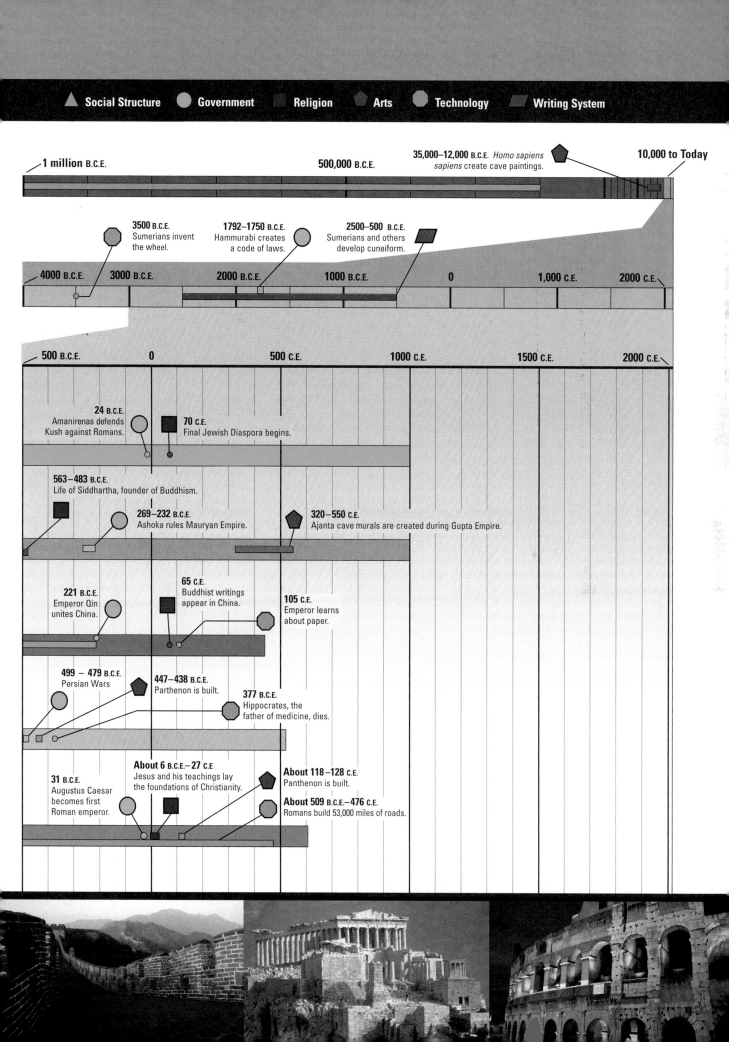

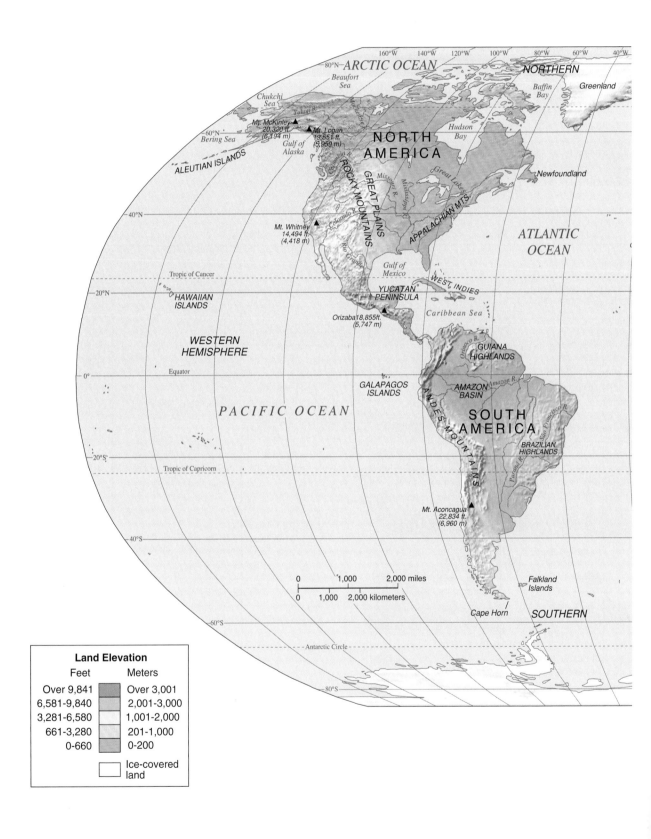

Land Elevation

Feet	Meters
Over 9,841	Over 3,001
6,581-9,840	2,001-3,000
3,281-6,580	1,001-2,000
661-3,280	201-1,000
0-660	0-200

Ice-covered land

HEMISPHERE

20°W 0° 20°E 40°E 60°E 80°E 100°E 120°E 140°E 160°E

SVALBARD
FRANZ JOSEF LAND SEVERNAYA ZEMLYA

Novaya Zemlya
Norwegian Sea
Barents Sea
Kara Sea

Laptev Sea
East Siberian Sea

Arctic Circle

North Sea
Baltic Sea
NORTHERN EUROPEAN PLAIN
Dvina R.
Volga R.
Ob R.
Yenisey R.
Angara R.
Lena R.
Aldon R.
Amur R.
Sea of Okhotsk
Bering Sea

EUROPE
ALPS
Don R.
Ural R.
URAL MOUNTAINS
ASIA
Lake Baikal
East Sea

Danube R.
Black Sea
Aral Sea
GOBI
Huang He
Yellow Sea

CANARY IS.
ATLAS MTS.
Mediterranean Sea
Caspian Sea
Amu Darya
K2
28,250 ft.
(8,611 m)
EASTERN HEMISPHERE

SAHARA
Nile R.
Red Sea
ARABIAN PENINSULA
THAR DESERT
HIMALAYAS
Ganges R.
Mt. Everest
29,035 ft.
(8,850 m)
Chang Jiang
East China Sea
PACIFIC OCEAN

SAHEL
Niger R.
AFRICA
White Nile R.
DECCAN PLATEAU
Arabian Sea
Bay of Bengal
South China Sea
Philippine Sea

Uele R.
CONGO BASIN
Congo R.
Mt. Kenya
17,058 ft.
(5,199 m)
Mt. Kilimanjaro
19,340 ft.
(5,895 m)
Celebes Sea

Prime Meridian
Zambezi R.
INDIAN OCEAN
EAST INDIES
MELANESIA

KALAHARI DESERT
Orange R.
Coral Sea

AUSTRALIA
GREAT VICTORIA DESERT
Darling R.
Tasman Sea
North Island

N
W E
S
South Island

HEMISPHERE

ANTARCTICA

Resources 379

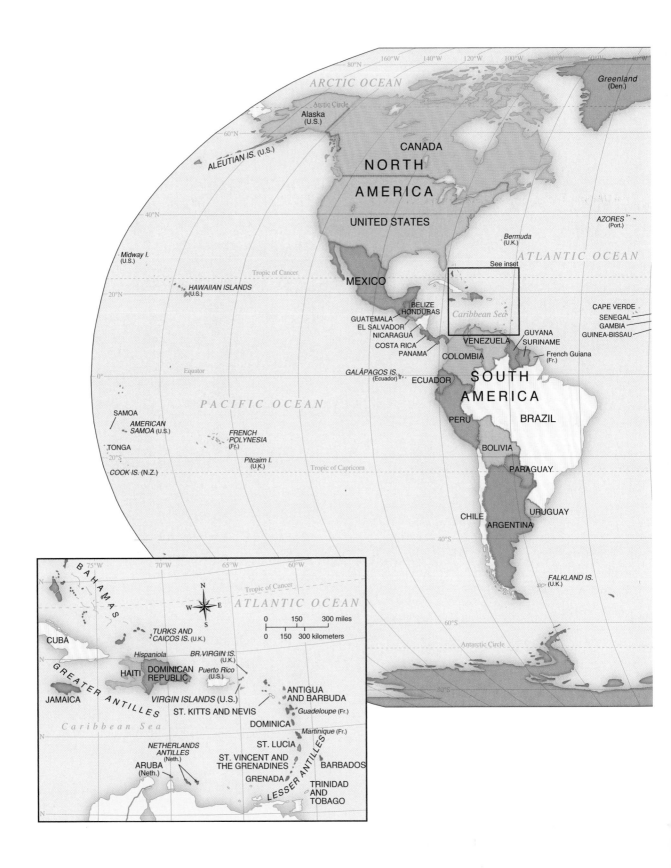

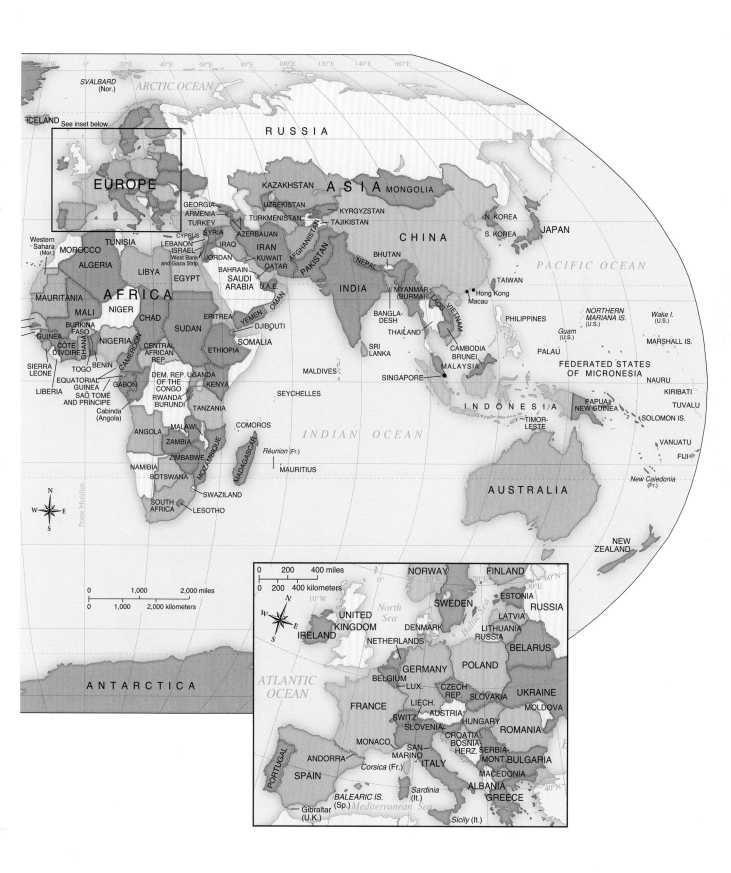

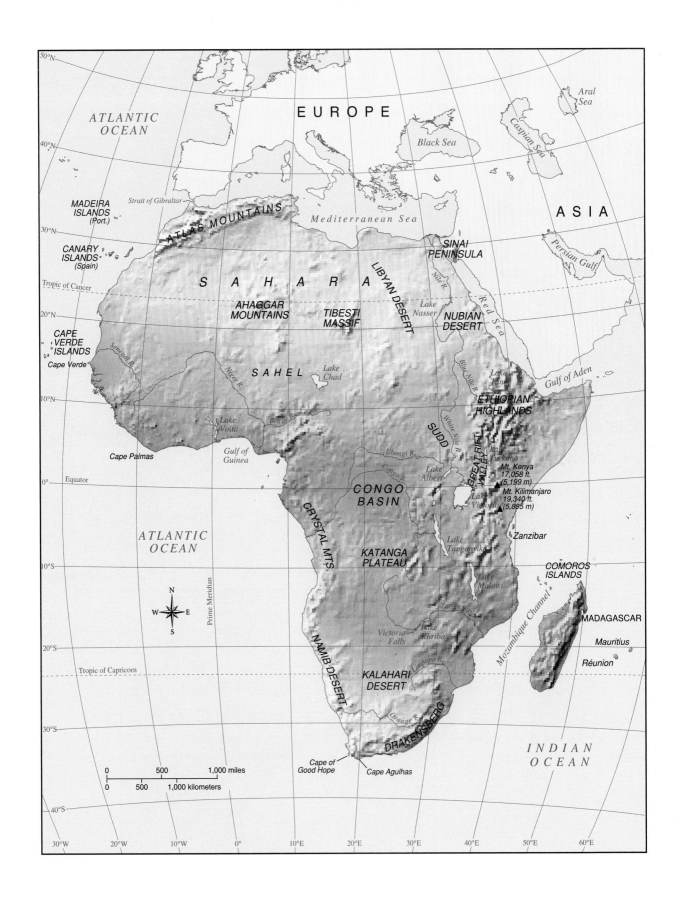

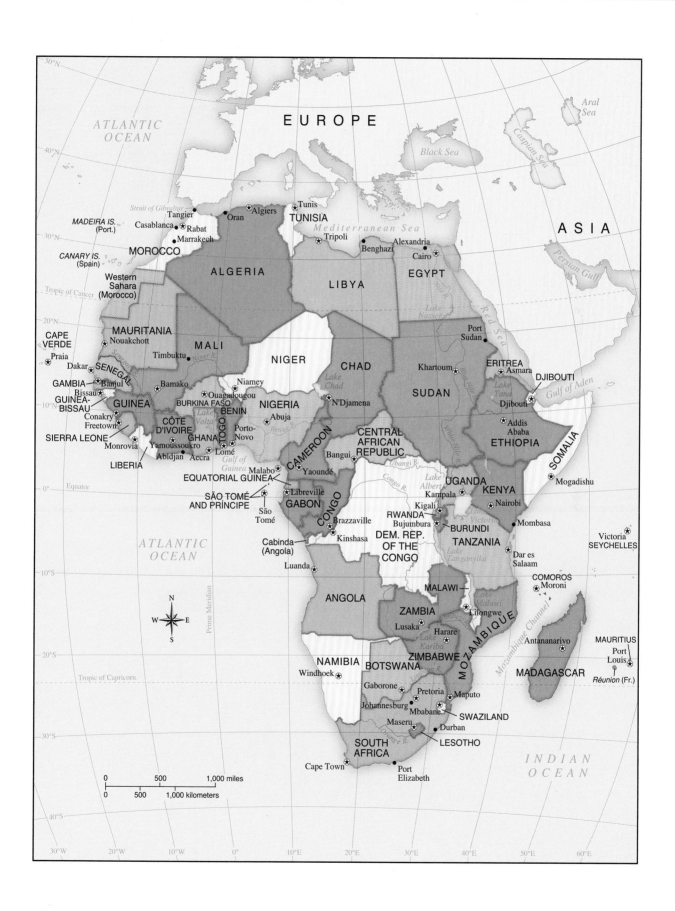

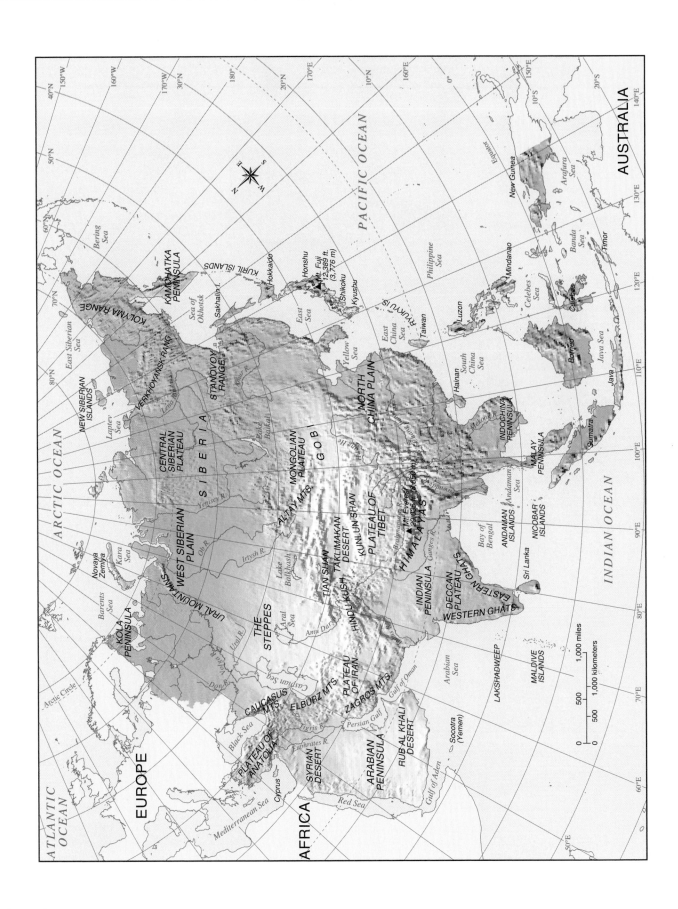

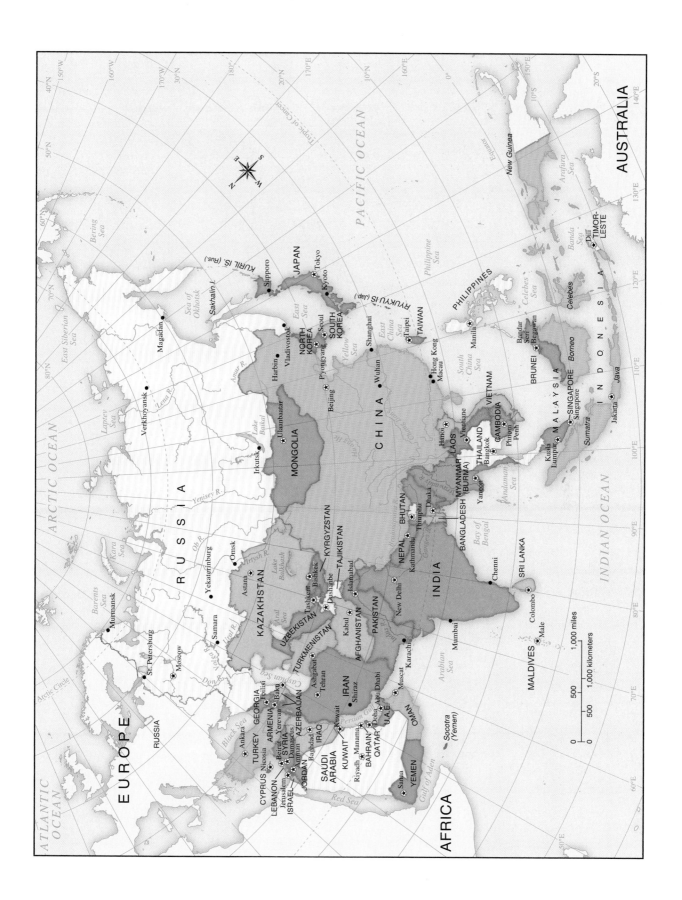

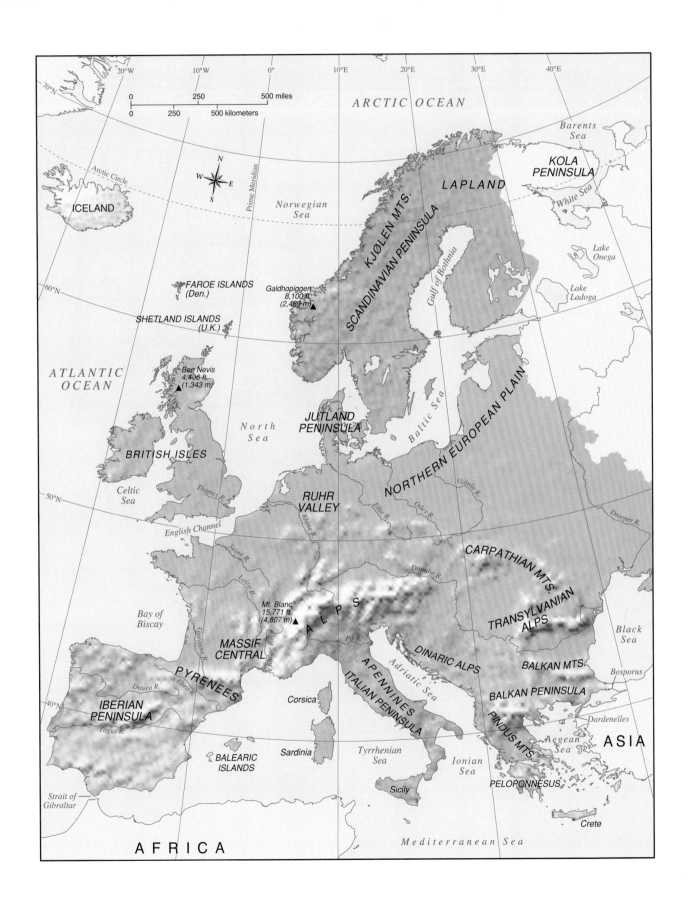

0 250 500 miles
0 250 500 kilometers

ARCTIC OCEAN

Barents Sea

KOLA PENINSULA

LAPLAND

White Sea

Lake Onega

Lake Ladoga

ICELAND

Arctic Circle

FAROE ISLANDS (Den.)

Galdhøpiggen 8,100 ft. (2,469 m)

SHETLAND ISLANDS (U.K.)

Norwegian Sea

KJØLEN MTS.

SCANDINAVIAN PENINSULA

Gulf of Bothnia

ATLANTIC OCEAN

Ben Nevis 4,406 ft. (1,343 m)

North Sea

JUTLAND PENINSULA

Baltic Sea

NORTHERN EUROPEAN PLAIN

Dnieper R.

Vistula R.

BRITISH ISLES

Celtic Sea

Thames R.

English Channel

RUHR VALLEY

Elbe R.

Oder R.

Rhine R.

Seine R.

CARPATHIAN MTS.

Danube R.

Loire R.

Mt. Blanc 15,771 ft. (4,807 m)

A L P S

TRANSYLVANIAN ALPS

Black Sea

Bay of Biscay

Garonne R.

MASSIF CENTRAL

Rhône R.

Po R.

DINARIC ALPS

Adriatic Sea

BALKAN MTS.

Bosporus

PYRENEES

Douro R.

Ebro R.

Corsica

APENNINES

ITALIAN PENINSULA

BALKAN PENINSULA

Dardenelles

IBERIAN PENINSULA

Tagus R.

BALEARIC ISLANDS

Sardinia

Tyrrhenian Sea

PINDUS MTS.

Aegean Sea

ASIA

Strait of Gibraltar

Sicily

Ionian Sea

PELOPONNESUS

Crete

AFRICA

Mediterranean Sea

70°N

60°N

50°N

40°N

20°W

10°W

0°

10°E

20°E

30°E

40°E

Prime Meridian

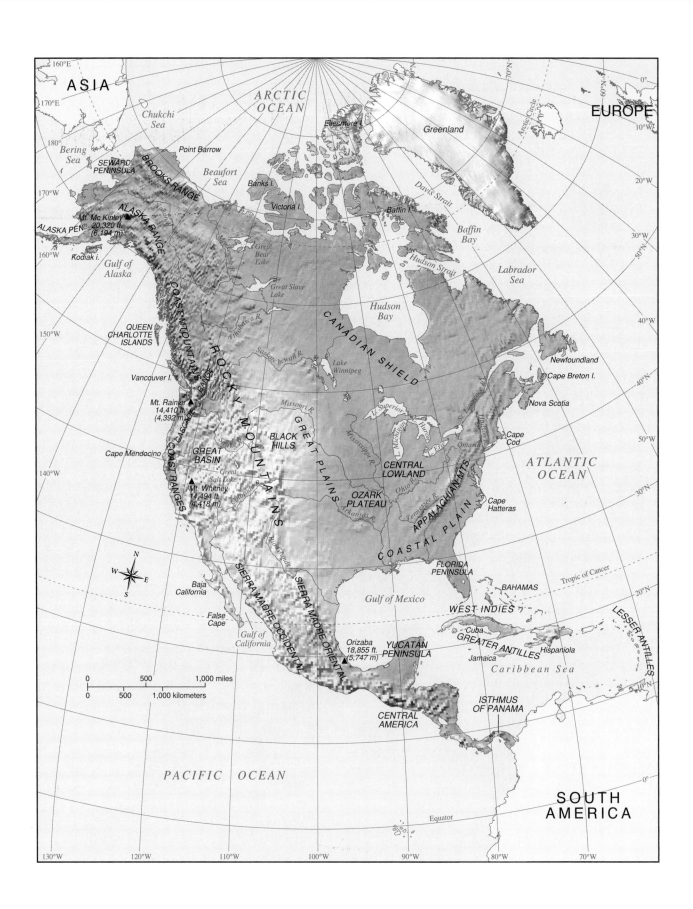

Political Map of North America

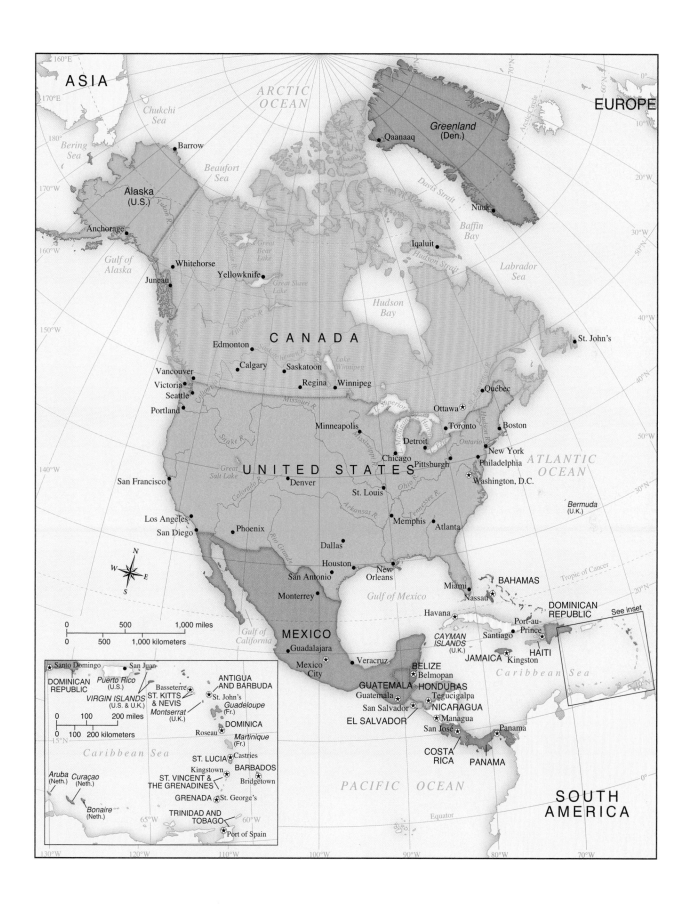

ASIA

ARCTIC OCEAN

EUROPE

Chukchi Sea

Bering Sea

Barrow

Beaufort Sea

Greenland (Den.)

Qaanaaq

Alaska (U.S.)

Anchorage

Gulf of Alaska

Whitehorse

Yellowknife

Juneau

Great Bear Lake

Great Slave Lake

Nuuk

Davis Strait

Baffin Bay

Iqaluit

Hudson Strait

Labrador Sea

Hudson Bay

CANADA

Edmonton

Calgary

Saskatoon

Regina

Winnipeg

Lake Winnipeg

St. John's

Vancouver

Victoria

Seattle

Portland

Québec

Ottawa

Toronto

Boston

Minneapolis

Detroit

Chicago

Pittsburgh

New York

Philadelphia

ATLANTIC OCEAN

San Francisco

Great Salt Lake

UNITED STATES

Denver

St. Louis

Washington, D.C.

Los Angeles

San Diego

Phoenix

Dallas

Houston

Memphis

Atlanta

Bermuda (U.K.)

San Antonio

Monterrey

New Orleans

Miami

BAHAMAS

Nassau

Tropic of Cancer

Gulf of California

MEXICO

Gulf of Mexico

Havana

Guadalajara

Mexico City

Veracruz

CAYMAN ISLANDS (U.K.)

Santiago

Port-au-Prince

DOMINICAN REPUBLIC

See inset

HAITI

JAMAICA Kingston

Caribbean Sea

BELIZE

Belmopan

GUATEMALA

HONDURAS

Guatemala

Tegucigalpa

San Salvador

EL SALVADOR

NICARAGUA

Managua

San José

COSTA RICA

Panama

PANAMA

PACIFIC OCEAN

Equator

SOUTH AMERICA

Inset (Caribbean)

Santo Domingo

San Juan

DOMINICAN REPUBLIC

Puerto Rico (U.S.)

VIRGIN ISLANDS (U.S. & U.K.)

Basseterre

ST. KITTS & NEVIS

Montserrat (U.K.)

ANTIGUA AND BARBUDA

St. John's

Guadeloupe (Fr.)

DOMINICA

Roseau

Martinique (Fr.)

Caribbean Sea

Aruba (Neth.)

Curaçao (Neth.)

ST. LUCIA

Castries

Kingstown

ST. VINCENT & THE GRENADINES

BARBADOS

Bridgetown

Bonaire (Neth.)

GRENADA St. George's

TRINIDAD AND TOBAGO

Port of Spain

0   500   1,000 miles
0   500   1,000 kilometers

0   100   200 miles
0   100   200 kilometers

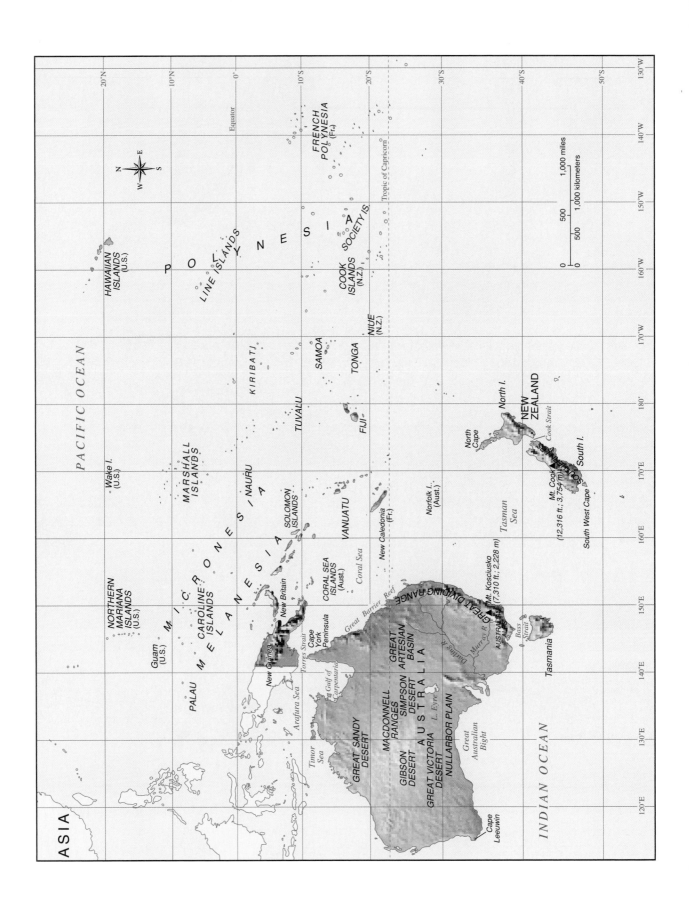

ASIA

PACIFIC OCEAN

N
E
S
W

HAWAIIAN
ISLANDS
(U.S.)

P O L Y N E S I A

LINE ISLANDS

Equator

FRENCH
POLYNESIA
(Fr.)

SOCIETY IS.

COOK
ISLANDS
(N.Z.)

Tropic of Capricorn

NIUE
(N.Z.)

KIRIBATI

SAMOA

TONGA

TUVALU

FIJI

NEW
ZEALAND

North I.

North
Cape

Cook Strait

South I.

Mt. Cook
12,316 ft.; 3,754 m
South West Cape

Wake I.
(U.S.)

MARSHALL
ISLANDS

M I C R O N E S I A / NAURU

SOLOMON
ISLANDS

VANUATU

New Caledonia
(Fr.)

Norfolk I.
(Aust.)

Tasman
Sea

NORTHERN
MARIANA
ISLANDS
(U.S.)

Guam
(U.S.)

CAROLINE ISLANDS

M E L A N E S I A

New Britain

Cape
York
Peninsula

CORAL SEA
ISLANDS
(Aust.)

Coral Sea

Great Barrier Reef

GREAT DIVIDING RANGE

Mt. Kosciusko
7,310 ft.; 2,228 m

Bass
Strait

PALAU

New Guinea

Torres Strait

Gulf of
Carpentaria

GREAT SANDY
DESERT

MACDONNELL
RANGES

SIMPSON
DESERT

GREAT
ARTESIAN
BASIN

Darling R.

Murray R.

AUSTRALIA

Tasmania

Arafura Sea

Timor
Sea

GIBSON
DESERT

GREAT VICTORIA
DESERT

A U S T R A L I A

L. Eyre

NULLARBOR PLAIN

Great
Australian
Bight

Cape
Leeuwin

INDIAN OCEAN

1,000 miles

1,000 kilometers

500

500

0

0

20°N

10°N

0°

10°S

20°S

30°S

40°S

50°S

120°E   130°E   140°E   150°E   160°E   170°E   180°   170°W   160°W   150°W   140°W   130°W

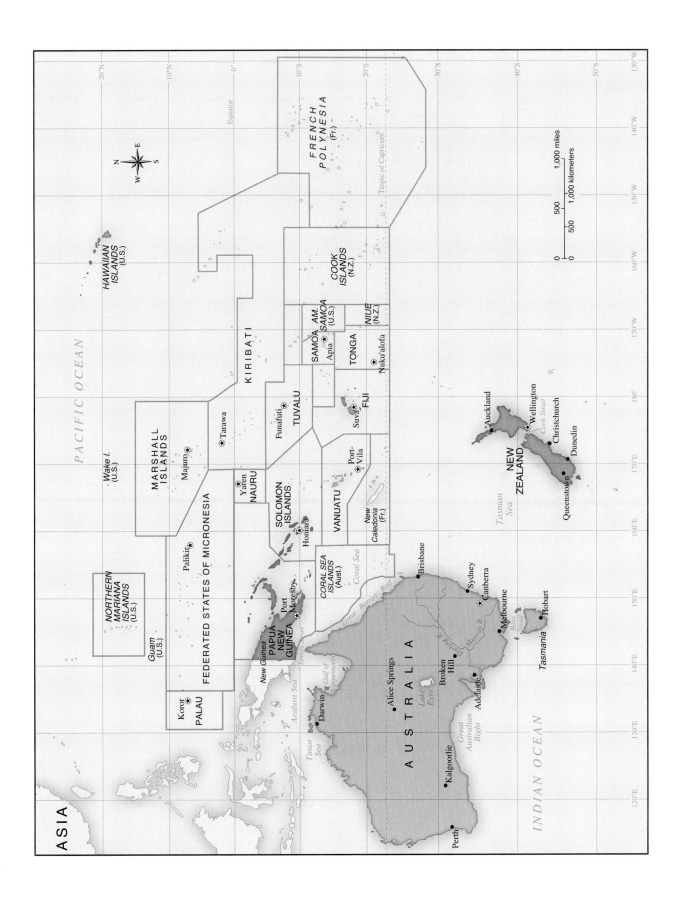

Physical Map of South America

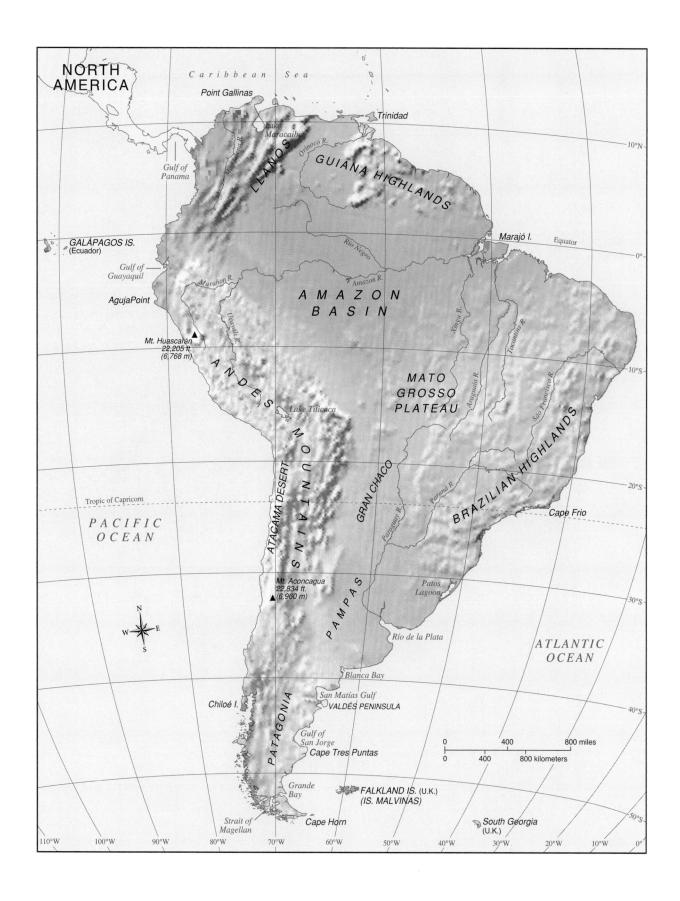

NORTH AMERICA

Caribbean Sea

Point Gallinas

Trinidad

LLANOS

Magdalena R.

Lake Maracaibo

Orinoco R.

GUIANA HIGHLANDS

Gulf of Panama

GALÁPAGOS IS.
(Ecuador)

Río Negro

Marajó I.

Equator

0°

Gulf of Guayaquil

Marañon R.

Amazon R.

AMAZON BASIN

Aguja Point

Ucayali R.

Mt. Huascarán
22,205 ft.
(6,768 m)

Xingu R.

Araguaia R.

Tocantins R.

10°S

A N D E S

Lake Titicaca

MATO GROSSO PLATEAU

São Francisco R.

BRAZILIAN HIGHLANDS

Tropic of Capricorn

M O U N T A I N S

ATACAMA DESERT

GRAN CHACO

Paraguay R.

Paraná R.

20°S

PACIFIC OCEAN

Cape Frio

Mt. Aconcagua
22,834 ft.
(6,960 m)

PAMPAS

Patos Lagoon

30°S

Río de la Plata

ATLANTIC OCEAN

N
W   E
S

Blanca Bay

Chiloé I.

PATAGONIA

San Matías Gulf

VALDÉS PENINSULA

40°S

Gulf of San Jorge

Cape Tres Puntas

0   400   800 miles
0   400   800 kilometers

Grande Bay

FALKLAND IS. (U.K.)
(IS. MALVINAS)

Strait of Magellan

Cape Horn

South Georgia
(U.K.)

50°S

110°W   100°W   90°W   80°W   70°W   60°W   50°W   40°W   30°W   20°W   10°W   0°

10°N

Online Resources

The Online Resources at www.teachtci.com/historyalive provide the following resources and assignments linked to the content of each unit in *History Alive! The Ancient World*:

* biographies of people important in the history of each area of the world
* excerpts from primary sources and literature
* an Internet research project and links to related Web sites for more in-depth exploration
* enrichment essays and activities

Below are brief descriptions of the biographies and excerpts from primary sources and literature for each unit.

Unit 1: Early Humans and the Rise of Civilization

Biography Kathleen Kenyon (1906–1978). This British archaeologist conducted excavations to learn about the ancient inhabitants of Jericho. Her discoveries have made a significant impact on the study of archaeology in the Middle East. (Chapter 1: Investigating the Past)

Primary Source *The Code of Hammurabi* (written c. 1792–1750 B.C.E.). Under the rule of King Hammurabi, the people of Babylonia were subject to this detailed code of laws. (Chapter 6: Exploring Four Empires of Mesopotamia)

Literature *The Epic of Gilgamesh* (c. 2000 B.C.E.). Perhaps the oldest written story on Earth, this myth from ancient Sumer was written in cuneiform script on 12 clay tablets. It tells the adventures of Gilgamesh, legendary King of Uruk. (Chapter 5: Was Ancient Sumer a Civilization?)

Unit 2: Ancient Egypt and the Near East

Biography Naomi and Ruth (Old Testament, Book of Ruth). This story from ancient Hebrew scriptures tells of a remarkable relationship between two women—one Jew and one gentile—and what they meant to the Jewish people. (Chapter 11: The Ancient Hebrews and the Origins of Judaism)

Primary Source *The Histories* by by Herodotus (c. 480–425 B.C.E.). An excerpt from the writings of this ancient Greek historian tells of a Persian expedition down the Nile to Kush. (Chapter 10: The Kingdom of Kush)

Psalm 137 (Old Testament, Book of Psalms). This moving song expresses the grief of the Jews being held captive in Babylon. (Chapter 12: The Struggle to Preserve Judaism)

Painted scenes from the Tomb of Rekhmire and Tomb of Nakht (c. 1550–1295 B.C.E.). These images from ancient Egyptian burials offer a glimpse into family life and the daily work of slaves. (Chapter 9: Daily Life in Ancient Egypt)

Literature *The Satire of the Trades* (c. 1950–1900 B.C.E.). This poem found on an ancient Egyptian papyrus describes the hardships faced by craftsmen and workers of all types. (Chapter 9: Daily Life in Ancient Egypt)

The Torah (from oral tradition, written down c. 5th century B.C.E.). Both Hebrew history and teachings of Judaic law are included in these ancient writings. (Chapter 11: The Ancient Hebrews and the Origins of Judaism)

Unit 3: Ancient India

Biography Mahavira (599–527 B.C.E.). Born an Indian prince, Mahavira gave up all his possessions to become a religious teacher. He spread the values of an ancient religion called Jainism, including respect for all forms of life (people, animals, birds, plants, insects). (Chapter 15: Learning About Hindu Beliefs)

Primary Source *The Travels or Fa-hsien or Record of Buddhistic Kingdoms* by Fa-hsien (written 394–414 C.E.). This is an excerpt from the journal of a Chinese monk who went to India to learn more about Buddhism. (Chapter 18: The Achievements of the Gupta Empire)

Literature *Ramayana* (from oral tradition; first written down c. 4th century B.C.E.). Hindus often teach religious beliefs to their children through stories. This excerpt from a modern Reader's Theater adaptation of the ancient Indian epic teaches about *dharma* (duty). (Chapter 15: Learning About Hindu Beliefs)

Unit 4: Ancient China

Biography Emperor Wu (156–87 B.C.E.). Wu ruled China for more than 50 years. His great army expanded the borders of the Han Dynasty, but he also supported Chinese art and culture. (Chapter 23: The Han Dynasty)

Primary Source *Lessons for Women* by Pan Chao (45–116 C.E.). In this excerpt from her handbook, China's first female historian describes the role of women in a Confucian society. (Chapter 21: Three Chinese Philosophies)

Literature *Ballad of Mulan* (c. 5 C.E.). This poem from the Han dynasty is an example of yuefu poetry, which often dealt with the emotions and daily lives of ordinary people. (Chapter 23: Three Chinese Philosophies)

Unit 5: Ancient Greece

Biography Pericles (c. 490–429 B.C.E.). Pericles helped rebuild Athens after the Persian Wars and led this city-state into its golden age. (Chapter 29: The Golden Age of Athens)

Plato (c. 427–347 B.C.E.). Founder of a school of philosophy called The Academy, Plato wrote many works about his political and scientific beliefs, some of which still influence modern thinkers. (Chapter 29: The Golden Age of Athens)

Literature *Aesop's Fables* (6th century B.C.E.). Fables are short tales that were once used to explain natural phenomena, and are now used to teach lessons. Three examples are presented. (Chapter 31: The Legacy of Ancient Greece)

"Some say..." by Sappho (born 612 B.C.E.). This Grecian woman wrote poems about love that were traditionally performed to music (a lyre). Only fragments of her work have survived. (Chapter 31: The Legacy of Ancient Greece)

Unit 6: Ancient Rome

Biography Tiberius Gracchus (163–133 B.C.E.) and Gaius Gracchus (153–121 B.C.E.). These two brothers both served in the Roman Senate, introducing a number of reforms that improved life for the people of Rome. (Chapter 34: From Republic to Empire)

Primary Source *Letter from Cicero to Brutus* (written 43 B.C.E.). After Julius Caesar's assassination by Brutus, the senator Cicero writes about his fears for the Roman republic. (Chapter 34: From Republic to Empire)

Literature: *Aeneid* by Virgil (70–19 B.C.E.). This epic poem glorifies the origins of the Roman Empire. In this excerpt, the goddess Venus brings gifts from the gods to her son Aeneas. (Chapter 37: The Legacy of Rome in the Modern World)

New Testament (c. 1st century C.E.). Parables and sermons from this collection of books and letters help explain the teachings of Jesus. Through the ages, they have offered Christians lessons for living. (Chapter 36: The Origins and Spread of Christianity)

Glossary

Teal words are defined in the margins of *History Alive! The Ancient World*.
Red words are key concepts in the chapter introductions.

A

Abraham the leader who led the Hebrews from Mesopotamia to Canaan

achievement an accomplishment

acropolis the hill above a Greek city on which temples were built

agora a marketplace in ancient Greece

agriculture the business of farming

Akkadian Empire a Mesopotamian empire

Alexander the Great the ruler of a vast empire from Macedonia to India in the 300s B.C.E.

alliance an agreement between nations to work together for common interests

ally a country or group that joins with another for a common purpose, such as to fight against a common enemy

alms goods given to the poor

ancestor worship honoring ancestors through rituals, such as offering food and wine to the dead

ancient history the study of the distant past, from the earliest humans through the first great civilizations

anesthetic something that takes away the feeling of pain

anthropologist a scientist who studies human development and culture

appoint to choose someone to fill an office or a position

aqueduct a pipe or channel that brings water from distant places

arch an upside-down U- or V-shaped structure that supports weight above it, as in a doorway

archeologist an expert who studies the past by examining objects that people have left behind

archer a person who shoots with a bow and arrow

architecture the art of designing buildings

aristocrat a member of the most powerful class in ancient Greek society

Ark of the Covenant the chest containing the Ten Commandments, written on stone tablets, that the Hebrews carried with them during their wanderings after their flight from Egypt

art human creations intended to express beauty and convey messages

artifact an object made or used by people in the past

artisan a craftsperson

ascetic a person who gives up worldly pleasures

Ashoka an Indian king who used Buddhist values to unify India from about 269 to 232 B.C.E.

assembly a group of citizens in an ancient Greek democracy with the power to pass laws

Assyrian Empire a Mesopotamian empire

astronomy the study of stars and planets

B

Babylonian Empire a Mesopotamian empire

baptize a ritual by which a person is welcomed into a religion

bas-relief a sculpture in which the image projects out from a flat surface

biped a two-footed animal

Brahman in Hinduism, the one supreme power, or divine force, that everything is a part of

Brahmanism an ancient Indian religion in which the Brahmins (priests and religious scholars) are the dominant class

Buddha a man originally named Siddhartha Gautama who lived in India from about 563 to 483 B.C.E. and began the religion of Buddhism

Buddhism a religion of India begun by Prince Siddhartha, or the Buddha

bureaucracy a form of government in which a few people rule many others

Glossary

C

calligraphy the art of fine handwriting

capability skill

capital a city that is the center of government

caravan a group of people traveling together

caste a class, or group, in Hindu society

cavalry soldiers who ride on horses

census an official count of the population or number of people living in an area

chariot a two-wheeled vehicle pulled by a horse

Christianity the religion based on the life and teachings of Jesus Christ

citadel a fortress built to protect a city

citizen a member of a democracy, who has certain rights and responsibilities

city-state an early city that was like a small, independent country with its own laws and government

civilization a culture marked by developments in arts, sciences, government, and social structure

civil servant a person who works for a government

civil war a war between regions of the same country

clan a large group of friends and family

climate the average weather conditions at a particular place

colonist a person who lives in a colony

colony a settlement in a distant place

compass an instrument for determining direction

Confucianism a Chinese philosophy that emphasizes proper behavior

consul one of two chief leaders in the Roman Republic

covenant an agreement or promise

culture a characteristic of civilization that includes the beliefs and behaviors of a society or group of people

cuneiform writing that uses wedge-shaped characters

cuniculus an irrigation system invented by the Etruscans

D

daily life the factors of everyday existence, including religion, recreation, housing, food and drink, and education

Daoism a Chinese philosophy that emphasizes living in harmony with nature

David the Hebrew king who established Jerusalem as a holy city

deities in Hinduism, the forms that represent the various qualities of Brahman

delta an area of sediment deposited at the mouth of a river

democracy a form of government in which the ruling power is shared by all citizens

descendant a daughter or son, granddaughter or grandson, and so on

dharma one of the basic beliefs of Hinduism that stands for law, obligation, and duty

disciple a person who helps spread the religious teachings of another

dome a half-round or hemisphere-shaped roof

domesticate to train a wild animal to be useful to humans

drama the art of writing, acting in, and producing plays

dynasty a family or group that rules for several generations

E

economy a system of managing the wealth of a community or region

edict a command that is obeyed like a law

education a system of learning

Glossary

Egyptian civilization a society of people who lived in the northeast corner of Africa from around 3100 B.C.E. to 350 C.E.

embalm to treat a dead body with preservatives to prevent it from decaying

empire a large territory in which several groups of people are ruled by a single leader or government

engineering the science of building structures and the like

environmental factors the water, topography (shape of the land), and vegetation (plant life) of an area or region

Etruscans inhabitants of Etruria, a land just north of the Palatine

execute to kill

exile living away from one's native country

Exodus the escape of the Hebrews from Egyptian slavery

expansion the process of becoming larger, such as of an empire

F

famine a severe shortage of food

fertilization the process of adding fertilizer, or plant food, to soil

feudalism a system of government based on landowners and tenants

G

gentile non-Jewish

geographer an expert who studies and creates maps of Earth's natural and humanmade features

geographic region an area of land that has its own geographic characteristics

geography the physical features of an area

geometry the branch of mathematics involving points, lines, planes, and figures

glacier a huge mass of ice that slowly slides over a land area

gladiator a person trained to fight another person to the death for public entertainment

golden age a time of great prosperity and achievement

gospel an account of the life and teachings of Jesus Christ

government the people or groups that rule a particular region

granary a place to store grain

Greco-Roman having the characteristics of Roman art with a strong Greek influence

Greek contribution influence from the Greeks that affects us today, as in the areas of language, government, medicine, mathematics and science, architecture, entertainment, and sports

Greek culture the features of Greek society, including religion, architecture, sculpture, drama, philosophy, and sports

Greeks inhabitants of Greece

Gupta Empire an empire that flourished in India from about 320 to 550 C.E.

H

Han dynasty the Chinese dynasty that ruled from about 206 B.C.E. to 220 C.E.

Hebrew civilization a society of people (ancient Israelites) who lived to the northeast of Egypt, in Canaan, from about 1800 B.C.E. to 70 C.E.

Hellespont the long, narrow body of water between Europe and Asia in present-day Turkey

hieroglyph a symbol used in hieroglyphics, a system of writing developed in about 3000 B.C.E.

Hinduism India's first major religion

historian an expert who studies and records the past

hominid a prehistoric human

human sacrifice a person who is killed as part of a religious ritual

I

immortal able to live forever

Indus-Sarasvati civilization a society of people who settled in the Indus River valley in India and were known for their advanced culture; also called the Harappan civilization

industry a business that manufactures a particular product, such as silk

irrigation system a means of supplying land with water

isolated community a settlement that is separated from other settlements by features such as mountains or oceans

J

Jesus a man who lived from about 6 B.C.E. to 27 C.E. and upon whose life and teachings Christianity is based. Christians refer to him as Jesus Christ.

Jewish beliefs the basis of Judaism, such as the belief in one God and the importance of following the Ten Commandments

Jewish Diaspora the scattering of the Jewish people to many lands

Judaism a major world religion that was founded by the Hebrews

K

kandake a powerful female leader who co-ruled Kush with her husband and sons

karma in Hinduism, the belief that how a person lives will affect their next life

Kush civilization a society of people who lived along the Nile, south of Egypt, from about 2000 B.C.E. to 350 C.E.

L

land bridge a piece of land connecting two continents

language spoken and written words used to communicate thoughts, ideas, and feelings

Latins people from the ancient country of Latium, an area in what is now the country of Italy

latitude a measure of how far a place on Earth is from the equator

law a legal system

legacy a contribution of one culture to another

Legalism a Chinese philosophy that emphasizes strict obedience to laws

levee a wall of earth built to prevent a river from flooding its banks

lodestone a type of iron ore

logograph a written character that represents a word

longitude a measure of how far a place on Earth is from an imaginary line that runs between the North and South Poles on the globe

M

Macedonia an ancient kingdom north of Greece

maize a type of corn

Mandate of Heaven a power or law believed to be granted by a god

Mauryan Empire an empire that flourished in India from about 322 to 187 B.C.E.

medicine the science of healing the body and preventing disease

merchant a person who makes money by selling goods

Mesopotamia in ancient times, the geographic area located between the Tigris and Euphrates Rivers

Messiah a savior that many Jews believed had been promised by God

Middle Kingdom a period in ancient Egyptian history that lasted from about 2000 to 1800 B.C.E.

migrate to move from one geographic region to another

millet a type of grain

mirage an image of something that isn't really there, such as water

missionary someone who tries to persuade others to believe in his or her religious teachings

Mohenjodaro one of the first great settlements in India and a center of the Indus-Sarasvati civilization

monarch a single ruler who holds all the power in a country or empire

monarchy a form of government in which the ruling power is in the hands of one person

monastery a home for monks

Glossary

monk a holy man who devotes his life to religious practice

monotheism the belief that there is only one God

monsoon a strong wind that brings heavy rain to southern Asia in the summer

Moses a Hebrew leader who led his people out of slavery in Egypt and brought Judaism its fundamental laws, the Ten Commandments

mural a wall painting

mutton meat from sheep

myth a traditional story that helps to explain a culture's beliefs

N

Neo-Babylonian Empire a Mesopotamian empire

Neolithic Age the later part of the Stone Age, called the New Stone Age, from 8000 to 3000 B.C.E.

New Kingdom a period in ancient Egyptian history that lasted from about 1600 to 1100 B.C.E.

nirvana an ideal state of happiness and peace

nomad a person who moves from place to place with no permanent home

O

oasis a place where water can be found in a desert

Old Kingdom a period in ancient Egyptian history that lasted from about 2700 to 2200 B.C.E.

oligarch one of several people who rule a country or empire together, sharing the power

oligarchy a form of government in which the ruling power is in the hands of a few people

ore a mineral mined for its valuable uses

P

Palatine one of the seven hills in ancient Rome

Paleolithic Age the first period of the Stone Age, called the Old Stone Age, from about 2 million years ago to around 8000 B.C.E.

papyrus a tough water plant used to make paper and rope in ancient times

parable a simple story that explains a moral or religious lesson

Parthenon the temple honoring the goddess Athena, built on the acropolis above Athens

patrician in the Roman Republic, a rich man who held power

peasant a person who does farmwork for wealthy landowners

Peloponnesian War conflict between Athens and Sparta (and other city-states) from 431 to 404 B.C.E.

Peloponnesus the peninsula forming the southern part of the mainland of Greece

Persian Empire at its height in the 400s B.C.E., the largest empire the world had ever known, ruling over land in Africa, the Middle East, and Asia

Persian wars the conflict between Persia and the Greek city-states between 499 and 479 B.C.E.

pharaoh an ancient Egyptian leader

philosophy a theory or set of values by which one lives; the search for wisdom or knowledge

physical feature an aspect of the land, such as mountains, plateaus, and rivers

pictograph a symbol that stands for an object

pilgrimage a journey to a holy place

plague a terrible disaster affecting many people and thought to be sent by God as a punishment

plateau a flat area of land that is elevated, or raised, above the land around it

plebeian one of the common people; in the Roman Republic, a person who had no say in government

prefect a high official in ancient Rome

prehistoric before written history

priestess a female priest

prophet a person who speaks or interprets for God to other people

province a territory that is part of a country or an empire

Punic Wars wars fought between Rome and Carthage

pyramid a huge, triangular-shaped monument of ancient Egypt built around a tomb

Q

Qin Shihuangdi the man who became emperor over a united China from 221 to 210 B.C.E.

R

rabbi a religious teacher who studies and teaches others about Jewish law

reincarnation the belief that a person's soul is reborn into a new body after death

relationship between Egypt and Kush how the cultures of Egypt of Kush influenced each other commercially, culturally, and politically

religion a set of spiritual beliefs, values, and practices

remains a dead body

Renaissance a period of European history around the 14th century in which there was a rebirth of interest and accomplishments in art, literature, and learning

republic a form of government with elected leaders

ritual relating to a ceremony, such as a religious ceremony

Rome a city in Italy

S

Sabbath the seventh day of the week to be used for rest and worship, according to one of the Ten Commandments

sacrifice a gift of an animal for slaughter as a way to honor gods

samsara in Hinduism, the belief in a continuous cycle of birth, death, and rebirth

Sanskrit an ancient language of India

sarcophagus a large stone coffin

science knowledge of the physical world

scribe a person who writes

scroll a roll of a material like paper or papyrus

sculpture the art of creating three-dimensional figures from such materials as wood, stone, and clay

seismograph an instrument for detecting earthquakes

Senate a group of 300 men elected to govern Rome in the Roman Republic

settlement a small community or village

sewer system a network of pipes that disposes of sewage, or waste water

shelter a place that provides protection from weather, such as a house

Shang dynasty the Chinese dynasty that ruled the area around the Huang He from 1700 to 1122 B.C.E.

siege a military blockade and attack on a city to force it to surrender

Silk Road a network of trade routes that stretched more than 4,000 miles across Asia

silt fine particles of rock

social class a group of society distinguished from other groups by such things as wealth, property, and rights

social pyramid a drawing of a pyramid shape with levels showing how social classes are positioned above and below one another regarding power and rights in the society

social structure the way a society or civilization is organized

Solomon the Hebrew king who built Jerusalem's first great temple; son of King David

standardize to make the same

status importance

Stone Age the first period of prehistoric human culture, from about 2 million years ago to around 3000 B.C.E.

struggle to preserve Judaism the effort of the Jews to preserve their religion after being scattered to many lands in the Diaspora

stylus a pointed instrument used for writing

Glossary

subcontinent a landmass, such as India, that is of great size but smaller than a continent

Sumer an area in the southern part of Mesopotamia, where cities first appeared

Sumerians ancient people who lived in the geographic region of Sumer

synagogue a place of Jewish worship

T

Talmud the collection of ancient Jewish writings that interpret the law of the Torah

technology the use of tools and other inventions for practical purposes

Ten Commandments the ten laws said to be given to Moses by God

toga a loose robe worn by men in Rome

topography the surface features of a place or region, such as mountains or deserts

Torah the first five books of the Jewish Bible

trade the business of buying and selling or exchanging items

trade route a network of roads along which traders traveled

treaty a written agreement by which two or more groups agree to be peaceful

tribune an official of the Roman Republic elected by plebeians to protect their rights

tributary a stream that feeds into a larger river

tribute wealth sent from one country or ruler to another as a sign that the other is superior

tyranny a form of government in which the ruling power is in the hands of one person who is not a lawful king

tyrant a person who seizes power illegally

U

unification of China the merging of Chinese government and culture that occurred during the reign of Qin Shihuangdi

unify to make into a whole

V

vault an arched structure used to hold up a ceiling or roof

Vedas a collection of Hindu sacred writings

vegetation the plant life of a place or region

veto to refuse to approve proposals of government made by the Senate

villa a large house in the country

vizier a high-ranking government official

W

warfare military struggle between enemies

writing letters, words, and symbols formed on a surface, using an instrument, to record or communicate information

Y

yang one half of the Daoist concept of opposing forces of nature; the opposite of yin

yin one half of the Daoist concept of opposing forces of nature; the opposite of yang

Z

ziggurat an ancient Mesopotamian temple tower

Zhou dynasty a line of rulers in China from about 1045 to 256 B.C.E.

A

B

Correlation of History Alive! Materials to State History–Social Science Standards

Below is a correlation of *History Alive! The Ancient World* to California Content Standards. For correlations to other state standards, go to **http://www.historyalive.com**.

California History–Social Science Standards, Sixth Grade	Where Standards Are Addressed
6.1 Students describe what is known through archaeological studies of the early physical and cultural development of humankind from the Paleolithic era to the agricultural revolution.	
1. Describe the hunter-gatherer societies, including the development of tools and the use of fire.	pp. 16–22
2. Identify the locations of human communities that populated the major regions of the world and describe how humans adapted to a variety of environments.	pp. 22, 26, 34–39 Online Resources: Ch. 3 Enrichment Essay 4
3. Discuss the climatic changes and human modifications of the physical environment that gave rise to the domestication of plants and animals and new sources of clothing and shelter.	pp. 25–31, 34–39 Online Resources: Ch. 3 Enrichment Essay 4
6.2 Students analyze the geographic, political, economic, religious, and social structures of the early civilizations of Mesopotamia, Egypt, and Kush.	
1. Locate and describe the major river systems and discuss the physical settings that supported permanent settlement and early civilizations.	pp. 33–35, 65–71
2. Trace the development of agricultural techniques that permitted the production of economic surplus and the emergence of cities as centers of culture and power.	pp. 27–31, 34–39, 42–43, 57
3. Understand the relationship between religion and the social and political order in Mesopotamia and Egypt.	pp. 44-46, 53-54, 57, 74–75, 81–87
4. Know the significance of Hammurabi's Code.	p. 54 Online Resources: Ch. 6 Primary Sources
5. Discuss the main features of Egyptian art and architecture.	pp. 75-76, 78–79, 90–91
6. Describe the role of Egyptian trade in the eastern Mediterranean and Nile valley.	pp. 77, 96 Online Resources: Ch. 8 Enrichment Essay 5
7. Understand the significance of Queen Hatshepsut and Ramses the Great.	pp. 77, 78-79
8. Identify the location of the Kush civilization and describe its political, commercial, and cultural relations with Egypt.	pp. 95–99
9. Trace the evolution of language and its written forms.	pp. 49, 53, 88–89, 99 Online Resources: Ch. 5 Literature

California History–Social Science Standards, Sixth Grade	Where Standards Are Addressed
6.3 Students analyze the geographic, political, economic, religious, and social structures of the Ancient Hebrews.	
1. Describe the origins and significance of Judaism as the first monotheistic religion based on the concept of one God who sets down moral laws for humanity.	pp. 101–105, 112-113
2. Identify the sources of the ethical teachings and central beliefs of Judaism (the Hebrew Bible, the Commentaries): belief in God, observance of law, practice of the concepts of righteousness and justice, and importance of study; and describe how the ideas of the Hebrew traditions are reflected in the moral and ethical traditions of Western civilization.	pp. 101–105, 107, 112–113
3. Explain the significance of Abraham, Moses, Naomi, Ruth, David, and Yohanan ben Zaccai in the development of the Jewish religion.	pp. 101–109, 116–117 Online Resources: Ch. 11 Biographies
4. Discuss the locations of the settlements and movements of Hebrew peoples, including the Exodus and their movement to and from Egypt, and outline the significance of the Exodus to the Jewish and other people.	pp. 102–107, 111, 114–115 Online Resources: Ch. 12 Primary Sources
5. Discuss how Judaism survived and developed despite the continuing dispersion of much of the Jewish population from Jerusalem and the rest of Israel after the destruction of the second Temple in A.D. 70.	pp. 116–117
6.4 Students analyze the geographic, political, economic, religious, and social structures of the early civilizations of Ancient Greece.	
1. Discuss the connections between geography and the development of city-states in the region of the Aegean Sea, including patterns of trade and commerce among Greek city-states and within the wider Mediterranean region.	pp. 247–251, 260, 262
2. Trace the transition from tyranny and oligarchy to early democratic forms of government and back to dictatorship in ancient Greece, including the significance of the invention of the idea of citizenship (e.g., from *Pericles' Funeral Oration*).	pp. 254–257 Online Resources: Ch. 29 Biographies (Pericles)
3. State the key differences between Athenian, or direct, democracy and representative democracy.	p. 257, 298
4. Explain the significance of Greek mythology to the everyday life of people in the region and how Greek literature continues to permeate our literature and language today, drawing from Greek mythology and epics, such as Homer's *Iliad* and *Odyssey,* and from *Aesop's Fables*.	p. 281-282, 284, 296 Online Resources: Ch. 31 Literature (Aesop); Enrichment Essay 10
5. Outline the founding, expansion, and political organization of the Persian Empire.	pp. 245, 272
6. Compare and contrast life in Athens and Sparta, with emphasis on their roles in the Persian and Peloponnesian Wars.	pp. 259–268, 273–277, 289–290
7. Trace the rise of Alexander the Great and the spread of Greek culture eastward and into Egypt.	pp. 290–295

California History–Social Science Standards, Sixth Grade	Where Standards Are Addressed
8. Describe the enduring contributions of important Greek figures in the arts and sciences (e.g., Hypatia, Socrates, Plato, Aristotle, Euclid, Thucydides).	pp. 283, 285, 298-9, 300-301 Online Resources: Ch. 29 Biographies (Plato); Ch. 31 Literature (Sappho); Enrichment Essay 10
6.5 Students analyze the geographic, political, economic, religious, and social structures of the early civilizations of India.	
1. Locate and describe the major river system and discuss the physical setting that supported the rise of this civilization.	pp. 124, 126, 129, 131, 133
2. Discuss the significance of the Aryan invasions.	p. 144 Online Resources: Ch. 15 Enrichment Essay 7
3. Explain the major beliefs and practices of Brahmanism in India and how they evolved into early Hinduism.	pp. 144–146
4. Outline the social structure of the caste system.	p. 145
5. Know the life and moral teachings of the Buddha and how Buddhism spread in India, Ceylon, and Central Asia.	pp. 121, 153–159, 163–164, 241
6. Describe the growth of the Maurya empire and the political and moral achievements of the emperor Asoka.	pp. 161–164
7. Discuss important aesthetic and intellectual traditions (e.g., Sanskrit literature, including the *Bhagavad Gita;* medicine; metallurgy; and mathematics, including Hindu-Arabic numerals and the zero).	pp. 167, 169-175 Online Resources: Ch. 15 Biographies; Literature; Ch. 18 Enrichment Essay 8
6.6 Students analyze the geographic, political, economic, religious, and social structures of the early civilizations of China.	
1. Locate and describe the origins of Chinese civilization in the Huang-He Valley during the Shang Dynasty.	pp. 191, 195–202
2. Explain the geographic features of China that made governance and the spread of ideas and goods difficult and served to isolate the country from the rest of the world.	pp. 183–191
3. Know about the life of Confucius and the fundamental teachings of Confucianism and Daoism.	pp. 205, 208–209, 210–211 Online Resources: Ch. 21 Primary Sources
4. Identify the political and cultural problems prevalent in the time of Confucius and how he sought to solve them.	pp. 205–209
5. List the policies and achievements of the emperor Shi Huangdi in unifying northern China under the Qin Dynasty.	pp. 215–221

California History–Social Science Standards, Sixth Grade	Where Standards Are Addressed
6. Detail the political contributions of the Han Dynasty to the development of the imperial bureaucratic state and the expansion of the empire.	pp. 223–225 Online Resources: Ch. 23 Biographies
7. Cite the significance of the trans-Eurasian "silk roads" in the period of the Han Dynasty and Roman Empire and their locations.	pp. 233–241
8. Describe the diffusion of Buddhism northward to China during the Han Dynasty.	p. 241
6.7 Students analyze the geographic, political, economic, religious, and social structures during the development of Rome.	
1. Identify the location and describe the rise of the Roman Republic, including the importance of such mythical and historical figures as Aeneas, Romulus and Remus, Cincinnatus, Julius Caesar, and Cicero.	pp. 309–310, 312, 317, 323–326, 330–331 Online Resources: Ch. 34 Primary Sources
2. Describe the government of the Roman Republic and its significance (e.g., written constitution and tripartite government, checks and balances, civic duty).	pp. 318–321
3. Identify the location of and the political and geographic reasons for the growth of Roman territories and expansion of the empire, including how the empire fostered economic growth through the use of currency and trade routes.	pp. 323–333 Online Resources: Ch. 34 Enrichment Essay 11
4. Discuss the influence of Julius Caesar and Augustus in Rome's transition from republic to empire.	pp. 330–333
5. Trace the migration of Jews around the Mediterranean region and the effects of their conflict with the Romans, including the Romans' restrictions on their right to live in Jerusalem.	pp. 114–117
6. Note the origins of Christianity in the Jewish Messianic prophecies, the life and teachings of Jesus of Nazareth as described in the New Testament, and the contribution of St. Paul the Apostle to the definition and spread of Christian beliefs (e.g., belief in the Trinity, resurrection, salvation).	pp. 347–359 Online Resources: Ch. 36 Literature, Ch. 36 Enrichment Essay 12
7. Describe the circumstances that led to the spread of Christianity in Europe and other Roman territories.	pp. 356–359 pp. 356–359
8. Discuss the legacies of Roman art and architecture, technology and science, literature, language, and law.	pp. 361, 364–371 Online Resources: Ch. 37 Literature

Historical and Social Science Analysis Skills

In addition to the content standards, students demonstrate the following intellectual reasoning, reflection, and research skills, which are reinforced throughout the program.

Chronological and Spatial Thinking

1. Students explain how major events are related to one another in time.

2. Students construct various time lines of key events, people, and periods of the historical era they are studying.

3. Students use a variety of maps and documents to identify physical and cultural features of neighborhoods, cities, states, and countries and to explain the historical migration of people, expansion and disintegration of empires, and the growth of economic systems.

Historical Research, Evidence, and Point of View

1. Students frame questions that can be answered by historical study and research.

2. Students distinguish fact from opinion in historical narratives and stories.

3. Students distinguish relevant from irrelevant information, essential from incidental information, and verifiable from unverifiable information in historical narratives and stories.

4. Students assess the credibility of primary and secondary sources and draw sound conclusions from them.

5. Students detect the different historical points of view on historical events and determine the context in which the historical statements were made (the questions asked, sources used, author's perspectives).

Historical Interpretation

1. Students explain the central issues and problems from the past, placing people and events in a matrix of time and place.

2. Students understand and distinguish cause, effect, sequence, and correlation in historical events, including the long- and short-term causal relations.

3. Students explain the sources of historical continuity and how the combination of ideas and events explains the emergence of new patterns.

4. Students recognize the role of chance, oversight, and error in history.

5. Students recognize that interpretations of history are subject to change as new information is uncovered.

6. Students interpret basic indicators of economic performance and conduct cost-benefit analyses of economic and political issues.

Chapter 1

pp. 2–3: Etosha National Park, Namibia; Jeremy Woodhouse/Getty Images/PhotoDisc. **p. 4:** Hall of Bulls, Lascaux cave, Lascaux, France; © Sisse Brimberg/National Geographic Image Collection. **p. 5:** Susan Jaekel. **p. 6:** Archeological dig in Gibraltar; © Bojan Bredelj/Corbis. **p. 7:** Depiction of Cro-Magnon man with pictographs; © Margaret Kyle McLellan/National Geographic Image Collection. **p. 8:** Magdalenian rock painting depicts scene from a hunt with human figure, Lascaux cave, Perigord, France; © Charles & Josette Lenars/Corbis. **p. 9, upper:** Prehistoric animals from Lascaux cave, France; © Sylvain Julienne/Woodfin Camp & Associates. **p. 9, lower:** Petroglyphs from Los Manos Cave, Patgonia, Santa Cruz Provience, Argentina; © Hubert Stadler/Corbis. **p. 10, upper:** Carving of horse on a spear thrower made of antler bone found in Bruniquel, France; Magdalenian period; Musée des Antiquites Nationales, St. Germain-en-Laye, France; © 1985 David Brill. **p. 10, lower:** Clay sculpture of two bison from the Tuc d'Audoubert cave, France; © Sisse Brimberg/National Geographic Image Collection. **p. 11:** Prehistoric artists' tools including grindstone with manganese, ocher, sculptor's pick, and an engraving burin; © Sisse Brimberg/National Geographic Image Collection.

Chapter 2

p. 12: Illustration of early man in fire-lit cave; © Bettmann/Corbis. **p. 13:** Susan Jaekel. **p. 14:** Susan Jaekel. **p. 15:** Susan Jaekel. **p. 16, left:** Susan Jaekel. **pp. 16–17:** Artist's rendition of *Homo habilis* group skinning a zebra; Robert Harding. **p. 18, left:** Susan Jaekel. **pp. 18–19:** Rendition of *Homo erectus* group around fire; Robert Harding. **p. 20, left:** Susan Jaekel. **pp. 20–21:** Rendition of the Shanidar Cave burial; Robert Harding. **p. 22:** Susan Jaekel. **p. 23:** Artist's rendition of *Homo sapiens sapiens* making cave paintings in Lascaux cave, France; © Jack Unruh/National Geographic Image Collection.

Chapter 3

p. 24: DJ Simison. **p. 25:** Doug Roy. **p. 27:** Detail of cattle, herdsmen, and women with children; cave painting of Tassili n'Ajjer, Algeria; 2nd millenium B.C.E.; Henri Lhote Collection, Musée de l'Homme, Paris, France; © Erich Lessing/Art Resource, NY. **p. 28:** Renate Lohmann. **p. 29:** Renate Lohmann. **p. 30:** Prehistoric man fashioning a cooking pot from clay; 19th C. engraving; The Granger Collection, New York. **p. 31:** Obsidian arrowhead; © Tom Bean/Corbis.

Chapter 4

p. 32: Excavated ruins at Dura Europus, near Mari, As Salihiyah, Syria; © Dean Conger/Corbis. **p. 33:** Doug Roy. **p. 35:** Zagros Mountains, Parawah, Iran; Robert Harding. **p. 36:** Euphrates River near Anah, Iraq; © V.

Southwell/The Hutchison Library. **p. 37:** Irrigated fields on the Euphrates' banks; © V. Southwell/The Hutchison Library. **p. 38:** Detail of armies from the Stele of the Vultures, ca. 2450 B.C.E.; © Gianni Dagli Orti/Corbis. **p. 39:** Artist's rendition of a Sumerian city-state; Teachers' Curriculum Institute.

Chapter 5

p. 40: Both sides of the Standard of Ur (detail), illustration of scenes of war and peace; worked in shell, red limestone, and lapis lazuli, bitumen inlay; © Trustees of the British Museum, London. **p. 41:** Doug Roy. **p. 42, left:** Reverse of U.S. penny; Teachers' Curriculum Institute. **p. 42, right:** Phoenician galley ship on a coin of Sidon, Mesopotamian period, ca. 4th C. B.C.E.; British Museum, London; © Winfield Parks/National Geographic Image Collection. **p. 43:** Boy plowing with buffalo in Azerbaijan area of Iran; © Roger Wood/Corbis. **p. 44:** Sumerian ruins of Uruk; © Nik Wheeler/Corbis. **p. 45:** Nebuchadrezzar II, Chaldean king of Babylon; North Wind Picture Archives. **p. 46:** Ziggurat of Ur, Iraq, Sumerian city ca. 4500–400 B.C.E.; Robert Harding. **p. 47:** Reconstruction of a lyre found in the grave of Queen Pu-abi, Royal Cemetery, Ur, Iraq; © Trustees of the British Museum, London. **p. 48:** Baked clay model of a chariot, 17 x 15 cm; period of the Amorite dynasties, 2000–1595 B.C.E.; © Erich Lessing/Art Resource, NY. **p. 49:** Relief of scribes using tablet and stylus; © Trustees of the British Museum, London.

Chapter 6

p. 50: Elamite warriors marching into battle against Ashurbanipal at the battle of Til Tuba, detail from stone bas-relief, palace in Miniveh, Mesopotamia, 7th C. B.C.E.; © Erich Lessing/Art Resource, NY. **p. 51:** Susan Jaekel. **p. 52:** Head of Sargon the Great, Nineveh, Akkadian, ca. 2300–2200 B.C.E., bronze, h: 12″ (30.7 cm); Iraq Museum, Baghdad, Iraq; © Scala/Art Resource, NY. **p. 53:** Victory Stele of Naram-Sin, ca. 2300–2200 B.C.E.; © Gianni Dagli Orti/Corbis. **p. 54:** Stele of Hammurabi, ca. 1780 B.C.E.; © Gianni Dagli Orti/Corbis. **p. 55:** Terra-cotta relief plaque of a woman weaving, early 2nd millenium B.C.E.; © Gianni Dagli Orti/Corbis. **p. 56:** Tower with defenders; Assyrians attack the Jewish fortified town of Lachish in 701 B.C.E.; detail of an Assyrian relief from the palace of Sennacherib at Ninveh, Mesotamia, 8th C. B.C.E., British Museum, London; © Erich Lessing/Art Resource, NY. **p. 57:** Colossal human-headed winged bull, Ashurbanipal, Nimrud, ca. 865 B.C.E.; © Boltin Picture Library. **p. 58:** Ishtar Gate, Babylon, Iraq; © Nik Wheeler/Corbis. **p. 59:** Hanging gardens of ancient Babylon; North Wind Picture Archives. **pp. 60–61, background:** Etosha National Park, Namibia; Jeremy Woodhouse/Getty Images/PhotoDisc. **pp. 60–61, details:** Len Ebert.

Chapter 7

pp. 62–63: Pyramid at Giza, sphinx in front; Neil Beer/Getty Images/PhotoDisc. **p. 64:** Nile River at Aswan, where prior to being dammed the river narrowed to the First Cataract, Egypt; © Nik Wheeler/Corbis. **p. 65:** Doug Roy. **p. 67:** Farmer in field, Nile, Egypt; © Staffan Widstrand/Corbis. **p. 68:** Farmland on banks of Nile, Egypt; © Yann Arthus-Bertrand/Corbis. **p. 69:** Desert near Aswan, Egypt; © Roger Wood/Corbis. **p. 70:** Jordan River valley, Galilee, Israel; © Richard T. Nowitz/Corbis. **p. 71:** Desert flowers bloom in Negev Desert, Israel; © Shai Ginott/Corbis.

Chapter 8

p. 72: Entrance to Nefertari and Hathor Temple, Abu Simbel, ca.1250 B.C.E.; colossal statues of Ramses II flank the entrance to the smaller of two temples cut into sandstone rock at Abu Simbel, on the Nile River; © Carmen Redondo/Corbis. **p. 73:** Len Ebert. **p. 75, upper:** Entrance to the Great Pyramid of Giza, Egypt, ca. 2525 B.C.E.; © Corbis. **p. 75, lower:** King Cheops or Pharaoh Khufu (2545–2520 B.C.E.), ivory statuette; Egyptian Museum, Cairo, Egypt; © Erich Lessing/Art Resource, NY. **p. 76:** Senusret I (reign 1964–1926 B.C.E.), from Osiride Pillar; © Richard T. Nowitz/Corbis. **p. 77:** Queen Hatshepsut seated, pink granite figure, 18th dynasty (16th–14th C. B.C.E.), New Kingdom, Egypt; Rijksmuseum van Oudheden, Egyptian Collection, Leiden, Netherlands; © Erich Lessing/Art Resource, NY. **p. 78:** Ramesses II and sons attacking Hittite fortress, painting; James Putnam. **p. 79:** Mummified face of Ramses II, New Kingdom, 19th dynasty (1550–1070 B.C.); © Roger Wood/Corbis.

Chapter 9

p. 80: Painting of ancient Egyptian architecture (detail), 1838, Antonio Basoli; © Massimo Listri/Corbis. **p. 81:** Len Ebert. **p. 82:** Len Ebert. **p. 83:** Nefertari playing senet, fresco, ca. 1320–1200 B.C.E.; © Gianni Dagli Orti/Corbis. **p. 84:** Imhotep, architect and minister of Djoser, with a dedication of Poumeh, son of Horsaiset; bronze, height 15 cm; © Réunion des Musées Nationaux, Paris/Art Resource, NY. **p. 85:** Banquet scene (detail), wall painting from the tomb of Nebamun, Dra Abu el-Naga, West Thebes, 18th dynasty; British Museum, London, Great Britain; Werner Forman/Art Resource, NY. **p. 86:** Priest and scribe, detail, F.A. Bridgman; © Bettmann/Corbis. **p. 87:** Purification of the dead before entombment, fresco wall painting, ca. 1550–1295 B.C.E.; © Gianni Dagli Orti/Corbis. **p. 88:** Scribes, bas-relief, Egypt, 18th dynasty; © Scala/Art Resource, NY. **p. 89:** Bas-relief with Egyptian scribes, ca. 2494–2345 B.C.; © Gianni Dagli Orti/Corbis. **p. 90:** Sculptors at work, detail, wall painting, tomb of Rekhmere, vizier under pharaohs Thutmosis III and Amenophis II, 18th dynasty, 16th–14th C. B.C.E.; tomb of Reckhmere, cemetery of Sheikh Abd

el-Qurnah, Tombs of the Nobles, Thebes, Egypt; © Erich Lessing/Art Resource, NY.
p. 91: Rekhmere inspects woodcarvers and carpenters, detail, wall painting, tomb of Rekhmere, vizier under Pharaohs Thutmosis III and Amenophis II, 18th dynasty, 16th–14th C. B.C.E.; tomb of Reckhmere, cemetery of Sheikh Abd el-Qurnah, Tombs of the Nobles, Thebes, Egypt; © Erich Lessing/Art Resource, NY. **p. 92:** Ancient Egyptian fresco of husband and wife plowing fields, ca. 1306–1290 B.C.; © Archivo Iconografico, S.A./Corbis. **p. 93:** Agricultural scene, wall painting, tomb of Mennah, scribe of the fields and estate inspector under pharaoh Thutmosis IV (18th dynasty, 16th–14th C. B.C.E.); cemetery of Sheikh Abd el-Qurna, Tombs of the Nobles, Thebes, Egypt; © Erich Lessing/Art Resource, NY.

Chapter 10
p. 94: Men bring the tribute of Black Africa for presentation to Pharaoh, fragment of painted plaster from the tomb of Sebekhotep; © Trustees of the British Museum, London. **p. 95:** Len Ebert. **p. 96:** Kushites bringing tribute to Ramesses II's governor of Kush; ©Trustees of the British Museum, London. **p. 97:** King Piye accepting the tribute of Egyptian princes (NGM 1990/11 104-5); © James Gurney. **p. 98:** Kush iron workers; © Lloyd Townsend/National Geographic Image Collection. **p. 99:** Kandake Amanirenas and her son Prince Akinidad direct a dawn attack on the Roman garrison at Syene, modern-day Aswan, Egypt; © David Blossom/National Geographic Image Collection.

Chapter 11
p. 100: Moses with the Ten Commandments; © Bettmann/Corbis. **p. 101:** Susan Jaekel. **p. 102:** Ceremonial reading of the Torah at the Western Wall, Jerusalem, Israel; © Bojan Brecelj/Corbis. **p. 103:** Jamb sculptures of Abraham, Isaac, Moses, Samuel, and David on north portal, Chartres Cathedral, Chartres, France; © Mary Ann Sullivan. **p. 105:** *Sacrifice of Isaac,* Giovanni Battista Tiepolo, panel from fresco cycle depicting scenes from the Old Testament, 1726; © Elio Ciol/Corbis. **p. 106:** *The Crossing of the Red Sea,* from *The Story of Moses,* school of Raphael (1483–1520), fresco, loggia, Vatican Palace, Vatican State; © Scala/Art Resource, NY. **p. 108:** King David leading the procession of the sacred Ark into Jerusalem, Luigi Ademollo, 19th C.; © Archivo Iconografico, S.A./Corbis. **p. 109:** Illustration of King Solomon's temple, updated illustration depicting John W. Kelchner's 1913 reconstruction; © Bettmann/Corbis.

Chapter 12
p. 110: Romans carrying Jewish spoils, replica of the Arch of Titus in the Diaspora Museum, Tel Aviv, Israel; © Richard T. Nowitz/Corbis. **p. 111:** Susan Jaekel. **p. 112:** *Moses and the Ten Commandments,* by James Jacques Joseph Tissot (1836-1902), c. 1896-1902, gouache on

board, 10 11/16 x 5 5/8 in. Gift of the Heirs of Jacob Schiff, x1952–190. Photo by John Parnell. ©The Jewish Museum of New York, NY/Art Resource, NY. **p. 113:** Bar/bat mitzvah class, Tel Aviv-Yafo, Israel; © David H. Wells/Corbis. **p. 115:** The Wailing Wall, Jerusalem, Israel; H. Wiesenhofer/PhotoLink/Getty Images/PhotoDisc. **p. 117:** Torah study group, Yeshiva Bircas Halorah, Jerusalem, Israel; © Bojan Brecelj/Corbis. **pp. 118–119, background:** Pyramid at Giza, sphinx in front; Neil Beer/Getty Images/PhotoDisc. **pp. 118–119, details:** Len Ebert.

Chapter 13
pp. 120–121: Amber Fort near Jaipur, India; Glen Allison/Getty Images/Photodisc. **p. 122:** River Ganges, Varanasi, India; © G. Hellier/Robert Harding. **p. 123:** Len Ebert. **p. 124:** Bangla Desh, Sundabarns fishing; Robert Harding **p. 125:** Deccan Plateau, Tamil Nadu, India; Robert Harding. **p. 126, upper:** Tea plantation, India; © R. & S. Michaud/ Woodfin Camp & Associates. **p. 126, lower:** Ganges River, Benares, India; © Andrea Pistolesi/Getty Images/The Image Bank. **p. 127:** Himalaya Mountains, Manaslu, Nepal; Robert Harding. **p. 128:** Hunza Valley, Karakoku Mountains, Pakistan; Robert Harding. **p. 129:** Indus River, Ladakh, Alchi, India; © John Elk III. **p. 130:** Sam Desert, Rajastahn, India; The Hutchison Library.

Chapter 14
p. 132: Pakistan, Mohenjodaro, citadel with Buddhist stupa, ca. 2nd C. C.E.; Robert Harding. **p. 133:** Renate Lohmann. **p. 134:** View from top of stupa/citadel of Mohenjodaro site, Mohenjodaro, Pakistan; © Randy Olson/National Geographic Image Collection. **p. 135:** Precision weights and measures, artifacts from Mohenjodaro, Pakistan; © Jehangir Gazdar/Woodfin Camp & Associates. **p. 136:** Great Bath at Mohenjodaro, Pakistan; © Borromeo/Art Resource, NY. **p. 137, upper left:** King-priest figure, Mohejodaro, Indus Valley civilization, C. 2000 B.C.E., limestone, height 6 7/8″ (17.5 cm); National Museum of Pakistan, Karachi, Pakistan; Robert Harding. **p. 137, upper right:** Necklace with carnelian beads, Mohenjodaro, Pakistan; Robert Harding. **p. 137, lower:** Steatite seals from Mohenjodaro (Indus Valley culture); National Museum of Pakistan, Karachi, Pakistan; © Borromeo/Art Resource, NY. **p. 138:** Ruins of sewer system, Mohenjodaro, Pakistan; © James P. Blair/National Geographic Image Collection. **p. 139:** Ruins of Mohenjodaro houses; © Robert Harding. **p. 140, upper:** Artifacts of game pieces, Mohenjodaro, Pakistan; © Jehangir Gazdar/Woodfin Camp & Associates. **p. 140, lower:** Sculpture from Mohenjodaro, Pakistan; Karachi Museum, Pakistan; © Corbis. **p. 141:** Aerial view of Mohenjodaro, Pakistan; © Randy Olson/National Geographic Image Collection.

Chapter 15
p. 142: Brahmin praying on ghats beside Ganges River, Varanasi, Uttar Pradesh, India; © Ric Ergenbright/Corbis. **p. 143:** Susan Jaekel. **p. 144:** Books of the Indian Vedas; © Milind A. Ketkar/Dinodia Photo Library. **p. 145:** Brahmins praying before eating, Pushkar, Rajasthan, India; © 2003 Anthony Cassidy/Getty Images/Stone. **p. 146:** Mobile pavement shrine, Mysore, India; © David Cumming; Eye Ubiquitous/Corbis. **p. 147:** Lighting of candles and sparklers to celebrate Diwali, Hindu festival of lights, commemorating Lord Rama's homecoming after overcoming the god-demon Ravana; Calcutta, India; © AFP Photo/Deshakalyan Chowdhury/Corbis. **p. 148:** Malaysian Indian Tamils during a traditional Tamil Hindu wedding ceremony; © Russell Gordon/Aurora Photos. **p. 149:** Hindu man praying; © Lindsay Hebberd/Corbis. **p. 150:** Ritual bathing in the Ganges, Varnasi, India; © 2003 Gavin Hellier/Getty Images/Taxi. **p. 151:** Member of brahmin class reading from sacred books to Hindu followers; © G. Corrigan/Robert Harding.

Chapter 16
p. 152: Buddha with halo, Gupta dynasty, 5th C., Mathura style; Archaeological Museum, Mathura, Sarnath, Uttar Pradesh, India; © Borromeo/Art Resource, NY. **p. 153:** Len Ebert. **p. 154:** A king enthroned in his palace; outside the palace gates his general on a white elephant and his army await orders. By permission of the British Library, London (manuscript number OR 14297, folios 10b–11, photo 1006304.011). **p. 155:** The prince shows his archery skill (upper left) and marries Princess Yasodhara (lower left). By permission of the British Library, London (manuscript number OR 14297, folios 10b–11, photo 1006301.011). **p. 156:** Prince Siddartha encounters an old man, a sick man, a corpse and a monk (on the right); and departs from his palace (on left). By permission of the British Library, London (manuscript number OR 14297, folios 10b–11, 1006350.011). **p. 157:** Buddhas, mounted asparas on white horses outside the walls of a Buddhist shrine. By permission of the British Library, London (manuscript number OR 14297, folios 10b–11, photo 1006670.011). **p. 158:** The Buddha is honoured by gods and men (on left); he meditates for seven days seated and for seven days standing (on right). By permission of the British Library, London (manuscript number OR 14297, folios 10b–11, photo 1006295.011).

Chapter 17
p. 160: Ashokan pillar, Lauriya, Nandangarth, India; by permission of the British Library, London (photo number 1002/C27). **p. 161:** Renate Lohmann. **p. 163:** Stupa III at Sanchi, ca. 1st C. B.C.E.–1st C. C.E., Sanchi, India; © Chris Lisle/Corbis. **p. 164:** 4th C. iron Gupta pillar with Sanskrit inscriptions, Delhi, India; © David Cumming/Eye Ubiquitous/Corbis.

p. 165, left: Lion capital of Ashoka's pillar, 3rd C. B.C.E., Sarnath, India; © John Elk III. p. 165, right: Indian flag; © Diondia Photo Library.

Chapter 18

p. 166: Prince Gautama/Buddha, Gupta cave painting, detail, Ajanta, India, 6th C.; © Charles & Josette Lenars/Corbis. p. 167: Susan Jaekel. p. 168: Coin with depiction of Chandragupta; National Museum, New Delhi, Delhi, India; © Scala/Art Resource, NY. p. 170: Ruins of University at Nalanda, India; © Lindsay Hebbard/Woodfin Camp & Associates. p. 171: Sanskrit with miniature painting of Vishnu, Brahma, and Sesha Nag from the *Bhagavata Purana,* 18th C.; © Archivo Iconografico, S.A./Corbis. p. 172: Anjanta cave painting of procession of elephants (detail), India; Robert Harding. p. 173, right: Tiver goddess Ganga on makara, 405–415 C.E., Gupta sculpture, Besnagar, India; © Bettmann/Corbis. p. 173, left: Buddha, from stupa of Mirpur-Khas, Gupta period, 4th–5th C. C.E., terracotta; Prince of Wales Museum, Bombay, Maharashtra, India. p. 174: Battle axe and temple lion coins, reign of Samudra Gupta; elephant and rhinoceros coins, reign of Kumara Gupta I; 4th–5th C. C.E.; National Museum, New Delhi, Delhi, India. p. 175: Temple at Shrirangam, India; © Adam Woolfitt/Woodfin Camp & Associates. p. 176: Hunza River Valley with Karakoram Highway connecting northern Pakistan with China; Jonathan S. Blair/National Geographic Image Collection. p. 177: Buddhas, wall painting, Gupta dynasty, 5th–6th C. C.E., cave no. 2, Ajanta Caves, Maharashtra, India; © Borromeo/Art Resource, NY. pp. 178–179, background: Amber Fort near Jaipur, India; Glen Allison/Getty Images/PhotoDisc. pp. 178–179, details: Len Ebert.

Chapter 19

pp. 180–181: Great Wall of China; Tim Hall/Getty Images/PhotoDisc. p. 182: Huang He (Yellow River) at Tengri Desert; © Liu Wen Min/ChinaStock. p. 183: Len Ebert. p. 184: Oasis along river, Xinjiang, Turpan (Turfan) at Jiahoe ruins; © 1995 Dennis Cox/ChinaStock. p. 185: Rice fields; © Corbis. p. 186: Karola Pass between Lhasa and Gyantse, Tibet; © 1994 Dennis Cox/ChinaStock. p. 187: Taklamakan Desert, Xinjiang Autonomous Region; © Song Shijing, Bejing Jabel/ChinaStock. p. 188: Manchurian farmland, Jilin province, China; © Liu Liqun/ChinaStock. p. 189: Irrigation system of Yellow River, Ningxia region, China; © Yang Xiuyun/ChinaStock. p. 190: Fields between Gweilin and Yangshuo, China; Digital Vision/Getty Images. p. 191: *Snow on Mount Tianshan,* Ha Yan, Qing dynasty; © Imperial Palace Museum, Beijing/ChinaStock. p. 192: *Nomadic Life in Western China* (detail), Qing dynasty; © Liu Liqun/ChinaStock. p. 193: Planting rice, stone brick rubbing, Qing dynasty; © Liu Liqun/ChinaStock.

Chapter 20

p. 194: Buried carriage (chariot), Shang dynasty (ca. 1324–1066 B.C.E.), Anyang, China; ©Yin Xu Museum/Wang Deying/ChinaStock. p. 195: Len Ebert. p. 196: Renate Lohmann. p. 198: Dragon shaped ornament. China. Shang dynasty (approx. 1600–1050 B.C.E.). Nephrite. Asian Art Museum of San Francisco, The Avery Brundage Collection, B60J702. Reproduced by permission. p. 199: Stone ox, ca. 1766–1045 B.C.E.; © Asian Art and Archaeology, Inc./Corbis. p. 200: Len Ebert. p. 201, upper: Ritual vessel (*zun* or *gui*) in the shape of a rhinoceros, probably late 1100s–1050 B.C.E. China; reportedly Shouchang, Shandong province. Shang dynasty (approx. 1600–1050 B.C.E.). Bronze. Asian Art Museum of San Francisco, The Avery Brundage Collection, B60B1+. Reproduced by permission. p. 201, lower: Bird-fish pendant, approx. 1100–900 B.C.E. China. Shang (approx. 1600–1050 B.C.E.) or Western Zhou dynasty (approx. 1050–771 B.C.E.). Nephrite. Asian Art Museum of San Francisco, The Avery Brundage Collection, B60J698. Reproduced by permission. p. 202: Chinese bronze dagger axes dating from the Shang through the Zhou dynasties, 13th–3rd C. B.C.E.; © Royal Ontario Museum/Corbis. p. 203: Excavation of a Shang tomb; courtesy of the Institute of History and Philology, Academia Sinica, Taipei, Taiwan.

Chapter 21

p. 204: Sages study and mediate upon the yin-yang symbol, Chinese scroll painting (OA 1881.1210.080); Trustees of the British Museum, London. p. 205: Len Ebert. p. 206: Emperor Wu, Chou dynasty, 1050–256 B.C.E.; © National Palace Museum, Taiwan/ The Art Archive. p. 208: Confucius (ca. 551– 479 B.C.E.), 17th C. scroll painting, Bibliotheque Nationale, Paris, France; © Snark/Art Resource, NY. p. 209: Candidates for civil service positions waiting for the posting of their exam results, Ch'iu Yin, Ming dynasty; National Palace Museum, Taipei, Taiwan, Republic of China. p. 210: Lao Tse riding on a water buffalo, Chinese figurine, Quing dynasty; Musée des Art Asiatiques-Guimet, Paris, France; © Giraudon/Art Resource, NY. p. 211: *The Thatched Hut of Dreaming of an Immortal* (detail). Tang Yin (1470–1523). Chinese, Ming dynasty, early 16th century. Handscroll: ink and color on paper; 28.3 x 103.0 cm. © Freer Gallery of Art, Smithsonian Institution, Washington, D.C.: Purchase F1939.60. p. 212: Chinese painting from Dunhuang caves showing tormentation in hell; The British Museum/The Art Archive. p. 213: *Lady Xuanwen Jun Giving Instructions on the Classics,* 1638. Chen Hongshou, Chinese, 1598–1652, Ming dynasty. Hanging scroll, ink and color on silk, 173.7 x 55.4 cm. ©The Cleveland Museum of Art, Mr. and Mrs. William H. Marlatt Fund, 1961.89.

Chapter 22

p. 214: Qin Shihuangdi, first emperor of China, Qin dynasty; © Liu Liqun/ChinaStock. p. 215: Susan Jaekel. p. 216: *Battle at Wu Yan,* Red-Eyebrow uprising, peasants fighting Han army, 22 C.E., Wu Yan battlefield, present-day Dong Pin County, Shandong province, China; © Liu Liqun/ChinaStock. p. 217: *Promenade of Qin Shi Huang Di* (Tsin dynasty emperor (221–206 B.C.E.)), from *The Lives of the Emperors of China,* Qing dynasty, 17th C., watercolor on silk; Bibliothèque Nationale, Paris, France; © Giraudon/Art Resource, NY. p. 218: The Great Wall; © Karen Su/Corbis. p. 219: *Killing of the Confucian Scholars by Order of Emperor Shihuangdi,* Qin dynasty, 221–206 B.C.E.; Sovfoto/Eastfoto/New China Pictures. p. 220: Warriors (detail), terracotta army, tomb of Qin Shihuangdi, Xianyang, China, Qin dynasty, 210 B.C.E.; © Bridgeman Art Library.

Chapter 23

p. 222: *Entry of Emperor Gaozu of Han into Guanzhong* (detail). Anonymous, 17th C., formerly attributed to Zhao Boju, d. ca. 1162. Chinese, Ming dynasty, 17th C. Handscroll; ink and color on silk, 29.7 x 312.8 cm (11 11/16 x 123 1/8 in.). © Museum of Fine Arts, Boston, William Armory Garner Fund and Annie Anderson Hough Fund; 31.910. Photograph © 2003 Museum of Fine Arts, Boston. p. 223: Doug Roy. p. 225: Horse carriage with driver and attendant, bronze model, Eastern Han dynasty (2nd C. C.E.), excavated 1969 at Wu-Wei, Kansu, China; National Museum, Beijing, China; © Erich Lessing/Art Resource, NY. p. 226: Rice culture and irrigation using endless chain pump, attributed to Cheng Chi, Yuan Dynasty, 13th–14th C. C.E.; © Freer Gallery of Art, Smithsonian Institution, Washington, D.C./The Art Archive. p. 227: "Chinese Civilizations: The Occupations of Women," ca. 1800, Bernisches Historisches Museum, Bern, Switzerland; © SEF/Art Resource, NY. p. 228: Papermaking, 19th C. Chinese woodblock print; ©The Art Archive. p. 229: Country doctor applying moxibustion, Song dynasty; © National Palace Museum, Taiwan/The Art Archive. p. 230: "South pointing spoon," oldest known compass; Chinese stamp; ©The Art Archive. p. 231: Emperor Wu-Di, detail from *Portraits of Thirteen Emperors,* attributed to Yen Li-pen; © Burstein Collection/Corbis.

Chapter 24

p. 232: Camel caravan crossing the Takla-makan Desert, Xinjiang Uygur Autonomous Region, China; © Keren Su/ Corbis. p. 233: Doug Roy. p. 234: The Hero Zhang Qian on his raft. China. Ming dynasty (1368–1644). Nephrite. Asian Art Museum of San Francisco, The Avery Brundage Collection, B60J162. Reproduced by permission. p. 235: Silkworm cultivation; Qing dynasty; © Liu Liqun/ChinaStock. **p. 236:** *The Caravan,* Alexandre Hecamps, 19th C.; © Archivo Iconografico, S.A./Corbis. **p. 237:** *Flying Horse,* one foot resting on swallow, bronze figure, Eastern Han dynasty, 34.5 x 45 cm, excavated 1969 at Wu-Wai, Kansu, China; National Museum, Beijing, China; © Erich Lessing/Art Resource, NY. **p. 238:** Camels on the Pamir Plateau, alongside the Karakoram Highway, Kashgar, China; © Alison Wright/Corbis. **p. 239:** Moustasha Kashan carpet, Persian; © Art Resource, NY. **p. 240:** Seated buddha, dated 338, China. Later Zhao dynasty (319–350). Gilt bronze. Asian Art Museum of San Francisco, The Avery Brundage Collection, B60B1034. Reproduced by permission. **p. 241:** Silk road, silk from Astana (386–581 C.E.); © Ru Suichu/ChinaStock. **pp. 242–243, background:** Great Wall of China; Tim Hall/Getty Images/Photo Disc. **pp. 242–243, details:** Len Ebert.

Chapter 25

pp. 244–245: View of the Parthenon and Acropolis, Athens, Greece; Scala/Art Resource, NY. **p. 246:** Olive trees, Crete; © Gail Mooney/Corbis. **p. 247:** Doug Roy. **p. 249:** Women gathering fruit; reverse side of red-figured cup, 5th C. B.C.E.; Musée Vivenel, Compiegne, France, Inv. ARV2 922,1; © Erich Lessing/Art Resource, NY. **p. 251:** Merchant ship of Athens, ca. 500 B.C.E.; hand-colored woodcut from a vase painting; North Wind Picture Archives.

Chapter 26

p. 252: Olympia, ancient Greece, site of the Olympic Games; North Wind Picture Archives. **p. 253:** Len Ebert. **p. 254:** Agesilaus II, king of Sparta; © Hulton-Deutsch Collection/Corbis. **p. 255:** Francois vase, details of Calydonian boar hunt/chariot race at the funeral games of Patroklos/gods arriving after the wedding of Peleus and Thetis; Ergotimos (potter, 6th C. B.C.E.) and Kleitias (vase painter, 575–560 B.C.E.); Attic black-figure volute krater, Chiusi, ca. 570 B.C.E.; Museo Archeologico, Florence, Italy; © Scala/Art Resource, NY. **p. 256:** Assasination of Hipparchus; Martin von Wagner Museum der Universität Würzburg, Würzburg, Germany; photograph K. Oehrlein. **p. 257:** "Vote of the Greeks," Greek pot illustrating quarrel between Ajax and Odysseus for the arms of Achilles, shown here solved in a novel way through the casting of votes by the Greek heroes under the supervision of the goddess Athena; vase E69; Trustees of the British Museum, London.

Chapter 27

p. 258, upper: Ancient Greek city of Sparta, viewed from Therapne; North Wind Picture Archives. **p. 258, lower:** Piraeus with ships and long walls to Athens; North Wind Picture Archives. **p. 259:** Renate Lohmann. **p. 261:** The

Greek assembly, oration of Demosthenes; Bettmann/Corbis. **p. 262:** Buyer inspecting a pot; large, red-figured amphora, ca. 480 B.C.E.; Musée du Louvre, Department des Antiquites Grecques/Romaines, Paris, France; © Erich Lessing/Art Resource, NY. **p. 263:** School scene in ancient Greece; North Wind Picture Archives. **p. 264, upper:** Women at their household occupations in ancient Greece; North Wind Picture Archives. **p. 264, lower:** 5th C. B.C.E. Greek pottery showing slave working with a pick; red-figured pottery; The Granger Collection, New York. **p. 265:** Market place of Sparta, ancient Greece; North Wind Picture Archives. **p. 266, upper:** Agricultural scene of plowing and sowing; black-figured cup with painted ribbon, 525 B.C.E.; Musée du Louvre, Department des Antiquites Grecques/Romaines, Paris, France; © Erich Lessing/Art Resource, NY. **p. 266, lower:** Iron spits used as currency in Sparta, ancient Greece, Sanctuary of Artemis, 9th–7th C. B.C.E.; Ronald Sheridan/Ancient Art & Architecture Collection. **p. 267:** Youths exercising, the Dromos, Sparta, ancient Greece; North Wind Picture Archives. **p. 268:** Women mixing with men in public in agora of Sparta; © Bettmann/Corbis. **p. 269, upper:** *Draped Warrior,* Greek, 510–500 B.C.E.; bronze/red marble, H: 5.938 in.; Wadsworth Antheneum, Hartford, Connecticut; gift of J. Pierpont Morgan (1917.815A). **p. 269, lower:** Pericles supervising building activities in Athens; © Bettmann/Corbis.

Chapter 28

p. 270: *The Greek and the Persian;* © The Trustees of the National Museums of Scotland. **p. 271:** Len Ebert. **p. 272:** Darius the Great in council before his expedition against Greece, detail, Apulian volute krater, 3rd quarter of 4th C. B.C.E.; National Museum of Naples, Italy; © Alinari/Art Resource, NY. **p. 273:** The Battle of Marathon; North Wind Picture Archives. **p. 274:** Defense of Thermopylae, Greeks checking Persian invasion, 480 B.C.E.; North Wind Picture Archives. **p. 275:** The Battle of Salamis, Greek fleet defeating the Persians, 480 B.C.E.; engraving; © Bettmann/Corbis. **p. 276:** The Spartans at Plataea, defeat of the Persian invasion of Greece by the Spartans, 479 B.C.; © Stock Montage.

Chapter 29

p. 278: A restoration of the Acropolis in Athens; Stock Montage. **p. 279:** Doug Roy. **p. 280:** Athens' agora; © Bettmann/Corbis. **p. 281:** The Delphic oracle; Stock Montage. **p. 282, upper:** Parthenon at the time of Pericles, ancient Athens; North Wind Picture Archives. **p. 282, lower:** Renate Lohmann. **p. 283:** Athena Varvakeion; copy of the Athena Parthenos by Pheidias (ca. 490–430 B.C.E.); National Archaeological Museum, Athens,

Greece; © Nimatallah/Art Resource, NY. **p. 284:** Theatre of Dionysos, Athens, Greece; North Wind Picture Archives. **p. 285:** *The Death of Socrates,* Jacques Louis David (1748–1825). Oil on canvas, H. 51 in. W. 77 1/4 in. (129.5 x 196.2 cm.). The Metropolitan Museum of Art, Catharine Lorillard Wolfe Collection, Wolfe Fund, 1931. (31.45) Photo © 1995 The Metropolitan Museum of Art. **p. 286:** Participants in foot race at Panathenaic Games, detail of black-figured amphora, 6th C. B.C.E.; © Erich Lessing/Art Resource, NY. **p. 287:** Model of the Acropolis of Athens in Roman times; © Gianni Dagli Orti/Corbis.

Chapter 30

p. 288: Battle between Alexander the Great and King Dareios (at Issos or Gaugamela), Roman mosaic replica of a painting by Philoxdilos of Emtrea (4th C. B.C.E.); © Erich Lessing/Art Resource, NY. **p. 289:** Susan Jaekel. **p. 290:** Coin showing Philip of Macedonia on horseback, 340 BC; Ronald Sheridan/Ancient Art & Architecture Collection. **p. 292:** Alexandria, Egypt; Byzantine (476–1453 C.E.), detail from floor mosaic in Saint John's Church, Gerasa, Jordan, 6th C. C.E.; Archaeological Museum, Gerasa (Jerash), Jordan; © Erich Lessing/Art Resource, NY. **p. 293:** Alexander the Great and Jewish high priest show mutual respect, 331 B.C.E.; engraving by White after Luyken; Mary Evans Picture Library, London, England. **p. 294:** *The Wedding of Alexander the Great (356–323 BC) and Roxana,* 1810, Baron Pierre-Narcisse Guerin (1774–1833), oil on canvas; Musée des Beaux-Arts, Rouen, France; The Bridgeman Art Library, New York. **p. 295:** Death of Alexander the Great; North Wind Picture Archives.

Chapter 31

p. 296: *The School of Athens,* detail, Raphael (1483–1520), Stanza della Segnatura, Vatican Palace, Vatican, Rome, Italy; © Scala/Art Resource, NY. **p. 297:** Susan Jaekel. **p. 298:** Thucydides (Greek historian), marble bust, 5th–4th B.C.E.; Musée du Louvre, Paris, France; © Erich Lessing/Art Resource, NY. **p. 299:** "Peytel Arybalos," doctor bleeding a patient, red-figured arybalos, 5th C. B.C.E.; © Erich Lessing/Art Resource, NY. **p. 300:** Statuette of Hypatia, female philosopher, leader of Neo-platonists at Alexandria, 370–415 C.E.; Ronald Sheridan/Ancient Art & Architecture Collection. **p. 301:** Aristotle describes the animals Alexander has sent him, Eugene Delacroix (1798–1860), fresco from the spandrels of the main hall of the Assemblee Nationale, Paris, France; © Erich Lessing/Art Resource, NY. **p. 302:** Actor holding a mask, fragment of a Greekkrater by painter of Pronomos, ca. 410 B.C.E.; The Granger Collection, New York. **p. 303:** Sacrifice of a pig; red-figure cup, 500 B.C.E.,

Epidronos painter, 5th–4th B.C.E.; photo: M. Chuzeville/Musée du Louvre, Paris, France; © Réunion des Musées Nationaux/Art Resouce, NY. **pp. 304–305, background:** View of the Parthenon and Acropolis, Athens, Greece; Scala/Art Resource, NY. **pp. 304–305, details:** Len Ebert.

Chapter 32
pp. 306–307: Colosseum, Rome, Italy; Sami Sarkis/Getty Images/PhotoDisc. **p. 308:** *Romulus and Remus Given Shelter by Faustulus,* Pietro da Cortona (1596–1669), oil on canvas, photographed by Jean Schormans; Musée du Louvre, Paris, France; © Réunion des Musées Nationaux, Paris, France/Art Resource, NY. **p. 309:** Len Ebert. **p. 311, upper:** City gate, Etruscan, 3rd–2nd C. B.C.E., Volterra, Italy; © SEF/Art Resource, NY. **p. 311, lower:** Etruscan wall painting of a man riding in a chariot; © David Lees/Corbis. **p. 312, upper:** The Parthenon, Athens, Greece; © Roger Wood/Corbis. **p. 312, lower:** Ostrakon of Themistocles; © Gianni Dagli Orti/Corbis. **p. 313, left:** Black-figure hydria with women running, ancient Greece; © Araldo de Luca/Corbis. **p. 313, right:** Domestic scene of a woman spinning and another holding a small hand-loom, centauromachy painter, 5th C. B.C.E., red-figure Greek vase painting on pyxis, ca. 430 B.C.E.; Musée du Louvre, Paris, France; © Erich Lessing/Art Resource, NY. **p. 314:** *Olympus,* Luigi Sabatelli (1772–1850), sala dell'Iliade, ceiling fresco, Palazzo Pitti, Florence, Italy; © Scala/Art Resource, NY. **p. 315:** Baths of Caracalla, Rome, 19th C. line engraving; The Granger Collection, New York.

Chapter 33
p. 316: *Cicero Denouncing Catalina Before the Senate,* Cesare Maccari (1840–1919), wall painting (detail), Palazzo Madama, Rome; © Scala/Art Resource, NY. **p. 317:** Len Ebert. **p. 318:** Lucius Junius Brutus declaring the new Roman republic; engraving, 18th C.; © Bettmann/Corbis. **p. 319:** Conflict between patricians and plebeians; North Wind Picture Archives. **p. 320:** Romans inspecting the Twelve Tables; © Bettmann/Corbis. **p. 321:** *Cicero Denouncing Catalina Before the Senate,* Cesare Maccari (1840–1919), wall painting, Palazzo Madama, Rome; © Scala/Art Resource, NY.

Chapter 34
p. 322: Roman emperor and his son triumphantly parade through Rome in a chariot, ca. 40 B.C.E., lithograph after painting by F.W. Topham; Mary Evans Picture Library, London, England. **p. 323:** Len Ebert. **p. 324:** Roman ships capturing part of a Carthaginian fleet; North Wind Picture Archives. **p. 325, upper:** Julius Caesar landing Roman army in Britain; North Wind Picture Archives. **p. 325, lower:**

Augustus (63 B.C.E.–14 C.E.) as Pontifex Maximus, also called Augustus of the Via Labicana; marble, 1st C.; Museo Nazionale Romano delle Terme, Rome, Italy; © Erich Lessing/Art Resource, NY. **p. 326:** Cincinnatus receiving the dictatorship of Rome; North Wind Picture Archives. **p. 328:** Hannibal and his troops crossing the Alps; North Wind Picture Archives. **p. 330:** Julius Caesar assassinated in the Roman senate, 44 B.C.E.; North Wind Picture Archives. **p. 332:** The Augustan Age, ancient Rome's flowering of literature and art; North Wind Picture Archives.

Chapter 35
p. 334: Forum of ancient Rome; North Wind Picture Archives. **p. 335:** Doug Roy. **p. 336:** Roman Forum under the Caesars; North Wind Picture Archives. **p. 337:** Roman court, 19th C., colored engraving; The Granger Collection, New York. **p. 338:** Taking of the census and a suovetaurilia (sacrifice of a bull, ram, and pig) in honor of the god Mars, altar of Domitius Ahenobarbus, ca. 100 B.C.E., L.: 205 cm; inv.: MA 975.; Musée du Louvre, Paris, France; © Réunion des Musées Nationaux/Art Resource, NY. **p. 339, upper:** Scenes in the life of a child, sarcophagus of M. Cornelius Statius (detail), mid 2nd C. C.E., marble, L: 148 cm, H: 47 cm; Musée du Louvre, Dept. des Antiquites Grecques/Romaines, Paris, France; © Erich Lessing/Art Resource, NY. **p. 339, lower:** Sculpture of Roman wedding ceremony, goddess Vesta blessing the ceremony; 2nd C. C.E.; Ronald Sheridan/Ancient Art & Architecture Collection. **p. 340:** Market scene with two monkeys to attract customers, funerary stele, 3rd C. C.E.; Museo Ostiense, Ostia, Italy; © Erich Lessing/Art Resource, NY. **p. 341, upper:** Interior of Roman house; North Wind Picture Archives. **p. 341, lower:** Decumano Massimo, Herculaneum, Italy; © Alinari/Art Resource, NY. **p. 342:** Neumagen school relief, 4th C. C.E.; © Bettmann/Corbis. **p. 343, upper:** Chariot race at the Circus Maximus; North Wind Picture Archives. **p. 343, lower:** Doomed gladiator, a scene in ancient Rome; Stock Montage. **p. 344:** Roman villa; North Wind Picture Archives. **p. 345:** Toilette of a Roman lady of rank; North Wind Picture Archives.

Chapter 36
p. 346: Christians hunted down in the catacombs of ancient Rome; North Wind Picture Archives. **p. 347:** Len Ebert. **p. 349:** First page of a religious codex made for the 73rd Jacobite Patriarch Michael son of Zaraa (detail). Egypt, Damietta, Mamluk dynasty, 1175–1200. Gold and color on parchment; 35.6 x 22.8 cm. © Freer Gallery of Art, Smithsonian Institution, Washington, D.C.: Purchase, F1955.11. **p. 350:** Nativity, colored engraving after Gustave Doré; The Granger Collection,

New York. **p. 351:** Star of the Nativity at the grotto of the Church of the Nativity, Bethlehem, West Bank, Israel; © Hanan Isachar/Corbis. **p. 352:** Sea of Galilee, also known as Lake Tiberias, Lake Gennesaret, or Yam Kinneret, Israel; © Dave G. Houser/Corbis. **p. 353:** Sermon on the Mount, colored engraving after Gustave Doré; The Granger Collection, New York. **p. 354:** *The Crucifixion,* 1457–1460, Andrea Mantegna, oil on panel; The Granger Collection, New York. **p. 355:** *The Resurrection of Christ,* Piero della Francesca (ca.1420–1492), fresco; Pinacoteca Comunale, Sansepolcro, Italy; © Scala/Art Resource, NY. **p. 356:** Paul in prison, writing the Epistles; North Wind Picture Archives. **p. 357:** Saint Paul Discussing with Jew and Gentiles, enamel plaque from a reliquary or altar, England, 1180–1185 C.E.; Victoria and Albert Museum, London, England; © Erich Lessing/Art Resource, NY. **p. 358:** Christian martyrs in Colosseum, ancient Rome; © North Wind Picture Archives. **p. 359:** Donation of Constantine the Great and Pope Sylvester I, 13th C. fresco; Quattro Santi Coronati, Rome, Italy; Scala/Art Resource, NY.

Chapter 37
p. 360: United States Capitol building, Washington, D.C.; Hisham F. Ibrahim/Getty Images/PhotoDisc. **p. 361:** Len Ebert. **p. 362:** Vandals sacking Rome; North Wind Picture Archives. **p. 364, left:** Roman Emperor Trajan (53–117 C.E.), Roman emperor 98–117 C.E.; © Bettmann/Corbis. **p. 364, right:** *George Washington,* Horatio Greenough (1805–1852), 1840, marble; © National Museum of American Art Museum/Smithsonian Institute, Washington, D.C. **p. 365:** Bedroom (cubiculum nocturnum) from the villa of P. Fannius Synistor, ca. 40–30 B.C.; Republican; Second Style. Mosaic floor, couch and footstool come from other Roman villas of later date. Fresco on lime plaster. H. 8 ft. 8-1/2 in. (262 cm) L. 19 ft. 1-7/8 in. (583 cm) W. 10 ft. 11-1/2 in. (334 cm) The Metropolitan Museum of Art, Rogers Fund, 1903 (03.14.13). Photograph by Schecter Lee. Photograph © 1986 The Metropolitan Museum of Art. **p. 366:** Pantheon, façade; Rome, Italy; © Scala/Art Resource, NY. **p. 367, upper:** Colosseum, 72–84 C.E.; Rome, Italy; © Archivo Iconografico, S.A./Corbis. **p. 367, lower:** West front, United States Capitol building, Washington, D.C.; © Corbis. **p. 368:** Front view of Acqua Paola, created by Roman emperor Trajan, 98–117 C.E.; Rome, Italy; © Araldo de Luca/Corbis. **p. 370:** Equestrian statue of Marcus Aurelius; Campidoglio, Rome; © Robert Frerck/Woodfin Camp & Associates. **p. 371:** Modern judge reviewing notes; © Corbis. **pp. 372–373, background:** Colosseum, Rome, Italy; Sami Sarkis/ Getty Images/PhotoDisc. **pp. 372–373, details:** Len Ebert.